Queen's
UNIVERSITY

OOL OF

blicy Studies

cations Unit
rt Sutherland Hall
Jnion Street
ston, ON, Canada
3N6
v.queensu.ca/sps/

referred citation for this book is:
ie, R., M. Frenette, R.E. Mueller, and A. Sweetman, eds. 2010. *Pursuing Higher Educa-*
n Canada: Economic, Social, and Policy Dimensions. Montreal and Kingston: Queen's
y Studies Series, McGill-Queen's University Press.

ary and Archives Canada Cataloguing in Publication

Pursuing higher education in Canada : economic, social, and policy dimensions /
d by Ross Finnie ... [et aI.].

des bibliographical references.
glish, abstracts also in French.
978-1-55339-277-4 (pbk.).—ISBN 978-1-55339-278-1 (bound)

1. Education, Higher—Canada. I. Finnie, Ross II. Queen's University (Kingston,
). School of Policy Studies

17.5.P87 2010   378.71   C2009-905666-6

Pursuing
Higher
Education
in Canada

Pursuing Higher Education in Canada

Economic, Social, and Policy Dimensions

Edited by

Ross Finnie, Marc Frenette,

Richard E. Mueller, and Arthur Sweetman

Queen's Policy Studies Series
School of Policy Studies, Queen's University
McGill-Queen's University Press
Montreal & Kingston • London • Ithaca

Contents

Acknowledgements

This volume, *Pursuing Higher Education in Canada: Economic, Social, and Policy Dimensions*, grew out of the Canada Millennium Scholarship Foundation's desire to better understand post-secondary access and persistence in order to aid Canadian policy-makers. The Education Policy Institute (EPI) and the School of Policy Studies at Queen's University partnered to create the Measuring the Effectiveness of Student Aid (MESA) project / le projet Mesurer l'efficacité de l'aide financière aux étudiants – MEAFE (http://www.mesa-project.org/) to study the issues, and this volume is one result. Another is the earlier collection of articles on which this one builds: *Who Goes? Who Stays? What Matters? Accessing and Persisting in Post-Secondary Education in Canada*, edited by Ross Finnie, Richard E. Mueller, Arthur Sweetman, and Alex Usher, also distributed by McGill-Queen's University Press in the School of Policy Studies Series.

We would like to thank Mark Howes and Valerie Jarus of the School of Policy Studies Publication Unit for their many efforts, as well as Maureen Garvie, who copy-edited the manuscript, and Jean Bernard, who translated the abstracts. Thanks also go to the research assistants for the MESA project, Stephen Childs, Viorela Diaconu, Theresa Hanqing Qiu, and Yan Zhang, for their excellent work with the YITS data. Academic guidance and peer review of the chapters were undertaken by the members of the MESA Research Advisory Committee, and for this we would like to thank Keith Banting, Charles Beach, Lorne Carmichael, Jane Friesen, Clément Lemelin, Daniel Parent, Garnet Picot, Michael Veall, and Hans Vossensteyn. Special thanks go to Anne Motte of the Foundation, who has been invaluable to the MESA project and in the preparation of this book. We warmly acknowledge the many contributions of our colleague Alex Usher to all aspects of the MESA project. Finally, we would like to thank all those responsible for the planning, development, and support of the Youth in Transition Survey (YITS) upon which most of the papers in this volume are based. The YITS data, arguably the best of this type in the world, have allowed us to gain important new insights into post-secondary education and post-secondary students.

Ross Finnie
Associate Professor
School of Public and International Affairs
University of Ottawa

Marc Frenette
Acting Director
Social Analysis Division
Statistics Canada

Richard E. Mueller
Associate Professor
Department of Economics
University of Lethbridge

Arthur Sweetman
Professor
School of Policy Studies
Queen's University at Kingston

1

Introduction: Deepening Our Understanding of Young Canadians' Participation in Post-Secondary Education

Marc Frenette, Richard E. Mueller, and Arthur Sweetman

Various economic and social phenomena have made post-secondary education (PSE) very valuable for both current students and graduates and – because of spillovers from graduates to others – for all levels of Canadian society. Globalization and technological change are influencing Canada's industrial and occupational structure, making higher order skills increasingly important not only for individual success but also for national economic growth and social development. In this context, access to PSE and persistence and completion have never been more important. Equity as well as efficiency may be an important motivation for policies regarding PSE access and completion.

Post-secondary participation rates for youth in their late teens and early twenties, and attainment rates for prime age workers, are high in Canada by international standards. Current PSE enrolment *levels* are at all time highs, but for those aged between 18 and 24, participation *rates* – defined as either pursuing or having completed post-secondary studies – have been trending down for at least a decade; in 2006 they were at least 10 percent lower than their peak. The baby boom "echo" generation now passing through the post-secondary system reconciles these last two observations that appear, at least initially, to be at odds with each other (Berger, Motte, and Parkin 2009). It is not yet clear how the recession of 2009 will affect participation rates, and whether the decade-long declining trend will be reversed, either temporarily or permanently. It is also not clear what will happen to enrolment levels and rates as the baby boom echo ages beyond the typical years of enrolment in PSE.

Pursuing Higher Education in Canada: Economic, Social, and Policy Dimensions, ed. R. Finnie, M. Frenette, R.E. Mueller, and A. Sweetman. Montreal and Kingston: Queen's Policy Studies Series, McGill-Queen's University Press.

Economic rates of return to PSE – that is, the earnings or wage premia of PSE graduates compared to those of otherwise similar high school graduates – are frequently used as indicators of the value of PSE in the labour market. Over the last 30 years, despite the increased supply of graduates, the premia have increased strongly, although there have been periods of stability and periods of stronger growth. In the early to mid-1980s, premia increased strongly, were relatively flat in the late 1980s, started increasing again in the early 1990s, and increased strongly in the late 1990s. Premia were then relatively flat in the early 2000s and declined slightly in 2005 and 2006.[1]

It seems plausible that business cycle fluctuations affect rates of return so that they reduce at the peak of booms and increase in busts, assuming that lower-wage individuals' labour market outcomes are more sensitive to the state of the economy. If this is correct, then we can expect rates of return to increase beyond our data period given the recent recession. In terms of the magnitude of the returns, in 2006 employed men with a bachelor's degree could expect to earn on an hourly or weekly basis on average about 33 or 34 percent more than those with a high school diploma; comparable numbers for women are roughly 44 to 46 percent (Boudarbat, Lemieux, and Riddell 2010; Berger, Mott, and Parkin 2009). These returns do not include the commensurate reduction in time spent in unemployment. When annual earnings are considered, thereby taking into account both average annual hours of work and dollars per hour, the gap is roughly 50 percent for males and 70 percent for females. Of course, these labour market returns do not include the many non-financial and non-economic private benefits, nor do they include the social benefits of education for the community. Overall in the past three decades, rates of return were very significant financially and saw a very large increase.

Within this broad context, *Pursuing Higher Education in Canada: Economic, Social, and Policy Dimensions* addresses a range of important topics related to PSE access and persistence that can help inform policy to improve both efficiency and equity. The volume does not primarily address financial issues such as tuition and student aid, which, as discussed by Finnie, Sweetman, and Usher (2008) in the previous volume in this series, *Who Goes? Who Stays? What Matters? Access and Persistence in Post-Secondary Education in Canada*, appear not to be the primary motivators of access and persistence in the current policy context. Thus in many ways this volume represents an evolution in thinking about PSE participation issues, moving away from debates on financial determinants – tuition, family income, and student financial aid – to a more in-depth discussion of the multitude of other factors that are at least as important. This emphasis does not imply that financial factors are irrelevant, nor that they might not become important as the context changes, but in the current context they appear to be crucial for only a small proportion of the population. What appear to be more broadly relevant for a larger group are factors related to family background, academic preparation, aspirations, and the like, which very early in life form the foundation for PSE readiness. There are also many issues relating to access and persistence about which we know very little, and the chapters in this volume contribute to sketching aspects of a fuller picture than has previously been available.

Both of these volumes rely heavily on the Youth in Transition Survey (YITS), an extremely valuable longitudinal data source collected by Statistics Canada and funded by Human Resources and Skills Development Canada (HRSDC). Motte et al. (2008) describe this data source and its relevance for the analyses conducted here.

Transitioning from high school to college or university is a big step for most young Canadians. Leaving high school – and perhaps moving away from family and friends – is a seminal moment replete with change. Ross Finnie and Felice Martinello address one such change that has garnered little attention: the tendency for high school grade averages to decline, in some cases substantially, at university. The authors find that grades drop by about 10 percentage points between high school and the first year of university. This drop is smaller for females, those living at home, those with high family incomes and more educated parents, and those who attend smaller universities. Perhaps the most interesting result is that better students – as measured by high school grades – tend to experience the largest percentage point drop in university. This may be the result of better students congregating at better universities, thus facing stiffer competition for grades that more were easily obtained in high school.

This drop in grades is an important phenomenon since its consequences can include increased stress, higher probability of dropping out, and loss of academic scholarships. Given the arbitrariness of grades, and differences in standards and policies across provinces, institutions, and academic disciplines, however, it is difficult to draw strong conclusions. Finnie and Martinello's work complements recent US research by Achen and Courant (2009) and Bar, Kadiyali, and Zussman (2009) looking at the impacts of grades on student choices. Together these papers explore many issues at the core of pedagogy that drive behaviour by PSE faculty and administrators. We hope that others pursue the topic of grades in general and various dimensions of gaps in grades in particular. As Sabot and Wakeman-Linn (1991) have pointed out, grades are extremely important information for students and have substantial incentive effects that affect persistence and student pathways through PSE; they can be instruments of social policy and/or can be leveraged to serve narrower interests.

Currently at Canadian universities, females outnumber males by a substantial margin. According to Statistics Canada, of the almost 1.07 million students enrolled at universities in Canada in 2007-08, 613,566 or 57.5 percent were female. The proportions are only slightly more balanced for college enrolments, where females account for 55.1 percent of total enrolments.[2] This pattern, of course, is a reversal of the historic gender imbalance in PSE and does not result from a decreasing male participation rate; rather, female enrolment rates have accelerated at a swifter pace than those for males. Understanding this differential is of clear social and economic importance, and in the related volume Frenette and Zeman (2008) argue that the gender university attendance gap can largely be explained by different high school grades. In this volume, Torben Drewes digs deeper into the source of these grade differences between the sexes. He observes that a significant proportion – about one-half – of the raw difference in the high school grade point average is the result of lower effort in high school (skipping classes, fewer hours spent performing schoolwork, etc.) What is perhaps more interesting is the finding that boys' grades would continue to lag even if they had worked the same hours as girls, since they also seem less effective at translating hours of work into grades.

The question that remains unanswered is: why do boys do less schoolwork than girls do? It is quite possible that the marginal boys are less interested in attending university and therefore do not put in the effort necessary to gain admission. Two possible explanations for this lag concern aspirations and participation in non-school activities. Christofides, Hoy, Li, and Stengos (2008) show that girls at age 15 have higher aspirations to attend university, and that the gap increases by age 17. While this gap may have a direct impact on university attendance, it may also have an indirect effect by reducing boys' effort in high school. In other words, aspirations are endogenous to Drewes's model. So too are non-school activities; Hansen (2008) shows that the ability to produce high school grades is positively related to non-work activities such as sports and volunteering but negatively related to paid work activities outside of school. Females have a larger probability of participation in both these areas, so we are not sure which effect prevails. Nor do we know if these effects are different for high school aged boys and girls. This is a critical area for further research, but Drewes makes an important contribution to moving forward what we know.

Kathleen Day's contribution (2008) looks at the importance of secondary school quality for PSE attendance by attempting to quantify the importance that various high school resources have for PSE access. Controlling for a variety of family background factors, she addresses the correlates of secondary school resources and various educational outcomes, including high school grades and scores in the PISA reading test at age 15, on educational attainment at age 21. This line of reasoning evolves out of a fairly simple yet profoundly important question: what is the best way to spend scarce education dollars to improve the educational outcomes of Canadian youth? Her results show that family characteristics have a much larger impact than do school characteristics. Day's approach here is novel in Canadian research in that it looks at the relationship between high school characteristics and PSE access; however, the general result of a very modest relationship between school resources and student outcomes is consistent with the broader Canadian research she cites in her paper, and with a very large international literature dating back to at least the seminal Coleman (1966) report in the United States. Of course, the impact of school resources on student outcomes has been the subject of intense debate in the last decade or two, and this literature is surveyed by Hanushek (2006). Two key interpretive issues as posited by Betts (1996a, 1996b) may make it difficult to observe a relationship between school resources and subsequent outcomes. First, there may be diminishing returns to increased investment in such resources, and Canada may be on the relatively flat portion of the curve relating inputs and outcomes. Second, and closely related to the first issue, the existing variation in school resources in Canada (and other OECD countries) may be too narrow to be associated with large changes in outcomes, making it difficult to statistically identify any effect on PSE attendance.

Another metric of success at high school is the completion rate. Related research at the PSE level on dropping out has shown that these rates can be very sensitive to the scope of the analysis. By viewing dropout behaviour through a wider prism, both Finnie and Qiu (2008) and Martinello (2008) show that the longer term college and university non-completion rates are lower than those generally reported in the media. The authors find that many of these young people switch programs and/or institutions, or they may temporarily withdraw from their program only to return and complete at a later date. While individual institutions and programs may be concerned about their own dropout rates, the PSE system as a whole seems to be doing well in terms of retaining and graduating Canadian youth.

Ross Finnie, Christine Laporte, and Arthur Sweetman address the dynamics of dropping out and of bouncing back – returning to high school or going directly to PSE without completing high school – at the high school level. They begin by arguing that, as with PSE dropout rates, a broad scope and longitudinal perspective can tell a fuller, and in this case very different, story than is evident in more limited analyses. As with PSE, high school dropout rates are estimated to be higher when short run measures rather than longer term ones are employed. This could be problematic if the limitations of various estimates are not fully understood by policy-makers.

Expanding the analysis to include bouncing back gives a very different picture than do simpler analyses that effectively count all those who ever dropped out. Finnie, Laporte, and Sweetman first observe that dropout rates have declined in the past decade and a half and that about half of dropouts consistently bounce back into the formal education system. Furthermore, an increasing share of those who bounce back return to complete high school rather than going straight to PSE programs that accept students with incomplete high school. They also find that family background factors – such as higher parental education, being raised in a two-parent family, and, to a lesser extent, higher parental income – are associated with low dropout rates and increased probabilities of continuing to PSE, but are not strongly related to bouncing back. Perhaps not surprisingly, the same factors are related to similar bouncing back and program switching behaviours at the PSE level (Finnie and Qiu 2008; Martinello 2008). Overall, as is well known from many people's experience but not incorporated in many statistics, the education system is flexible and provides students with opportunities to get back on track.

While this body of work suggests that flexibility in the Canadian education system at both secondary and post-secondary levels ensures that there is a good match between students and programs and prevents short term errors from becoming "locked in," this flexibility is not costless. Andres and Adamuti-Trache (2008) show that at the PSE level, in addition to administrative costs and the foregone earnings of the participants, the longer the time to degree completion, the more student debt tends to be accumulated; this debt, along with the increased time to program completion, may be related to paid work behaviour during post-secondary as well as post-graduation life course outcomes such as marrying, having children, and owning a home.

Four chapters in *Who Goes? Who Stays? What Matters?* are directly devoted to financial issues and their relationship to PSE participation. Johnson (2008) finds that there is little evidence suggesting that tuition fees are linked to either accessing or persisting in PSE. Similarly, Day (2008) fails to find any conclusive evidence of a relationship between financial aid and persistence behaviour.

A third chapter by Frenette (2008) suggests that the gap in university attendance among high school graduates in the top and bottom quartiles of the income distribution can be almost fully explained by differences in academic performance, parental education, and parental expectations. As reported by the students themselves, only 12 percent of the gap is related to differences in the incidence of facing financial constraints. However, Frenette notes three crucial caveats to his findings. First, some youth do report being financially constrained. Second, money may matter at an earlier point in life: for example, richer families may be more likely to hire a tutor or take their children to a museum, both of which may be associated with academic performance. Third, he notes that his results are conditional on the current level of financial aid available to students. While many studies have linked changes in student aid to changes in enrolment patterns, Frenette's findings show that, given the current state of affairs, money does not seem to be holding back most youth from paying the costs associated with attending university.

A fourth paper by Finnie and Carmichael (2008) highlights another financial dimension. They argue that even if the cost of post-secondary education is the same for everyone, students from low income families are less likely to receive the same amount of parental transfers and therefore are likely to have a higher debt burden. As a result, students from low income backgrounds require higher rates of return to education to choose to attain the same amounts of education. To the extent that there are decreasing returns to each additional year of education, a pattern which is identical for all individuals, the student from the low income family will elect a lower level of total educational attainment.

In this volume, several papers further our knowledge of financial factors, using different lenses. These papers specifically examine the relationship between labour market returns and attendance decisions. While the research presented thus far has included a host of family background and school related variables, here the authors look at the state of the economy and the rate of return to education for Aboriginal youth as related to PSE attendance.

Christine Neill and Michal Burdzy look at the recent resource booms, with a focus on the energy sector and oil prices, to explore the effects of varying opportunity costs on continuing in school. They find that oil prices have the largest impact on PSE enrolment rates in those provinces with the highest share of economic activity derived from the energy sector; in Alberta, the province with the largest energy sector, a US$50 increase in the price of oil will reduce university enrolments by about 3 percentage points. However, the authors find no impact on college enrolments. Higher energy prices result in lower demand for university spots since the opportunity cost of attending PSE increases when there is a robust job market for unskilled labour. This is not only the result of higher wages but also because the probability of employment is enhanced. Consequently, demand for PSE is countercyclical on the margin (since the magnitude of the impact is modest). This pattern is well known, but an economic downturn largely caused by low energy prices will result in enrolment effects that are larger still in energy dependent provinces. The authors offer a straightforward policy recommendation: financing to public postsecondary institutions should be increased during recessionary periods in order to accommodate the increased number of qualified students who apply for admission. Another important result in the paper is that these oil price effects are not temporary but are likely to be permanent. This finding casts doubt on the argument that young people may seek employment during boom periods and save for their future return to school. Certainly the low historical university participation rates in Alberta offer more evidence in support of permanent effects of energy sector booms.

In the first of two related pieces, Marc Frenette investigates whether low rates of return to education can explain the low levels of education for those with Aboriginal backgrounds. However, he shows with the 2006 Census data that the returns to higher education are as high amongst Aboriginal people (defined as North American Indians, Métis, and Inuit) as among non-Aboriginals. Further, pursuing higher education is associated with a larger decline in unemployment rates among Aboriginal people. These results hold for those who live off reserve, on reserve, or in northern communities. It is theoretically possible that Aboriginal people positively select into higher education much more strongly than do non-Aboriginals. If this is the case, then those with characteristics that are rewarded in the labour market will be more likely to attend PSE. To address this possibility, Frenette uses the PISA reading test score results contained in the YITS-A. He finds no difference in test scores by highest level of education among Aboriginal and non-Aboriginal people. Even when he compares the perceptions of the benefits of education, he finds no meaningful difference between the two groups across educational attainment. He concludes that there must be some other reason for the observed lower levels of educational attainment among Aboriginal people, a topic he explores in a second paper described below.

The next two papers in this volume look at the PSE experiences of Aboriginal people and the children of immigrants. While previous research has often included control variables for ethnicity or immigrant status (e.g., Finnie and Mueller 2008), these papers attempt to explain differences between the two groups and their counterparts. Frenette's second paper here, closely related to his first, tackles the question of why there is an educational attainment gap between Aboriginal and non-Aboriginal youth in Canada. Using the YITS-A survey, he shows that by the age of 21 years, about 94 percent of non-Aboriginal youth have completed high school, while the comparable Aboriginal rate is 84 percent. Conditional on graduating from high school, college attendance rates are fairly similar between the two groups. However, at the university level a differential opens up, with Aboriginal youth having about a 30 percent probability of attending university by age 21, some 17 percentage points below that for non-Aboriginal youth. The gap is interesting given that Frenette's first paper shows that financial returns to university are similar for both groups.

Searching for alternative explanations, Frenette breaks down the gap in high school and university attendance. He finds that many of the well-known factors that determine educational success at both high school and university levels are not working in favour of Aboriginal youth. These factors include greater incidences of low parental education and income, lower grades in high school and on the PISA reading test, and relatively poor study habits. Taking these factors into consideration, the author finds that about one-half of the high school graduation gap and about 90 percent of the university attendance gap are explained. Stated differently, it appears that Aboriginal status per se does not explain the total gap; rather, family and environment factors contribute to limiting the educational success of this population.

The contribution by Ross Finnie and Richard Mueller shows that the children of immigrants are more likely to attend PSE – university in particular – compared to children born in Canada to Canadian born parents. Even after controlling for a variety of family background and education variables, first and second generation Canadians show higher university participation rates. This result, however, does not hold for immigrants from all source regions. Those from China, some other parts of Asia, and Africa are more likely to attend university compared to third generation or higher Canadians (i.e., those born in Canada to Canadian born parents). The only group that consistently displays a lower probability of attendance is individuals from the Americas (excluding the United States). Immigrants and their children from traditional European and English-speaking regions generally show similar attendance rates compared to the control group of Canadian born children of Canadian born parents.

These regional effects persist even after controlling for parental aspirations regarding their children's level of schooling. Certain groups simply go to university, and the precise reasons cannot be ascertained with these data. Despite the difficulties that some immigrants face in integrating into the Canadian labour market, more recent immigrants may do quite well, given that a university education (particularly one obtained in Canada) is viewed as the key to economic success in the new global economy. The authors argue that the total impact of recent immigration should be measured over a longer time period, thus allowing the children of immigrants to be considered in evaluations of immigration policy.

The next three papers are concerned with factors related to individual and family characteristics in the decision to participate in PSE. Pierre Lefebvre and Philip Merrigan use the National Longitudinal Survey of Children and Youth (NLSCY) to study the relationships between a number of cognitive and non-cognitive factors and the educational pathways of Canadian youth. This is an important extension of the work by Finnie and Mueller (2008) looking at effects of family background. Like Finnie and Mueller but using a different dataset, the authors model the PSE choices of Canadians aged 18 to 21 in 2005 as a function of various family background and education related variables, but they expand the analysis to include a host of health and behavioural characteristics. Their results generally confirm that low family incomes (albeit defined over a longer period than is usually the case, given the longitudinal nature of their data), single-parent status, and low parental education all contribute to lower probabilities of PSE attendance. The addition of behavioural and health variables are the real contributions of the paper. A low self-perception of health, aggression in young girls (but not boys), and hyperactivity in boys (but not girls) are all solid predictors of a diminished probability of PSE attendance.

The paper by Stephen Childs, Ross Finnie, and Richard Mueller further extends our knowledge of family background factors related to postsecondary attendance. Aside from improving cognitive and non-cognitive abilities in order to better the chances of attending PSE, are there other methods by which parents may be able to enrich their children's lives and enhance the probability of attendance? Although the authors are only able to look at correlations and not causes, they find evidence suggesting the answer is yes. Borrowing from the sociology literature, they use the concept of "cultural capital," defined very broadly as "the knowledge, experiences, and connections that help individuals succeed in life." If the correlations are taken as causal, and since higher educated parents tend to provide their children with more of this capital, inequalities in society – such as access to PSE – could be perpetuated by this mechanism. The authors find that many cultural capital factors have a positive association with PSE attendance (especially university), and that these associations exist even after controlling for parental education and income. While the results are not conclusive enough to offer any meaningful policy advice, they point to an area where more research is required.

Addressing a different dimension related to the family, Dianne Looker asks whether rural students are at a disadvantage compared to their urban counterparts. As with many others in this volume, this paper starts with a stylized fact: rural students have lower PSE participation rates. However, once Looker controls for family income, parental education, and other factors, she finds that the urban-rural divide disappears. Thus, characteristics that are correlated with rural status seem to be driving the differences in rural participation rates. This result holds at both the national and provincial levels. However, the story changes somewhat in relation to the proportion of PSE attendees who go to university. In that case, the rural-urban divide persists even after accounting for student and family background variables. Although these results cannot definitively say that rural students per se are disadvantaged in terms of university access, it does suggest that rural students may have less access than urban youth.

While the papers in this volume greatly contribute to our knowledge of the dynamics of post-secondary education participation, in some ways we are only beginning to understand the motivations of young Canadians in this regard and the incentives they receive. While there is increasing consensus in the literature that, in the current context, financial factors are not as important as previously thought, there are many family background and contextual factors whose influence on PSE decisions we do not yet fully understand. However, it is increasingly clear that outcomes of youth at the PSE age are strongly influenced, although certainly not predetermined, by factors that are in place many years earlier. Although external factors such as energy cycles driving employment demand have some impact on enrolment rates, their impact is relatively modest. Similarly, school resources have an impact but one that seems to be quite small. In contrast, parental education and factors inside the home appear to be key determinants of children's educational aspirations and outcomes.

As with much research, the papers in this volume collectively raise as many questions as are answered. With datasets such as the YITS continuing to follow young Canadians through this important period of their lives, researchers will continue to exploit these data in search of answers to many of these important questions.

Notes

1. Canadian census data show that this small decline in the gap is the result of the real earnings of those with a high school degree increasing more quickly than the real earnings of those with a university degree, rather than a decline among the more educated.
2. These data include both full and part time enrolments and are from CANSIM, Table 477-0013 (for universities) and Table 477-0015 (for colleges). The gender breakdown by full time status is almost identical.

References

Achen, A.C., and P.N. Courant. 2009. "What Are Grades Made Of? *Journal of Economic Perspectives* 23 (3): 77-92.

Andres, L., and M. Adamuti-Trache. 2008. "University Attainment, Student Loans, and Adult Life Course Activities: A Fifteen Year Portrait of Young Adults in British Columbia. In *Who Goes? Who Stays? What Matters?*, 239-75.*

Bar, T., V. Kadiyali, and A. Zussman. 2009. "Grade Information and Grade Inflation: The Cornell Experiment." *Journal of Economic Perspectives* 23 (3): 93-108.

Boudarbat, B., T. Lemieux, and W. C. Riddell. 2010. "The Evolution of Returns to Human Capital in Canada: 1980-2005." CLSRN Working Paper no. 53. Accessed at http://www.clsrn.econ.ubc.ca/workingpapers.php.

Berger, J., A. Motte, and A. Parkin, eds. 2009. *The Price of Knowledge: Access and Student Finance in Canada.* 4th ed. Montreal: Canada Millennium Scholarship Foundation.

Betts, J. 1996a. "Do School Resources Matter Only for Older Workers?" *Review of Economics and Statistics* 78 (4): 638-52.

– 1996b. "Is There a Link between School Inputs and Earnings? Fresh Scrutiny of an Old Literature." In *The Effect of School Resources on Student Achievement and Adult Success*, ed. G. Burtless, 141-91. Washington, DC: Brookings Institution.

Christofides, L.N., M. Hoy, Z. Li, and T. Stengos. 2008. "The Evolution of the Aspirations for University Attendance." In *Who Goes? Who Stays? What Matters?*, 109-34.*

Coleman, J.S. 1966. *Equality of Educational Opportunity*, Washington, DC: National Council for Educational Statistics.

Day, K. 2008. "A Tangled Web: The Relationship between Persistence and Financial Aid." In *Who Goes? Who Stays? What Matters?*, 327-46.*

Finnie, R., and L. Carmichael. 2008. "Family Income, Access to Post-Secondary Education, and Student Grants: Why Equal Access Requires More Than Loans." In *Who Goes? Who Stays? What Matters?*, 347-68.*

Finnie, R., and R.E. Mueller. 2008. "The Backgrounds of Canadian Youth and Access to Post-Secondary Education: New Evidence from the Youth in Transition Survey." In *Who Goes? Who Stays?*, 79-107.*

Finnie, R., and H.T. Qiu. 2008. "Is the Glass (or Classroom) Half-Empty or Nearly Full? New Evidence on Persistence in Post-Secondary Education in Canada." In *Who Goes? Who Stays? What Matters?*, 179-207.*

Finnie, R., A. Sweetman, and A. Usher. 2008. "Introduction: A Framework for Thinking about Participation in Post-Secondary Education." In *Who Goes? Who Stays? What Matters?*, 3-32.*

Frenette, M. 2008. "Why Are Lower-Income Students Less Likely to Attend University? Evidence from Academic Abilities, Parental Influences, and Financial Constraints." In *Who Goes? Who Stays? What Matters?*, 279-97.*

Frenette, M., and K. Zeman. 2008. "Understanding the Gender Gap in University Attendance: Evidence Based on Academic Performance, Study Habits, and Parental Influences." In *Who Goes? Who Stays? What Matters?*, 135-52.*

Hansen, J. 2008. "The Effect of School and Non-School Activities on High School Performance in Canada." In *Who Goes? Who Stays? What Matters?*, 153-75.*

Hanushek, E.A. 2006. "School Resources." In *Handbook of the Economics of Education*, vol. 2, ed. E.A. Hanushek and F. Welch, 865-908. Amsterdam: Elsevier.

Johnson. D. 2008. "How Is Variation in Tuition across Canadian Provinces Related to University Participation in the Youth in Transition Survey?" In *Who Goes? Who Stays? What Matters?*, 299-326.*

Martinello, F. 2008. "Transitions and Adjustments in Students' Post-Secondary Education." In *Who Goes? Who Stays? What Matters?*, 209-38.*

Motte, A., H.T. Qiu, Y. Zhang, and P. Bussière. 2008. "The Youth in Transition Survey: Following Canadian Youth through Time." In *Who Goes? Who Stays? What Matters?*, 63-75.*

Sabot, R., and J. Wakeman-Linn. 1991. "Grade Inflation and Course Choice." *Journal of Economic Perspectives* 5 (1): 159-70.

* In *Who Goes? Who Stays? What Matters? Accessing and Persisting in Post-Secondary Education in Canada*, edited by R. Finnie, R.E. Mueller, A. Sweetman, and A. Usher (Montreal and Kingston: Queen's Policy Studies Series, McGill-Queen's University Press).

Part I

Transitioning from Secondary to Post-Secondary Education

2

"I Lost My Scholarship": Changes in Grades from High School to First Year University[1]

Ross Finnie and Felice Martinello

Dans cet article, nous analysons la baisse des notes moyennes d'un échantillon d'étudiants, de la dernière année du secondaire à la première année d'université, grâce aux données de la cohorte A de l'Enquête auprès des jeunes en transition (EJET). Cette baisse moyenne est de près de 10 points de pourcentage ; toutefois, elle est moins importante chez les filles, ainsi que chez les jeunes de familles à revenu plus élevé et dont les parents sont plus scolarisés, qui vivent avec leurs parents et qui fréquentent de plus petites universités – les autres variables étant gardées fixes. Les baisses varient aussi selon les provinces, et selon les champs d'études. De plus, les caractéristiques des étudiants, prises individuellement, ne produisent que peu de différences (un ou deux points) ; cependant, la combinaison de certaines caractéristiques peut entraîner une variation de plus d'un degré (en notes littérales). Par ailleurs, ce sont les étudiants qui ont les plus hautes notes au secondaire qui subissent la plus forte baisse, ce phénomène étant possiblement dû au fait que les universités sélectionnent les étudiants qu'ils acceptent sur la base des notes obtenues au secondaire. Enfin, plusieurs facteurs – comme le type de famille (si les deux parents sont présents ou non, par exemple), l'obligation ou non de quitter le foyer familial pour fréquenter une université, le fait de vivre en milieu urbain ou en milieu rural, et l'appartenance à une minorité visible ou le fait d'être issu de l'immigration – n'ont aucun effet significatif sur la baisse des notes.

We examine the decrease in average grades from students' last year of high school to their first year of university. The average drop is almost 10 percentage points, but students who are female with higher family incomes, more educated parents, living at home, or attending smaller universities have smaller decreases, holding other factors constant. Decreases also vary by province and major. Differences for individual characteristics are generally estimated to be small (one to two marks), but they can accumulate to more than a letter grade in total for certain combinations of characteristics. Stronger students (as measured by high school grades) experience much larger decreases than weaker students,

Pursuing Higher Education in Canada: Economic, Social, and Policy Dimensions, ed. R. Finnie, M. Frenette, R.E. Mueller, and A. Sweetman. Montreal and Kingston: Queen's Policy Studies Series, McGill-Queen's University Press.

perhaps reflecting sorting of students across universities by high school grades. Family status, moving to start university, urban/rural background, and being a visible minority or immigrant have no significant effect.

Introduction

Most students receive significantly lower grades in their first year of university than they achieved in high school. These grade decreases often come as a personal shock, and reactions can include increased anxiety and declines in the student's sense of self-worth and confidence. Gilbert et al. (1997, 56), for example, cite a retrospective study of second year students at Queen's University where 54 percent of males and 82 percent of females identified the decrease in their grades from high school to university as a stressor. These effects are important on their own as they directly affect students' well-being and can also affect students' ability to perform in school or function more generally.

Furthermore, based upon their high school grades, students often earn entrance scholarships and secure places in competitive university programs. Any significant decrease in their performance can put scholarships at risk or cause students to be disqualified from their programs of study, placed on academic probation, or suspended. As one student expressed it in a note sent to a professor (paraphrased and changed to protect the anonymity of the individual): "I really am an excellent student. I got an academic scholarship to come to [name of university] as well as a few other schools I applied to … But because of my mistakes I have lost my scholarship and face academic probation and possible suspension. I need a minimum of 60% in your class to even have a chance of escaping the hole I've dug for myself. I have learned from my mistakes and if you could give me a 60 and thereby the opportunity to continue on at [name of university] I promise to somehow prove to you I learned from my errors and took full advantage of the chance you gave me. I feel embarrassed even having to write this letter but I have no other choice given the severity of my situation." Other schooling opportunities such as cooperative education programs, internships, or athletic eligibility may be affected negatively as well.

As a large research literature suggests, grades are important to students' persistence in university or college; for example, see Pascarella and Terenzini (1991), Adelman (2006), Martinello (2008), Finnie and Qiu (2008b) and references cited therein. Pascarella and Terenzini (2005) survey the American literature and observe that "grades may well be the best single predictors of student persistence, degree completion, and graduate school enrolment" (396). Finnie and Qiu (2008a) do multivariate analysis on a large sample of Canadian post-secondary students and find that first year grades are strongly related to staying in school and program completion. They do, however, caution that these "grade effects" are almost certainly not entirely causal and may reflect students' commitment to their studies rather than an actual determinant of dropping out (i.e., those on the way to leaving may obtain lower grades along the way). Grade changes may also reflect other omitted (or imperfectly measured) factors such as ability or motivation that are also related to persistence and other outcomes.

Better understanding of the grade changes from high school to first year university and how these changes relate to student, family, program, university, and other characteristics would be of value to the various stakeholders in post-secondary education (PSE). Students would be able to make more informed choices, and their parents, high school counsellors, and others would be more able to help them in these decisions. University admissions officers would have better information on how students would likely perform, and academic advisors would be able to design and target relevant assistance programs more effectively. Government policy-makers would have a more accurate idea of how institutional characteristics and schooling experiences affect schooling outcomes and act accordingly. Lastly, all stakeholders would be able to place the observed outcomes in a more informed perspective.

The main contribution of this paper is to provide what is to our knowledge the first general, detailed study of Canadian students' grade changes from high school to university. Specifically, data on individual students from the Youth in Transition Survey (Cohort A, or "Reading Cohort") are used to examine the change in average grade that first year students experience from their last year of high school. Regression analysis is employed to estimate how these grade changes are related to students' personal characteristics, parental and family attributes, decisions about field of study and residence, and university characteristics.

Our paper also contributes to the literature by considering a larger set of potential determinants or co-variates of student grades than has typically been the case, this being possible due to the richness of the YITS data. In addition to the usual personal and family characteristics such as gender, parents' education, and belonging to a visible minority, we include variables for family structure, parents' income, being an immigrant to Canada, having been raised in a rural setting, and major field of study. We also examine other factors that may have particular relevance for university and government policy-makers, including the size of the university, first year class sizes, and students' living arrangements (e.g., living with parent(s) or in a student residence). Our findings are instructive and potentially policy relevant along all of these dimensions.

The next section reviews the literature. This is followed by a discussion of the data, including the average grades and changes in grades found in our sample. A short section on the methodology employed is followed by the empirical findings. A short concluding section summarizes the main results, draws some implications, and points to avenues for further research.

Previous Studies of Students' Academic Performance in PSE

Previous studies in the literature examine levels of grades but do not deal with their changes as is done here; however, the overall subject matter and method of many of these studies are not very different from this paper. Hence a brief summary of their findings provides some useful context and comparisons for the estimates presented below.

Virtually all studies include gender in their analysis, and all find that females achieve higher university grades than males. Almost all studies also include in their analysis some combination of high school grades or test scores (SAT or ACT). Some (Rothstein 2004; Smith, Yun Dai, and Szelest 2006) include both high school grades and test scores, and others include verbal and math test scores (Arcidiacono 2004; Betts and Morell 1999; Hotchkiss, Moore, and Pitts 2006; Mouw and Khanna 1993, who survey the earlier literature; Stinebrickner and Stinebrickner 2003). In all cases, high school grades and all of the included test scores are estimated to have large, positive, and strongly statistically significant relations to post-secondary grades.

Most of the studies use data on students in the United States and include variables indicating whether the students are black or belong to other visible minorities (often with separate categories for Hispanic and/or Asian). Blacks and other visible minorities are consistently found to have lower grades after controlling for other factors. One exception is Betts and Morell (1999), who report that the estimate for blacks becomes statistically insignificant once high school grades and math and verbal SAT scores are added to the regression. (They review other work on this issue as well.)

Grades in PSE are also reported to vary with family background. Monks (2000), Stinebrickner and Stinebrickner (2004), and Win and Miller (2005) report that students' grades are higher if their parents have greater levels of education. Win and Miller (2005) show that parents' occupation is statistically significant, and Betts and Morell (1999) and Monks (2000) find that students' grades rise with parents' income.

The majority of studies concentrate on the grades of first or second year students, but in their samples Betts and Morell (1999) and Horowitz and Spector (2005) include undergraduates at all levels. Both studies find that grades increase as students progress through their post-secondary education, and Horowitz and Spector (2005) report that grades increase with students' age, even after controlling for the number of years in PSE. Betts and Morell (1999), Hotchkiss et al. (2006), Rothstein (2004), and Win and Miller (2005) include the student's major field of study; all but the last study find statistically significant differences. Win and Miller (2005) also test for grade differences across students living in urban or rural areas and find no statistically significant differences.

Terenzini, Pascarella, and Blimling (1996) survey estimates of the effects of out-of-class experiences on grades and report that students living in residence tend to have slightly higher grades than those living in fraternity/sorority houses or on their own off campus. There are generally no significant differences between students living in residence and those living with their parents off campus, but there is evidence that students in residences with academic and intellectual development programs (e.g., living-learning centres) perform better academically than those in conventional residences.

The Data, Average Grades, and Grade Changes

The information on individual students is taken from the Youth in Transition Survey, Cohort A. The YITS-A is a representative national sample of youth aged 15 as of 31 December 1999 who were interviewed along with their parents and high school administrators in the spring of 2000.[2] Those data comprise the first cycle of the YITS-A, and the same youth were re-interviewed every two years thereafter to produce the subsequent cycles of the YITS-A. The cycles can be merged to produce a panel or longitudinal data set in which researchers can follow the activities of individual youths over time. The many other interesting components in the YITS-A include student assessment (Programme for International Student Assessment, or PISA) scores, detailed background variables, and other data on students' experiences and attitudes, but these are not used in this project, as the goal here is to establish a set of benchmark numbers and otherwise conduct an analysis in the spirit of the existing literature.

Data from the first three cycles of YITS-A are used, and students are retained in the sample only if they were interviewed in all three cycles. Further, students are included only if they attended university and enrolled in a bachelor's level program that was expected to take at least three years with full-time enrolment. Students in Quebec are excluded from the dataset because their CEGEP system provides an intermediate step between high school and university that has no equivalent in other provinces. Students with average grades below 60 percent in their last year of high school are excluded from the analysis, but this makes no difference to the results, since virtually none of them attended university. This yields a dataset consisting of more than 5,200 students. All observations in the data are weighted by the Cycle 3 population weights to account for student attrition across the cycles and thus provide a representative sample of the underlying Canadian student population.

Given the ages of the students and the timing of their interviews, most of those in the sample were in their first or second year of university from 2002-03 to 2003-04 (inclusive), which are the years covered by the third cycle of YITS. Table 1 shows the characteristics of the students in the sample and the relevant grade distributions.

TABLE 1
Student Characteristics and Grades

	Percentage	Standard Error
Sex		
Male	41.0	1.1
Female	59.0	1.1
High school location		
Rural	17.3	0.7
Urban	82.7	0.7
High school province		
Newfoundland and Labrador	2.8	0.2
Prince Edward Island	1.1	0.1
Nova Scotia	6.4	0.3
New Brunswick	4.6	0.2
Ontario	53.6	1.1
Manitoba	5.1	0.3
Saskatchewan	5.1	0.3
Alberta	8.9	0.5
British Columbia	12.3	0.6
Visible minority		
Visible minority	20.3	0.9
Non-visible minority	79.7	0.9
Immigrant status		0.0
Canadian by birth	86.7	0.8
Not Canadian by birth	13.3	0.8
Family type		
Single parent or other	13.0	0.8
Two parents	87.0	0.8
Parental/guardian's education		
Less than HS	2.8	0.4
HS completed	12.6	0.7
Some PSE	5.5	0.5
Trade/college	24.6	0.9
University – below BA	5.8	0.5
University – BA	29.2	1.0
Post-graduate study	19.4	0.9
Parental income level		
Extremely low ($0-$5,000)	0.9	0.2
$5,000 to $25,000	5.0	0.5
$25,000 to $50,000	18.7	0.8
$50,000 to $75,000	25.2	0.9
$75,000 to $100,000	27.6	1.0
$100,000 and above	22.5	0.9
Moved to another city/province to start PSE		
No	46.0	1.1
Yes	54.0	1.1

... continued

TABLE 1
(Continued)

	Percentage	Standard Error
Overall grade of 1st year PSE		
90% or above	3.3	0.3
80% to 89%	20.8	0.9
70% to 79%	48.8	1.1
60% to 69%	22.9	0.9
50% to 59%	3.5	0.4
Under 50%	0.7	0.1
Overall grade of last year HS		
90% to 100%	18.3	0.8
80% to 89%	56.8	1.1
70% to 79%	23.4	0.9
60% to 69%	1.4	0.2
Grade changes		
Increase	2.5	0.3
Same	24.7	0.9
Decrease by 1 category	49.8	1.1
Decrease by 2 category	19.9	0.9
Decrease by 3 category or more	3.1	0.3
Number of observations	5,246	

Note: The data represent of respondents who participated in the first three cycles of YITS-A and enrolled in a bachelor's level PSE program that required at least three years of study if taken full time.

Source: Authors' compilation.

Students' average grades in their last year of high school and first year of university are reported in ten-mark categories (90-100, 80-89, 70-79, etc.) in the YITS. The exceptions are grades under 50 percent, which are grouped into one category. Although marking schemes vary from school to school, the differences between categories can reasonably be considered the differences between letter grades. Table 1 shows that a substantial majority of the students who attended university have an average grade in the 80s in their last year of high school. Eighteen percent have high school grades of 90 or above, while slightly less than a quarter have grades in the 70s, and only 1.4 percent were admitted with high school averages in the 60s. Table 1 also shows that almost half of all students experience a decrease of one grade category from high school to their first year of university. Only 2.5 percent receive higher grades in university than in high school, while roughly one-quarter manage to keep their averages within the same ten-mark category. Approximately 20 percent of students see their grades fall by two categories, and another 3.1 percent experience decreases of three or more categories. If numerical grades equal to the midpoint of their grade category are assigned to each student, then the average decline is 9.7 marks (with a standard error of 0.12).

The size of the university attended, as measured by the number of full-time equivalent (FTE) students enrolled at the institution, is included as an explanatory variable in the analysis. University enrolment figures for the 2003-04 academic year are taken from the 2006 Canadian Association of University Teachers (CAUT) Almanac, but their original source is Statistics Canada (CAUT 2006). These enrolment figures are linked to individuals' records in the YITS-A based on the institutional identifier available in the data.[3] All other variables used in the analysis are taken from the YITS-A.

Empirical Methodology

Regression analysis is used to estimate how the changes in grades are related to each student, parent, and school characteristic, while simultaneously controlling for all the other influences included in the analysis. The regression estimates are reported in the Appendix, while the text presents the findings using graphs.

The variable of interest is the difference between the students' average grades in their last year of high school and their average grades in the first year of university. Only grade categories (not actual specific number grades) are known, so if students' high school and university averages are in the same category (between 70 and 79, for example), then we know that their university grades are at most nine marks higher or nine marks lower than their high school grades. The upper bound of this range occurs if the high school average was 70 and the university average was 79. The lower bound occurs if the university and high school averages are reversed. If students' university grades are one category lower, then we know that their university average is from one mark to 19 marks lower than their high school average. This reasoning is used to calculate the range or interval of the change in grades for every student. The statistical method set out in the Appendix uses the grade change intervals to estimate how the *actual* grade changes are related, on average, to the characteristics included in the analysis, even though only the grade change intervals (and not the actual grade changes) can be calculated from the data.

Our study differs from most of the literature in that it specifies the *change* in grades from high school to university as the variable of interest or dependent variable. Other work in the literature typically examines the *level* of post-secondary grades rather than the change, but high school grades are almost always included as an explanatory variable in any related regression analysis, and the estimated coefficients on high school grades are always large, positive, and overwhelmingly statistically significant.

Thus, examining the level of university grades *relative to* (or controlling for) the level of high school grades in this way is actually not very different from looking at the change in grades from high school to university. Our approach (i.e., the latter) essentially stems from our emphasis on the *transition* perspective we prefer, in contrast to the *first year outcomes* perspective of others.[4]

In our case the outcome variable (i.e., the *change* in grades) is generally negative, and we look at how various student characteristics and the other variables included in the models result in more or less negative outcomes (i.e., smaller or larger grade decreases), rather than looking at the *level* of grades in university (which are of course always positive) and how they are higher or lower depending on the various influences. In any event, we are able to relate the findings gained with our approach to the existing literature, since a positive or negative effect in the one kind of specification will typically generate a similar effect in the other.

In addition, previous work in this area generally specifies a linear relationship between high school and university grades, whereas we essentially test this specification by including the level of high school grades as an explanatory variable in our change-of-grades model with a set of dummy variables, thus allowing for non-linear effects. Grades are therefore allowed to decrease to a greater or lesser degree depending on the high school grade level. For example, grades may generally drop less – or more – for students with higher high school grades than for those with lower high school grades. Our results are quite interesting in this regard.

Empirical Findings

Since the estimates control simultaneously for all of the variables included in the analysis, the estimates are relative to a baseline or comparison set of characteristics. The baseline characteristics correspond to a student who is female, attended a high school in an urban location in Ontario, is not a visible minority or an immigrant, lived with two parents in high school, had parents whose highest education level is completed high school and a family income level of $50,000 to $75,000, did not move to start PSE and lived with parents during first year of university, had a grade average in the last year of high school between 80 and 89, had sciences, engineering, or health as major field of study at university, was at a university with an overall enrolment of 10,000 to 14,999 students, and had no first year classes with fewer than 35 students and less than half with fewer than 75 students.

The results discussed below are taken from the coefficient estimates shown in the far right column of Table A1 in the Appendix. This specification (column) includes all of the variables considered in the estimation. The other specifications exclude different sets of characteristics, and they are reported to show whether the estimates are sensitive to those exclusions and provide alternative perspectives on the relationships in question.

Given the baseline characteristics listed above and the coefficient estimates in that final column of Table A1, the predicted average decrease in grades from high school to first year university for the baseline student is 9.2 marks. This is close to but slightly less than the actual 9.7 mark overall average decrease in grades cited above. The difference occurs because the latter represents the average change in grades over all individuals, and thus corresponds to the mean characteristics in the sample; namely, a student who would be 59 percent female and 41 percent male, 83 percent urban and 17 percent rural, etc. The average predicted grade change, in contrast, corresponds to the baseline individual described above (female, high school in urban Ontario, etc.). Just the difference in gender (i.e., making the baseline student female rather than considering the "average" gender, or actual male-female mix in the sample) accounts for more than half of the difference between the estimate of the overall average and the baseline student's decline in grades.

Figure 1 shows the predicted average decline in grades for the female baseline student and a male student who possesses all of the characteristics of the baseline student except gender. Male students experience on average a 0.7 mark larger decrease in average grades after controlling for all of the other student, parent, and university characteristics, and the difference is statistically significant at the 5 percent level. This is a robust result consistent across all of the different regression specifications that were estimated (i.e., the other columns of Table A1).

FIGURE 1
Average Grade Change by Gender

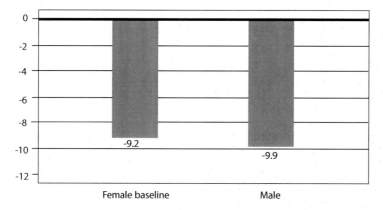

Note: Difference between males and females is statistically significant at the 5 percent level.
Source: Authors' compilation.

Given our approach of studying changes in grade levels versus the grade level effects typically generated in the literature, we interpret the smaller estimated grade decrease for women to be consistent with the results cited in the literature: namely, that women earn higher post-secondary grades than do men after controlling for high school grades. The same sort of comparison is made for the other results from the literature cited below. Specifically, smaller decreases in grades for a given characteristic (such as gender) are considered comparable to the findings of higher levels of grades for that same characteristic in the literature, with analogous comparisons for changes in the opposite directions (i.e., greater decreases correspond to negative effects).

Figure 2 shows a more tentative result from the regression equation. Students who attend high schools in rural areas are estimated to receive a 0.7 mark larger decrease in grades than those who attend high schools in urban areas. The estimated difference, however, is only significant at the 12 percent level, but all of the other specifications (shown in Table A1) yield estimates that are statistically significant at conventional significance levels.

Differences across provinces account for some of the largest variations in predicted grade changes, and these are shown in Figure 3. The largest grade decreases, after controlling for the other factors, are found in Newfoundland, Nova Scotia, and Saskatchewan. The differences between those provinces and Ontario (the comparison category) are statistically significant at the 1 percent level and are consistent across all of the

FIGURE 2
Average Grade Change by Urban vs. Rural

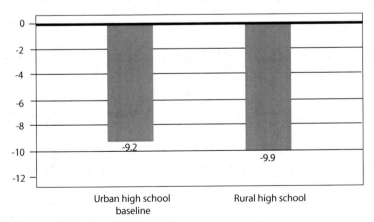

Note: Difference between urban and rural high schools is not statistically significant.
Source: Authors' compilation.

FIGURE 3
Average Grade Change by Province

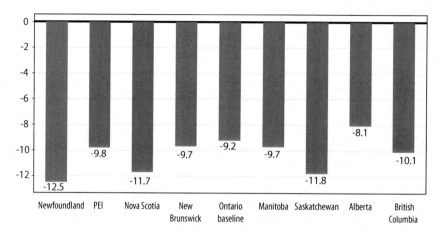

Notes: Differences between Newfoundland, Nova Scotia, and Saskatchewan and baseline Ontario are significant at the 1 percent level. Differences between Alberta and British Columbia and baseline Ontario are significant at the 10 percent level.

Source: Authors' compilation.

specifications. Alberta is estimated to have the smallest decline in grades. It is only different from the baseline Ontario at the 10 percent significance level in the final specification, but it is consistently significant at the 5 or 1 percent levels in all of the other specifications. The decrease in grades in British Columbia is intermediate between the smaller decreases in Ontario and Alberta and the larger decreases mentioned above, and it is also only statistically significant (compared to the baseline Ontario) at the 10 percent level.

The regression analysis investigates whether grade changes vary according to whether the student was a visible minority, whether he or she was an immigrant to Canada, and what the family status was while the student was in high school (two parents present versus other family types). The estimated coefficients on these variables are small and very far from statistically significant in all of the specifications (and are therefore not graphed), so it is reasonable to conclude that grade changes from high school to university are not related to any of these factors. The insignificant result for visible minority is inconsistent with much of the literature cited above, but most of the other studies use data on American students where visible minorities (mainly blacks and Hispanics) are generally disadvantaged groups, which is not the case for Canada, especially among this sample of youth who completed high school in Canada.[5]

A variable indicating whether students moved to start PSE is also included in the analysis. The results are mixed and generally statistically insignificant, so we conclude that moving to start PSE is not estimated to be related to changes in grades in any clear fashion.

Figure 4 shows the predicted grade changes for different categories of parental education. The predicted grade decreases are smaller when parents report high levels of education, and this is consistent with the results found in the literature. Most of the differences across parent education categories are not statistically significant, although the estimated 1.4 mark difference between post-graduate studies and the baseline of completed high school is significant at the 5 percent level, and the estimated 1 mark difference in grade decreases between completed high school and a bachelor's degree is significant at the 10 percent level. We thus conclude that parental education has an effect, but one that is limited to the highest (parental) schooling levels.

FIGURE 4
Average Grade Change by Parents' Education

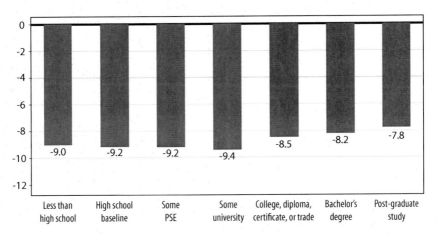

Notes: Difference between completed high school and post-graduate study is significant at the 5 percent level. Difference between completed high school and a bachelor's degree is significant at the 10 percent level.
Source: Authors' compilation.

Consistent with the literature, family income is also estimated to be related to grade decreases. The predicted grade changes for family income categories, arranged from lower to higher, are reported in Figure 5. Although the predicted impact of higher income is not monotonic, it is clear that there are at least some differences between higher and lower family incomes. Average grade decreases are estimated to be 1.2 marks greater when family income is $25,000 to $50,000 compared to the baseline income of $50,000 to $75,000, and the difference is statistically significant at the 5 percent level. Students with family income between $5,000 and

FIGURE 5
Average Grade Change by Family Income

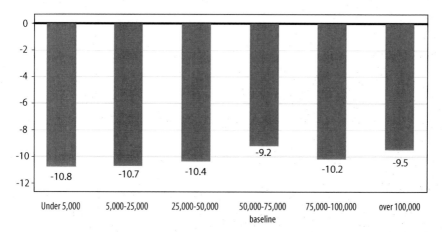

Notes: Differences between 25K-50K and 75K-100K and the baseline 50K-75K category are significant at the 5 percent level. Difference between 5K-25K and the baseline 50K-75K category is
significant at the 10 percent level.
Source: Authors' compilation.

$25,000 experience a 1.5 mark larger decrease in grades than the baseline
group, although this estimate is only significant at the 10 percent level.
An exception to the lower income–larger grade decrease tendency occurs
for students with family income in the $75,000 to $100,000 range. Their
grades decline one mark more on average than the lower income baseline
group, and the difference is significant at the 5 percent level. Furthermore,
the decrease of 9.5 for the highest income group (over $100,000) is also
greater than the baseline group ($50,000 to $75,000), although this difference is not statistically significant. We conclude that there appears to
be some relationship between family income and grade changes, but it
is mixed and seems strongest for lower income groups.[6] The association
is not, in any event, as strong as some might have expected or as some
others have previously found.[7]

Interestingly, the largest differences in grade changes occur across different levels of high school grades. Figure 6 shows that students with the
highest category of high school average grades (90 to 100) experience,
on average, an 11.9 mark decrease in their grades after controlling for
the other variables in the analysis. Students in the middle category, with
high school averages in the 80s, experience the baseline 9.2 mark decline.
Students who went on to university with the lowest high school averages (i.e., in the 60s and 70s, but almost all in the 70s) experience a much
smaller decline of only 4.4 marks. All of the differences are statistically
significant at the 1 percent level.

FIGURE 6
Average Grade Change by High School Grade

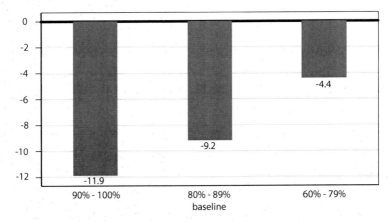

Note: Differences between all of the grades changes are statistically significant at the 1 percent level.

Source: Authors' compilation.

Thus, students in different high school grade categories do not experience the same decreases in grades, nor even the same percentage decreases, and the hypothesis that there is a linear relationship between university and high school grades is rejected. More importantly, it is not the weaker (academically) high school students who experience the largest decreases in grades when they attend university. Instead, the highest achieving group (in high school) has the largest decrease in grades – both proportionately as well as in absolute changes in marks – while the group with the lowest high school grades in this sample experiences the smallest decrease in grades from high school to the first year of university.

Note, however, that the differences in the sizes of the grade changes (across high school grade categories) are less than 10 marks, so students with higher high school grades still receive higher university grades; they are just not as much higher as they were in high school.

A possible explanation for these estimated grade changes, and those presented below for university size (Figure 7), is that students may be sorted across universities. Specifically, high school students with higher grades may tend to go to one set of "better" (and likely larger) universities, while those with lower grades go to a different set of (likely smaller) universities. High grade students are then compared to other high grade students at their universities, while low grade students are compared to other low grade students at their universities – but with the final grade distributions at each kind of university not being that different, i.e., with similar proportions of As, Bs, and so on, regardless of the "quality."

FIGURE 7
Average Grade Change by University Enrolment/Size

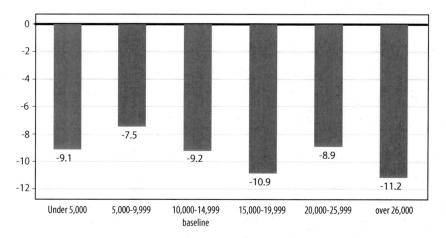

Notes: Grade decreases for the under 5,000 category are significantly different than those for the over 26,000 and 15,000-19,999 categories at the 1 percent level. Difference between under 5,000 and 5,000-9,999 is statistically significant at the 1 percent level.
Source: Authors' compilation.

The university grades that students receive in "higher entering grade universities" might in a sense be more meaningful and represent a higher level of absolute achievement, since they are gained in what is essentially a more competitive environment. By this reasoning, higher grade students experience greater decreases in grades when moving from high school to university because they are fitted into university grade curves generated by higher proportions of students with better high school records. The reverse may occur at "lower entering grade" universities (again, as defined by the high school marks of the student body). Investigating student sorting across universities, whether different universities have different grading standards, and the extent to which students' work is graded on a relative (to other students) rather than absolute basis are interesting and important topics, but they are left for future work.[8]

As suggested by the argument above, the regression estimates show that the size of the university attended (as measured by student enrolments) is related to the average decrease in grades experienced by students. The predicted grade changes are shown in Figure 7, with university size increasing from left to right. As with family income and parents' education, the estimated effects are not monotonic across the categories, but there is a difference between the larger and smaller size categories. In general, students at larger universities experience larger decreases in grades than those attending smaller universities. Specifically, students at universities with 15,000 to 20,000 students or over 26,000 students see their grades decrease on average by 1.8 and 2.1 marks (respectively) more than students at universities with under 5,000 students, and the differences are significant at the 1 percent level. The average decline in grades is even smaller at universities with 5,000 to 9,999 students, and the difference, compared to the smallest schools, is statistically significant at the 1 percent level. Students at the smallest universities of all, however, have grade changes close to the baseline change. Whether these patterns reflect differences in actual performance or the sorting effects mentioned just above with respect to the grade effects cannot be determined.

As reported in most of the literature cited above, there are also differences in the grade decreases across students' fields of study. Figure 8 shows that the average grades of students enrolled in the social sciences or business decline by 8.1 marks on average, while the average decline for students in sciences, engineering, or health is the baseline 9.2 marks, and the difference is statistically significant at the 5 percent level. Students enrolled in humanities, fine arts, communications, or education are estimated to experience an intermediate decline of 8.5 marks on average. Students who declare themselves as undecided or undeclared, or in "other" disciplines, experience the largest decrease in grades (10 marks), which is significantly larger than the decline for social sciences and business students at the 1 percent level.

FIGURE 8
Average Grade Change by Major Field of Study

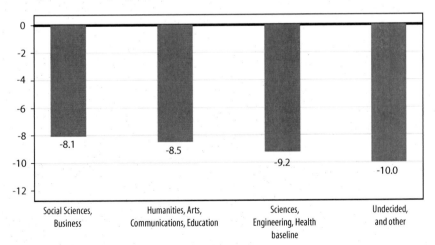

Notes: Difference between social sciences and sciences is statistically significant at the 5 percent level. Difference between social sciences and undecided is statistically significant at the 1 percent level.

Source: Authors' compilation.

Living arrangements are also related to the average decline in grades. Figure 9 shows that students' grades decline less in first year university on average if they live with their parents compared to all of the other living arrangements, and most of the differences are statistically significant. In particular, the average decline in grades is estimated to be 2.1 marks larger, after controlling for all of the other factors in the analysis, if students lived in a student residence compared to living with their parents, and the difference is statistically significant at the 1 percent level. This is contrary to the Terenzini et al. (1996) summary of the literature that concludes that students living with their parents off-campus do no better than those in residence. The same study reports that students in residence earn higher grades than those living off-campus (with other students or alone), while the differences are insignificant here. Again, the difference may result because the literature cited above considers mostly students in the United States, where universities and colleges are likely to be more residential than universities in Canada and have fewer commuter students.

The last factors considered are measures of first year class sizes. These are coded as numerical values rather than categories, so it is difficult to express their estimates graphically. In general, the average decline in grades is smaller if students are enrolled in more classes with fewer than 35 students and fewer than 75 students (i.e., smaller classes). The estimate for the 75 student threshold, however, is not statistically significant in any

FIGURE 9
Average Grade Change by Student Habitation in First Year

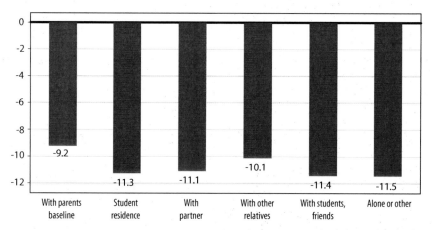

Notes: Difference between living with parents and in student residence is statistically significant at the 1 percent level. Difference between living with parents and with students or friends is statistically significant at the 5 percent level. Difference between living with parents and alone or other is statistically significant at the 10 percent level.

Source: Authors' compilation.

of the specifications, and the estimate for the 35 student threshold is only significant at the 10 percent level.[9]

Conclusion and Policy Implications

This paper has presented an empirical examination of the change in grades experienced from the last year of high school to the first year of university for a representative sample of Canadian students. The topic is important because the change in grades that students experience can affect their well-being directly by causing stress and affecting their level of self-confidence; can negatively impact scholarships, program eligibility, and other academic options; and can affect various schooling outcomes, including academic advancement and degree completion (i.e., persistence). Studying students' grade changes can help predict how individual students are likely to do, help put any given student's performance in perspective, and perhaps lead to improvements in these grade outcomes through policy interventions of various types.

Consistent with what one would expect from the literature, female students and students with more educated and higher income parents generally experience smaller decreases in average grades from high school to university. Changes in average grades also vary across major fields of study, with undeclared students experiencing the largest decreases and social sciences and business students the smallest. Students attending the largest universities experience the largest decreases in grades, while students who live with their parents see their grades fall by less than students with other living arrangements. Decreases in grades are not uniform across different levels of high school grades, and stronger students (as measured by high school grades) suffer the largest decreases in grades. Contrary to the US evidence, grade changes for visible minorities in Canada are not different from those for other students.

The regression estimates show that while many of the individual characteristics are associated with only small changes in grades, the accumulated effects can be substantial. For example, the average grade of a rural male student, living in Newfoundland, with family income below $25,000 and parents having completed high school, is predicted to decline by over 8 marks more than an urban female living in Alberta, with family income greater than $100,000 and whose parents have a post-graduate level of schooling, other factors held constant. Note that this example does not include the substantial further differences estimated for differences in major, university size, or living arrangements, which could account for a further 8 mark difference in the predicted change in grades.

These empirical results represent a simple first attempt to study Canadian university students' grade changes and are mainly intended to be descriptive. In particular, we advise caution in inferring causality from the findings. The estimates may be biased due to the omission of other factors that are correlated with the explanatory variables included here and with the change in grades. There may also be selection or sorting of students across major fields of study, university sizes, first year living arrangements, and some of the other explanatory variables such that the differences in grade changes across those variables are actually due to different characteristics of the students or universities that are not controlled for in the analysis.

Notwithstanding these caveats, if we entertain at least the possibility of some causality in the estimated relationships, then the results may not only provide a better understanding of the grade change process and allow for better predictions of how individual students might be expected to do but may also have certain policy implications. Consistent with an emerging literature regarding gender differences, male students, especially those with less educated and lower income family backgrounds and possibly certain other characteristics, should perhaps be monitored in university more carefully and targeted for academic support programs more than others, although this would of course have to be done in a sensitive and respectful manner. Indeed, it is not even clear that any given intervention would necessarily have positive outcomes (one can think of negative stigma effects, for example), and the effects of any initiatives should be tested using rigorous scientific methods, preferably before being rolled out in a general way.

For provincial governments, the results offer an argument to have more and smaller (but not too small) universities in more cities. According to the estimates, this strategy would lessen the decrease in grades directly (the university size effect) and likely enable more students to continue to live with their parents (i.e., if there were more local institutions), leading to a further decline in the grade decrease due to the estimated living arrangement effect. Furthermore, high school counsellors might be enlisted to encourage students to continue to live with their parents – again to capitalize on the living arrangements effects found here. Of course, students' living arrangements evolve for many reasons and likely have many effects (including those not related to their schooling outcomes – personal growth, for instance), so potential grade effects would be just one consideration among others in the development of any policy initiative aimed in this direction.

A final policy prescription possibly implied by the estimates is for high schools to change their grading scales and bring them more into line with what is found at universities (i.e., lower grade distributions), thus diminishing the (average) grade decreases that would be experienced when students attend university. While some may consider this approach a meaningless "re-nominalizing" of grades, it might not be the case if "grade shock" is a real and significant effect. In fact – especially in the absence of students' having full command of the regression model presented here and thus not being as able to predict their own university grades and not otherwise being aware of what grade changes typically occur – a revision of high school grading scales may provide more realistic signals to students about whether to attend university, what sorts of programs to attempt, and what to expect when they get there, which in turn should reduce disappointment and failed attempts at unsuitable programs.

Further research could go in many directions. One avenue would be to add more variables to the models, including the PISA scores available in the YITS. Another would be to explore the various sorting mechanisms discussed in this paper, especially those that involve higher and lower high school grade students going to institutions with proportionately greater numbers of their "type" and affecting their average grade changes accordingly (e.g., greater drops for better students). A final strategy might be to follow this point and investigate how university grades and the quality of the institution attended affect job market outcomes. For example, when it comes to getting a job and moving up the job ladder, is it more advantageous to go to a harder, better university and not do so well, or go to an easier, "poorer" institution? The richness of the YITS data suggest these possibilities among others.[10]

Notes

We would like to thank Yan Zhang of the MESA Project for her invaluable help with the YITS dataset and the estimation. We would also like to thank the editors of this book for their very helpful comments on earlier drafts and suggestions for further research. Support of this project by the Canada Millennium Scholarship Foundation through the MESA Project is also gratefully acknowledged.

1. The quote is from a liaison officer representing a Canadian university (not Brock or the University of Ottawa). Speaking to a group of high school students about the difficulties they might encounter on starting university, she explained that she had lost her own university entrance scholarship because she had not maintained the required 80 percent average in her first year. She said that it was not uncommon for students to lose entrance scholarships, and while it had been a real setback for her, she persevered and went on to complete a degree at that university.

2. The YITS-A was built up from the Canadian PISA (Program for International Student Assessment) sample in that year. See Motte et al. (2008) for detailed discussion of the YITS-A as well as the slightly older YITS-B cohort (aged 18-20 in December 1999).

3. We are grateful to the Education Division at Statistics Canada for facilitating this linkage.

4. Arguments can be made for either specification. Technically speaking, our approach is consistent with considering both high school grades and university grades to be separate outcomes of related (statistical) processes, where both are assumed to be determined by underlying forces, such as an

(unobserved) "ability" effect (plus other factors); thus we gather these two dependent variables together to form a single composite "change in grades" dependent variable, which has desirable statistical properties. Treating the level of university grades as the dependent variable and including high school grades as an explanatory variable is, conversely, consistent with high school grades being truly exogenous to university grades. In practice, such models typically generate comparable estimates after adjusting for the interpretation of the results as described here. As noted, the additional advantage of our approach is that it puts the emphasis on focusing on the changes we are interested in as part of the school-to-university transition.

5.   See Finnie and Mueller (2010) for patterns of access to post-secondary education among the children of immigrants. They find generally high university (rather than college) participation rates among immigrant youth, including both those who came to Canada with their immigrant parents and those born in Canada to immigrant parents.

6.   The less than $5,000 income group may include zeros that represent non-responses, and so the results for this category should be read with caution.

7.   The result is, however, consistent with Finnie and Qiu (2008a, 2008b), who find only a weak relationship between parental education and the persistence of university students.

8.   We are grateful to Arthur Sweetman for discussions on this issue. See Anglin and Meng (2000) regarding the related issue of differential grade inflation across disciplines over time, and Bishop (2002) on high school grades, standardized tests, and related issues.

9.   Furthermore, if the class size measures are coded as categories (an alternative specification not shown here), then none of the estimated coefficients are statistically significant.

10.   The authors are grateful to Rick Mueller and Arthur Sweetman for discussions regarding these future research ideas.

References

Adelman, C. 2006. "The Toolbox Revisited: Paths to Degree Completions from High School through College." Washington, DC: US Department of Education.

Anglin, P.M., and R. Meng. 2000. "Evidence on Grades and Grade Inflation at Ontario's Universities." *Canadian Public Policy / Analyse de Politiques* 26 (3): 361-8.

Arcidiacono, P. 2004. "Ability Sorting and the Returns to College Major." *Journal of Econometrics* 121: 343-75.

Betts, J.R., and D. Morell. 1999. "The Determinants of Undergraduate Grade Point Average." *Journal of Human Resources* 34 (2): 268-92.

Bishop, J. 2002. "School Choice, Exams and Achievement." In *Towards Evidence-Based Policy for Canadian Education*, ed. P. de Broucker and A. Sweetman, 385-417. Montreal and Kingston: John Deutsch Institute for the Study of Economic Policy, McGill-Queen's University Press.

Canadian Association of University Teachers. 2006. *CAUT Almanac of Post-Secondary Education in Canada* Ottawa: CAUT.

Finnie, R., and H.T. Qiu. 2008a. "The Patterns of Persistence in Post-Secondary Education in Canada: Evidence from the YITS-B Dataset." MESA Project

Research Paper. Toronto, MESA Project. http://www.mesa-project.org/pub/pdf/MESA_Finnie_Qiu_2008Aug12.pdf

– 2008b. "Is the Glass (or Classroom) Half-Empty or Nearly Full? New Evidence on Persistence in Post-Secondary Education in Canada." In *Who Goes? Who Stays? What Matters? Accessing and Persisting in Post-Secondary Education in Canada*, ed. R. Finnie, R.E. Mueller, A. Sweetman, and A. Usher, 179-208. Montreal and Kingston: Queen's Policy Studies Series, McGill-Queen's University Press.

Finnie, R., and R.E. Mueller. 2010. "They Came, They Saw, They Enrolled: Access to Post-Secondary Education by the Children of Canadian Immigrants." In *Pursuing Higher Education in Canada: Economic, Social, and Policy Dimensions*, ed. R. Finnie, M. Frenette, R.E. Mueller, and A. Sweetman, 191-216. Montreal and Kingston: Queen's Policy Studies Series, McGill-Queen's University Press.

Gilbert, S., J. Chapman, P. Dietsche, P. Grayson, and J. Gardver. 1997. *From Best Intentions to Best Practices: The First-Year Experience in Canadian Postsecondary Education*. Columbia, SC: University of South Carolina National Resource Center for the Freshman Year Experience and Students in Transition.

Horowitz, J.B., and L. Spector. 2005. "Is There a Difference between Private and Public Education on College Performance?" *Economics of Education Review* 24 (2): 189-95.

Hotchkiss, J., R. Moore, and M. Pitts. 2006. "Freshman Learning Communities, College Performance, and Retention." *Education Economics* 14 (2): 197-210.

Martinello, F. 2008. "Transitions and Adjustments in Students' Post-Secondary Education." In *Who Goes? Who Stays? What Matters? Accessing and Persisting in Post-Secondary Education in Canada*, ed. R. Finnie, R.E. Mueller, A. Sweetman, and A. Usher, 209-38. Montreal and Kingston: Queen's Policy Studies Series, McGill-Queen's University Press.

Monks, J. 2000. "The Academic Performance of Legacies." *Economics Letter* 67 (1): 99-104

Motte, A., H.T. Qiu, Y. Zhang, and P. Bussière. 2008. "The Youth in Transition Survey: Following Canadian Youth through Time." In *Who Goes? Who Stays? What Matters? Accessing and Persisting in Post-Secondary Education in Canada*, ed. R. Finnie, R.E. Mueller, A. Sweetman, and A. Usher, 63-78. Montreal and Kingston: Queen's Policy Studies Series, McGill-Queen's University Press.

Mouw, J.T., and R.K. Khanna. 1993. "Prediction of Academic Success: A Review of the Literature and Some Recommendations." *College Student Journal* 27 (1): 228-36.

Pascarella, E.T., and P.T. Terenzini. 1991. *How College Affects Students*. Vol. 1. San Francisco: Jossey-Bass.

– 2005. *How College Affects Students*. Vol. 2. San Francisco: Jossey-Bass.

Rothstein, J.M. 2004. "College Performance Predictions and the SAT." *Journal of Econometrics* 121: 297-317.

Smith, J.S., D. Yun Dai, and B.P. Szelest. 2006. "Helping First-Year Students Make the Transition to College through Advisor-Researcher Collaboration." *NACADA Journal* 26 (1): 67-76.

StataCorp. 2003. *Stata Statistical Software: Release 8*. College Station, TX: StataCorp LP.

Stinebrickner, R., and T.R. Stinebrickner. 2003. "Working during School and Academic Performance." *Journal of Labor Economics* 21 (2): 473-91.

– 2004. "Time Use and College Outcomes." *Journal of Econometrics* 121: 243-69.

Terenzini, P.T., E.T. Pascarella, and G.S. Blimling. 1996. "Students' Out-of-Class Experiences and Their Influence on Learning and Cognitive Development: A Literature Review." *Journal of College Student Development* 37 (2): 149-62.

Win, R., and P.W. Miller. 2005. "The Effects of Individual and School Factors on University Students' Academic Performance." *Australian Economic Review* 38 (1): 1-18.

TECHNICAL APPENDIX

As noted in the text, the dependent variable is the change in average grade from the last year of high school to the first year university. It is calculated as the university grade minus the high school grade. Since only 10-mark grade categories (e.g., 70-79) are known, it is expressed as a range with endpoints:

lower bound = lower endpoint of university grade range minus upper endpoint of high school grade range

upper bound = upper endpoint of university grade range minus lower endpoint of high school grade range

For example, if high school grades are in the 80-89 range, and university grades are in the 70-79 range (a decrease of one grade category), then the range of the actual underlying grade change is -19 to -1. If university grades are two categories lower, then the range of the dependent variable is -29 to -11, and so on.

Specify a regression equation:

$$y_i = X_i \beta + \varepsilon_i \qquad (1)$$

where y_i is the actual change in grades experienced by student i, X_i is a row vector containing the values of the right hand side variables for student i, β is a column vector of regression coefficients, and ε_i is a random variable with distribution $N(0, \sigma^2)$. For any student i, y_i is not known; only the upper bound (y_{ui}) and lower bound (y_{li}) are known, and these are calculated using the definitions given above. Given this, estimates of the elements of β can be calculated by maximizing the following log likelihood function

$$1nL = \sum_{i=1}^{N} w_i 1n \left\{ F\left(\frac{y_{ui} - X_i \beta}{\sigma} \right) - F\left(\frac{y_{li} - X_i \beta}{\sigma} \right) \right\} \qquad (2)$$

where w_i is the population weight on student i and $F()$ is the cumulative normal distribution function. Essentially, the regression estimates are calculated by integrating over the range of the dependent variable interval in the same way that tobit analysis integrates over the censored range of a dependent variable. The coefficient and standard error estimates can be interpreted as if the regression is a standard linear OLS regression with the actual numerical change in grades as the dependent variable. The only difference from OLS is that the regression explicitly accounts for the fact that the actual numerical grade change is not known – only a range for the change is known.

The estimates are calculated using the *intreg* regression command in Stata (published by StataCorp), which implements this method. Robust estimates of the standard errors are calculated using the Huber/White adjustment for arbitrary heteroscedasticity, which is an option in the *intreg* command.

The estimated coefficients and robust estimates of their standard error are reported in Table A1 for various specifications. The specification at the far right is used for the analysis in the text since it includes all of the right hand side variables. The estimates in the other columns exclude different sets of right hand side variables and are reported to show the stability of the estimates across alternative specifications.

Two other estimations methods were tried, and they yielded similar results. One method set students' grades equal to the midpoint of their category, and calculated OLS estimates with the dependent variable defined to be the difference between the university and high school average grades. Another method defined the dependent variable to be the number of categories that grades changed (e.g., 0 if grades stayed in the same category, 1 if grades increased by one category, -1 if grades decreased by one category, and so on). Ordered multinomial probit estimation was then applied to calculate the coefficient estimates. The results from the interval regression method are reported and used here because: (a) unlike the OLS estimates, they explicitly account for the fact that grade averages are reported as categories and the actual numerical value of the grade change is not known, and (b) unlike the ordered probit, the estimated coefficients are easy to interpret since they provide the estimated marginal effects in terms of actual marks.

Finally, note that the omitted categories for the sets of dummy variables in the regression equation do not always correspond to the baseline or comparison characteristics used in the text above. Different baseline characteristics are used for the graphs and discussion in the text so that the predicted decrease in grades for the baseline student is close to the overall average decrease in grades. This is done in an attempt to make the explanation of the regression results in the text easier and more intuitive and makes no difference for the actual results.

TABLE A1
Regression Coefficient Estimates (omitted category is shown in parentheses)

Variable	Specifications					
Female (male)	0.466	0.442	0.462	0.644*	0.688**	0.666**
	[0.362]	[0.361]	[0.362]	[0.342]	[0.337]	[0.337]
HS location – urban (rural)	1.217***	1.183***	1.182***	0.721*	0.796*	0.695
	[0.435]	[0.437]	[0.432]	[0.433]	[0.431]	[0.438]
HS province (Ontario)						
Newfoundland and Labrador	-1.732***	-1.657***	-1.768***	-2.497***	-3.163***	-3.291***
	[0.635]	[0.642]	[0.649]	[0.643]	[0.736]	[0.736]
Prince Edward Island	0.613	0.676	0.634	0.256	-0.449	-0.604
	[0.515]	[0.525]	[0.526]	[0.511]	[0.635]	[0.632]
Nova Scotia	-1.393***	-1.344***	-1.381***	-1.259**	-2.404***	-2.489***
	[0.489]	[0.493]	[0.495]	[0.496]	[0.56]	[0.558]
New Brunswick	0.856*	0.936*	0.893*	0.38	-0.356	-0.475
	[0.492]	[0.502]	[0.505]	[0.499]	[0.572]	[0.57]
Manitoba	1.592***	1.609***	1.616***	1.005*	-0.382	-0.539
	[0.526]	[0.527]	[0.527]	[0.529]	[0.605]	[0.607]
Saskatchewan	-3.083***	-2.947***	-2.955***	-2.591***	-2.418***	-2.588***
	[0.543]	[0.549]	[0.551]	[0.523]	[0.545]	[0.566]
Alberta	1.679***	1.676***	1.635***	1.412**	1.227**	1.129*
	[0.623]	[0.622]	[0.624]	[0.596]	[0.62]	[0.63]
British Columbia	-1.492***	-1.47***	-1.466***	-1.065**	-0.814	-0.89*
	[0.534]	[0.533]	[0.53]	[0.498]	[0.498]	[0.499]
Visible minority (all others)	0.082	0.216	0.241	0.311	0.596	0.531
	[0.565]	[0.571]	[0.57]	[0.529]	[0.532]	[0.528]
Immigrant (non-immigrant)	-1.101	-0.976	-1.021	-0.587	-0.4402	-0.468
	[0.722]	[0.736]	[0.744]	[0.694]	[0.6979]	[0.694]
Family type (not two parents present)						
Two parents	0.006	-0.232	-0.195	0.021	0.1901	0.159
	[0.527]	[0.574]	[0.578]	[0.528]	[0.5161]	[0.519]
Moved to start PSE (did not move)				-0.468	-0.618*	1.105
				[0.373]	[0.372]	[0.758]
Parent/guardian's education (HS complete)						
Less than HS			0.832	0.1949	0.238	0.178
			[0.979]	[1.0269]	[1.024]	[1.022]
Some PSE			-0.398	-0.001	0.134	-0.013
			[0.922]	[0.7917]	[0.794]	[0.8]
Trade/college			0.292	0.6202	0.795	0.731
			[0.611]	[0.5839]	[0.580]	[0.58]
University – below BA degree			-1.221	-0.3221	-0.177	-0.227
			[0.981]	[0.9244]	[0.908]	[0.903]
University – BA			0.168	0.8646	1.046*	0.959*
			[0.588]	[0.5769]	[0.575]	[0.578]
Post-graduate study			-0.11	1.2030*	1.482**	1.45**
			[0.685]	[0.6577]	[0.65]	[0.652]
Family income level ($50,000 to $75,000)						
Extremely low ($0-$5000)		-2.561	-2.649*	-1.94	-1.791	-1.587
		[1.579]	[1.582]	[1.291]	[1.369]	[1.424]
$5,000 to $25,000		-1.019	-1.052	-1.864**	-1.629**	-1.511**
		[0.904]	[0.916]	[0.841]	[0.831]	[0.842]
$25,000 to $50,000		-1.242**	-1.282**	-1.249**	-1.203**	-1.167**
		[0.53]	[0.533]	[0.491]	[0.49]	[0.489]
$75,000 to $100,000		-0.748	-0.679	-0.906**	-1.029*	-0.963**
		[0.495]	[0.495]	[0.451]	[0.448]	[0.446]
$100,000 and up		-0.337	-0.293	-0.408	-0.352	-0.294
		[0.52]	[0.555]	[0.513]	[0.503]	[0.506]

... continued

TABLE A1
(Continued)

Variable	Specifications					
Overall grade of last year HS (60% to 79%)						
90% to 100%			-8.023***	-7.52***	-7.512***	
			[0.514]	[0.512]	[0.512]	
80% to 89%			-5.254***	-4.82***	-4.809***	
			[0.399]	[0.405]	[0.406]	
Major field of study in 1st year of university (social sciences and business)						
Humanities, arts, communications, and education			-0.505	-0.445	-0.457	
			[0.45]	[0.445]	[0.447]	
Sciences, engineering, and health			-1.175**	-1.166**	-1.15**	
			[0.475]	[0.469]	[0.469]	
Undecided and other			-1.912***	-1.978***	-1.956***	
			[0.569]	[0.554]	[0.556]	
2003-2004 FTE students (0 - 5,000)						
26,000 and up				-1.904***	-2.077***	
				[0.653]	[0.647]	
20,000 to 25,999				0.333	0.183	
				[0.683]	[0.677]	
15,000 to 19,999				-1.721***	-1.766***	
				[0.636]	[0.634]	
10,000 to 14,999				0.01	-0.112	
				[0.547]	[0.544]	
5,000 to 9,999				1.756***	1.623***	
				[0.635]	[0.627]	
Living arrangements in first year (with parent /guardian)						
In a student residence					-2.074***	
					[0.804]	
With girlfriend/boyfriend/spouse and/or children					-1.889	
					[1.574]	
With other relatives, e.g., brother, aunt					-0.925	
					[0.962]	
With students or friends, off campus					-2.226**	
					[0.894]	
On own / boarding house / other					-2.267*	
					[1.252]	
Proportion of 1st year classes less than 35 students[a]						
None = 1; less than half = 2; about half = 3; more than half = 4; all = 5			0.433*	0.431*	0.448*	
			[0.235]	[0.234]	[0.235]	
Proportion of 1st year classes less than 75 students[a]						
None = 1; less than half = 2; about half = 3; more than half = 4; all = 5			0.273	0.231	0.204	
			[0.172]	[0.172]	[0.171]	
Constant	-10.702***	-9.926***	-10.005***	-6.279***	-6.095***	-5.508***
	[0.706]	[0.815]	[0.908]	[1.053]	[1.13]	[1.154]
Number of observations	5,215	5,215	5,215	5,203	5,203	5,203

Note: Dependent variable is the range of the change in average grades from the last year of high school to first year of university, defined as the university grade minus the high school grade.
Robust standard errors are shown in square brackets.

[a] Variable is coded as a continuous number, according to definitions given in the line below, and not a set of dummy variable categories.

***, **, * indicate statistically significant at the 1 percent, 5 percent, or 10 percent levels, respectively.

Source: Authors' compilation.

3

Gender Differences in High School Grades: Causes and Possible Impacts on the University Gender Gap

Torben Drewes

Étant donné que, parmi les jeunes qui obtiennent un diplôme d'études secondaires, les résultats des garçons sont inférieurs à ceux des filles, les critères d'admission minimums qu'utilisent les universités pourraient être la cause du déséquilibre dans le nombre d'hommes et de femmes que l'on observe parmi les étudiants des universités canadiennes. Dès lors, il serait intéressant d'établir pourquoi les garçons obtiennent des notes inférieures à celles des filles au secondaire. Dans cet article, j'estime une fonction de production des notes afin d'analyser l'incidence de l'intensité de l'effort fourni par les élèves sur l'écart entre les notes des garçons et celles des filles. Les données de l'Enquête auprès des jeunes en transition nous permettent ainsi d'observer que plus de la moitié de l'écart entre les notes moyennes des garçons et des filles s'explique par des différences dans l'intensité de l'effort fourni. Le fait que ce facteur n'explique qu'une partie de l'écart implique également que les garçons sont moins susceptibles que les filles d'obtenir de bonnes notes.

Given the different distributions of high school grades for male and female graduates, rationing of university places using minimum admissions standards could potentially produce the gender imbalance observed in Canadian universities. Why high school marks are lower for males then becomes a question of some interest. This paper estimates a grades production function to examine the role of different effort levels in generating gender differences in high school grades. Using data from the Youth in Transition Survey, it finds that over half of the difference in mean grades between males and females can be accounted for by different levels of effort. The remaining difference suggests that boys are less able to produce good grades in high school.

Pursuing Higher Education in Canada: Economic, Social, and Policy Dimensions, ed. R. Finnie, M. Frenette, R.E. Mueller, and A. Sweetman. Montreal and Kingston: Queen's Policy Studies Series, McGill-Queen's University Press.

Introduction

In a single generation, women have moved from minority representation in Canada's universities to a significant majority, accounting in 2006 for 58 percent of full-time undergraduate enrolment (AUCC 2007). The phenomenon is not unique to Canada. Women now form a majority of university students in 19 out of 22 OECD countries. The dramatic evolution of gender patterns in university enrolment is a fascinating social and economic phenomenon, but its causes and consequences are as yet not entirely understood.

Most of the research on the causes of the changing gender gap has focused on demand-side explanations, trying to understand why males are now less likely than females to *want* to continue on to a university education. Possible explanations range from sociological perspectives on the failure of schools to instill a desire for education among males to more orthodox economic paradigms suggesting that males face lower rates of return. This paper takes as its point of departure the question of why males are less likely to be *able* to pursue a university education. University spaces are rationed on the basis of high school averages, a practice that is gender neutral on the surface but may play a role in the gender gap since males have lower high school grades than females.[1]

Current admissions standards coupled with observed gender differences in high school grades have the potential to generate observed gender differences in university participation rates even if both males and females are equally likely to apply to university. Since obtaining the grades necessary for admission requires effort, however, lower high school grades among males may not necessarily be the *cause* of their lower participation rates. Rather, they may result from decisions made by them not to attend university and, consequently, not to expend the effort required to meet admissions standards.

This paper exploits the rich data in the Youth in Transition Survey (YITS) on high school behaviour and grades to explore the process by which high school grades are produced. In particular, the paper estimates the relationship between grades and effort levels to determine the extent to which the lower high school performance of males can be attributed to lower effort levels. If all of it can be attributed, then the observed gender gap in universities may be the result of males' choices not to participate, for whatever reason. If none of it can, then males and females differ in the efficiency with which they can produce the entrance requirements, and those requirements become culprits in the gender imbalance. Males should then be included with other under-represented groups about whom current educational policy is concerned.

The following section briefly reviews the very small literature on rationing by grades and on the educational production function applied at the individual level. After a brief overview of the data, a simple model of grades production is presented, followed by the empirical findings. Approximately half of the observed difference in mean grades between males and females can be accounted for by lower effort levels on the part of males. The other half is attributed to a lower efficiency among high school boys in converting effort into grades in the sense that boys exerting the same level of effort as girls obtain lower grades. This lower efficiency may then explain part of the gender gap in university participation.

Background

If lower high school grades among males are to play any role in the university gender gap, it must be true that rationing on the basis of those grades actually occurs. Some indirect evidence can be produced that this indeed is the case. Coelli (2005) found a significant negative relationship between cohort size and university attendance and interpreted this as evidence of rationing of university places. Fortin (2005) concurred, arguing that tuition levels are too low to clear the market in the face of large increases in the demand for university education, leaving the short side of the market to determine enrolment. That is, universities may use rationing on the basis of grades to allocate spaces, the number of which may be largely determined by the operating funds they receive from provincial governments.

Direct evidence of rationing is much harder to come by, as it requires information on individuals who applied to universities but were denied admission as well as those who may not have bothered to apply in expectation of not meeting admissions requirements. However, the application process in Ontario produces a set of data that can directly show the existence of rationing in that province. All high school graduates seeking admission to any of the province's universities must apply through a centralized application centre, the Ontario Universities Application Centre (OUAC). Applicants supply the centre with personal data, including financial information, which is used to determine financial assistance, and they make unlimited choices[2] of universities and programs to which they wish to apply. The high schools they attend supply the centre with information on the grades they obtained in their final twelve credits. Universities use these data to decide upon which students are offered admission and then report back to the centre on which students were offered admission into the program of choice and whether or not individuals eventually registered at the university. All of this information is used to construct a microdata file on applicants, which has been made available to some researchers. Figure 1 illustrates the number of applicants who received an offer of admission from at least one of their choices and the number who were entirely unsuccessful, by grade average in the final year of high school.[3]

FIGURE 1
Admissions and Denials, Ontario Universities, 2005

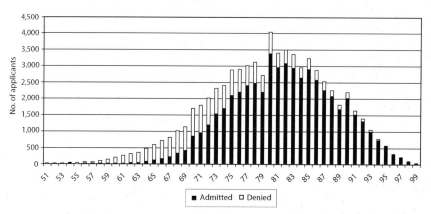

Source: OUAC data, 2005.

Not all applicants to Ontario universities in 2005 were offered admission, with 6.5 percent not receiving an offer from any institution. Since different universities and programs have different admissions requirements, there is no clear demarcation of a single cut-off grade in Figure 1. Nevertheless, it is clear that rationing does take place, largely on the basis of high school averages. Since the application process is costly in terms of time and money, and since students have fairly good information on minimum entrance requirements, OUAC applicants are self-selected in the sense that high school graduates with low grades may choose not to incur the cost if there is no reasonable hope of success. With lower grades, males are less likely to apply (and to appear in the data), even if they have aspirations for higher education similar to females. Therefore, one cannot simply compare the gender distribution of applicants to that of successful applicants to determine the impact of rationing on the gender gap. The high school grades (and the potential for successful application to university) must be examined for a representative sample of males and females.

The YITS data do not report unsuccessful applications for admission to university but do report high school grades for all individuals, whether or not they are applicants. Table 1 reports the distribution of high school grades by gender.

Now, suppose that all males and females wanted to go to university but faced a minimum grade of 70 percent for admission. For each 100 males and 100 females, 74 males and 86 females would have been accepted, and the proportion of females in university would be 54 percent. If the cut-off grade were 80 percent, the proportion of females would be 60 percent. Hypothetically, then, the use of high school grades to ration places in universities has the potential to generate the gender gap actually observed in Canada's universities.

TABLE 1
High School Grade Distributions

Grade %	Males %	Females %
90 +	5.8	8.7
80-89	26.4	37.8
70-79	41.8	39.1
60-69	21.4	12.3
55-59	3.1	1.5
50-54	0.9	0.4
< 50	0.6	0.3

Source: Author's compilations.

The YITS data thus show that gender-blind rationing on the basis of high school averages is theoretically capable of producing the observed gender gap in university participation, even if males are as likely to apply as females. But it is also theoretically possible that the grade distributions above are the result of grade targeting by males, many of whom had no intention of pursuing a university education and therefore had no reason to exert the effort required to obtain the minimum admissions cut-offs.[4] In fact, the reality is likely to be a combination of these two phenomena, which presumably explains Frenette and Zeman's (2007) allocation of underlying reasons for the gender gap to both grades and personal characteristics. Indeed, their results indicate that slightly more than 30 percent of the gap is caused by differences in high school grades although they did not account for the possibility of grade targeting.

Determining whether males are prevented from attending university due to low grades or whether males have low grades because they do not intend to go to university is a very difficult econometric problem and one that is not solved in this paper. Instead, the more modest objective is to determine whether males would have achieved high school grades similar to those of females had they worked as hard. An education production function approach is used here to address this issue.

Several authors have taken into account the active role that learners play in producing outcomes and have sought to model effort levels in a choice-theoretic framework. For example, Cho (2007) treats high school average as an outcome that can be increased through greater effort. The optimal level of effort is chosen to balance marginal benefits and costs, where the benefit produced by more effort is a higher probability of admission to post-secondary education (PSE) and the subsequent enjoyment of higher incomes. The model is used to examine how the increase in women's high school performance has contributed to the changing gender composition of American university students. This improved high school performance is found to explain more than half of the change in the university enrolment gender gap over the past 30 years. The improvement in women's high school achievement is partly due to exogenous changes in how high schools prepare women for university and partly due to increased effort levels induced by the greater benefits produced by expanded labour market opportunities for women.

Bishop (2006) argues that most of the education production function literature treats students as "goods in process" rather than active participants in the production of academic achievement. He provides evidence that student effort accounts for an important share of the variance in achievement across individuals but unfortunately does not investigate gender differences. A Cobb-Douglas specification of the learning function is used to derive theoretical results such as the optimal effort level, but the model is not implemented empirically.

Numerous studies find that indicators of student effort such as hours spent on studying or homework assignments have significant effects on learning.[5] Although multivariate methods are used to control for prior achievement and family background, effort indicators are typically regarded as exogenously determined. The fairly large literature on the relationship between performance and working while in school is more directly related to the research in this paper, since the connection between working and performance is derived from choices of time allocation within a fixed time budget. The findings on the impact of working on academic achievement (and, by extension, the impact of time available for studies) tend to be ambiguous.[6]

Stinebrickner and Stinebrickner (2004, 2007) have produced research most directly related to the estimates that follow here. In both papers, the objective is to estimate the relationship between educational outcomes and students' study time and effort. The authors acknowledge endogeneity of effort but contend that the causal effect of studying can be identified by using a unique feature of the institution-specific data available to them. At this particular institution, roommates are assigned randomly, and the data allow observation of certain characteristics of roommates. Specifically, some individuals found themselves housed with roommates who brought video games with them, while others did not. The resulting exogenous variation in the quantity and quality of studying induced by the presence or absence of such distractions allows the authors to conclude that study efforts have a substantial causal role to play in the grades production function.

Data and Descriptive Statistics

The Youth in Transition Survey (YITS) is a longitudinal survey designed to provide information about education, training, and work experiences of two target populations: a cohort of individuals who were 18 to 20 years old on 31 December 1999 (Cohort B) and a cohort who were 15 years old on that date (Cohort A).[7] This paper uses Cohort A. YITS has now gone through four cycles, with the first conducted in 2000 on almost 30,000 students and the latest follow-up done in 2006 when respondents were 21 years of age. Since almost all respondents were finished high school by the time of the last cycle, only the first three are used in this paper in order not to lose observations through attrition between Cycles 3 and 4. In the first cycle, YITS obtained information from students, parents, and school administrators to produce a rich set of information on student behaviours and aspirations, family background, school resources available, and so on. In addition, Cohort A participated in the OECD's Programme for International Student Assessment (PISA) evaluations, writing standard tests in the areas of reading, mathematics, and science skills.

YITS respondents were asked their overall grade average in their last year of high school in all cycles, with the results reported by grade category, as in Table 1. This self-reported measure serves as the dependent variable. Three measures of effort are used in the estimates of the grades production function. First, YITS respondents were asked to report the number of weekly hours spent studying outside of class.[8] Second, the YITS reports the number of times the individual skipped classes. Finally, among measures of behaviour, respondents were asked to report how often the statement that "they did as little work as possible, wanting to just get by" applied to their studies. All three effort variables apply to the final year of high school. Other variables to be included in the grades production function are derived from information on parental financial resources, education, and support, as well as school resources. The YITS gathered this information directly from parents and school officials, but only in the first cycle of the survey, so that this information may apply to the student's background several years before the last year of high school (when the high school grade used in this paper is measured). The same is true of the PISA scores, which were determined at age 15.

Figures 2 through 5 provide a statistical preview of differences in grades and effort levels between males and females in their final year of high school. The descriptive statistics are also broken down by aspirations for a university education, to get some preliminary sense of whether effort levels might be driven by the need to satisfy university entrance requirements. Clearly, simultaneity will be a problem here, since effort may be motivated by aspirations for higher education, but those aspirations may in turn be affected by the student's assessment of his or her ability, as measured by high school grades. University aspirations used here are those reported only in the first YITS cycle, to try to avoid as much as possible the kind of dynamic endogeneity resulting from revisions to aspirations as the individual moves through high school and through periodic assessments of ability.

Figure 2 repeats the information in Table 1 and adds a comparison of grades distributions for only those males and females with stated

FIGURE 2
High School Grade Distributions

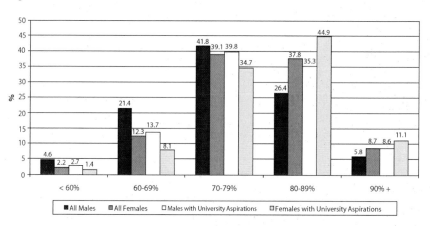

Source: Author's compilations.

aspirations for at least a university degree.[9] Within each of the five possible grade ranges, the height of each bar represents the proportion of each of the four possible combinations of gender and university aspiration achieving that grade. The proportion with grades of at least 80 percent are significantly higher when only those with university aspirations are considered, rising from 32.2 percent to 43.9 percent for males and from 46.5 percent to 56.0 percent for females. Again, whether higher grades among those with aspirations for university were the result of students working harder in the knowledge that they would need to meet admissions standards or, rather, higher grades were causing those aspirations is a question not settled in this paper. It is interesting to note, however, that the gender gap in the proportion of "A" students (those with grades of 80 percent or higher) falls from 14.3 percentage points in the population as a whole to 12.1 percentage points among those with university aspirations. If hopes for a university education drive efforts to earn grades in high school, this is the first sign that differences in those efforts matter.

The next three figures provide tabulations of the three measures of effort in the YITS data to be used in the estimates of the education production function. Figure 3 reports the most direct measure of effort by tabulating the number of hours of study outside the classroom. A disappointing 16 percent of males, compared to 6 percent of females, reported spending less than one hour of study per week. Using mid-points of the categories and 17.5 hours for the top open-ended category, the average number of hours spent studying would be 4.7 for males and 6.4 for females. Among those with university aspirations, the number of hours would be 5.5 and 7.1 hours, respectively.

FIGURE 3
Weekly Hours of Study

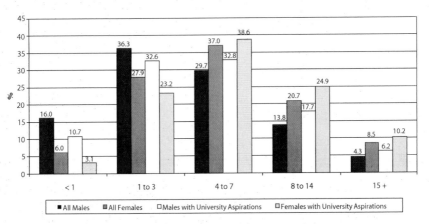

Source: Author's compilations.

Time spent on studies outside the classroom is one measure of effort. So too is time spent inside the classroom, which is apparently a choice variable for many high school students. Over 21 percent of males reported skipping classes at least once a week, compared to 15 percent of females. Those with university aspirations are somewhat less likely to skip class as frequently, but the practice was clearly not uncommon among both genders.

FIGURE 4
Incidence of Skipping Classes

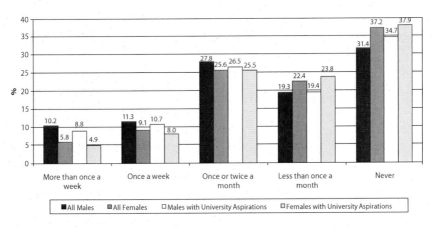

Source: Author's compilations.

Figure 5 reveals significant gender differences in respondents' self-assessment of their effort. While almost 60 percent of males stated that they had worked at less than full capacity at some point, only 40 percent of females reported this behaviour.

FIGURE 5
Work Effort

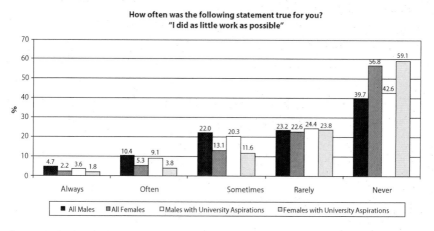

Source: Author's compilations.

By all three measures or proxies for effort exerted in high school, females worked harder and longer than males. Had males worked as hard as females, would they have been able to generate similar grades? Or are there gender differences in the efficiency with which grades are produced? To examine this question, the next section estimates a grade production function.

The Grade Production Function

The general form of the grade production function relates the final year high school average to a set of current and past family inputs, school resources, and measures of student effort. Following the literature, the educational production function is estimated using a simple linear form relating high school grades to a set of explanatory variables. Note that the YITS data report high school grades as a categorical variable while the estimates in this paper use the mid-points of each category as the dependent variable.

The specific explanatory variables used are listed in the table of sample means, Table 2.[10] In terms of family inputs, the model includes measures of the capacity to provide support for the educational process, measures of indirect parental influence, and measures of parental activity. Capacity is measured using combined parental income in 1999 as reported in Cycle 1 of the survey. All sources of income are accounted for, including government transfers. The educational attainments of parents or guardians are included to capture, separately from financial capacity, the indirect influence of parental education in terms of expectations, understanding of the PSE sector, and so on. While income and education may capture the environment in which the respondents grew up, they do not measure proactive involvement and encouragement on the part of parents. To proxy for active support of their children's education, the estimates use the PISA variable on the frequency with which the mother or the father work with the student on school work (ranging from never to several times a week).[11]

TABLE 2
Sample Means

Variable	Males	Females
PISA reading score	520.78	551.72
Mother's education		
High school or less	0.523	0.539
Some post-secondary: incomplete	0.035	0.028
College	0.262	0.257
University	0.180	0.176
Father's education		
High school or less	0.541	0.568
Some post-secondary: incomplete	0.019	0.018
College	0.244	0.225
University	0.196	0.189
Parents' combined income (,000's)	71.441	68.001
Frequency of mother's help (1 = never, 5 = several times/wk)	2.520	2.667
Frequency of father's help (")	2.319	2.361
School's physical infrastructure index (SCMATBUI)	-0.358	-0.338
School's educational resources index (SCMATEDU)	-0.243	-0.236
Student teaching staff ratio	17.00	16.99
Nfld	0.018	0.021
PEI	0.004	0.004
NS	0.033	0.034
NB	0.026	0.027
QUE	0.228	0.220
ONT	0.382	0.390
MAN	0.036	0.036
SASK	0.043	0.042
ALTA	0.102	0.101
BC	0.129	0.125
No. of observations	8,131	8,500

Note: Descriptive statistics for effort level variables are reported in Figures 3, 4, and 5.
Source: Author's compilations.

School resources available to support student learning and grade achievement are captured in three variables from the PISA school survey. An index of the quality of school infrastructure is based on principals' reports concerning building conditions and instructional space. The index ranges from -1.12 to 3.38, with higher values implying better conditions. Similarly, the availability of educational resources (including computers, library resources, science equipment, and so on) is captured by an index with a range of -1.9 to 3.22. Teaching support is measured by the student-teaching staff ratio: the number of students in the school divided by the number of full-time equivalent teachers. Again, these measures are available only for Cycle 1.

Provincial dummies are used to pick up any differences in the way in which grading occurs, provincial variations in resources not captured in the school resource variables, and any other province-specific influences not explicitly accounted for by other explanatory variables.

As discussed above, students' own effort is measured using three proxies: hours of study per week, incidence of skipping classes, and the degree to which they agree that they did as little work as possible.

Most variables in Table 2 should have means that are not significantly different for males and females, since gender has no role in their determination. There are only two comparisons of interest. First, males and females receive about the same amount of help from their parents, so there appears to be no gender difference in the investment of time made by parents. Second, the mean family income for women is lower than that for men, which is consistent with the marginally lower levels of educational attainment among the parents of females in the sample. Why this occurs is not clear. In the empirical work to follow, parental education and family income are used as controls so that these differences should not affect the outcomes derived below.

Effort and Causality

Effort levels are clearly endogenous values chosen by students. There is a strong possibility that they are correlated with academic ability, which in turn is likely to be a determinant of high school grades. Without a measure of this ability, it winds up in the error term, and OLS estimates of the effects of included effort variables on grades will be biased, a problem akin to the standard ability bias issue in estimating the effects of education on earnings. For example, if more able students devote greater effort to earning grades, perhaps because learning activities are more enjoyable for them, we would expect an upward bias in the estimated effort effect. In this scenario, the higher grades of the students who exert greater levels of effort may actually be caused by their greater ability and not by their effort levels. Without controlling for ability, the effort variables would falsely pick up the impact of ability leading to an over-estimate of the impact of effort on grades.

As Stinebrickner and Stinebrickner (2004) point out, however, the bias story is unlikely to be that simple when we take the human capital model of learning activity seriously. High school averages may not be the ultimate goal of students' optimizing calculations. Instead, their decisions about effort may be based on the probability of entry into post-secondary education and the higher income that results from that entry. It is plausible to suppose, as they point out, that high ability students with grade targets in mind exert less effort than those with lower ability as they aim only to achieve the minimum grades required for admission into PSE. As we compare the grades of higher effort/lower ability students to those of lower effort/higher ability students, estimates of the effect of effort are downward biased.

The YITS data contain the results of standardized PISA scores, measured at age 15, and these scores have some potential to act as proxies for ability. PISA tests in the areas of reading, mathematics, and science are intended to assess students' mastery of school curriculum as well as knowledge and skills needed to perform real world tasks. Only the reading test was administered to the full YITS sample. Unquestionably, PISA test scores are correlated with innate ability, but they are also very likely to be correlated with how much a student has learned in the classroom and, therefore, with effort levels. Note, however, that PISA performance will be influenced by effort levels in the past, while the effort variables used in the grades production equation are measured in the last year of high school. If the correlation between past and current effort levels is less than perfect, using PISA reading scores as a plug-in solution to the omitted ability variable problem will not eliminate the bias caused by endogenous effort levels but may reduce it.

Estimates

This paper first provides estimates of the grades production function without the PISA reading score proxy for ability in the spirit of a descriptive model, without claiming a measure of causality. The production functions are then re-estimated after including the PISA reading score as the only feasible approach to addressing the omitted ability variable problem. Results are reported in Table 3. Recall that YITS reports grade averages in the final year of high school as a categorical variable (the categories are found in Table 1 and Figure 2). Students are assigned numerical values equal to the mid-points of the grade category, and the grade production functions are estimated by OLS applied to each gender separately.

Many of the explanatory variables in Table 3 are categorical and easily interpreted. For example, in the equation without PISA scores as controls, boys who study one to three hours per week have high school grades that are 1.8 percentage points above the grades of boys who report not studying at all. The corresponding increase in grades for girls who study one to three hours per week instead of no hours is 2.0 percentage points.

TABLE 3
Regression Results

Dependent Variable: Final Year High School Average Grade	Males		Females	
	Without PISA Score	*With PISA Score*	*Without PISA Score*	*With PISA Score*
Explanatory Variables				
Hours of study per week (ref. group: 0 hrs.)				
Less than 1 hour	0.933	-0.050	2.027	0.680
1 – 3 hours	1.827**	0.661	2.046	0.190
4 – 7 hours	2.837**	1.223*	4.071*	1.268
8 – 14 hours	4.635**	2.437***	5.981**	2.678
15 + hours	6.879**	4.854***	5.875**	2.810
Did as little work as possible (ref. group: never)				
Rarely	-1.208**	-1.572***	-0.402	-0.771***
Sometimes	-3.294**	-3.332***	-2.732**	-2.537***
Often	-4.060**	-4.130***	-4.426**	-3.936***
Always	-3.843**	-3.937***	-6.520**	-5.381***
Incidence of skipping classes (ref. group: never)				
Less than once per month	-1.329**	-0.987***	-1.558**	-1.591***
Once or twice per month	-2.749**	-1.946***	-2.397**	-2.272***
Once per week	-3.842**	-3.114***	-3.465**	-3.512***
More than once per week	-5.563**	-4.508***	-5.045**	-5.120***
PISA reading score		0.0358***		0.0388***
Mother's education (ref. group: HS or less)				
Some post-secondary: incomplete	-0.270	-0.135	0.202	-0.091
College	1.221**	0.654**	1.393**	0.604**
University	3.045**	1.649***	2.806**	1.401***
Father's education (ref. group: HS or less)				
Some post-secondary: incomplete	-0.321	-0.773	0.289	-0.191
College	0.446	0.091	0.912**	0.342
University	3.013**	2.104***	3.397**	2.251***
Parents' combined income (,000's)	0.003	-0.002	0.006*	0.000
Frequency of mother's help (1 = never, 5 = several times/wk)	-0.395**	-0.092	-0.488**	-0.049
Frequency of father's help (")	-0.342**	-0.213	-0.120	-0.070
School's Physical Infrastructure Index (SCMATBUI)	-0.155	-0.292	0.242	0.161
School's Educational Resources Index (SCMATEDU)	-0.004	0.223	-0.060	0.014
Student teaching staff ratio	-0.074	-0.169***	0.006	-0.067
Province: (ref. group: Ontario)				
NFLD	-2.115**	-1.380**	-2.167**	-2.048***
PEI	1.402*	2.080***	1.284*	2.016***
NS	0.820	1.182***	1.405**	1.445***
NB	0.823	1.884***	0.598	1.191***
QUE	1.866**	1.478***	-0.128	-0.895**
MAN	0.021	-0.238	0.453	0.016
SASK	0.335	0.283	1.020*	0.634
ALTA	-1.077*	-1.737***	-3.996**	-4.753***
BC	0.491	0.503	-0.834	-0.925**
Constant	77.82**	61.85***	77.18**	59.82***
R^2	0.204	0.317	0.223	0.341
No. of observations	8,131	8,118	8,500	8,493
Mean of dependent variable	75.92	75.92	78.95	78.95

Notes: *** significant at the 3 percent level; ** significant at the 5 percent level; * significant at the 10 percent level.
Source: Author's compilations.

All three effort measures are strongly correlated with the level of high school average in the regressions that exclude the PISA score ability control. Additional time spent studying has significant and large coefficients that tend to be smaller for males than for females, except for the highest category. Males who sometimes, often, or always did as little work as was necessary to get by earned lower grades than those who claimed to always have worked hard. The same is true for females. For both genders, skipping classes is negatively correlated with grades. Effort therefore matters for both males and females.

Compared to children whose mother had no more than a completed high school education, children of college educated mothers achieved higher grades, and those with university educated mothers earned even higher averages. The effect of mother's education is similar for males and females. A comparable pattern is seen in the impacts of father's education, although the estimated coefficient on the indicator for father's college education is insignificant. When we control for parental education, the effect of income is statistically significant only for females and is small in magnitude. As discussed above, the frequency with which parents helped their children is used to capture parental involvement. As it turns out, high school performance is negatively related to parental help with school work except for females, where a father's help has no significant impact. The obvious interpretation is that parents intercede when their children are having difficulty with school.

None of the three measures of school quality appears to have an effect on high school performance. This is not entirely inconsistent with other findings in the literature on school quality but might also be attributable in this case to the inclusion of provincial controls. If provincial funding schemes are uniform so that school resources vary by province but not within provinces, there will be little independent variation in the quality measures. Turning to the estimates on those provincial controls, compared to Ontario, high school averages for both males and females are significantly lower in Newfoundland and Labrador as well as in Alberta, especially for females in the latter province. Relative high school performance is higher in Prince Edward Island than in Ontario. It is also higher in Nova Scotia for females only, and in Quebec for males only.

Turning to the model with PISA scores serving as proxies for ability, the impact on grades of spending time studying diminishes for males and becomes statistically insignificant for females. This is consistent with the simpler ability bias story discussed above: effort and ability are positively correlated, leading to an upward bias in the estimated causal effect of effort when controls for ability are not included. The deleterious effects of shirking work and skipping classes, on the other hand, remain largely unaffected by the inclusion of the PISA reading score.

Not surprisingly, the PISA scores themselves are highly significant determinants of high school averages. A standard deviation increase in the PISA reading score is estimated to add 3.6 percentage points to that average for males and 3.8 percentage points for females.[12] The scores are also clearly correlated with measures of family background and support, reducing the estimated impact of parental education, income, and assistance. With the inclusion of the PISA score, most of the provincial coefficients become significant, and tend to increase in size.

Decomposition Analysis

With these estimates in hand, we turn to the question of the extent to which the gender gap in high school grades can be attributed to differences in effort levels, using a standard Blinder-Oaxaca decomposition. Knowing how the observable characteristics and effort levels of males are related to high school grades, and having measures of these explanatory variables for males and females, we can estimate the high school grades that males would have received if their characteristics and effort levels were the same as for females. In essence, the mean levels of the explanatory variables for females are plugged into the male grade equation. Any remaining gap between this hypothetical grade and actual grades is attributed to differences in the efficiency with which males and females convert inputs into the grades production function for high school averages.[13] In other words, if the female grades are higher than they are for males when we compare observationally equivalent individuals, females are somehow able to obtain higher grades for the same effort levels. Borrowing from the production function literature, this unexplained difference is considered a difference in the productivity with which a given set of inputs is converted into outputs – or efficiency.

The Blinder-Oaxaca analysis allows a decomposition by each of the variables included in the regression in Table 3 separately. However, Table 4 aggregates the contribution of the three effort variables and then aggregates the contribution of all remaining explanatory variables.[14] Consider first the specification without the PISA score proxy for ability. Differences in effort levels account for slightly over half of the 3 percentage point gap in final high school grades and more than all of the portion of the gap that is "explained" by differences in the explanatory variables. The explanatory variables not related to effort levels, when taken together, actually work in favour of males, although marginally so. According to this specification, then, if males worked as hard as females in high school, the gender gap in averages would be cut in half. It would not be eliminated, as females appear to be able to convert inputs into the production of high school averages more effectively than males. In other words, if the average male exerted the same effort (and possessed the same value of all other explanatory variables) as females, he would receive a grade 1.577 points lower than a female.

Introducing the PISA reading score as a proxy for ability reduces the contribution of the effort variables to the gender gap, but only marginally to about 44 percent of the gap. The PISA score is, in this application, considered part of the endowment of an individual, and (not surprisingly) the total contribution of endowment differences to average grade differences increases to almost 80 percent of the overall gender difference. The finding that there are gender differences in the ability to convert inputs into grade averages after controlling for the PISA score strengthens the conclusion that females are better able to earn the high school grades required for entry into post-secondary education.

TABLE 4
Decomposition of Mean Grade Differences

	Without PISA Score	With PISA Score
Mean prediction for females	78.945	78.957
Mean prediction for males	75.922	75.930
Raw difference	3.023	3.027
Due to different effort levels	1.598	1.335
Due to differences in other endowments	-0.153	1.052
Total due to endowments	1.445	2.387
Due to differences in coefficients (evaluated at females' means)	1.577	0.640

Source: Author's compilations.

Math versus Reading Grades[15]

Given that this paper is interested in the ability of high school students to pass minimum entry requirements for universities, the focus so far has been on final high school averages. We can delve a little deeper into gender differences by examining differences in grades by subject, however. The YITS asked students about the last mathematics, language, and science courses taken in high school, and we have final grades for the mathematics and language courses. Table 5 repeats the decomposition procedure used for overall high school averages to see if the difficulties among males are general or specific to the kind of subject matter.[16] The specifications used for the individual course grades results do not include PISA scores, given the results discussed in the previous paragraph.

Clearly, subject matters. There is almost no gender difference in grades obtained in mathematics courses but a very substantial advantage for females in language courses. Interestingly, lower effort in high school

TABLE 5
Decomposition of Mean Grade Differences in Math and Language Courses

	Mathematics	Language
Mean prediction for females	74.995	79.592
Mean prediction for males	74.536	74.892
Raw difference	0.459	4.700
Due to different effort levels	1.132	1.235
Due to differences in other endowments	-0.128	-0.071
Total due to endowments	1.004	1.106
Due to differences in coefficients (evaluated at females' means)	-0.545	3.594

Source: Author's compilations.

produces a similar grade point penalty for males in both mathematics and language courses.[17] However, males appear to be slightly more efficient at translating effort into mathematics grades, with their mathematics grade production function lying higher at the mean of female endowments, and this partially offsets the loss of grades through lower effort. In the case of language courses, however, the effect of males' lower effort is compounded by a lower ability to convert their efforts into good grades. A male who is observationally equivalent to the average female in the sample is predicted to earn a language course grade 3.6 percent lower.

Yet caution should be exercised in interpreting these disaggregated results since the effort variables do not refer to effort in particular courses but rather to overall attention to studies. The two genders may have different comparative advantages or "comparative interests," leading them to allocate effort differently across these kinds of courses.[18] If, for example, males took a particular interest in mathematics courses and dedicated a disproportionately large share of their overall study time to those courses, effort levels in those courses would be higher than those used to produce the decomposition in Table 5. This would in turn produce overestimates of their efficiency advantage in converting effort into mathematics grades. Figure 6 reports the distribution by gender across four categories of time spent on homework, disaggregated by the three PISA test areas. In all three, a greater proportion of males than females spend no hours at all doing homework, with the difference being the greatest in science subjects. Females spent more time studying in all three test areas, and among those students spending at least three hours per week, both genders apply more time to mathematics than language or science. There is, however, no clear evidence of "comparative interests" among boys.

FIGURE 6
Weekly Hours of Study Time in Language, Mathematics, and Science

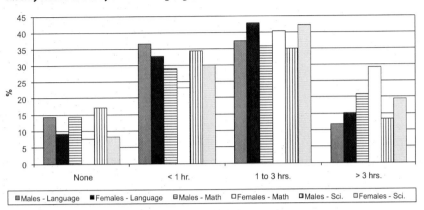

Source: Author's compilations.

Conclusion

The gender gap in university participation is a remarkable sociological and economic phenomenon. To the extent that it reflects differential access to universities, it is also an important problem that needs to be addressed. Undoubtedly, part of the explanation for lower participation rates by males lies in a lower desire on their part to pursue a university education, whether that is because the returns they earn are lower than for women or because their "taste" for education is somehow lower. Even if the desire for further education were the same, however, entrance standards set by Canadian universities could represent a greater barrier for males than for females, given the lower high school grades achieved by the former. Before coming to that conclusion, we need to consider the possibility that those lower grades are themselves an artifact of a lower effort by boys in generating them.

The YITS data show that males do exert lower effort levels than females in high school and that this accounts for 52 percent of the gap in the observed difference in mean grades. The remainder of the gap is mostly attributable to differences between the genders in the ability to produce high school grades. Had males worked as hard at producing high school grades, any gender gap in university participation attributable to rationing by entrance standards would be lessened but would not disappear. The obvious next step is to understand why the genders differ in the efficiency with which they produce grade outcomes. A preliminary examination of mathematics and language course grades indicates quite clearly that the difficulties for males lie not in the former types of courses but very much in the latter.

This paper raises a number of policy implications. First, although there has been considerable interest in access issues, research has been almost exclusively focused on why some individuals are unable to afford higher education or are uninterested in continuing education beyond high school. Almost no consideration has been given to supply constraints in the market for higher education,[19] but Figure 1 suggests that such constraints may play a role. Similarly, post-secondary education policy-makers frequently refer to under-represented groups in post-secondary education, but the list of those groups rarely if ever includes males. Yet if male participation rates could be brought up to the level of female rates, there would be a significant increase in educational attainment in the Canadian labour force. Admittedly, this paper does not quantify the extent to which rationing of university spaces by grades affects male participation; however, if it introduces these two dimensions into the debate on university accessibility, it will have made a contribution.

As for the specific question of rationing by high school grades and the more general, oft-heard discussion about the so-called failure of high schools to educate boys, the results suggest the direction that remedial efforts should take. The relative disadvantage that boys face in high school stems not only from lack of effort but also from an inefficiency in the translation of those efforts into measures of success, particularly in language courses. Increasing boys' motivation will therefore only partially close the gender gap.

Notes

This research was financed by the Canada Millennium Scholarship Foundation through the MESA project. I wish to thank Ross Finnie for his advice and Stephen Childs for his excellent research assistance. Helpful comments were received from Felice Martinello, Lorne Carmichael, David Johnson, Richard Mueller, Marc Frenette, and other participants in the MESA sessions in Vancouver and Montreal, as well as the MESA research committee. Any errors are the sole responsibility of the author.

1.   This is, of course, true only for individuals seeking direct entry into universities from high schools. A small minority of university students are admitted as mature students.
2.   A fixed fee permits three choices, with each additional choice adding to the cost. The great majority of applicants make no more than three choices.
3.   In the past, Ontario universities typically made conditional offers of admission based on high school grades available early in the spring. When final grades became available, these conditional offers were withdrawn if the final high school average fell below the cut-off for the program. Recently, universities

vying for students have made commitments to students based on grades in the penultimate year of high school.

4. See Allgood (2001) for a model of grade targets.
5. See, for example, Betts (1996).
6. See Oettinger (1999) for a careful analysis that takes into account choice-based endogeneity.
7. A complete description of the YITS is available in Motte et al. (2008).
8. Individuals are asked to report this information for the last year of high school, so effort levels are tied to the high school average in the same year.
9. In the sample used to estimate the grades production function below, 56.5 percent of males and 66.9 percent of females have university aspirations.
10. The effort variables have already been described statistically in Figures 3 through 5, and their means are not reported in Table 2.
11. Note that, being a PISA variable, this measure applies at the time of Cycle 1 and is not contemporaneous with high school averages in the final year of high school.
12. PISA results are scaled in such a way that the scores should have a mean of 500 and a standard deviation of 100. Since the scores are fairly close to being normally distributed, a standard deviation would represent the difference, for example, between a student with the mean score and a student at the 84th percentile.
13. This assumes that the set of controls is sufficiently rich to capture all relevant characteristics related to grades that might differ between genders.
14. In keeping with the jargon of this literature, the explanatory variables are termed "endowments." Complete results reporting the contribution of each individual explanatory variable to the decomposition outcomes are available from the author.
15. I am grateful to Felice Martinello for suggesting separate estimates for language and mathematics grades.
16. The regression results are not reported here but are available from the author upon request.
17. The similarity of mathematics grades between the genders is consistent with the findings of national assessments through the School Achievement Indicators Program. See Lauzon (2001, 4).
18. I am indebted to Lorne Carmichael for making this point.
19. Finnie (2005) is an important exception.

References

Allgood, S. 2001. "Grade Targets and Teaching Innovations." *Economics of Education Review* 20 (5): 485-93.

Association of Universities and Colleges of Canada 2007. *Trends in Higher Education 2007*, vol.1 . Ottawa: AUCC.

Betts, J. 1996. "The Role of Homework in Improving School Quality." Discussion Paper 96-16, Department of Economics, University of California at San Diego.

Bishop, J. 2006. "Drinking from the Fountain of Knowledge: Student Incentive to Study and Learn – Externalities, Information Problems and Peer Pressure."

In *Handbook of the Economics of Education,* vol. 2, ed. E. Hanushek and F. Welch, 909-44. Amsterdam: Elsevier.

Cho, D. 2007. "The Role of High School Performance in Explaining Women's Rising College Enrollment." *Economics of Education Review* 26 (4): 450-62.

Coelli, M. 2005. "Tuition, Rationing and Equality of Access to Postsecondary Education." Discussion Paper, Department of Economics, University of Melbourne.

Ehrenberg, R., and D. Brewer. 1994. "Do School and Teacher Characteristics Matter? Evidence from High School and Beyond." *Economics of Education Review* 13 (1): 1-17.

Finnie, R. 2005. "Access and Capacity in the Canadian Post-Secondary Education System: A Policy Discussion Framework." In *Preparing for Post-Secondary Education: New Roles for Governments and Families,* ed. P. Anisef and R. Sweet, 17-54. Montreal and Kingston: McGill-Queen's University Press.

Fortin, N. 2005. "Rising Tuition and Supply Constraints: Explaining Canada-U.S. Differences in University Enrollment Rates." In *Higher Education in Canada.* ed. C. Beach, R. Boadway, and R. McInnis, 369-413. Montreal and Kingston: McGill-Queen's University Press.

Frenette, M., and K. Zeman. 2007. "Why Are Most University Students Women? Evidence Based on Academic Performance, Study Habits, and Parental Influences." Research Report 11F0019MIE2007303. Ottawa: Statistics Canada.

Goldin, C., L. Katz, and I. Kuziemko. 2006. "The Homecoming of American College Women: The Reversal of the College Gender Gap." *Journal of Economic Perspectives* 20 (4): 133-56.

Hanushek, E. 1986. "The Economics of Schooling: Production and Efficiency in Public Schools." *Journal of Economic Literature* 24 (3): 1141-77.

Lauzon, D. 2001. "Gender Differences in Large-Scale, Quantitative Assessments of Mathematics and Science Achievement." In *Towards Evidence-Based Policy for Canadian Education,* ed. P. deBroucker and A. Sweetman, 355-72. Kingston: John Deutsch Institute for the Study of Economic Policy.

Motte, A., H. Qui, Y. Zhang, and P. Bussière 2008. "The Youth in Transition Survey: Following Canadian Youth through Time." In *Who Goes? Who Stays? What Matters? Accessing and Persisting in Post-Secondary Education in Canada,* ed. R. Finnie, R. Mueller, A. Sweetman, and A. Usher, 63-78. Montreal and Kingston: Queen's Policy Studies Series, McGill-Queen's University Press.

Oettinger, G. 1999. "Does High School Employment Affect High School Academic Performance?" *Industrial and Labor Relations Review* 53 (1): 136-51.

Stinebrickner, T., and R. Stinebrickner. 2004. "Time-Use and College Outcomes." *Journal of Econometrics* 121 (1-2): 243-69.

– 2007. "The Causal Effect of Studying on Academic Performance." Discussion Paper 13341. Cambridge: National Bureau of Economic Research.

4

Teachers, Books, or Mortar?
High School Resources and
Educational Outcomes in Canada

KATHLEEN DAY

Quelle serait la façon la plus efficiente d'améliorer les résultats scolaires au niveau post-secondaire : dépenser plus d'argent en éducation au niveau postsecondaire, ou bien investir plus au niveau secondaire, pour ainsi tenter de mieux préparer les élèves aux études post-secondaires ? C'est à cette question que je tente de répondre dans cet article, en utilisant la riche information sur les ressources existantes au niveau secondaire que l'on trouve dans l'Enquête auprès des jeunes en transition (EJET), cohorte A. Après avoir brièvement passé en revue les différences entre les systèmes d'éducation provinciaux, j'analyse le lien entre, d'une part, les ressources au niveau secondaire et, d'autre part, les résultats scolaires et aux tests PISA des élèves à l'âge de 15 ans, ainsi que la fréquentation scolaire à partir de l'âge de 21 ans. J'observe ainsi qu'il existe peu de corrélations statistiques significatives entre les ressources au niveau secondaire et les résultats scolaires. Par contre, on peut établir de très fortes corrélations entre les résultats scolaires et d'autres facteurs, comme le rang de naissance, les aspirations des parents au sujet de leurs enfants, et le niveau de scolarité des parents. En conclusion, j'apporte des pistes qui pourraient servir à de futures recherches et à la mise en place de politiques.

What would be the most cost-effective way to improve post-secondary educational outcomes: to spend more money on post-secondary education or to spend more on secondary education in the hopes of better preparing students for post-secondary studies? This paper addresses this issue by exploiting the wealth of information on high school resources that is available in the Youth in Transition Survey, Cohort A. After briefly reviewing provincial differences in educational systems, the paper examines the relationship between high school resources and high school grades at age 15, PISA scores at age 15, and educational attainment as of age 21. While few statistically significant correlations between high school resources and educational outcomes are observed, the paper highlights other factors such as birth order, parental aspirations for children, and parental education that are highly

Pursuing Higher Education in Canada: Economic, Social, and Policy Dimensions, ed. R. Finnie, M. Frenette, R.E. Mueller, and A. Sweetman. Montreal and Kingston: Queen's Policy Studies Series, McGill-Queen's University Press.

correlated with educational outcomes. The paper concludes by suggesting avenues for future research and policy development.

It is common knowledge that acquiring an education is a cumulative process: one cannot complete high school without first learning to read, and few go on to university without completing the equivalent of a high school diploma.[1] Consequently, few would dispute that the quality of the education received at the elementary and secondary levels is an important determinant of a student's success at higher levels of education. It might even be the case that improving the quality of education at elementary and secondary levels would have a bigger impact on educational outcomes at the post-secondary level than pouring more resources directly into post-secondary education (PSE).

Unfortunately, little is known about the effect of school resources at earlier levels on post-secondary educational attainment in Canada, as few if any studies directly address the issue.[2] A number of studies do, however, investigate the relationship between school characteristics and educational outcomes below the post-secondary level, although as both Crocker (2007) and Morgan and McKerrow (2007) note, they are not numerous. Some of these studies, including Zhang (2002), Bertrand (2002), and Jones (2002), examine only simple correlations between school characteristics and student performance at the elementary level. Zhang (2002) reports positive correlations between the degree of math instructional resources and math teachers' familiarity with the curriculum, on the one hand, and on the other hand, Grade 8 students' test scores in the Third International Mathematics and Science Study (TIMSS) conducted in 1995. Bertrand (2002) finds a positive correlation between access to computers and student performance as measured by the School Achievement Indicators Program (SAIP) in 1996. Similarly, Jones (2002) reports that an analysis of the TIMSS data carried out for Ontario's Education Quality and Accountability Office found that shortages of instructional materials were correlated with poorer performance on the TIMSS math test.

Several other studies carry out more sophisticated statistical analyses that control as well for individual, family, and/or other possible influences on educational outcomes. For example, Ma and Klinger (2000) look at the effect of several school variables – school size, average socio-economic status of school families, disciplinary climate, academic press, and parental involvement – on student performance on achievement tests administered to Grade 6 students in New Brunswick during the 1995-96 academic year. They find that disciplinary climate is the most important of the three school climate variables included in their hierarchical linear models, although the average socio-economic status of families is also positively related to student scores in reading and writing (but not math and science). In the economics literature, Bedard (2003) uses Census data to investigate the relationship between provincial average measures of class size, school size, and relative teacher earnings on the earnings of Canadian men. Although she finds some effects at the extremes of the earnings distribution, her reliance on provincial average measures of school resources means that those measures may not accurately reflect the resources available to the specific individuals in her sample. Johnson (2005) considers the influence of some types of school resources in Ontario on the performance of elementary students. Corak and Lauzon (2002, 2005) employ a data set that provides more accurate measures of school resources than does Bedard, but they examine only student performance at age 15.

This lack of empirical evidence on the impact of school resources on educational outcomes in Canada is particularly striking when one compares the number of Canadian studies to the number of studies available for other countries, particularly the United States. Hanushek (2006) reviews 276 studies of the effect of school resources alone on educational outcomes, while the survey papers of Hanushek and Rivkin (2006) and Speakman and Welch (2006) on the effects of teacher quality and the relationship between school characteristics and wages also include lengthy bibliographies. However, the results of these studies are very mixed. Hanushek (2006, 892) notes that 72 percent of the 276 studies he reviewed find that the teacher-pupil ratio has no statistically significant impact on student outcomes. Even worse, of the 28 percent of studies that found a statistically significant effect, only half found that increasing the teacher-pupil ratio would improve student performance. The other half reached the conclusion that increasing the teacher-pupil ratio would actually lead to deterioration in student performance. Similarly, 66 percent of 163 studies of the effects of expenditure per pupil on student outcomes reviewed by Hanushek (2006) find no statistically significant effect.

The lack of consensus on the impact of school resources in general and the dearth of empirical studies for Canada in particular suggest a need for further research on this topic, especially for Canada. The availability of new datasets that contain information on both school characteristics and student outcomes, such as Cohort A of Statistics Canada's Youth in Transition Survey (YITS-A), provides new opportunities for such research. In fact, Corak and Lauzon (2002, 2005) use data from the first cycle of this panel dataset to generate their results. More recently, Day (2009) combined data from several cycles of YITS-A to examine the effect of a wide range of school resource measures on not only student performance at age 15 but also educational attainment after high school.

This paper highlights and discusses some of the most policy-relevant results of Day (2009) in an attempt to shed new light on the question of the importance of high school resources to post-secondary educational outcomes. Briefly, the principal findings are that there is little empirical evidence of a strong relationship between the available measures of high school resources and three measures of educational success: either high school grades, or standardized test scores at age 15, or educational attainment as of age 21. Instead, individual characteristics and family background play far more important roles. However, these findings should not necessarily be interpreted as implying that school resources are unimportant to educational outcomes; due to data limitations, information regarding school resources is available for only one point in time, meaning that many school-related inputs consumed in earlier years are missing from the models. Furthermore, the models estimate only the average impact of school resources; it is quite possible that certain school resources are more important to particular subgroups of the population, as the results of Bedard (2003) and Corak and Lauzon (2002, 2005) for Canada and Rangvid (2007) for Denmark suggest. Finally, there may simply not be enough heterogeneity of resources across schools in Canada to measure their effects with any degree of precision. Provincial government control over educational policy at the elementary and secondary levels, coupled with the fact that there are only ten Canadian provinces, as compared to fifty US states, means that there may be less variation in resources across schools in Canada than in the United States, where differences in average levels of high school resources may be more important.

The next section of this paper provides some background on differences in school systems across Canada that could potentially lead to differences in student outcomes. The third section discusses the problem of how to measure the effect of school resources on student outcomes. The fourth and fifth sections discuss some of the empirical evidence derived from YITS-A by Day (2009) regarding the effect of school resources on student performance at age 15 (as reflected in the overall average grade and PISA scores) and educational attainment as of age 21.[3] The last section of the paper summarizes the results and their policy implications, and suggests directions for future research.

Background

Under the Canadian constitution, responsibility for education is allocated to the provincial governments. Today each province has its own ministry of education that is responsible for policy with respect to not only the funding of education but also the design of the curriculum. As noted by the Council of Ministers of Education (2008, 2), "while there are a great many similarities in the provincial and territorial education systems across Canada, there are significant differences in curriculum, assessment, and accountability policies among the jurisdictions."

Although it would be impossible in this short paper to catalogue all the differences in provincial education systems and their evolution over time, it is instructive to highlight a few important ones. For example, although in most provinces a student must complete twelve grades to obtain a high school diploma, students in Quebec graduate from high school after only eleven grades. However, in contrast to other provinces, where students can proceed directly from high school to university, Quebecois students who wish to continue on to university must first complete two years of study in a college (or CEGEP).[4] In Ontario before 2002, most students heading for university completed thirteen years of schooling, not twelve, until modifications to the secondary system made it possible to enter university after twelve years.

Another important difference involves charter schools, which were introduced in Alberta in 1994. To date Alberta remains the only province of Canada that permits charter schools. Charter schools are publicly funded, non-profit schools that are not administered by school boards.[5] Although Alberta's Ministry of Education still dictates standards of student achievement, charter schools have considerably more flexibility and autonomy when it comes to determining how those standards are met.

Other differences involve the funding of schools. Some provinces such as Ontario have a fully funded, parallel Roman Catholic school system, while others such as Newfoundland have only one publicly funded school system.[6] In addition, provinces differ in the extent to which school boards raise their own funds through property taxes and other sources as opposed to receiving government grants. As Figure 1 shows, school board own-source revenue as a percentage of total school board revenue varies greatly across provinces, from a low of zero in New Brunswick (which explains why it does not appear in the figure) to a high of 54.5 percent in Saskatchewan in 2007, the most recent year for which data were available. The figure also shows important changes in the extent to which school boards have relied on own-source revenues over time; in particular, in Alberta and British Columbia, the proportion of school board funding derived from the boards' own revenue sources dropped precipitously in the early 1990s. Even in Ontario, which still relies relatively heavily on the own-source revenues of school boards, there was a drop of almost 16 percentage points in the importance of this revenue source between 1988 and 2007 as the provincial government sought to equalize school funding across boards.[7] Transfers from the provincial government now account for more than 50 percent of school board funding in all provinces except Saskatchewan, presumably leaving school boards in those provinces with less autonomy than those in Saskatchewan.[8]

Exactly how these provincial differences in school administration and funding have affected school resources in Canada is not clear. What is clear is that provincial governments differ in the extent to which they invest resources in elementary and secondary schools. Figure 2 shows that relative to per capita provincial GDP, expenditures per student were higher in New Brunswick than in any other province in both the 1999-2000 and 2005-06 academic years, the two years compared in the

FIGURE 1

School Board Own-Source Revenue as a Proportion of Total Revenue, 1988-2007

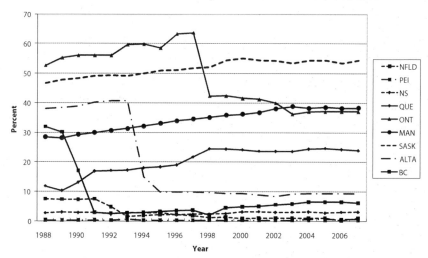

Data source: CANSIM Table 3850009..

FIGURE 2

Total Expenditure Per Student as a Percentage of Per Capita Provincial GDP

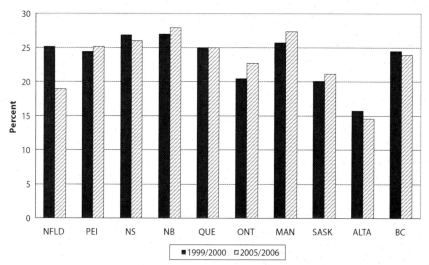

Data source: Table A.25 of Blouin, 2008.

figure. By contrast, in Alberta expenditures per student constituted the lowest proportion of provincial GDP – about 15 percent in both years. However, these numbers do not imply that Alberta is neglecting its elementary and secondary school students; in fact, as Figure 3 shows, total real expenditures per student in Alberta were actually higher than those in New Brunswick in 2005-06. Prince Edward Island was the province in which real per student expenditures were lowest in 2005-06; at $5,957, they were more than $1,600 less than the Canadian average of $7,625 per student (in 1992 constant dollars). Although the relative positions of the provinces changed slightly between 1999-2000 and 2005-06, total real expenditures per student were higher in all provinces in 2005-06 than they had been six years earlier.

FIGURE 3
Total Expenditure Per Student, by Province

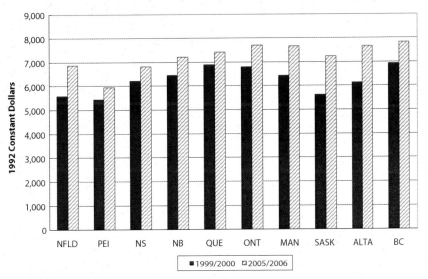

Data source: Table 17.2 of Blouin, 2008.

Because there are many reasons why the per-student cost of education might vary across provinces, such as differences in population density or in the age distribution of the population, it is also interesting to look at provincial differences in a quantitative rather than a dollar measure of inputs into education, namely the student-educator ratio. Here an educator is defined broadly to include school principals and other non-teaching staff, although it does not include classroom assistants and volunteers.[9] As Figure 4 shows, in 1999-2000 the student-educator ratio varied from a low of 14.1 in Newfoundland and Labrador to a high of 17.1 in Alberta and British Columbia. By the 2005-06 school year, the ratio had dropped in all provinces, although the drop in British Columbia, from 17.1 to 17, was very small.[10] However, a comparison of Figures 3 and 4 shows that low expenditures per student are not necessarily associated with a low student-educator ratio. The ratios in the three Maritime provinces are among the highest in Canada, even though expenditures per student in these provinces are relatively low.

FIGURE 4
Student-Educator Ratio, by Province

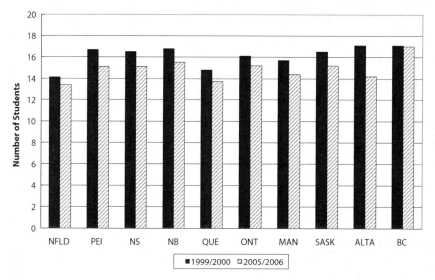

Data source: Table A.11 of Blouin, 2008.

Simply looking at average expenditure per student or the student-educator ratio at the provincial level, however, is not sufficient to determine which province might be doing the best job of educating its elementary and secondary students. The real measures of the success of the educational system are how well students perform in school and how well they succeed later in life. Are schools providing students with the skills they need to succeed at the post-secondary level? The remaining sections of this paper look at what YITS-A can tell us about this issue.

Measuring the Effect of School Resources on Educational Outcomes

Most empirical studies of the effect of school resources on educational outcomes are based on the idea of an educational production function that takes inputs supplied by the school and the student and transforms them into an educational outcome. But while this idea seems straightforward, implementing it is not. First, one must decide on an outcome measure. Grades, standardized test scores, the level of educational attainment, and earnings have all been used as outcome measures in different studies, depending on the focus of the study and the data available.

Second, one must measure the inputs into the educational production function. This is even more difficult, since many potential inputs are difficult to observe directly. Student ability is obviously an important factor, but few datasets include independent measures of individual ability. The measurement of school inputs is also fraught with difficulties; while smaller classes may allow any teacher to devote more time to each student in the class, teachers may differ in their ability to stimulate learning. Similarly, using expenditures per student as an educational input measure overlooks the fact that outcomes are likely to depend on how the money is spent.

Thirdly, econometric problems arise from the fact that student outcomes may be jointly determined with some of the inputs into the educational production function – for example, because parents explicitly take school characteristics into account when choosing a neighbourhood to live in, or because schools and school boards may take student performance into account in allocating students to classes or resources to schools. Peer influences may also be bi-directional; for example, it is illogical to argue that student A's performance is influenced by student B while ignoring student A's potential reciprocal influence on student B.

Regardless of the cause of the endogeneity problem, if school resources and educational outcomes are indeed jointly determined, estimates of the effect of school resources are likely to be biased unless steps are taken to deal with the problem. One option would be to randomly allocate students to schools with different levels of resources; this was the approach of Project STAR in the United States, but very few such experiments exist, necessitating the use of appropriate statistical techniques instead.[11] Some researchers have tackled the problem using instrumental variables methods (e.g., Akerhielm 1995). Dearden, Ferri, and Meghir (2002) recommend instead the inclusion in the empirical model of explanatory variables that account for as many other influences on educational outcomes as possible, arguing that this is a better strategy because it is extremely difficult to find instrumental variables that are highly correlated with school characteristics but not with educational outcomes.[12]

In this paper the outcome measures examined include self-reported grades at age 15, PISA scores at age 15, and educational attainment as of ages 19 and 21. Although the primary objective of the study is to examine the relationship between high school resources and educational attainment – because educational attainment has the most direct bearing on future labour market outcomes – academic performance at age 15 was also examined because the school data available in YITS-A pertain only to that particular year.[13] This is one of the principal limitations of YITS-A as a source of data for this type of research; ideally a study of the effect of school resources on educational attainment should include information on the resources of all the schools attended by the individual prior to beginning post-secondary education, since in principle all contribute to the individual's preparation for post-secondary study. Nonetheless, since there are few other Canadian datasets that contain any information about school characteristics, the advantages of using YITS-A for the purposes of examining the role of school resources in Canada would seem to make doing so worthwhile.[14]

Complete details regarding the econometric modelling of the three different outcome measures can be found in Day (2009). Here it suffices to say that in addition to a variety of school resource measures, all equations included a large number of control variables derived from YITS-A. These included indicators of sex, visible minority status, immigrants to Canada, learning and other types of disabilities, and the individual's smoking behaviour. Smoking behaviour was included because it is likely correlated with other factors that may influence the respondent's ability to make decisions that involve trade-offs between current and future benefits. Family background is taken into account by including variables for the number of schools attended, the number of siblings, the number of older siblings, family structure (single parent, two birth parents, etc.), parental education, family income, and the parents' educational aspirations for their child. Peer influences are represented by indicators of the proportion of the respondent's friends who were troublemakers and the extent to which bullying, drugs and alcohol, and poor home environments interfered with learning at the respondent's school. Finally, neighbourhood characteristics include variables indicating the province of schooling, the size of the community in which the respondent's school was located, and, for each school included in YITS-A, average family income, the proportion of students with at least one parent employed, and the proportion of students with at least one university-educated parent.[15]

The focus of this paper, however, is on school characteristics. Thanks to a school administrator questionnaire completed by school principals as part of the PISA data collection process in Cycle 1 of YITS-A, a wealth of information about the schools of the respondents is available. From these variables an attempt was made to select a series that best reflected the educational resources provided by the school: the school size, the student-teacher ratio, the proportion of teachers with a teaching qualification (a B.Ed., or in some models, the proportion of teachers with a university degree in their area of specialization), the ratio of students to computers in the school, an index of the quality of the school's physical resources (i.e., condition of building, space, lighting, etc.), an index of the quality of the school's educational resources (e.g., library, lab equipment, computers), and a dummy variable indicating whether the school offers special courses on study skills. Three additional variables related to the teaching climate are also included: an index of teacher morale, an index of teacher participation, and an index of school autonomy.[16] Since Dearden, Ferri, and Meghir (2002) in their study of educational attainment in Britain found that the type of school attended seemed to affect educational attainment, three indicators of the type of school – co-educational, private, and/or with a religious affiliation – were also included.

While the large number of school characteristics included in the estimated models is one of the strengths of this study, it could also be a weakness if the included measures were so highly correlated with one another that it would be statistically impossible to distinguish their independent effects. In such a case it would be better to reduce the number of measures included. However, it turns out that the various school measures included in the model are not in fact highly correlated, and thus all are included in all the models estimated.

Finally, two additional explanatory variables were included in the models of educational attainment that did not appear in the models of academic performance at age 15: the number of high schools attended and the PISA reading score. The PISA reading score serves as an indicator of student ability. Otherwise, the set of explanatory variables is the same for all the models estimated.

Because the nature of the dependent variable was different for PISA scores and the other educational outcome measures, different econometric models were used for each. In the case of PISA scores, an actual numerical score was available for each student in the sample. Hence relatively simple linear regression models could be estimated in which the dependent variable was the PISA score and the various individual, school, family, and neighbourhood characteristics served as right-hand side variables. However, both grades and educational attainment are reported in YITS-A as categorical variables that take on only a limited number of possible values. Since the use of categorical variables as dependent variables can lead to statistical problems, ordered probit models were employed instead of linear regression models for the analysis of grades and educational attainment. Ordered probit models (and related models such as the ordered logit model) were specifically developed for the analysis of categorical variables whose categories reflect the natural ordering of an unobservable underlying variable. In the cases of grades and educational attainment, an increase in the value of the corresponding categorical dependent variable reflects an increase in an underlying, but unobservable, continuous variable – the numerical grade in the case of grades, and "human capital" in the case of educational attainment. Consequently, ordered probit models are well suited to the analysis of these two dependent variables.[17]

For all the models, the results should be interpreted in terms of a comparison with a reference student. In other words, they reflect differences between the reference student and a student who differs from the reference student only with respect to the highlighted characteristic. This reference student is a male who was born in Canada, is not a member of a visible minority, attended three different schools up to age 15, and does not have any disabilities or health problems. He is a non-smoker with one younger sibling. His parents do not want him to achieve anything beyond a high school diploma. At least one parent has graduated from high school, but neither parent has a post-secondary education. He lives in an urban area in Ontario and attends a boys-only public school with no religious affiliation that does not offer any special courses in study skills, and none of his friends are troublemakers.[18] The next two sections of the paper highlight some of the most interesting results.

High School Resources and Educational Outcomes at Age 15

YITS-A contains data on not just the student's overall average grade at age 15 but also grades in math, science, and language/literature courses. In addition, it contains the PISA reading score for all students and PISA scores in math and science for a subset of the respondents.[19] Due to space limitations, the discussion here focuses on the overall average grade and the PISA reading scores, although a few of the most interesting results for the PISA math and science scores will also be presented. As a preliminary to the more complete statistical analysis, Figure 5 compares the average values of six school resource measures across levels of grades and PISA scores.[20] The six measures of school resources examined are the proportion of teachers with a teaching qualification (i.e., a B.Ed.), the school size, the ratio of students to computers, the index of school physical resources, the index of school educational resources, and the student-teacher ratio.

The figure shows that the PISA reading level appears to decrease with the proportion of qualified teachers, while the overall average grade decreases and then increases sharply at the highest grade level. The PISA reading level also appears to increase with school size, while there does not appear to be any particular relationship between school size and overall average grades. However, neither the overall average grade nor the PISA reading level appears to be strongly correlated with the ratio of students to computers, although it is true that the highest ratio of students to computers observed in the figure is associated with the lowest PISA reading level. Similarly, there is no discernible relationship between the PISA reading level and either measure of school resources (i.e., physical or educational), although there appears to be a slightly U-shaped relationship between high school grades and both measures. Finally, the student-teacher ratio, a widely used measure of school resources, appears to be slightly negatively related to overall average grades but positively related to the PISA reading level.

FIGURE 5
Comparison of Six School Resource Measures across Levels of Grades and PISA Scores

a. Proportion of Qualified Teachers

b. Proportion of Qualified Teachers

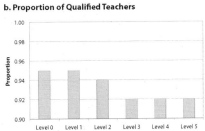

c. School Size

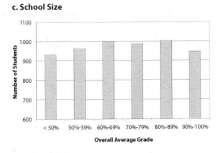

d. School Size

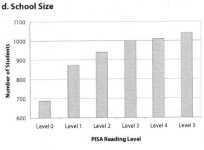

e. Ratio of Students to Computers

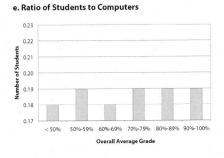

f. Ratio of Students to Computers

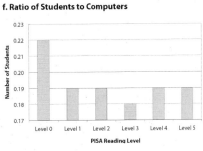

g. Index of Quality of School Physical Resources

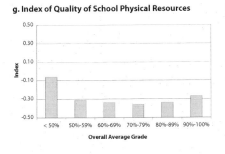

h. Index of Quality of School Physical Resources

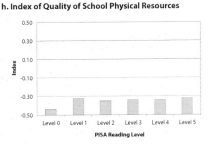

... continued

FIGURE 5
(Continued)

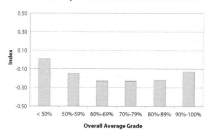

i. Index of Quality of School Educational Resources

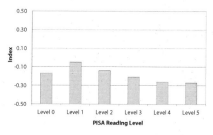

j. Index of Quality of School Educational Resources

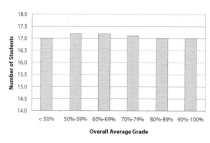

k. Student-Teacher Ratio

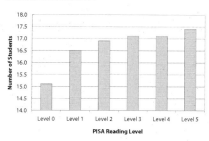

l. Student-Teacher Ratio

Source: Author's compilation.

Not only do these graphs suggest that PISA scores and overall average grades behave somewhat differently, but the relationships they imply between the PISA reading score and school resources measures such as the student-teacher ratio, the proportion of qualified teachers, and school size are somewhat counter-intuitive. However, the graphs do not control for other factors that may affect educational outcomes, such as individual characteristics and family background, as do the models estimated. The estimation results for these models are summarized in graphical presentations of the predicted effects on the outcome measures of changes in variables with statistically significant coefficients.[21] In the case of the overall average grade, Figure 6 shows the difference in the predicted probability of obtaining an average of at least 70 percent between the reference student and a student who differs from the reference student with respect to just one characteristic.[22] Similarly, in the case of the PISA reading score, Figure 7 shows the difference in the predicted score between the reference student and a student who differs with respect to just one characteristic.[23] The results with respect to the explanatory variables included in the figure were similar for the PISA math and science scores. Figure 8 provides some additional statistically significant results with

FIGURE 6
Predicted Difference in Probability of an Overall Average Grade of at Least 70 Percent

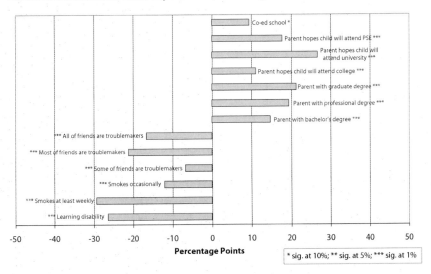

Source: Author's compilation.

FIGURE 7
Predicted Difference in Pisa Reading Score

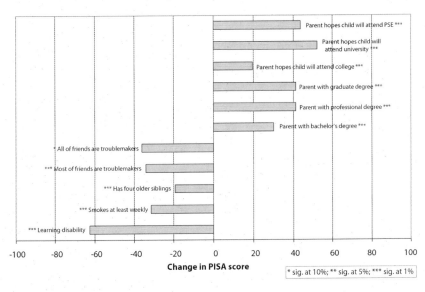

Source: Author's compilation.

FIGURE 8

Predicted Difference in Pisa Reading Scores Due to a One-Unit Change in Variable

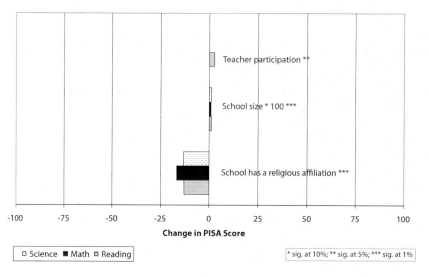

Source: Author's compilation.

respect to the effects of school characteristics on PISA scores in math and science as well as reading. (The corresponding results for the overall average grade were not statistically significant and are not presented.) For the reference student, the predicted probability of an overall average grade of at least 70 percent is 58 percent, while his predicted PISA reading, math, and science scores are 486.7, 506.6, and 511.0, respectively.[24]

The first thing to note about the results is that although a relatively large number of school characteristics were included in the overall average grades model, only one of them – the indicator of attending a co-educational school – proved to have a statistically significant relationship with the overall average grade, and hence the others are not included in Figure 6. According to the results, attending a co-educational school is associated with an increase of 9.4 percentage points in the probability of receiving a grade of at least 70 percent. However, there is no evidence that other school resources measures – not even the student-teacher ratio – have an important impact on student grades.

The story is a little different when one looks at PISA scores. Recall that for the reference individual, the predicted value of the PISA reading score is 486.7, which would put the student in Level 3. As Figure 8 indicates, school size, school type, and teacher participation are the only three school-related variables that appear to be significantly related to PISA scores, with the third variable having an effect only on reading scores. Once again, however, the effects are not large – for example, holding all

that the determinants of smoking behaviour and educational investment decisions are similar, success in identifying these factors could lead to health benefits as a result of reduced smoking, and to better educational outcomes as well. Finally, improvements in treating mental health disorders, included in the category "other disabilities," might also lead to improvements in educational attainment. The fact that learning disabilities are negatively related to educational outcomes at age 15 but not at age 21 suggests that, on average, the educational system has arguably made progress in the treatment of such disabilities. While it would be difficult to design policies to deal with the other issues singled out here, the empirical results derived from YITS-A suggest that tackling these issues rather than making small changes in high school resources might lead to greater improvements in educational attainment.

Notes

I would like to thank the Canada Millennium Scholarship Foundation and the Educational Policy Institute for research support through the MESA project, and Statistics Canada's COOL RDC for providing access to the data. I would also like to thank Theresa Qiu for assembling the data and doing much of the initial programming; without her assistance this paper would not have been completed. Finally, I thank the MESA Research Review Committee, Kim Foley, David Johnson, Ross Finnie, the editors of this volume, and participants at the MESA sessions of the 2008 Canadian Economics Association Meetings for their helpful comments and suggestions.

1. Although it is possible to enter some post-secondary programs in Canada as a mature student without a high school diploma, this rarely happens at the university level. However, Ferrer and Riddell (2002) found that in 1995 Canadian Census data, almost 30 percent of full-time, full-year workers with a college diploma or trades certificate did not have a high school diploma.
2. There is, of course, a large economic literature on the effect of education on earnings and other social outcomes. This literature is reviewed in a number of sources, including Lemieux (2002), Sweetman (2003), and Riddell (2003, 2007).
3. PISA stands for Programme for International Student Assessment. Under this program, the OECD administers standardized tests of reading, math, and science skills to a random sample of students of member countries. The data used herein are from the 2000 assessment. See OECD (2003) for further details.
4. See Ministère de l'Éducation, du Loisir et du Sport (2006) for further details on the Quebec education system.
5. See Alberta Learning (2002) for more information on charter schools in that province.
6. Schools affiliated with other religious denominations are generally not funded.

7. Although school boards in Ontario still receive funding from property taxes, since 1998 they no longer have the authority to set education tax rates. See chapter 2 of Rozanski (2002) for further details.

8. Calculation based on data from CANSIM table 3850009, accessed 29 March 2009.

9. Blouin (2008, 19) defines the term "educator" to include "all employees in the public school system who are required to have teaching certification as a condition of their employment." Thus it includes school principals and various types of counsellors, making the student-educator ratio smaller than a student-teacher ratio. However, it also excludes classroom assistants and volunteers who do not have a teaching certification. The importance of each of these different types of human resources to each province's school system is unknown.

10. Note that while there appears to have been a considerable drop in the student-educator ratio in Alberta over the period examined, the Alberta data for 1999-2000 to 2003-04 are not comparable to those of the two later years due to a change in the methodology used to compute the number of educators. See Blouin (2008) for more information.

11. Project STAR was a large-scale experiment carried out over four years by the State Department of Education in Tennessee to investigate the effects of class sizes in kindergarten to grade 3 on academic achievement. The results of the experiment have been studied extensively. For further information, see http://www.heros-inc.org/star.htm.

12. While instrumental variables estimators are widely used and have some good theoretical properties, those properties vanish in the absence of a strong correlation between the instrumental variables and the endogenous explanatory variables.

13. Note that it would also have been possible to examine the effect of high school resources at age 15 on grades upon high school graduation, or on grades obtained in the first year of PSE. These extensions were not pursued due to time limitations.

14. The National Longitudinal Survey of Children and Youth (NLSCY) also contains some information on the characteristics of schools attended by respondents, but fewer school characteristics are available. The sample size is also smaller.

15. The last three variables were constructed by averaging over students in the sample who attended the same school. Individuals were excluded from the samples used for estimation if less than 20 individuals from their school were included in the calculation of these averages.

16. All these measures are based on the responses of the school principal to the School Administrator Questionnaire. The index variables are constructed by the OECD; for further details regarding their construction, see chapter 17 of OECD (2003).

17. The ordered probit model is distinguished from the ordered logit model by the assumption that the random errors underlying the model have a normal distribution, not an extreme value distribution. For further details regarding ordered probit and logit models, see Greene (2008) or Cameron and Trivedi (2005). Both the ordered probit and linear regression estimates are weighted using sampling weights, with a correction for clustering at the school level.

18. All other explanatory variables not mentioned in this paragraph are continuous variables that are set equal to their sample means for the calculation of marginal effects.
19. While the PISA reading test was administered to all participants in YITS-A, only about half of the students wrote either the math or science tests.
20. The categorization of PISA reading scores into levels is that developed by the OECD. See OECD (2003) for details regarding the definitions of the levels. Levels were proposed by the OECD for reading scores only.
21. Note that although the factors highlighted in Figures 6 and 7 are not identical, the same explanatory variables were included in the models for PISA scores and overall average grades. The difference is due to the fact that some explanatory variables had a statistically significant coefficient in one model but not the other.
22. After estimating an ordered probit model, one can use the estimates to predict the probability of observing any particular value of the categorical variable for an individual with a specified set of characteristics. When the dependent variable has six categories, as is the case in the model of high school grades, this means that one can predict the probability of each of the six outcomes. Here the probabilities of the last three possible outcomes – a grade of 70%-79%, 80%-89%, or 90%-100% – are summed to reduce the volume of information to a more manageable amount. A grade of 70% was chosen as the cut-off because it is usually considered to be the dividing line between "good" and "not good" students.
23. In this case it is possible to predict the actual numerical PISA score associated with a particular set of individual characteristics, rather than the probability of obtaining a specific score, because the dependent variable was the actual numerical value of the PISA score rather than a categorical variable.
24. The PISA scores may range in value from 0 to over 900. It should be noted that the OECD normalizes PISA scores so as to ensure that the mean over all participating countries is 500 and the standard deviation is 100. For individual countries such as Canada, however, the mean and standard deviation may differ from these values. Furthermore, the predicted means reported in the text may differ from means constructed from the raw data because they have been derived from statistical models that standardize over a variety of respondent characteristics using the estimated parameters of those characteristics.
25. Since many individuals are unlikely to have completed even one post-secondary program as of age 21, the level of educational attainment is defined as the highest level of education attempted, rather than the highest level of education completed. The level of educational attainment ranges from not having graduated from high school to a graduate degree or above, depending on the YITS-A variable used (HEDLD4 or HLPSD4). HLSPD4 includes 14 possible levels of educational attainment, which were aggregated into 11 for the purposes of the econometric analysis.
26. Note that the marginal effect of the PISA score is not shown in Figure 9, due to the fact that it is a continuous variable rather than a dummy variable.
27. I thank Ross Finnie for this possible explanation of the result.

References

Akerhielm, K. 1995. "Does Class Size Matter?" *Economics of Education Review* 14 (3): 229-41.

Alberta Learning. 2002. *Charter Schools Handbook*. Edmonton: Alberta Learning, Special Programs Branch, December. At http://education.alberta.ca/media/434258/charter_hndbk.pdf (accessed 7 May 2009).

Bedard, K. 2003. "School Quality and the Distribution of Male Earnings in Canada." *Economics of Education Review* 22: 395-407.

Bertrand, R. 2002. "L'accès aux ressources pédagogiques: Commentaire." In *Towards Evidence-Based Policy for Canadian Education*, ed. P. de Broucker and A. Sweetman, 294-304. Montreal: McGill-Queen's University Press for the John Deutsch Institute for the Study of Economic Policy and Statistics Canada.

Blouin, P. 2008. *Summary Public School Indicators for the Provinces and Territories, 1999/2000 to 2005/2006*. Statistics Canada Catalogue no. 81-595-M – No. 067. Ottawa: Minister of Industry.

Cameron, A.C., and P.K. Trivedi. 2005. *Microeconometrics: Methods and Applications*. Cambridge: Cambridge University Press.

Corak, M., and D. Lauzon. 2002. "Provincial Differences in High School Achievement: For Whom Do Schools Matter?" *Proceedings of Statistics Canada Symposium 2002: Modeling Survey Data for Social and Economic Research*. At http://www.statcan.ca/english/freepub/11-522-XIE/2002001/session9/lauzon.pdf.

– 2005. "Differences in the Distribution of High School Achievement: The Role of Class Size and Time-in-Term." Analytical Studies Branch Research Paper Series, Statistics Canada, Catalogue no. 11F0019MIE – No. 270. November.

Council of Ministers of Education. Canada. 2008. *Education in Canada*. Toronto: Council of Ministers of Education, July. At http://www.cmec.ca/Publications/Pages/default.aspx (accessed 8 May 2009).

Crocker, R. 2007. "Human Capital Development and Education." In *Fulfilling Potential, Creating Success: Perspectives on Human Capital Development*, ed. G. Picot, R. Saunders, and A. Sweetman, 143-84. Montreal: McGill-Queen's University Press for the School of Policy Studies, Queen's University.

Day, K. 2009. "The Effect of High School Resources on Investment in Postsecondary Education in Canada." A MESA Project Research Paper. Toronto: Educational Policy Institute.

Dearden, L., J. Ferri, and C. Meghir. 2002. "The Effect of School Quality on Educational Attainment and Wages." *Review of Economics and Statistics* 84 (1): 1-20.

Ferrer, A.M., and W.C. Riddell. 2002. "The Role of Credentials in the Canadian Labour Market." *Canadian Journal of Economics* 35 (4): 879-905.

Greene, William H. 2008. *Econometric Analysis*. 6th ed. Upper Saddle River, NJ: Prentice Hall.

Hanushek, E.A. 1996. "School Resources and Student Performance." In *Does Money Matter? The Effect of School Resources on Student Achievement and Adult Success*, ed. G. Burtless, 43-73. Washington, DC: Brookings Institution.

Hanushek, E.A. 2006. "School Resources." In *Handbook of the Economics of Education*, vol. 2, ed. E.A. Hanushek and F. Welch, 865-908. Amsterdam: Elsevier.

Hanushek, E.A., and S.G. Rivkin. 2006. "Teacher Quality." In *Handbook of the Economics of Education*, vol. 2, ed. E.A. Hanushek and F. Welch, 1051-78. Amsterdam: Elsevier.

Johnson, D. 2005. *Signposts of Success: Interpreting Ontario's Elementary School Test Scores*. C.D. Howe Institute Policy Study 40. Ottawa: Renouf Publishing.

Jones, R.M. 2002. "TIMSS in Ontario: Providing Information for Educational Improvement." In *Towards Evidence-Based Policy for Canadian Education*, ed. P. de Broucker and A. Sweetman, 304-20. Montreal: McGill-Queen's University Press for the John Deutsch Institute for the Study of Economic Policy and Statistics Canada.

Lemieux, T. 2002. "The Causal Effect of Education on Earnings in Canada." In *Towards Evidence-Based Policy for Canadian Education*, ed. P. de Broucker and A. Sweetman, 105-16. Montreal: McGill-Queen's University Press for the John Deutsch Institute for the Study of Economic Policy and Statistics Canada.

Ma, X., and D.A. Klinger. 2000. "Hierarchical Linear Modelling of Student and School Effects on Academic Achievement." *Canadian Journal of Education* 25 (1): 41-55.

Ministère de l'Éducation, du Loisir et du Sport. Quebec. 2006. *Education in Quebec: An Overview*. Quebec: Gouvernment du Québec. At http://www.mels.gouv. qc.ca/daic/pdf/educqceng.pdf (accessed 7 May 2009).

Morgan, S.L., and M.W. McKerrow. 2007. "Human Capital Development and the Frontiers of Research in the Sociology of Education." In *Fulfilling Potential, Creating Success: Perspectives on Human Capital Development*, ed. G. Picot, R. Saunders, and A. Sweetman, 185-226. Montreal: McGill-Queen's University Press for the School of Policy Studies, Queen's University.

OECD. 2003. *PISA 2000 Technical Report*. Centre for Research and Innovation, SourceOECD Education, vol. 2002, no. 11.

Rangvid, B.S. 2007. "School Composition Effects in Denmark: Quantile Regression Evidence from PISA 2000." *Empirical Economics* 33: 359-88.

Riddell, W.C. 2003. "The Role of Government in Post-Secondary Education in Ontario." Research Report No. 29. Panel on the Role of Government in Ontario. At http://www.law-lib.utoronto.ca/investing/research_papers.htm (accessed 26 June 2009).

– 2007. "Impact of Education on Economic and Social Outcomes: An Overview of Recent Advances in Economics." In *Fulfilling Potential, Creating Success: Perspectives on Human Capital Development*, ed. G. Picot, R. Saunders, and A. Sweetman, 55-100. Montreal: McGill-Queen's University Press for the School of Policy Studies, Queen's University.

Rozanski, M. 2002. *Investing in Public Education: Advancing the Goal of Continuous Improvement in Student Learning and Achievement*. Report of the Education Equality Task Force. Toronto. At http://www.edu.gov.on.ca/eng/document/reports/task02/.

Speakman, R., and F. Welch. 2006. "Using Wages to Infer School Quality." In *Handbook of the Economics of Education*, vol. 2, ed. E.A. Hanushek and F. Welch, 813-64. Amsterdam: Elsevier.

Sweetman, A. 2003. "Ontario's Kindergarten to Grade 12 Education System: Some Thoughts for the Future." Research Report No. 25. Panel on the Role of Government in Ontario. At http://www.law-lib.utoronto.ca/investing/research_papers.htm (accessed 26 June 2009).

Zhang, Y. 2002. "The Distribution of Access to Educational Resources for 8th Grade Math in Canada: How Equitable Is It?" In *Towards Evidence-Based Policy for Canadian Education*, ed. P. de Broucker and A. Sweetman, 271-93. Montreal: McGill-Queen's University Press for the John Deutsch Institute for the Study of Economic Policy and Statistics Canada.

5

Dropping Out and Bouncing Back: New Evidence on High School Dynamics in Canada

ROSS FINNIE, CHRISTINE LAPORTE, AND ARTHUR SWEETMAN

On parle beaucoup de décrochage chez les jeunes du secondaire, mais les statistiques disponibles sont souvent imprécises et ne donnent pas l'heure juste, puisque, après avoir abandonné leurs études, certains jeunes les reprennent et obtiennent un diplôme, et d'autres entreprennent des études postsecondaires (EPS) sans diplôme de niveau secondaire. Dans cet article, à partir de trois ensembles de données longitudinales couvrant une période allant du début des années 1990 au milieu des années 2000, nous apportons de nouveaux résultats empiriques sur ces phénomènes, ainsi que sur les contextes individuels et familiaux qui y sont associés. Nous montrons ainsi que le taux de décrochage a baissé de façon notable, alors que le taux de retour aux études est resté stable (à environ 50 %). Toutefois, parmi les jeunes qui ont repris récemment les études, un plus grand nombre fréquentent de nouveau un établissement de niveau secondaire ; et ceux qui entreprennent directement des EPS sont moins nombreux. Le contexte familial et les facteurs qui y sont reliés ne constituent pas des variables explicatives importantes dans les cas de retour aux études (secondaires ou aux EPS) ; par contre, elles le sont quand on observe les jeunes qui décrochent et ceux qui entreprennent des EPS après avoir repris des études secondaires et avoir obtenu un diplôme.

Dropping out of high school is often discussed, but the underlying statistics are frequently confusing and rarely give just due to the phenomenon of "bouncing back" – defined here as either returning to high school and graduating, or going directly to post-secondary education (PSE) without completing secondary school. Using three longitudinal datasets from the early 1990s through to the mid-2000s, we provide new empirical evidence on the frequency of these events and their associated personal and family background characteristics. We find that dropout rates have fallen appreciably; nonetheless the rate of bouncing back remains constant at about 50 percent. However, more recently, a greater share of those who dropped out bounced back to high school, and fewer went directly to PSE.

Pursuing Higher Education in Canada: Economic, Social, and Policy Dimensions, ed. R. Finnie, M. Frenette, R.E. Mueller, and A. Sweetman. Montreal and Kingston: Queen's Policy Studies Series, McGill-Queen's University Press.

Family background and related variables are not strong predictors of bouncing back to either destination, but they are important predictors of who drops out and who continues to PSE after bouncing back to high school graduation.

In an environment where schooling is more than ever a determining factor of labour market opportunities, high school completion is an important indicator of both an individual's later economic prospects and society's future prosperity. This paper provides new empirical evidence on the high school dropout phenomenon and especially on the related, but generally neglected, dynamic of "bouncing back," defined here as either returning to and subsequently graduating from high school, or going straight to post-secondary education (PSE) without completing high school.

This paper thus provides a broader view of educational outcomes – dropping out, bouncing back, going on to PSE – that are too often looked at in isolation, and does so for three points in time from the early 1990s up to the recent past. It also explores the relationships of these pathways to various individual and family characteristics and other background factors such as parental education, family income, family structure, immigrant status, province, and language.

Our analysis is based on the two waves of the School Leavers Surveys (SLS) and both cohorts of the Youth in Transition Survey, YITS-A and YITS-B. Together, these datasets allow us to analyze and compare the dynamics at three points in time, first in the early 1990s and then a decade, and a decade and a half, later.

We first present simple descriptive statistics of high school dropout rates when the respondents are in their late teens, and subsequent rates of bouncing back by the time the respondents are in their early twenties. Next, we model these processes, first looking at who drops out, using a simple logit regression approach, and then analyzing the rates of bouncing back using a multinomial logit regression that allows for the three possible trajectories: (1) remaining out of school, (2) bouncing back to high school graduation, and (3) bouncing directly to PSE without completing high school. Finally, we use a similar logit set-up to look at who pursues PSE after bouncing back to high school graduation. While all three datasets have fairly extensive information on family backgrounds, only the YITS-A includes parental income as well as self-reported measures of parental education to go along with the student-reported measure, and these are explored in the last portion of the paper.

High school dropout rates stand at 16.6 percent for women and 23.9 percent for men in the earliest period, declining to 9.4 percent and 14.6 percent, respectively, by the latest point in time (we discuss the exact comparability of these rates). In each period, however, approximately 50 percent of these dropouts bounce back, thus introducing an appreciable wedge between dropout and ultimate high school graduation rates.

However, the nature of bouncing back does change over time. Early in the study period, about 15 percent of all dropouts bounce directly to PSE, whereas by the end of the study period, only about 5 percent do so. Meanwhile, the percentage of those who pursue PSE after bouncing back to high school graduation seems to increase slightly.

Family background characteristics are strongly related to dropping out. For example, in the YITS-A even controlling for other factors, young men whose parents have less than a high school diploma are about 14 percent more likely to drop out than those whose parents' highest level of education is high school; those whose parents have some or completed PSE are about 5 or 6 percent less likely to do so – a 20 percentage point difference. The rate of pursuing PSE after bouncing back is also related to family background, although not quite as strongly. Bouncing back itself, however, is not as clearly related to background characteristics, even as some generally weaker patterns are identified.

Overall, the predictors are in the expected directions. With respect to parental education, individuals with more highly educated parents drop out less and, having dropped out, are somewhat more likely to bounce back. In terms of family income, youth in higher income families are less likely to drop out, although the relationship with bouncing back is less than clear. But some of the estimated effects are likely to hold surprises for some readers, if only in the magnitudes of the effects rather than necessarily in their direction. Dual parent families have much lower dropout rates, but family structure does not appear to affect bouncing back. Female immigrants drop out at lower rates than non-immigrants and seem more likely to bounce directly to PSE, but rates do not appear to differ for immigrant and non-immigrant males. Interestingly, it is difficult to find any clear differences for urban and rural students once other factors (including parental education) are controlled for. Certain patterns also emerge by province and language groups, with Quebec having a somewhat higher dropout rate and minority language students (English in Quebec, French elsewhere) mostly having lower dropout rates.

The downward trend in dropout rates may be seen as a positive development, while the lack of movement in the rates of bouncing back must be interpreted carefully, since those who do drop out have likely become a more disaffected group as those rates have fallen – and so mere stability in rates might be a good thing here. The association of these rates with family and other related characteristics points to where the gaps are greater.

The Context

Public discussion often focuses on various measures of "dropout rates" that confuse more than they elucidate. At one extreme, these statistics count all instances where a student leaves high school before graduation (in, for example, a given province or school board). Among other issues, particular individuals may be counted multiple times if they drop out, re-register, and then drop out again; students are sometimes counted as being permanent dropouts if they do not graduate (close to) on time; and non-completion may be confused with a move to a different jurisdiction. The resulting "dropout rates" can be extremely high, and while they may be useful if regarded appropriately, they do not reflect the final outcomes of the education system and are both prone to misinterpretation and subject to sensationalist reporting.

Alternative, more comprehensive measures, sometimes called high school non-completion (or the complement – high school graduation) rates, typically look at the proportion of those in some age group, commonly 20-24 years old, who have not completed high school. They find much lower "permanent" dropout rates, although even here some may bounce back after age 24, as emphasized by Richards (2009). However, both these approaches typically ignore the possibility that some students never complete high school but nevertheless pursue PSE, and in any event both approaches ignore the underlying dynamics by which some individuals drop out and then successfully return to their studies.

For example, O'Sullivan et al. (2009), in a report for Canada's Council of Ministers of Education which was widely publicized in the media, declared, "Approximately one-quarter of Canadian youth do not graduate from secondary school" (5). Ménard (2009), looking exclusively at Quebec, reports that only 69 percent of youth complete high school by age 20. In contrast (although for a few years earlier), Statistics Canada (Bowlby 2005) reports dropout rates of just over 9 percent for Ontario and just under 12 percent for Quebec. Richards (2009) uses 2006 Census data to look at completion rates by age 20-24 as well as by age 25-34 to find rates just a little above Bowlby's for the first group and rates similar to Bowlby's for the older group. These dramatic differences are not because of a gap in the years being analyzed; rather, they reflect fundamentally different ways of viewing the system (or viewing parts of the system in isolation) and measuring outcomes.

Many other examples of such divergences in dropout rates could be noted, as could the general lack of attention paid to the bouncing back phenomenon per se, including the different routes young people take in making their way back into the education system. There is, therefore, a need for more clearly defined analysis of dropout rates and for more comprehensive approaches that include the bouncing back dynamic. In particular, there is a need for a "person-based" and "system-wide" perspective that does not double count, that takes transfers into account, and that even goes beyond analysis such as Bowlby's by recognizing bouncing back to PSE.

One of the very few studies that takes a broad, system-wide view of education, and then links it to labour market outcomes, is that of Ferrer and Riddell (2002). They look at the earnings associated with different educational pathways, although not at the dynamics and determinants of the process that are the focus of the current analysis, so it is highly complementary to this study. "For those who did not complete high school," they find, "receipt of a college diploma or trades certificate raises earnings by approximately 6 per cent for both men and women" (903). This is roughly comparable to the earnings increment associated with high school graduation. High school graduation combined with a community college degree provides an increment that is at least twice as large. This suggests that bouncing back to high school graduation is the preferred path in terms of labour market outcomes for the average person, other things being equal. It should be noted that their analysis is complex; for example, it separates out years of education from the so-called "sheepskin effects" of degree completion.

The literature closest to our study includes Raymond (2008), who discusses the possibility of bouncing directly to PSE but does not isolate and model this trajectory. Finnie, Lascelles, and Sweetman (2005) and Finnie and Mueller (2008) look at the determinants of PSE attendance and show the importance of factors that occur early in a youth's life (including many of those considered here), but ignore whether the person has finished high school and the related dynamics. Youth PSE pathways in articulated systems, such as those in Western Canada, are discussed by Andres and Krahn (1999). Dagenais, Montmarquette, and Viennot-Briot (2007) look at dropping out and allow for returning in a structural model of student choice. For a general introduction to issues regarding access to PSE, see Finnie, Sweetman, and Usher (2008).

The Data[1]

The Surveys and Samples Employed

Our analysis is based on three longitudinal Statistics Canada surveys that were designed to address issues regarding youth transitions through school and into the labour market. The first is the School Leavers (SLS) and School Leavers Follow-Up (SLFS) surveys. The former was conducted in 1991 when respondents were 18 to 20 years of age, and the follow-up took place in 1995 when respondents were 22 to 24. The sampling frame for the SLS was the family allowance file, which comprised the universe of relevant youth.

The two other datasets we employ are the Youth in Transition Surveys – Cohorts A and B. Individuals were first interviewed in 2000, capturing representative samples of youth who were age 15 (YITS-A) or 18 to 20

(YITS-B) as of the preceding 31 December. Subsequent interviews have been conducted every two years.

In the SLS-SLFS, we identified those individuals who had (ever) dropped out of high school in the first interview when they were age 18 to 20, and then looked at who had bounced back to high school or directly to PSE by the second interview, when they were age 22 to 24. To generate comparable samples using the YITS-B, we used Cycle 1 (2000), when individuals were age 18-20, and then Cycle 3 (2004), both to measure dropout rates and to see who had bounced back by (again) age 22-24.[2]

For the YITS-A, dropouts are measured in Cycle 3 (2004), and bouncing back is determined by looking at Cycle 4 (2006), when respondents were 19 and 21, respectively. The YITS-B represents a random sample of youth using the Labour Force Survey frame, while the YITS-A sampled children within randomly selected elementary school classrooms, along with their parents and principals.

Restrictions in selecting the samples used in the analysis are kept to a minimum in order to make the analysis as representative as possible. We thus delete only those who indicated they did no high school in Canada, those who came to the country after 10 years of age,[3] those whose families (in the YITS-A) had exactly zero total income (the reported income does not appear to reflect the families' actual resources), and those who gave unclear responses, or who had missing, "don't know," or "does not apply" responses for the key variables used in the analysis. These amount to a very small number of deletions. Only those individuals included in all cycles of their respective datasets are included in the analysis, and we rely on the survey weights provided by Statistics Canada to adjust for attrition across the cycles and to address other sample design issues. The YITS-A standard errors are adjusted for the survey design that "clusters" on schools. For more information on the SLS and the SLFS, see Statistics Canada (1993). For the YITS see Shaienk, Eisl-Culkin, and Bussière (2006) and Motte et al. (2008).

Definitions of Dropping Out and Bouncing Back

We define dropouts as those who left high school, either permanently or temporarily, before completing. This is operationalized by identifying all those who drop out prior to the first interview for the SLS and YITS-B, and by the third interview for the YITS-A. Bouncing back is measured by using the respondents' status at the time of the subsequent interview two years later. Respondents' ages at each point seem appropriate to the purpose, although we do miss those who both drop out and then bounce back between interviews. Also, we do not observe beyond the last interview to know the ultimate status of those who have dropped out (and might in the future bounce back), and the very few who are still enrolled (who might drop out permanently). Hence, our count of both those who drop out and bounce back may be too low.

We define three trajectories for those who have dropped out, two of which we jointly label as bouncing back:

- *No bounce*: These individuals are still high school dropouts. This trajectory includes those who have returned to high school after dropping out but have not yet obtained their diploma.
- *Bounce to high school graduation*: These high school dropouts became graduates.
- *Bounce to post-secondary education*: These high school dropouts did not obtain their high school diploma by the second period but were observed to move directly to PSE. In most cases, these individuals were in a trade school or community college program.

Number of Dropouts and Bouncers

Figure 1 illustrates the distribution of the individuals in the three samples with respect to the different pathways for dropping out and bouncing back. As of the first interview (age 18-20 in 1991), 20.3 percent of the SLS sample had dropped out, and of these approximately half (49.4 percent) had bounced back by the second interview (age 22-24 in 1995), the majority to high school (34.5 percent) rather than directly to PSE (14.9 percent). Of those who bounced back to high school completion, 55.4 percent had also gone on to PSE by the time of the second interview.

Nine years later, as seen in the YITS-B (age 18-20 as of 31 December 1999), overall dropout rates had fallen by a quarter, to 15.5 percent (age 22-24 in 2003), but among these, bounce back rates were almost exactly the same, at 50.0 percent. Also, more of these represented high school completion rather than bouncing directly to PSE (40.8 percent versus 9.2 percent), while the number of high school finishers who had already gone on to PSE was about the same as in the earlier period (58.6 percent). The YITS-A (age 19 in December 2003, and 21 in 2005) shows a similar pattern as the YITS-B, although the dropout rate is lower yet, while the bounce back rate is again comparable. Again, over half of those who bounce back to high school graduation subsequently continue on to post-secondary education.

Overall, then, there appears to be a marked decline in the dropout rate over the data period, but the percentage of dropouts who bounce back remains stable. The latter finding should be seen in the context of the declining dropout rate, whereby a smaller, more select group of dropouts is perhaps characterized by greater disaffection or other characteristics that make them less likely to return to school. Interestingly, there is also an increase in the percentage of dropouts who return to complete high school.

FIGURE 1
Pathways for Dropping Out and Bouncing Back

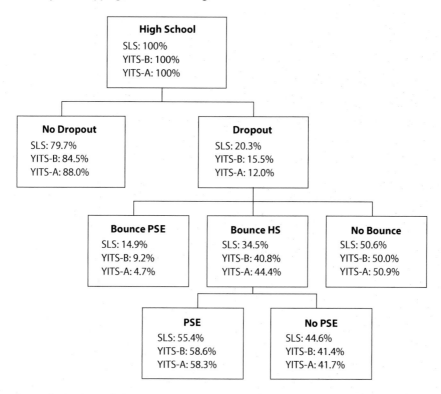

Source: Authors' compilation.

In these patterns, we cannot explicitly separate secular trends from business cycle effects or any other potential influences such as changes in the minimum wage. However, Raymond (2008), using the Labour Force Survey to look at trends in the high school dropout rate between 1990 and 2005 among 20 to 24 year olds, shows only very modest business cycle effects (although she does not discuss them). Also, in accord with our results, she observes a roughly 5 percentage point decrease in high school non-completion. She does not address the issue of bouncing directly to PSE.

Descriptive Statistics and Variable Definitions

Table 1 displays the sample means for the three datasets, and we need not discuss them in detail. Instead, we focus on describing the construction of the variables and differences across the datasets that are most pertinent to our analysis.

TABLE 1
Sample Means

	SLS		YITS-B		YITS-A	
	Women	*Men*	*Women*	*Men*	*Women*	*Men*
			Mean (%)			
Parental education (by student)						
Unknown	12.8	13.8	2.5	4.5	0.7	1.1
Less than high school	23.8	20.6	13.4	11.8	8.1	7.0
High school completed	24.1	27.2	26.7	26.6	26.4	25.7
Some or completed college	16.9	15.4	28.8	26.1	...	...
Some or completed university	22.4	23.1	28.5	30.9	...	...
Some or completed PSE	...	...	...	...	64.9	66.2
Parental education (by parent)						
Unknown	...	...	...	...	1.2	1.3
Less than high school	...	...	...	...	8.7	7.6
High school completed	...	...	...	...	22.1	20.8
Some or completed college	...	...	...	...	36.7	38.2
Some or completed university	...	...	...	...	31.4	32.2
Parental income (by parent)						
$1-$4,999	...	...	...	...	0.3	0.2
$5,000 to $24,999	...	...	...	...	7.8	6.3
$25,000 to $49,999	...	...	...	...	25.9	23.7
$50,000 to $74,999	...	...	...	...	28.9	29.7
$75,000 to $99,999	...	...	...	...	22.2	24.8
$100,000 to $300,000	...	...	...	...	15.0	15.3
Family type						
Two parents	79.1	82.1	79.1	81.6	81.6	83.6
Don't live 2-parents	20.9	17.9	20.9	18.5	18.4	16.4
Mother only	11.1	9.8	16.3	13.4	14.6	12.4
Father only	2.3	3.6	3.1	3.6	2.6	2.7
Other	7.5	4.6	1.5	1.4	1.2	1.3
Region						
Atlantic	10.7	10.6	8.3	8.5	8.8	8.1
Quebec	24.1	23.1	24.7	24.5	22.6	23.7
Ontario	37.3	36.3	36.6	36.5	37.1	36.8
Prairies	17.4	18.4	17.4	17.9	18.5	18.7
British Columbia	10.6	11.6	13.1	12.7	13.9	12.7
Language						
English	73.6	76.0	64.2	63.2	72.4	73.5
French	23.6	21.0	25.0	24.7	25.5	25.0
Bilingual	2.7	2.9	...	...	2.0	1.2
Other	x	x	10.8	12.2	x	x
Urban/rural						
Rural	23.5	25.0	20.1	22.8	28.0	26.7
Urban	76.5	75.0	79.9	77.2	72.0	73.3
Immigrant status						
Non-immigrant	93.4	92.5	91.9	90.2	94.2	94.4
Immigrant	6.6	7.5	8.1	9.8	5.9	5.6
# of observations	3,238	3,012	7,396	7,240	8,179	7,625

Notes: Women represent 50.11 percent of the weighted sample. Men represent 49.89 percent.
... = not applicable. x = suppressed to meet the confidentiality requirements of the *Statistics Act*.
Source: Authors' compilation.

The first set of family background variables represents the highest level of parental education (mother or father) as reported by the student or, in the case of the YITS-A, also by the parent(s). The information pertains to the parental relationships and associated education levels at the point when the student left high school. "Unknown" includes those with parental education unclassified or unknown, and those not living with at least one of their parents.[4] In the YITS-A, students were given a category that combined college and university, but parents were asked a question that differentiated the two.[5] One important pattern is the clear increase in parental education levels between the SLS and the YITS-B. Although this is somewhat confounded by the SLS having a much larger "unknown" category, to the degree that there are increasing levels of parental education and parental education is negatively related to dropout rates (as we in fact find), we would expect dropout rates to have been driven downward over time by this change. As previously noted, family income is not available on either the SLS or the YITS-B.

Family type is defined by the living arrangements at the time of leaving high school. A large majority of our sample lived with two parents (around 80 percent for all three surveys). The percentage of respondents who lived in some "other" situation decreased markedly between the SLS and both YITS. We are, however, reluctant to give too much importance to these familial shifts based on these data because the variables in the SLS and the YITS are not exactly identical. In the regression analysis we group the remaining categories as "don't live with two parents," based on an exploratory analysis.[6]

Region (or province) represents where the student last went to high school. Language is defined differently in the different datasets. The SLS and YITS-A measure language spoken when last in high school as French, English, or bilingual. In the YITS-B, language is defined as mother tongue, and we are unable to replicate the bilingual category since the questionnaire forces the respondent to choose only one. For the regression analysis, interactions between region and language were created to identify the English minority in Quebec and the French minority in the rest of Canada to take into account the specificities between the two populations and their school systems, cultures, and any other related factors.

In the SLS, the urban-rural variable applies to when the respondent left school, whereas in the YITS it refers to the time of the first interview. Table 1 shows only small changes in the proportion of each category between the surveys. Immigrants represent 7 percent of our SLS sample and about 9 percent of the YITS-B, but a smaller fraction of the YITS-A who are younger at the first interview. This accords with age-at-migration patterns whereby relatively few immigrants arrive at an age younger than their early twenties.

In the regressions that follow, for the SLS and the YITS-B we also control for age using a set of dummy variables. However, we view these regressors as controls for a background factor and do not present their results or discuss them in analysis.

Dropping Out and Bouncing Back: How Many and Who

Dropping Out

Dropout rates are shown in Table 2. In the SLS, 16.6 percent of female respondents and 23.9 percent of male respondents had dropped out of high school. These figures decrease to 13.7 percent and 17.2 percent, respectively, in the YITS-B, and 9.4 and 14.6 in the YITS-A. Thus, rates are substantial but lower than many of those sometimes reported, as mentioned in the introduction; also the rates fell appreciably over time and are higher for men than women.

Higher levels of parental education are strongly associated with lower dropout rates for both women and men, as is parental income (YITS-A only). The income profile appears to be steeper for women. Interestingly, the male-female differences emerge only for higher income households; male-female rates are similar in lower income households.

Living with both parents is associated with much lower dropout rates, and, although a small group in the three surveys, living with neither parent at the relevant point in time is associated with extremely high dropout rates. (Recall that the definition of family type "other" differs across the surveys.)

Dropout rates also vary significantly between regions, with Quebec having the highest rate, particularly for men. The Atlantic region follows closely in 1991, but its rate decreases sharply in the two YITS surveys. Note that there are significant differences in the male-female dropout gaps across regions. It is difficult to separate the influence of language from region on the dropout rate, but the results do show higher dropout rates for francophones.

Those living in rural areas have higher dropout rates. Immigrants (remember that in these data this includes only those who arrived in Canada when young) are less likely to drop out, but the effect is much greater for women than men.

Bouncing Back

Table 3 shows the rates of bouncing back. About half of those students who dropped out of high school before completing (as identified above) subsequently bounced back either to high school graduation or directly to PSE. Men are significantly less likely to bounce back than women, which, in combination with their higher dropout rate, makes them much more likely to finish their schooling without a high school diploma.

TABLE 2
Dropout Rates

	SLS		YITS-B		YITS-A	
	Women	Men	Women	Men	Women	Men
			Dropout rates (%)			
Total	16.6	23.9	13.7	17.2	9.4	14.6
Parental education (by student)						
Unknown	46.1	41.8	21.5	27.3	4.7	17.8
Less than high school	23.1	32.4	27.9	36.5	22.3	36.5
High school completed	13.2	22.6	16.8	21.5	10.7	17.6
Some or completed college	4.6	13.1	9.5	12.8	...	...
Some or completed university	5.5	14.3	7.7	8.3	...	...
Some or completed PSE	...	...	...	...	7.2	11.0
Parental education (by parent)						
Unknown	...	...	...	...	28.5	32.8
Less than high school	...	...	...	...	21.0	39.2
High school completed	...	...	...	...	12.9	19.5
Some or completed college	...	...	...	...	8.4	12.8
Some or completed university	...	...	...	...	4.0	7.0
Parental income (by parent)						
$1-$4,999	...	...	...	...	25.0	14.4
$5,000 to $24,999	...	...	...	...	22.1	23.9
$25,000 to $49,999	...	...	...	...	12.5	20.2
$50,000 to $74,999	...	...	...	...	7.9	15.3
$75,000 to $99,999	...	...	...	...	7.1	10.1
$100,000 to $300,000	...	...	...	...	3.0	7.7
Family type						
Two parents	12.1	20.5	10.2	14.4	7.4	13.0
Don't live 2-parents	46.1	39.3	26.9	29.3	17.9	22.8
Mother only	23.3	38.5	24.6	28.8	16.9	21.1
Father only	21.3	37.6	26.5	30.6	18.9	24.9
Other	52.8	42.2	52.6	30.4	28.0	34.1
Region						
Atlantic	18.1	26.2	7.4	16.1	6.9	10.4
Quebec	18.9	29.0	14.9	24.0	11.7	22.9
Ontario	14.8	22.2	13.1	12.0	9.1	13.2
Prairies	15.8	23.5	15.6	18.0	10.1	12.7
British Columbia	17.6	17.4	14.5	18.4	6.5	8.5
Language						
English	15.3	22.0	13.8	14.9	9.0	12.3
French	20.4	29.7	14.6	22.6	11.0	21.8
Bilingual	17.6	17.4	...	...	2.2	4.9
Other	x	x	11.0	18.0	x	x
Urban/rural						
Rural	18.1	28.0	15.5	21.3	10.2	14.7
Urban	16.2	22.5	13.2	16.0	9.0	14.5
Immigrant status						
Non-immigrant	17.4	24.0	14.1	17.2	9.6	14.7
Immigrant	5.9	22.7	8.5	16.7	6.0	12.6

Notes: ... = not applicable. x = suppressed to meet the confidentiality requirements of the *Statistics Act.*

Source: Authors' compilation.

TABLE 3
Bouncing Back Rates

	SLS		YITS-B		YITS-A	
	Women	*Men*	*Women*	*Men*	*Women*	*Men*
	Bouncing back rates (%)					
Total	51.6	47.9	59.4	42.8	55.5	45.0
Parental education (by student)						
Unknown	44.9	33.1	48.1	25.1	x	32.4
Less than high school	47.2	37.2	50.8	31.9	40.6	26.4
High school completed	52.5	54.9	52.6	43.8	51.9	41.3
Some or completed college	82.8	49.4	72.1	50.1	...	...
Some or completed university	81.7	81.9	75.0	58.0	...	...
Some or completed PSE	...	...	...	...	63.7	54.2
Parental education (by parent)						
Unknown	...	...	...	...	69.3	42.5
Less than high school	...	...	...	...	44.6	28.4
High school completed	...	...	...	...	47.3	40.7
Some or completed college	...	...	...	...	61.6	52.7
Some or completed university	...	...	...	...	71.7	58.3
Parental income (by parent)						
$1-$4,999	...	...	...	...	x	x
$5,000 to $24,999	...	...	...	...	45.1	40.6
$25,000 to $49,999	...	...	...	...	61.4	40.4
$50,000 to $74,999	...	...	...	...	49.0	37.4
$75,000 to $99,999	...	...	...	...	60.3	59.1
$100,000 to $300,000	...	...	...	...	62.5	67.5
Family type						
Two parents	54.5	48.1	51.6	43.3	56.7	43.9
Don't live 2-parents	47.7	47.6	61.4	41.7	53.3	48.3
Mother only	46.9	52.0	51.6	39.2	51.6	51.6
Father only	59.8	45.9	77.6	46.0	53.6	36.3
Other	46.8	40.1	72.3	52.5	66.2	46.9
Region						
Atlantic	52.7	52.4	50.3	40.9	60.3	38.9
Quebec	45.7	34.1	50.0	38.7	49.9	40.3
Ontario	57.6	55.1	68.3	49.3	59.3	54.6
Prairies	49.4	46.1	53.2	47.6	54.5	35.9
British Columbia	50.5	63.3	66.8	35.3	56.7	50.1
Language						
English	52.9	53.8	65.2	42.4	57.0	47.6
French	47.5	34.9	48.4	39.1	51.6	40.6
Bilingual	60.0	31.8	...	...	93.6	89.1
Other	x	x	49.8	53.9	x	x
Urban/rural						
Rural	40.3	44.3	45.7	32.9	53.0	38.7
Urban	55.5	49.4	63.4	46.7	56.6	47.3
Immigrant status						
Non-immigrant	51.6	47.0	58.5	41.7	55.5	44.4
Immigrant	50.0	60.1	75.8	52.7	56.6	56.2

Notes: ... = not applicable. x = suppressed to meet the confidentiality requirements of the *Statistics Act.*

Source: Authors' compilation.

Parental education, as reported by either parent or child, is related to bouncing back, but the relationship is not as smooth as it was in the case of dropping out. Still, the likelihood of bouncing back is about twice as high for the sons of university educated parents as for the sons of parents with less than high school education. For women, with their higher overall bounce back rates, the gradient is not quite as steep. Parental income is also related to bouncing back, although again the effect does not seem to be as strong or as consistent as it was for dropping out.

For men, the regional bounce back rates generally accentuate the dropout rates: regions with high dropout rates also tend to have lower bounce back rates. Plausibly, the same factors that cause students to drop out in the first place lead them to stay out, although our analysis cannot say what those factors are. Interestingly, the regional profile is flatter, although Quebec appears to have a lower rate. Language is again difficult to disentangle from region here, but those who speak English seem to have higher bounce back rates. (The changing definition of the bilingual/ other category along with its smallish number of observations makes the results for that group difficult to interpret.)

While the urban-rural dropout rate gap was not seen to be particularly large (Table 2), the pattern is unusual in that the differences for the bounce back rates are actually greater than for the dropout rates. It could be that the greater educational opportunities in an urban area facilitate these returns to school. In most cases, immigrants have a higher bounce back rate.

The Regression Analysis

Specification of the Models

For the regression analysis we first employ a standard logit model to treat the decision to drop out as opposed to continuing on to high school graduation. For those who drop out, we then use a multinomial logit to allow for the choices among not bouncing back (the base or comparison option), bouncing to high school graduation, and bouncing to PSE. Finally, we use another simple logit to see who among those who bounce back to high school subsequently go on to PSE. In each case the explanatory variables are the same as those discussed above, with a few modifications of the precise specifications as appropriate (the inclusion of the language-region interactions, the combination of certain categories, etc.). Parental income and parental education as reported by the parent, both of which are available only in the YITS-A, are not included in these initial regressions but are explored later. Separate regressions are run for men and women. For all of the regressions we report the marginal effects at the means, which are interpretable in a straightforward way: the (average) effect on the probability of the indicated outcome associated with a one unit change in the explanatory variable.

Dropping Out

Table 4 presents the logit results for dropping out. There is a clear pattern across all three surveys, whereby those whose parents have less education are more likely to drop out. In fact, the differences are almost as large as in Table 2 where the other factors taken into account in the regression approach are not considered. Compared to those whose parents completed high school (the omitted group), those whose parents had less than high school are between 7.5 and 14.0 percentage points more likely to drop out, and those whose parents had some or completed college, or some or completed university, are between 7 and 11.5 percentage points less likely to do so. Interestingly, where community college can be distinguished from university (in the SLS and the YITS-B), there is relatively little difference between the two. Overall, there seems to be a clear distinction between less than high school, high school, and PSE, but not much difference among PSE levels. Of course, the data cannot distinguish between complete and incomplete degrees.[7]

Using the regression set-up, not living with both parents at the end of high school is again associated with appreciably higher rates of dropping out. Region and language are intimately related, and the set-up of this regression is such that that the regional effect reflects the majority language group in each area: English outside of Quebec, and French within it. The minority language groups in each case are captured by the region-language interactions. (Note that this forces the difference between the English and non-English groups to be the same in all the provinces outside Quebec.) For the SLS, once the other factors are statistically controlled for, there are no regional differences for the primary language groups; however, in the YITS-B, some differences are statistically significant, with Quebec having high and the Atlantic and Western provinces having low dropout rates. In the YITS-A, even greater regional differences are identified. These results would suggest that differences by region – after controlling for other factors – have been increasing over time.

Minority language groups, with the possible exception of women who are bilingual outside of Quebec, actually have dropout rates similar to, or lower than, the comparable majority language groups in each region.

Urban-rural differences are, for the most part, not statistically significant, except for the case of men in the YITS-B, where there is a modest difference favouring urban dwellers. Immigrant women appear less likely to drop out of high school, although this gap has declined over time and is particularly small in the YITS-A. For men there is no statistically significant immigrant effect.

In summary, the results indicate a strong relationship between dropping out and parental education, which is consistent with the findings of Finnie and Mueller (2008) and other researchers using the YITS-A when looking at access. Other effects are identified, but there are few consistent patterns

TABLE 4
Logit on Dropping Out of High School

	SLS		YITS-B		YITS-A	
	Women	Men	Women	Men	Women	Men
Parental education (high school)						
Unknown	0.272***	0.139***	0.114**	0.101*	-0.050**	-0.003
	[0.061]	[0.049]	[0.053]	[0.054]	[0.023]	[0.063]
Less than high school	0.093**	0.082**	0.075***	0.112***	0.068***	0.140***
	[0.037]	[0.039]	[0.028]	[0.033]	[0.020]	[0.034]
Some or completed college	-0.088***	-0.087**	-0.062***	-0.078***	...	...
	[0.020]	[0.034]	[0.016]	[0.018]		
Some or completed university	-0.074***	-0.075**	-0.070***	-0.115***	...	...
	[0.022]	[0.032]	[0.015]	[0.016]		
Some or completed PSE	...	...	...	...	-0.029***	-0.057***
					[0.011]	[0.013]
Don't live 2 parents	0.099***	0.136***	0.127***	0.104***	0.084***	0.068***
	[0.035]	[0.037]	[0.021]	[0.020]	[0.014]	[0.017]
Region (Ontario)						
Atlantic	0.003	0.010	-0.069***	0.030	-0.041***	-0.061***
	[0.031]	[0.034]	[0.013]	[0.020]	[0.010]	[0.012]
Quebec	0.061	0.068	-0.007	0.097***	0.075***	0.149***
	[0.040]	[0.044]	[0.020]	[0.021]	[0.026]	[0.029]
Prairies	0.010	0.000	0.014	0.052***	-0.013	-0.039***
	[0.033]	[0.034]	[0.019]	[0.019]	[0.012]	[0.014]
British Columbia	0.030	-0.051	0.008	0.055*	-0.039***	-0.072***
	[0.044]	[0.041]	[0.024]	[0.030]	[0.012]	[0.014]
Language interactions						
Quebec x English	-0.204***	-0.082	-0.059*	-0.047	-0.040**	-0.047*
	[0.018]	[0.065]	[0.034]	[0.053]	[0.020]	[0.024]
Quebec x Bilingual	-0.222***	-0.184**	...	...	#	-0.074**
	[0.011]	[0.081]	[0.033]			[0.033]
Quebec x Other	...	...	0.023	0.030	...	...
	[0.073]	[0.064]				
Outside Quebec x French	-0.093*	-0.131***	-0.056***	-0.074**	-0.037***	0.000
	[0.054]	[0.042]	[0.021]	[0.033]	[0.010]	[0.017]
Outside Quebec x Bilingual	0.190**	0.157	...	...	-0.062***	-0.064
	[0.091]	[0.100]	[0.021]	[0.053]		
Outside Quebec x Other	...	...	-0.020	0.013	...	...
			[0.027]	[0.037]		
Urban	0.005	-0.051	-0.015	-0.034**	-0.004	0.015
	[0.027]	[0.031]	[0.014]	[0.015]	[0.012]	[0.011]
Immigrant	-0.133***	0.035	-0.052**	-0.008	-0.031**	-0.024
	[0.038]	[0.064]	[0.026]	[0.038]	[0.015]	[0.023]
Pseudo R²	0.169	0.072	0.085	0.089	0.079	0.080
Observations	3,238	3,012	7,396	7,240	8,160	7,625

Notes: Also included in the regressions for SLS and YITS-B are two age indicator variables.
Omitted categories in parentheses. Results shown are marginal effects evaluated at the sample mean.
Standard errors, adjusted for clustering in the YITS-A, are in brackets. *** p<0.01, ** p<0.05, * p<0.1.
implies insufficient variation in the data to produce an estimate.
Source: Authors' compilation.

and the magnitudes are generally not nearly as strong as those found in the simple correlations, precisely because those simple correlations do not take account of other factors such as parental education.

Bouncing Back

The results of a series of multinomial logit regressions representing the probability that an individual bounces back after dropping out of high school are presented in the three panels of Table 5. Each set of two columns (Women, Men) portrays a single regression over the three choices, with "no bounce" being the baseline or comparison choice, and the two kinds of bouncing back (to PSE, to high school graduation) being the outcomes shown. The marginal effects shown represent the change in the probability of the indicated outcome associated with a one unit change in the relevant explanatory variable. These models are estimated only for those individuals previously observed to have dropped out.

The results do not generally paint as clear a picture of the determinants of bouncing back as was the case for the dropping out regressions seen previously, although the pseudo-R^2s suggest comparable explanatory power. Of course, one reason for this lack of clarity and for the general lack of statistical significance of many of the specific variables stems from the relatively modest sample sizes (i.e., a given effect will have lower statistical significance in a smaller sample) as well as our attempt to identify two different pathways of bouncing back. Still, if there were an effect of appreciable magnitude, it has the potential of showing up.

In this context we find that increased parental education is somewhat related to a higher probability of bouncing back, but the effects are uneven across levels of education, models (women vs. men), and datasets (i.e., over time), and many of the effects are not statistically different from zero. Similarly, although not living with two parents is an important predictor of dropping out, it has no statistically significant effect on the probability of bouncing back.

There are few systematic differences across regions, except that those in Quebec (the Quebec variable represents francophones in the province with the interaction variable indicating "minority" anglophones there) are generally less likely to bounce back directly to college than are those in other provinces. The minority language group effects are mixed – this after these groups were generally associated with lower rates of dropping out. The urban variable similarly does not have a consistent pattern, with the marginal effects being only statistically significant for women returning directly to PSE in the SLS. There is some evidence that immigrants are less likely to return directly to PSE but more likely to return to high school graduation than non-immigrants.

TABLE 5
Multinomial Logit on Three Choices of Bouncing Back (1 of 3)

| | SLS | | | |
| | Women | | Men | |
	Bounce PS	HS Graduate	Bounce PS	HS Graduate
Parental education (high school)				
Unknown	-0.010	-0.013	-0.014	-0.194**
	[0.057]	[0.168]	[0.059]	[0.091]
Less than high school	0.007	-0.029	-0.012	-0.120
	[0.054]	[0.137]	[0.069]	[0.097]
Some or completed college	0.122	0.169	-0.051	-0.011
	[0.107]	[0.146]	[0.067]	[0.149]
Some or completed university	-0.044	0.362**	0.304***	-0.040
	[0.064]	[0.174]	[0.114]	[0.117]
Some or completed PSE	...	...	...	...
Don't live 2-parents	-0.007	-0.043	-0.017	0.052
	[0.045]	[0.112]	[0.051]	[0.073]
Region (Ontario)				
Atlantic	0.050	-0.047	0.029	0.042
	[0.048]	[0.122]	[0.080]	[0.086]
Quebec	0.122	-0.184	-0.118***	-0.054
	[0.078]	[0.117]	[0.042]	[0.132]
Prairies	-0.015	-0.048	0.012	-0.085
	[0.039]	[0.154]	[0.065]	[0.084]
British Columbia	0.129	-0.192	0.051	-0.037
	[0.096]	[0.124]	[0.085]	[0.112]
Language interactions				
Quebec x English	-0.098***	-0.225*	0.260	-0.172
	[0.017]	[0.129]	[0.236]	[0.137]
Quebec x Bilingual	-0.098***	0.046	-0.160***	0.539***
	[0.017]	[0.225]	[0.017]	[0.164]
Quebec x Other	...	...	...	...
Outside Quebec x French	0.410**	-0.142	0.087	-0.088
	[0.172]	[0.167]	[0.079]	[0.139]
Outside Quebec x Bilingual	0.017	0.006	-0.034	-0.245***
	[0.080]	[0.210]	[0.064]	[0.056]
Outside Quebec x Other	...	...	...	...
Urban	0.122***	0.065	-0.027	0.086
	[0.025]	[0.122]	[0.056]	[0.076]
Immigrant	-0.104***	0.166	0.002	0.002
	[0.020]	[0.298]	[0.092]	[0.138]
Pseudo R²	0.116		0.116	
Observations	1,187		1,238	

TABLE 5
Multinomial Logit on Three Choices of Bouncing Back (2 of 3)

	YITS-B			
	Women		Men	
	Bounce PS	*HS Graduate*	*Bounce PS*	*HS Graduate*
Parental education (high school)				
Unknown	-0.020	-0.001	-0.102***	-0.082
	[0.060]	[0.177]	[0.019]	[0.122]
Less than high school	-0.048	0.079	-0.067**	-0.061
	[0.034]	[0.121]	[0.033]	[0.097]
Some or completed college	-0.035	0.236**	-0.006	0.072
	[0.044]	[0.114]	[0.039]	[0.075]
Some or completed university	0.030	0.184	-0.055*	0.161*
	[0.074]	[0.117]	[0.033]	[0.097]
Some or completed PSE	...	...	...	...
Don't live 2 parents	0.010	0.042	-0.002	0.003
	[0.037]	[0.093]	[0.032]	[0.078]
Region (Ontario)				
Atlantic	-0.110***	0.006	0.029	-0.035
	[0.030]	[0.169]	[0.050]	[0.099]
Quebec	-0.093***	-0.060	-0.014	-0.023
	[0.034]	[0.128]	[0.030]	[0.091]
Prairies	-0.027	-0.110	0.046	-0.007
	[0.056]	[0.101]	[0.048]	[0.092]
British Columbia	-0.056	0.042	-0.020	-0.146
	[0.055]	[0.126]	[0.036]	[0.103]
Language interactions				
Quebec x English	-0.096***	0.357***	-0.098***	-0.088
	[0.016]	[0.110]	[0.013]	[0.124]
Quebec x Bilingual	...	...	...	...
Quebec x Other	-0.096***	-0.082	-0.097***	-0.039
	[0.016]	[0.206]	[0.013]	[0.233]
Outside Quebec x French	-0.034	-0.212	-0.075***	-0.152
	[0.066]	[0.192]	[0.028]	[0.148]
Outside Quebec x Bilingual	...	...	...	...
Outside Quebec x Other	-0.073***	-0.136	0.010	0.137
	[0.023]	[0.160]	[0.067]	[0.144]
Urban	0.029	0.074	0.042	0.092
	[0.030]	[0.092]	[0.030]	[0.074]
Immigrant	-0.004	0.262**	-0.086***	0.108
	[0.060]	[0.125]	[0.017]	[0.217]
Pseudo R^2	0.082		0.067	
Observations	757		1035	

TABLE 5
Multinomial Logit on Three Choices of Bouncing Back (3 of 3)

	YITS-A			
	Women		Men	
	Bounce PS	HS Graduate	Bounce PS	HS Graduate
Parental education (high school)				
Unknown	-0.072***	-0.260	-0.023***	-0.074
	[0.009]	[0.266]	[0.004]	[0.193]
Less than high school	-0.050**	-0.069	-0.015*	-0.122
	[0.024]	[0.178]	[0.009]	[0.193]
Some or completed college	...	...	...	...
Some or completed university	...	...	...	...
Some or completed PSE	0.018	0.083	0.025	0.096
	[0.044]	[0.123]	[0.022]	[0.172]
Don't live 2 parents	0.009	-0.025	-0.020	0.077
	[0.036]	[0.119]	[0.014]	[0.202]
Region (Ontario)				
Atlantic	-0.036	0.264*	-0.020*	0.066
	[0.035]	[0.138]	[0.012]	[0.158]
Quebec	-0.086***	0.220	-0.064***	0.124
	[0.013]	[0.251]	[0.008]	[0.278]
Prairies	-0.023	0.229**	0.004	0.000
	[0.035]	[0.117]	[0.023]	[0.138]
British Columbia	0.047	0.129	0.065	0.049
	[0.071]	[0.148]	[0.069]	[0.183]
Language interactions				
Quebec x English	-0.078***	-0.064	0.729***	-0.350***
	[0.013]	[0.293]	[0.011]	[0.058]
Quebec x Bilingual	#	#	-0.030***	0.040
	[0.007]	[0.340]		
Quebec x Other	...	...	...	...
Outside Quebec x French	-0.076***	0.007	-0.016	-0.227
	[0.016]	[0.248]	[0.017]	[0.187]
Outside Quebec x Bilingual	-0.079***	0.412***	-0.030***	0.550***
	[0.013]	[0.080]	[0.007]	[0.075]
Outside Quebec x Other	...	...	...	...
Urban	-0.047	0.051	0.003	0.030
	[0.033]	[0.112]	[0.014]	[0.113]
Immigrant	0.028	0.040	-0.030***	0.127
	[0.091]	[0.229]	[0.007]	[0.144]
Pseudo R²	0.084		0.089	
Observations	539		765	

Notes: Also included in the regressions for SLS and YITS-B are two age indicator variables.
Omitted categories are in parentheses. Results are marginal effects evaluated at the sample mean.
Standard errors, adjusted for clustering in the YITS-A, are in brackets. *** p<0.01, ** p<0.05, * p<0.1
implies insufficient variation in the data to produce an estimate.

Source: Authors' compilation.

Overall, it seems that bouncing back is a more idiosyncratic process than dropping out. Given the "selection" involved with dropping out and thus being included in these regressions, this is perhaps not a surprising result and compares to persistence rates in PSE often having very different determinants than those that affect entry into PSE (Finnie and Qiu 2009).

Continuing on to PSE after Bouncing Back to High School

In Table 6 we explore continuing on to PSE among those who have bounced back to high school graduation (above). Perhaps surprisingly, the PSE attendance rate for this group is quite high at 55 to 58 percent for men and women, respectively, compared to national averages of 55.9 percent for men and 69.2 percent for women (Finnie and Mueller 2009, Table 1).

The YITS-A and the YITS-B show that higher parental educational attainment is at least in some cases associated with increased PSE participation, especially for men, although in the SLS there is no clearly defined gradient. Family structure seems important for men in the YITS-A but not elsewhere. In terms of region, other jurisdictions generally have lower rates of going on to PSE after bouncing back to high school than Ontario. For the majority language groups, and like the bouncing back regressions, the minority language effects are mostly negative. The urban and immigrant marginal effects are for the most part not different from zero. These estimates are even more handicapped by small sample sizes, as also represented in some of the effects simply not being estimable using the non-linear maximum likelihood methods that underlie the logit approach.

Exploring Parental Income and Education in the YITS-A

Since the YITS-A has both student and parent reported measures of parental education, as well as family income (parent reported), the analysis can be extended for this dataset beyond that possible for the other two. Results that parallel Tables 4 through 6 are presented in Table 7. Parent reported education is compressed into the categories reported by the students for comparison purposes.

We expect to find two effects, likely countervailing, at play for the parental education effects compared to those found earlier that used student-reported parental education and did not include the family income variable. First, parent reported education is likely to have less measurement error, in which case the related dropout profile should be steeper, since measurement error tends to bias estimated effects toward being flatter. Secondly, based on previous research, it is expected that adding family income to the regression will tend to reduce the effects of parental education, with which it is positively correlated – even though by the same reasoning the education effect is expected to dominate. The net effect is uncertain.

TABLE 6
Logit on Bouncing Back to PSE for Those Who Bounced Back to High School

	SLS		YITS-B		YITS-A	
	Women	Men	Women	Men	Women	Men
Parental education (high school)						
Unknown	-0.013	0.074	-0.393*	0.218	#	-0.183***
	[0.168]	[0.158]	[0.235]	[0.211]	[0.044]	
Less than high school	0.097	0.118	-0.310***	0.143	0.056	0.011
	[0.149]	[0.133]	[0.097]	[0.110]	[0.112]	[0.110]
Some or completed college	0.184	0.100	0.007	0.203**	...	...
	[0.154]	[0.218]	[0.086]	[0.081]		
Some or completed university	-0.079	0.239	0.057	0.441***	...	...
	[0.212]	[0.178]	[0.088]	[0.087]		
Some or completed PSE	...	...	...	...	0.046	0.237***
					[0.080]	[0.078]
Don't live 2 parents	-0.053	-0.088	0.013	0.035	-0.010	-0.221***
	[0.126]	[0.116]	[0.067]	[0.075]	[0.077]	[0.065]
Region (Ontario)						
Atlantic	-0.151	-0.126	-0.055	0.003	-0.254**	-0.078
	[0.130]	[0.134]	[0.088]	[0.105]	[0.118]	[0.079]
Quebec	0.110	-0.335**	-0.129	-0.034	-0.324***	-0.096
	[0.110]	[0.156]	[0.095]	[0.095]	[0.095]	[0.079]
Prairies	-0.293**	-0.058	-0.121	-0.150*	-0.331***	-0.058
	[0.126]	[0.134]	[0.092]	[0.077]	[0.098]	[0.098]
British Columbia	0.000	-0.311*	0.096	-0.162	-0.320**	-0.180*
	[0.163]	[0.183]	[0.078]	[0.112]	[0.144]	[0.105]
Language interactions						
Quebec x English	-0.431**	#	-0.544***	0.245	0.236	0.116
	[0.209]	[0.136]	[0.262]	[0.259]	[0.184]	
Quebec x Other	...	...	0.207	0.013	...	...
			[0.165]	[0.324]		
Outside Quebec x French	-0.248	0.462***	0.073	-0.064	-0.305***	0.058
	[0.259]	[0.085]	[0.162]	[0.186]	[0.082]	[0.130]
Outside Quebec x Bilingual	-0.572***	-0.169	...	...	#	#
	[0.045]	[0.255]				
Outside Quebec x Other	...	...	-0.159	0.217	...	...
			[0.175]	[0.141]		
Urban	0.202*	0.042	0.020	0.075	0.130	-0.015
	[0.113]	[0.129]	[0.070]	[0.070]	[0.092]	[0.067]
Immigrant	0.126	0.013	-0.005	-0.191	0.143	0.259**
	[0.177]	[0.334]	[0.156]	[0.137]	[0.345]	[0.130]
Pseudo R²	0.186	0.099	0.135	0.120	0.108	0.103
Observations	375	284	369	381	268	296

Notes: Also included in the regressions for SLS and YITS-B are two age indicator variables.
Omitted categories are in parentheses. Results are marginal effects evaluated at the sample mean.
Standard errors, adjusted for clustering in the YITS-A, are in brackets. *** p<0.01, ** p<0.05, * p<0.1
implies insufficient variation in the data to produce an estimate.

Source: Authors' compilation.

TABLE 7
Parental Education and Income Reported by the Parent, YITS-A

| | Dropout | | Bouncing Back | | | | Bounce then PSE | |
| | Women | Men | Women | | Men | | Women | Men |
			Bounce PS	HS Graduate	Bounce PS	HS Graduate		
Parental education (high school)								
Unknown	0.088	0.085	0.000	0.203	-0.014	-0.056	0.318**	#
	[0.066]	[0.086]	[0.024]	[0.255]	[0.023]	[0.387]	[0.156]	
Less than high school	0.040	0.153***	0.043	-0.045	-0.022**	-0.062	0.015	-0.035
	[0.025]	[0.036]	[0.043]	[0.195]	[0.010]	[0.215]	[0.132]	[0.090]
Some or completed PSE	-0.033***	-0.058***	0.083**	0.052	0.024	0.088	-0.049	0.202**
	[0.011]	[0.015]	[0.036]	[0.172]	[0.024]	[0.164]	[0.081]	[0.083]
Parental income ($25,000 to $49,999)								
$0-4,999	0.056	-0.032	0.680***	-0.322***	0.315	0.216	#	#
	[0.124]	[0.079]	[0.145]	[0.032]	[0.233]	[0.187]		
$5,000 to $24,999	0.040*	-0.004	0.054	-0.146	0.011	0.004	0.197*	0.176
	[0.022]	[0.027]	[0.057]	[0.131]	[0.053]	[0.251]	[0.104]	[0.150]
$50,000 to $74,999	-0.021*	-0.011	-0.037	-0.091	-0.037**	0.004	0.113	0.216**
	[0.012]	[0.014]	[0.037]	[0.161]	[0.019]	[0.156]	[0.102]	[0.102]
$75,000 to $99,999	-0.021*	-0.044***	-0.051	0.023	-0.044***	0.211	0.214*	0.064
	[0.012]	[0.016]	[0.034]	[0.210]	[0.014]	[0.210]	[0.113]	[0.098]
$100,000 to $300,000	-0.059***	-0.058***	-0.020	-0.017	-0.013	0.231	0.230*	0.363***
	[0.010]	[0.016]	[0.057]	[0.237]	[0.034]	[0.201]	[0.139]	[0.126]

Notes: All the same regressors as in Table 4, 5, and 6 are included.
Omitted categories are in parentheses. Results are =marginal effects evaluated at the sample mean.
Standard errors, adjusted for clustering in the YITS-A, are in brackets. *** p<0.01, ** p<0.05, * p<0.1.
implies insufficient variation in the data to produce an estimate.

Source: Authors' compilation.

In the first set of columns the dependent variable is dropping out, and these columns compare to the last set in Table 4. Overall, the parental education effects differ only marginally for women and men, perhaps being slightly flatter for the former but almost exactly the same for the latter.[8]

Parental income is also related to dropping out, with young women from the higher income families being 9 to 10 percentage points less likely to drop out than those from the lowest income families, the difference being around half that for men. For men, but not for women, low income does not appear to be a detriment as much as high income is an advantage. For women, the effect is comparable to that for parental education, but for men education has the larger substantive relationship. As mentioned earlier, this gender pattern mirrors what others have found looking at access to PSE, regardless of the underlying high school dynamics. Of course, these are (conditional) correlations and do not speak directly to causality.

In terms of bouncing back, the four middle columns of Table 7 are comparable to the third part of Table 5. For women, the overall slope of the education profile does not change much, but what matters now is the advantage of youth from highly educated families in bouncing back to PSE as opposed to the disadvantage of those from families with less education in their background. Overall, as was the case in Table 5, parental education is not as strong a predictor of bouncing back as it was of dropping out. Similarly, except for women with extremely low family income backgrounds, parental income does not appear to influence bouncing back. For men, those from middle income categories appear less likely to bounce back directly to post-secondary education, but other than that none of the coefficients are statistically significant, the standard errors being quite large.

Finally, looking at PSE attendance among those who have bounced back to high school completion, although parental education appears to have a strong effect for men, it does not appear to have as strong an effect for women. Men from more highly educated family backgrounds are about 20 percentage points more likely to go on to PSE than those from families where the highest level of education is a high school diploma. In terms of family incomes, there are some significant differences, but the patterns are mixed, with lower income students in some cases having higher PSE rates than those from middle income families. It is not clear why this should be so, although one possibility is that student aid and other programs facilitate PSE attendance for those from lower income backgrounds; those from higher income backgrounds have the family resources to support them, but those from the middle (lower middle in particular) may be squeezed out. It would be interesting to see how these results compare to those from more recent years, after changes in the student financial aid system were made out of concerns along these lines.

Conclusion

A substantial number of students drop out of high school before completing their diplomas. This fact has significant repercussions for both the individuals who do so and for the broader society to which they belong, since a high school diploma is typically the bare minimum education level required for getting anything but the lowest paying jobs. This is especially so in the new knowledge economy, where schooling credentials are of great importance. The dropout rates reported here, however, representing the experiences of specific cohorts of particular individuals tracked over time, are considerably lower than some of the inflated estimates sometimes reported that are based on double counting, mixing dropouts with those who move from one jurisdiction to another, and other empirical problems.

Furthermore, from the early 1990s into the middle part of the first decade of the new millennium, there was a substantial decline in high school dropout rates for both men and women, although the former continue to have much higher rates than the latter. By the most recent period, high school dropout rates as we calculate them were 9.4 percent for women, and 14.6 percent for men.

But dropping out of high school can be far from a permanent transition, and by their early to mid-twenties, about 50 percent of those who dropped out of high school have bounced back into the education system, either completing their high school programs or, less commonly, going straight on to PSE. These numbers again favour women over men but, in contrast to dropout rates, have changed relatively little over time.

Clearly, a wide lens and dynamic framework are needed to understand the basic educational pathways of youth as they relate to high school completion and going on to PSE – perhaps especially when these dynamics include dropping out of high school at some point.

In terms of dropping out, family background – including parents' education, family income, and family structure – all matter enormously. For example, even after controlling for a range of related factors, there is a gap of about 20 percentage points in dropout rates between young men in households where the highest level of education is less than high school completed and those where the highest level is some or completed PSE – a huge difference, given the overall rates just cited. The range across the family income distribution is 5 to 10 percentage points, and not living with both parents is associated with another 7 to 12 percent gap. Immigrant women drop out less than the native-born, but this pattern does not hold for men. Other factors that matter, although more unevenly, include region and language (minority language groups actually tend to drop out less than others), while urban-rural differences are small once these other factors are taken into account.

Among those who drop out, bouncing back appears to exhibit far fewer clear patterns with respect to these background variables than does dropping out. Parental education remains a clear factor, but other influences tend to be weaker and/or less consistent than in the case of dropping out itself. Pursuing PSE after bouncing back to high school graduation is not quite as idiosyncratic as only bouncing back, and the influences are broadly similar – although naturally in the opposite direction – to those related to dropping out.

Establishing a firmer empirical foundation for dropping out of high school – and bouncing back in one way or another – should be helpful to discussions related to these dynamics, as well as to any related policy considerations. But they also point to the need for further research. What are the actual factors – the causal relationships – that underlie the patterns we identify? These are directions for future study.

Notes

Arthur Sweetman thanks SSHRC for financial support. The authors are grateful to Marc Frenette and Richard Mueller for their comments on an earlier draft of this paper.

1. See Finnie, Laporte, and Sweetman (2008) for further discussion of the data.
2. YITS-A and YITS-B interviews were conducted in March of the years indicated, but the information about dropping out and bouncing back pertains to the preceding year ending 31 December, which is the reference point for the YITS surveys.
3. As shown by Schaafsma and Sweetman (2001), for those who immigrate in their teens, the post-secondary transition process, including lower high school graduation rates, is very different from that of those who arrive at an earlier age.
4. Although we have information on parental education of "less than Grade 9" and "did not complete high school," separating these variables did not contribute to the analysis. In the case of the SLS, "mother" means birth mother or stepmother. In the case of the YITS, "mother" means birth mother, stepmother, adoptive mother, or foster mother. Congruent categories apply for fathers.
5. Though parental education is specified categorically, we also constructed a linear "years of education" variable using midpoints of the ranges, since we expect a single parameter (the linear variable) to be more precisely estimated than a set of parameters (the categorical variables). As the standard errors were only a bit smaller in the former, we continue to use the series of dummy variables, since it allows for non-linearities in the relationship to be observed.
6. The SLS variables are quite simple, presenting only a few possible family types from which the above categories were created. The YITS, on the other hand, has upwards of 30 different categories, and while many of these are clear and well defined, others include uncommon situations that are difficult to compare.

7. For both the SLS and the YITS-B, those students who were unable or unwilling to report their parents' education, or who did not live in a circumstance that allowed it to be reported, have a much higher probability of dropping out. This is not the case for the YITS-A, possibly due to its sampling design and the younger age at which the questions are posed.
8. See Appendix 2 of Finnie, Laporte, and Sweetman (2009) for a more detailed exploration of measurement error related to these two different measures of parental education.

References

Andres, L., and H. Krahn. 1999. "Youth Pathways in Articulated Post-Secondary Systems: Enrolment and Completion Patterns of Urban Young Women and Men." *Canadian Journal of Higher Education* 29 (1): 47-82.

Bowlby, G. 2005. "Provincial Drop-Out Rates: Trends and Consequences." *Education Matters: Insights on Education, Learning and Training in Canada.* Catalogue 81-004-XIE, vol. 2, no. 4. Ottawa: Statistics Canada.

Dagenais, M., C. Montmarquette, and N. Viennot-Briot. 2007. "Dropout, School Performance, and Working While in School." *Review of Economics and Statistics* 89 (4): 752-60.

Ferrer, A.M., and W.C. Riddell. 2002. "The Role of Credentials in the Canadian Labour Market." *Canadian Journal of Economics* 35 (4): 879-905.

Finnie, R., C. Laporte, and A. Sweetman. 2009. "Bouncing Back: Dropping out of High School and Dropping in Again." MESA working paper. At http://www.mesa-project.org/.

Finnie, R., E. Lascelles, and A. Sweetman. 2005. "Who Goes? The Direct and Indirect Effects of Family Background on Access to Post-Secondary Education." In *Higher Education in Canada*, ed. C. Beach, R. Boadway, and M. McInnis, 295-338. Montreal and Kingston: McGill University Press.

Finnie, R., and R.E. Mueller. 2008. "The Backgrounds of Canadian Youth and Access to Post-Secondary Education: New Evidence from the Youth in Transition Survey." In *Who Goes? Who Stays? What Matters? Accessing and Persisting in Post-Secondary Education in Canada*, ed. R. Finnie, R.E. Mueller, A. Sweetman, and A. Usher, 79-108. Montreal and Kingston: Queen's Policy Studies Series, McGill University Press.

Finnie, R., and T.(H.) Qiu. 2008. "Is the Glass (or Classroom) Half-Empty or Nearly Full? New Evidence on Persistence in Post-Secondary Education in Canada." In *Who Goes? Who Stays? What Matters? Accessing and Persisting in Post-Secondary Education in Canada*, ed. R. Finnie, R.E. Mueller, A. Sweetman, and A. Usher, 179-208. Montreal and Kingston: Queen's Policy Studies Series, McGill University Press.

Finnie, R., A. Sweetman, and A. Usher. 2008. "Introduction: A Framework for Thinking about Participation in Post-Secondary Education." In *Who Goes? Who Stays? What Matters? Accessing and Persisting in Post-Secondary Education in Canada*, ed. R. Finnie, R.E. Mueller, A. Sweetman, and A. Usher, 3-32. Montreal and Kingston: Queen's Policy Studies Series, McGill University Press.

Ménard, L.J. 2009. "Savoir pour pouvoir: Entreprendre un chantier national pour la persévérance scolaire." Rapport du Groupe d'action sur la persévérance et

la réussite scolaires au Québec. At http://catalogue.cdeacf.ca/Record.htm?id
list=6&record=19228594124910467769 (accessed 1 September 2009).

Motte, A., H.T. Qiu, Y. Zhang, and P. Bussière. 2008. "The Youth in Transition
Survey: Following Canadian Youth through Time." In *Who Goes? Who Stays?
What Matters? Accessing and Persisting in Post-Secondary Education in Canada*,
ed. R. Finnie, R.E. Mueller, A. Sweetman, and A. Usher, 63-78. Montreal and
Kingston: Queen's Policy Studies Series, McGill University Press.

O'Sullivan, J., P. Canning, L. Siegel, and M.E. Oliveri. 2009. "Key Factors to
Support Literacy Success in School-Aged Populations: A Literature Review."
Report for the Canadian Education Statistics Council, the Council of Ministers
of Education, Canada, and Statistics Canada.

Raymond, M. 2008. "High School Dropouts Returning to School." Catalogue no.
81-595-M – No. 055. Ottawa: Statistics Canada.

Richards, J. 2009. "Dropouts: The Achilles' Heel of Canada's High-School System."
C.D. Howe Institute, Commentary No. 298 (October).

Schaafsma, J., and A. Sweetman. 2001. "Immigrant Earnings: Age at Immigration
Matters." *Canadian Journal of Economics* 34 (4): 1066-99.

Shaienks D., J. Eisl-Culkin, and P. Bussière. 2006. "Follow-Up on Education and
Labour Market Pathways of Young Canadians Aged 18 to 20: Results from
YITS Cycle 3." Catalogue no. 81-595-MIE – No. 045. Ottawa: Statistics Canada.

Statistics Canada. 1993. "Leaving School: Results from a National Survey Comparing School Leavers and High School Graduates 18 to 20 Years of Age."
Catalogue no. MP43-303. Ottawa: Statistics Canada.

Part II

Economic Incentives
and the Decision
to Pursue More
Schooling

general business cycle effects, when there tends to be a high degree of correlation between labour market conditions across Canada, making it more difficult to examine relative effects on post-secondary enrolments. In some ways we could consider this to be akin to a natural experiment approach, since oil prices are large, discontinuous, and clearly exogenous to the Canadian economy.

A first step is to identify a measure of the oil intensity of each province's economy. We use the share of oil and gas extraction in gross provincial product in the 1990s. This period was chosen because we want to ensure we do not use a measure of oil intensity of production that is sensitive to oil prices, and the 1990s were a period of relative stability in oil prices. Figure 1 shows the estimates of the oil intensity of provincial economic activity used in this paper. They range from 0.007 percent in New Brunswick to 20.5 percent in Alberta. While the share of oil and gas extraction has remained fairly constant in most provincial economies, this is not true of Newfoundland, where recent offshore oil field development has led to a dramatic increase in the share of gross provincial product accounted for by the energy sector. In the 1980s and 1990s, only around 5 percent of

FIGURE 1
Percentage of Provincial Economic Activity Accounted for by Oil and Gas Extraction (Average, 1984-1994)

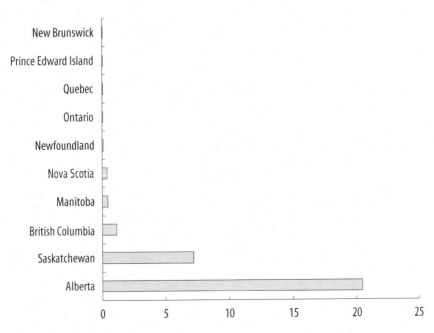

Source: CANSIM Table 3790025.

Newfoundland's economic activity was in the energy sector, and much of that was coal based. By 2002, more than 20 percent of economic activity in the province was energy based, with the vast bulk of the increase coming from the oil and gas sector. This is somewhat problematic for the estimation here. Given that Newfoundland's oil and gas sector has developed relatively recently, we use the same measure of oil and gas intensity as for the other provinces, but this measure would need to be changed for future studies on the same topic.

Clearly, given the figures above, the province most likely to see a labour market boom following an oil price shock is Alberta, with a somewhat smaller effect in Saskatchewan. The empirical techniques used in this paper can thus be said roughly to identify the extent to which enrolments in Alberta (relative to provinces that have no oil) fall as oil prices increase. Note that we do not interpret this as a direct causal relationship – that is, the argument is not that if oil prices increase, this would lead students in Alberta to change their post-secondary enrolment decisions if everything else stayed the same. Rather, the interpretation is that changes in the economy of Alberta (relative to other provinces) induced by oil price increases would have an effect on post-secondary enrolments. Oil prices act as a proxy for other changes in the economy for which we do not have good measures.

Figure 2 shows the relationship between the gap in enrolment rates in Alberta and the rest of Canada, along with the oil price in Canadian 2002 dollar terms (solid line). Enrolments shown in this figure are (1) the percentage of 17-24 year olds enrolled in any educational program (high school, college/CEGEP, university, or private colleges, and includes both full time and part time students); and (2) the percentage of 17-24 year olds enrolled in university full time. The gap is simply the enrolment rate in Alberta minus the enrolment rate in the rest of Canada. As can be seen, in general Alberta has a relatively low raw enrolment rate – both in any education and in university in particular – compared with the rest of Canada. Alberta's relative enrolment rates have also declined over time. Before 2004, the gap between Alberta's full time enrolment rate and that in the rest of Canada was never more than about 5 percentage points. In 2008, Alberta's full time university enrolment rate was 12.2 percent, compared with the rest of Canada at 20.6 percent, a gap of 8.5 percentage points.

More importantly, however, the figure shows a clear negative relationship between the gap in enrolment rates and real oil prices. In both of the two periods of oil price hikes – in the late 1970s and the years since 2005 – enrolments in university and any educational institution declined in Alberta relative to the rest of Canada. Overall enrolments declined by considerably more (in relative terms) than did university enrolments during the first oil price shock, while during the second it appears that the two have declined at more similar rates.

FIGURE 2
Gaps between Enrolment Rates of 17-24 Year Olds in Alberta Relative to the Rest of Canada (% Pts) and Real Oil Prices (2002 C$)

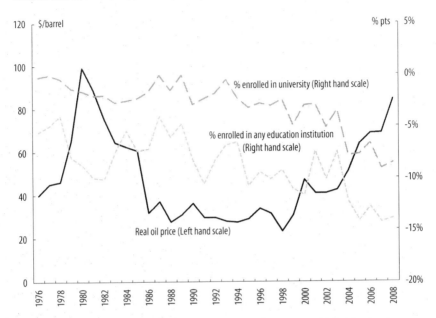

Note: The enrolment rate figures are the enrolment rate of 17-24 year olds in Alberta minus the enrolment rate of 17-24 year olds in the rest of Canada. The figure -0.1 would indicate an enrolment rate in Alberta that is 10 percentage points below the enrolment rate in the rest of Canada.

Source: St Louis Federal Reserve and Statistics Canada, Labour Force Survey.

It is worthwhile seeing whether the results hold up when we consider other factors that might have been changing at the same time and affecting enrolments, and also trying to get a feel for the magnitude of the enrolment effects following an oil price increase. In order to do so, we employ public use microdata files of the Labour Force Survey (LFS) to estimate a probit model of individual enrolment decisions.

Specifically, we use data on individuals aged 17 to 24 surveyed in the October LFS from 1976 to 2008 to estimate the probability that a given individual of that age is enrolled in an educational program. Because we want to focus on post-secondary education, we specifically examine college/CEGEP and university enrolments, but we also examine enrolments in any program (including high school and private colleges, and including both full time and part time enrolments). The dependent variable is a dummy variable equal to 1 if the individual is enrolled in any educational program (for the first set of columns), and 0 otherwise. For the second set of columns, the dependent variable is a dummy variable equal to 1 for those enrolled full time in a college program and 0 otherwise. For the third set of columns, the dependent variable is a dummy variable equal to 1 if the individual is enrolled full time in a university program, and 0 otherwise.

For the most part we concentrate on full time enrolments. Part time university-level study in Alberta appears to have increased compared with that in other provinces in the past decade, and although much of this increase occurred during a period of relatively low oil prices, it is possible that a strong labour market might encourage students to study part time rather than full time. Unfortunately, relatively few individuals in the LFS identify themselves as part time students, and so it is difficult to get reliable estimates for part time enrolments. We did, however, estimate models separately for part time enrolments, and found no effect of oil prices in those models. Models including both part and full time enrolments together yield very similar results to the estimates from models of full time enrolments only.[3]

In our analysis we include as determinants of post-secondary enrolments two key economic variables: the provincial minimum wage, and sex-specific provincial unemployment rates of 25-34 year old high school graduates.[4] We do not include tuition fees for colleges or universities here. Data on college tuition fees are not reliably available over this period. Real average university tuition fees are available from 1979, but as previous studies have found, including provincial average tuition fees has little effect on other results in these types of analyses. Including tuition fees here makes little difference to the key results, but being able to use the additional three years of data provides considerably more variation in oil prices, making the estimated effects of that variable more reliable.[5] All specifications include a full set of year and province fixed effects, so that we control for any particular oddities associated with specific provinces or specific years. For instance, Figure 2 shows that Alberta typically has lower enrolment rates than other provinces, which is dealt with by having province fixed effects. We also include province specific time trends (linear, quadratic, and cubic), to allow for the possibility that there may be some unobserved factors changing over time within provinces that are causing different trends in enrolment rates in different provinces. The key results do not, however, change very much when we introduce those time trends. We estimate the models separately for males and females and for each age group available in the public use microdata files of the LFS.

The focus of interest in this paper, though, is whether oil price increases affect enrolments in the relatively oil rich provinces. To examine this question, we create an interaction variable – the oil price multiplied by the oil intensity of gross provincial product. The estimated marginal effect of this variable then shows how much an increase in oil prices affects enrolments in provinces where much of economic activity is based on the oil sector relative to provinces that have relatively little oil production. These oil intensity estimates are those shown in Figure 1, and the oil price data are those shown in Figure 2. During the period under study, oil prices peaked twice – in 1980 and 2008 – with a long period of relatively low and fairly stable prices in the interregnum. From their low point in 1999 to the oil price peak in 2008, prices rose from an annual average of just under C$31 per barrel to C$91 per barrel.[6]

To give a simple summary of what has just been described, we estimate the following equation using a probit model:

$$E_{ipt} = \alpha + \beta OilInter_{pt} + X_{pt}\gamma + Y_t\rho + P_p\lambda + e_{ipt} \tag{1}$$

where E_{ipt} is a dummy variable equal to one if individual i whose usual place of residence is province p, in year t; $OilInter_{pt}$ is the product of the oil intensity of production in province p and oil prices in year t; X_{pt} includes the real (C$1992) minimum wage, and the sex-specific unemployment rate for 25-34 year olds in province p at time t; P_p is a full set of province dummies; and Y_t is a full set of year dummies. As noted earlier, some specifications also include province-specific time trends.[7]

Regression Results

The key estimated marginal effects from the probit models are shown graphically in Figures 3 and 4. Full estimates are in the Appendix tables. The estimated effects of the unemployment rate and the minimum wage are fairly small, and mostly not statistically significant for women. An increase in the male unemployment rate of 10 percentage points is estimated to increase the overall male enrolment rate by 4 percentage points, college enrolments by 1.2 percentage points, and university enrolment rates by about 1 percentage point. For 17-24 year old men, a $1 increase in the minimum wage is estimated to increase overall enrolments by 1 percentage point but to reduce college enrolments by 0.5 percentage points. University enrolments are less affected. Chan, Morisette, and Frenette (2009) also find that college enrolments are more affected by changes in the minimum wage than are university enrolments, and that women may in general be less sensitive to minimum wage changes than men, a pattern that is consistent with the results here. Landon (1997) finds that higher minimum wages reduce enrolments in Canada, and Neumark and Wascher (1995a, 1995b, 1995c, 2003) find similar effects in the United States.[8]

The estimates of the relationship between oil prices and enrolments in oil intensive provinces have been scaled to show the effect of a C$50 per barrel increase in the real oil price on enrolments in Alberta relative to provinces with no oil sector (that is, in effect, all provinces other than Saskatchewan and British Columbia). Oil prices from the most recent trough to the most recent boom in 2008 increased by around C$60 per barrel and are on track to be around C$40-$50 lower per barrel in 2009 than in 2008; this scaling means that we can interpret the effects of a move from an oil price peak to an oil price trough on enrolments.

Figure 3(a), then, shows that an increase in oil prices of $50 per barrel would decrease the overall rate of enrolment of 17-24 year old male Albertans by around 5 percentage points relative to the non-oil provinces. The full time university enrolment rate would decline by a little over 3 percentage points. These are large effects – in the LFS, the overall enrolment rate of all 17-24 year olds in Alberta averaged 43 percent between 2000 and 2005, while the university enrolment rate was 14.6 percent. Supposing that oil prices did not affect enrolments in provinces other than Alberta,[9] a $50 per barrel increase in oil prices would reduce the enrolment rate to around 52 percent – close to a 10 percent decline in enrolments – while university enrolments would fall to around 11.6 percent – close to 20 percent. The estimated effects are consistently smaller for women. Overall female enrolments, are estimated to decline between 2 and 4 percentage point, with university enrolments falling about 2.5 percentage points. College enrolments, interestingly, are estimated to increase slightly for women, by about 1 percentage point.

FIGURE 3
Marginal Effects of Oil Prices on Enrolments: 17-24 Year Olds

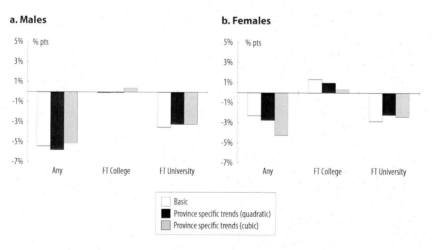

Notes: Bars show the estimated effects of a $50 per barrel oil price increase on enrolment rates in Alberta relative to provinces with no oil sector. Thus, an oil price increase of $50 per barrel is estimated to reduce the enrolment rate of 17-24 year old Albertan males in any educational program by about 5 percentage points relative to enrolment rates of 17-24 year old males in the rest of Canada. Not all estimated effects are statistically significant – see Tables A1 and A2 for details.

Source: Authors' estimates, as shown in Tables A1 and A2.

Figure 4 breaks the results down by age group. The patterns shown in Figure 3 are quite consistent across age groups for males. For women, though, by far the biggest and the only statistically significant effects appear to be on the group closest to the age when they are first able to enter post-secondary education when the oil price increases hit (17-19 year olds). Other studies have found somewhat larger effects of economic conditions and tuition fees on post-secondary enrolment among those individuals closer to the usual age of first entry (e.g., Card and Lemieux 2001). Further, there is some evidence that women are less likely than men to drop in and out of post-secondary programs (Martinello 2008). Perhaps this differential gender profile arises because of a lock-in effect for women who choose early whether or not to enrol and then remain enrolled regardless of changes in outside opportunities, while men are more willing to drop out of and back into education as economic conditions change. Some

FIGURE 4
Marginal Effects of Oil Prices on Enrolments: By Age Group and Sex

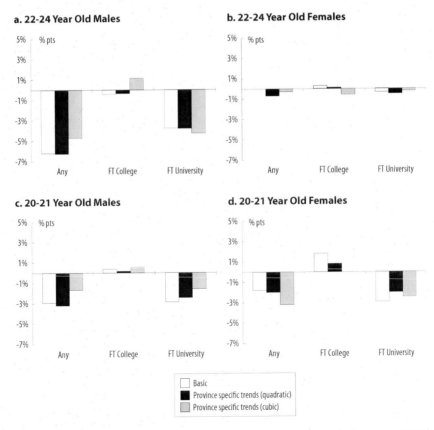

... *continued*

FIGURE 4
(Continued)

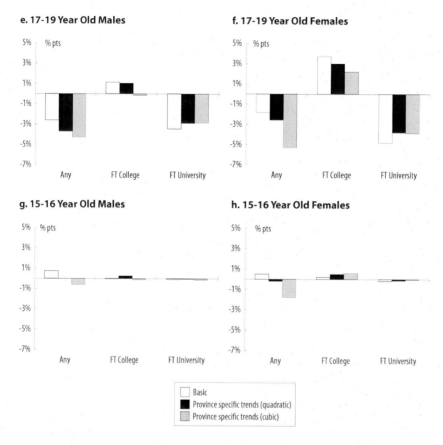

Notes: Bars show the estimated effects of a $50 per barrel oil price increase on enrolment rates in Alberta relative to provinces with no oil sector. Not all estimated effects are statistically significant – see Table A3 for details.
Source: Authors' calculations.

further supporting evidence for this possibility is that female enrolments in both college and university appear to be less sensitive to changes in the unemployment rate than are male enrolments (Tables A1 and A2).

As an exercise to check that the results here are not being driven by confounding factors, we also consider whether there is any estimated effect on enrolments of 15-16 year olds. For the most part, and during most of the period under study, youth of this age have been expected to remain in school, with some exceptions.[10] The estimated effects on this group are very close in magnitude to zero, and are statistically indistinguishable from zero. Oil prices do not appear to have changed their school enrolments to any important degree.

A point to note in interpreting the results is that, since we control for unemployment rates, the estimated effects of oil prices on enrolments in oil-intensive provinces are interpreted as the effects over and above whatever effect they may have via unemployment rates. Since a higher unemployment rate makes it harder for school-leavers to find jobs and therefore reduces the incentive to leave school, economic theory predicts higher unemployment will lead to higher enrolments. Consistent with similar empirical studies, we find that higher unemployment rates are associated with higher post-secondary enrolment rates. Thus, an oil price bust in Alberta that was associated with a larger increase in unemployment rates (for high school graduates) in Alberta than in other provinces would lead to an increase in university enrolments that is larger than the effect reported here. That said, the estimated coefficients on the oil price interaction variable do increase when we do not control for the sex-specific unemployment rate, but only by about 1 percentage point for overall male enrolments, and by less than half a percentage point for male university enrolments. The estimated effects on females barely shift – which is perhaps unsurprising, given the smaller estimated effects of unemployment rates on females. This suggests that unemployment rates are not the main channel through which an oil price shock affects post-secondary enrolments. We discuss other possible causal channels later in the paper.

The finding that there is little effect on college enrolments – except perhaps an increase in college enrolments among younger women – is also interesting. It may reflect the fact that a typical college program is shorter than most university programs, and – particularly in Alberta – is often more flexible in terms of both entry and taking short breaks from study, making it easier for college students to maintain enrolments during an oil price boom. Or colleges may provide training in skills that are complementary to those required during an oil price boom – if, say, college completion significantly improves the chances of finding a high paying job in the oil sector or related service sectors. The result that some female college enrolments increase suggests some support for the complementarity of college training and oil sector jobs hypothesis, with higher oil prices leading to a switch in the oil-rich provinces in the types of programs being undertaken by women but not so much those being undertaken by men.

What Is the Likely Cause of These Results?

Clearly, oil price increases in and of themselves are not the proximate cause of a decline in post-secondary enrolments in oil-rich provinces. Further, the effects estimated here are over and above any effect due to unemployment rate changes. What else could be driving the relative decline in enrolments in Alberta relative to non-oil provinces when oil prices go up? Three potential channels were described above as potential mechanisms through which higher oil prices might affect enrolments: (a) higher wages, (b) higher family incomes, and (c) increased government funding for post-secondary education. The regressions described above do not control for any of these factors.[11] Could one of them be responsible for the negative relationship between oil prices and Albertan educational enrolments? An increase in family incomes or in government funding for post-secondary education would be expected to be associated with a rise, not a decline, in post-secondary enrolment.

Of the three identified channels, the only really likely candidate is wages. Higher oil prices do appear to have driven up wages in Alberta – and interestingly, particularly for men relative to women. Between 2000 and 2008, average wages for 15-24 year old males in Alberta rose from $11.60 an hour to $18.20 an hour, while across the whole of Canada they rose from $11.40 to $14.80. For Albertan women, wages increased from $10.00 to $15.40, while for women in Canada as a whole they rose from $10.20 to $13.30.[12] Rising wages would thus increase the incentive for young Albertans – particularly males – to work rather than to continue with their education, consistent with the economic model set out earlier.

Robustness Checks

There are two possible concerns with this analysis. First, a high degree of inward migration among youth from other provinces in search of work would itself cause Alberta's enrolment rate to fall relative to other provinces. Suppose all youth who want to study stay in their home province, and that an oil price shock has no effect on the percentage of Albertan youth who continue on to post-secondary education. But suppose also that youth who want to work migrate to areas with the best job prospects: this would mean that the number of youth in Alberta studying would not change with an increase in oil prices, but the number of youth living in Alberta and not studying (working) would increase with an increase in oil prices. So there would be a mechanical decrease in the measured enrolment rate in Alberta – the numerator of the enrolment rate would remain the same, while the denominator increased. This could potentially be sufficient to explain our finding of a negative relationship between oil prices and Albertan enrolment rates. We explore this possibility by estimating the effect of higher oil prices on net inter-provincial migration to Alberta.

A second possible objection is that the effects described here are short term only – youth might rationally decide to go to work in the oil fields during a boom, stockpile their earnings, and then enrol in school later. This would make a lot of sense if youth expected the boom to be temporary, since the opportunity cost of studying is high during a boom and low during a bust. To examine this possibility, we do two things. First, we examine whether oil price increases are followed by a short run decrease in enrolments, which are then offset by increases in enrolments after a few years. Second, we use Census data as a secondary source of information on completed education levels. For reasons explained later, these data also provide some information on the extent to which the earlier results may be driven by inter-provincial mobility.

How Much of the Enrolment Effect Could Be Due to Inter-Provincial Migration?

A key concern with these estimates is that a high degree of inward migration among youth from other provinces in search of work could itself cause Alberta's enrolment rate to drop in response to an increase in oil prices. Suppose that higher oil prices have no effect on the propensity of Albertan students to enrol in a course of study. If, however, the higher prices lead to an influx of youth from other provinces seeking employment in Alberta, then the overall population will increase. The ratio of students to total numbers of youth would then fall.

Coulombe (2006) finds that improvements in provincial labour markets are indeed associated with increases in net inward migration, particularly among 18-24 year olds. He argues that the magnitudes are not particularly important economically: "Even the migration response of the 18-24 age group to business cycle shocks is very weak since less than 7 percent of the cyclical migration is explained by the business cycle" (219). However, his analysis is not focused on the question of responses to oil price shocks. Figure 5 shows a clear relationship between oil prices and net migration to Alberta. At the peak of the late 1970s oil price boom, net flows of 17-24 year olds into Alberta accounted for 12 percent of that age population in the province, compared with negative net migration rates for the same age group during the later period of declining oil prices.

We use much the same framework of analysis described above to estimate how much an oil price shock increases migration of 17-24 year olds into Alberta during an oil price boom. Specifically, we calculate net inter-provincial migration of 17-24 year olds for each province as a percentage of the total population of 17-24 year olds. We then use a cross-section time-series approach to estimate how much net migration into an oil-intensive province increases in response to an oil price shock, controlling for minimum wages, unemployment rates, and fixed effects at the province and year level. The results are that a C$50 per barrel oil price increase would lead to an increase in net migration into Alberta as a percentage of the 17-24 year old population of around 1.5 percentage points for women and 2.1 percentage points for men.[13]

FIGURE 5
Oil Prices and Net Inward Migration to Alberta

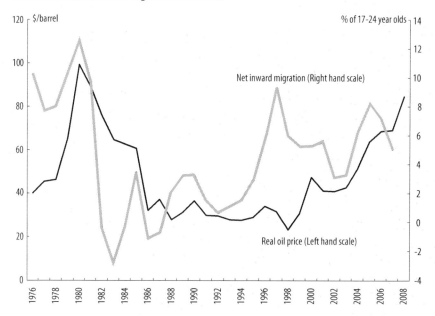

Note: Net inward migration shows the number of 17-24 year olds moving into Alberta in a given year divided by the total population of 17-24 year olds residing in Alberta.

Source: St Louis Federal Reserve and CANSIM Table 510012.

How large a change in measured enrolment rates could this inward migration explain? Suppose that all of the increase in net migration were due to individuals moving to Alberta to work rather than to study. That in itself would tend to decrease the average university enrolment rate in Alberta from around 14.6 (the average university enrolment rate for 17-24 year olds in the LFS data for Alberta for the period 2000-05) to 14.3 percent, or around 0.3 percentage points. It would reduce the overall enrolment rate (all types, full time and part time) from 42.6 percent to 41.8 percent, or around 0.8 percentage points. These figures, although not trivial in magnitude, are much smaller than the estimated effects of oil prices on enrolments of 3 percentage points and 5 percentage points, respectively. Indeed, a swing in net migration of 12 percentage points (the biggest seen in the data shown in Figure 5) would only just explain the estimated effects on overall enrolments, and could still only explain around 1 percentage point of the estimated effect on university enrolments. That would be an upper bound on the possible effects of migration on enrolments, since the figures assume that all of the swing in net migration was attributable to youth who moved to Alberta in order to work, and that none would have gone to Alberta to study.

So, even though it is clear that higher oil prices are indeed associated with an increase in migration of 17-24 year olds into Alberta, it does not appear that migration of young workers is sufficiently large to explain the greatest part of the estimated effects of higher oil prices on university enrolments.

The Lagged Effects of Oil Price Shocks on Enrolments

A second possibility is that although higher oil prices might lead to short-term reductions in enrolment rates in Alberta, this effect may be reversed as youth return to study after a few years of working in the oil fields (and perhaps accumulating savings to fund their education). Such an effect would reduce possible concerns that a resource boom would lead to longer-term losses in human capital and therefore potentially reduce long-run productivity. Even so, however, it would still be useful for government policy-making to factor in short-term fluctuations in enrolment demand.

The results on the lags are easily stated: there does not appear to be any consistent increase in enrolments among the group of 15-24 year olds even four years after an oil price boom. Figure 6 shows the lags estimated for males and females graphically, for the case of overall enrolments (at any institution and on either a full time or part time basis) of 17-24 year olds. For both men and women, the lagged values of the oil interaction variable have negative estimated coefficients. The magnitudes are smaller than the initial impact, and none of the lagged estimates is statistically significant. That is, there is no evidence in the data that although enrolments drop off in the first year of an oil price boom, they will pick up a few years later once youth have spent a couple of years working and then decide that they would like to return to study. The results suggest that if there were a permanent increase in oil prices, enrolments of Albertan students would fall very quickly relative to enrolments of Canadians in other provinces – by about 4 percentage points in the first year of the oil price rise and then by another 1-2 percentage points in the next two years – and remain permanently lower.

In the interests of brevity, we do not report results for all combinations of sex, age group, and type of enrolment studied here.[14] In all cases except one, the inclusion of lagged oil prices makes almost no difference to the estimates. Only in the case of 22-24 year old women does the estimated pattern of lags look different to that above. In that case an increase in oil prices has a small positive effect on university enrolments in the year it occurs (the opposite of the more usual case found in this paper), which is offset by similarly sized drop in university enrolments in the very next year. There also appears to be some small pickup in college enrolments among 22-24 year old women four years after an oil price increase. But these cases should probably be seen as outliers that do not affect the broad thrust of the results shown in Figure 6.

FIGURE 6
Lagged Effects of an Oil Price Rise on Attendance at Any Educational Institution

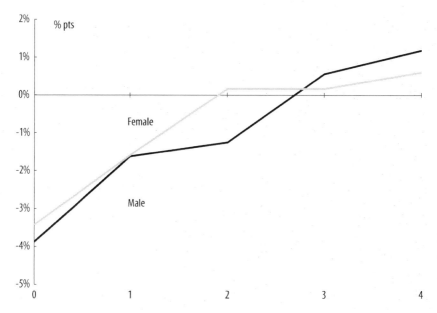

Note: The graph shows the impacts in the year oil prices go up (year zero) and then in subsequent years. The results show that in a year in which oil prices increase by $50 per barrel, male and female enrolments decrease by about 4 percentage points in Alberta relative to other provinces. In the year after the oil price increase (if oil prices stay up) both fall again by 1.5 percentage points. There is a further 1.2 percentage point decline in male enrolments in the second year after the oil price increase, followed by slight rebounds in the third and fourth years. These estimated effects of the lags are, however, not statistically significantly different from zero.

Source: Authors' calculations.

Effects on Long-Run Educational Attainment

A second way of examining the longer-term effects is to see whether these results persist through to completed education levels in the adult population. In order to examine this, we employ the public use microdata files of the 2001 Census to obtain information on the educational attainment of individuals aged 25 and over at the time of the 2001 Census by province of birth, and we match those data to the oil price when the person turned 18, interacted by their province of birth. We use the oil price at age 18 because for most youth this is around the age at which they are making a first decision on post-secondary attendance after completing (or in some provinces being about to complete) high school. Unfortunately, the Census data does not include information on the place of residence of an individual at age 18. Consequently, we use province of birth as a proxy for province of residence at age 18 with the individual's province of birth. This has the advantage that these estimates are not subject to the concerns for the enrolment rate estimates that they may be contaminated by inter-provincial mobility. The use of province of birth as a proxy for province of residence around the time of post-secondary education entrance, however, also introduces a degree of measurement error. If effectively random, this measurement error will tend to result in estimates that are biased towards zero, making any effect of oil prices on enrolments seem smaller. Consequently, we restrict the sample to individuals currently residing in their province of birth, which lessens the likelihood that individuals in the sample were not resident in their province of birth at age 18. Nonetheless, estimates from this model are likely to be conservative; if anything, they likely understate the effects of an oil price shock on completed education of those living in oil-rich provinces.

Results from regressions using these data provide corroboration of the enrolment results described earlier. These are shown in Figure 7. Specifically, individuals born in oil rich provinces and aged 18 during an oil price boom have less education on average than those who turned 18 during a

FIGURE 7
Effect of a $50 per Barrel Increase in Oil Prices on Completed Years of Schooling (Alberta Relative to Non-Oil Provinces)

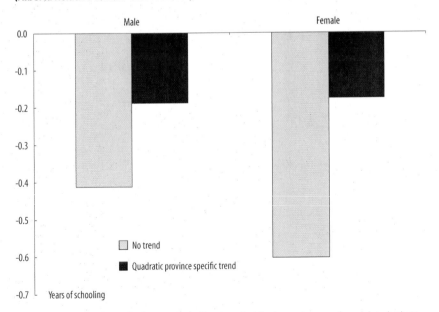

Notes: Estimated effects of a $50 per barrel increase in oil prices on years of completed education for Albertan-born individuals relative to those born in the rest of Canada. Not all estimated effects are statistically significant; see Table A4 for details.

Source: Authors' calculations.

period of low oil prices. An oil price increase of C$50 leads to a reduction in the years of schooling of the cohort of Alberta-born youth who were 18 when the oil price shock hit (relative to those in non-oil provinces) of around 0.4 to 0.2 years, using estimates from a model including province-specific trends.

Figure 8 shows the estimates for highest completed level of schooling, broken down into three categories for men and women: (1) at least graduated from high school; (2) highest level of education is a college diploma or trades certificate; and (3) highest level of education is a university degree (BA or above). Albertan males who turned 18 during an oil price boom are slightly more than 3 percentage points less likely to have at least graduated from high school. While the point estimates show a negative effect of higher oil prices on university and college completion for both men and women, these effects are not statistically distinguishable from zero, and the magnitudes are fairly small – about a 1-2 percent reduction in the probability of completing a university degree for those whose post-secondary education decisions were affected by a $50 per barrel oil price increase relative to those who were not. This is somewhat smaller than the estimated effect on university enrolment rates of 3 percentage

FIGURE 8
Effect of a $50 per Barrel Increase in Oil Prices on Highest Completed Level of Schooling (Alberta Relative to Non-Oil Provinces)

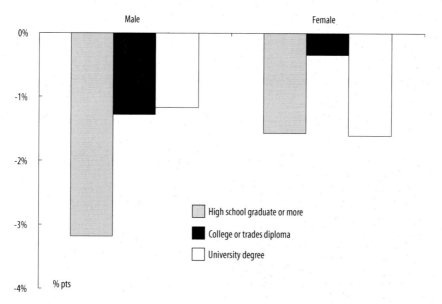

Notes: Estimated effects of a $50 per barrel increase in probability of an Alberta-born individual completing a particular level of education compared with those born in the rest of Canada. Not all estimated effects are statistically significant; see Table A4 for details.

Source: Authors' calculations.

points. As with the enrolment effects, the estimated effects on long-term educational outcomes are typically smaller for women than for men, except regarding university.

The effects on post-secondary education completion are small in magnitude compared with the enrolment effects. There are likely several possible reasons for this.

First, unlike the estimates from the LFS data, the estimates from the Census data cannot plausibly be attributed to inter-provincial migration of youth seeking employment in Alberta during an oil price boom. If this differential mobility were the main reason for the estimated decline in enrolments in the LFS, we would expect to see no effect in the Census data. However, this is unlikely to be the full story – as discussed above, the estimated extent of the inter-provincial migration response to oil prices is not sufficient to explain a large proportion of the estimated enrolment effects.

Second, as suggested earlier, it is possible that cohorts that experience an oil price boom when they are considering entry to post-secondary choose to delay for several years and return to school when oil prices subsequently decline. Alternatively, youth may choose to enrol part time rather than full time. That said, there is little evidence in the LFS data to suggest that this is the case.

Third, the estimates here attribute all the effects of an oil price rise to individuals turning 18 in the year that prices increase. The enrolment data above, however, suggest that the effects of an oil price rise are felt by older cohorts as well. Thus the estimates here – which do not allow for that possibility – will by construction understate the overall effects on educational attainment.

Finally, the estimates also likely understate the true effects on educational attainment, because the use of province of birth to proxy for province of residence at post-secondary entrance age likely introduces some measurement error. As the Census estimates cannot take into account the effects of the most recent oil price shock – and therefore really do capture only one price shock episode – some caution should be used in relying on these estimates.

Overall, then, it is probably reasonable to see the estimates of the effects of oil price shocks on educational attainment using Census data as a lower-bound estimate of the long-run effects on educational attainment of an oil price shock, while the estimated effects on enrolments from the LFS may constitute an upper bound on the true long-run effect.

Conclusion

This paper has clear implications for the timing of Alberta's (and to a lesser extent Saskatchewan's and in the future Newfoundland's) spending on post-secondary education. There is likely to be a need to increase spending on education not during an economic boom when revenues are flowing into provincial coffers but rather in periods of recession, when the demand for university access among youth is higher. Recognizing that decisions on the timing of post-secondary enrolments respond to broader economic conditions is important given the mounting evidence – particularly from the cohort crowding literature – that post-secondary institutions do not expand enrolments perfectly to meet increases in demand for post-secondary education. Without an increase in government funding, or other sources of university financing such as tuition fees, educational attainment may be negatively affected among young people in oil rich provinces during economic downturns associated with oil price declines.

Emery and Kneebone (2009) note, "The recent crash in energy prices threatens the [Alberta] government with repeating the earlier experience of deficits followed by dramatic spending cuts" (1). This boom-bust cycle is particularly inappropriate in the post-secondary sector. The Alberta government does appear to have recognized this dilemma and attempted to increase capital funding to post-secondary institutions during the oil price boom, rather than increasing operating funds only. But Emery and Kneebone's analysis suggests that more needs to be done to keep in mind the lessons of previous oil price booms – that maintaining or even increasing spending on post-secondary education in Alberta during oil busts is likely to be important to ensure that post-secondary institutions are able to meet the resulting increase in demand for post-secondary education.

This is potentially a general principle that governments may wish to follow. Demand for post-secondary education is likely to be higher during an economic downturn because it is a relatively low-cost time to be seeking more education – and this is true for society as a whole as much as it is true for the individual. Add to that the potential macroeconomic benefits of higher government spending during a recession, and there is a strong argument that funding to post-secondary institutions should be counter-cyclical. Note that this is not an argument for increasing funding to the post-secondary education sector. It is only a suggestion that whatever the decision on overall funding to post-secondary education, that funding should be provided in a counter-cyclical pattern: governments should expect that funding needs will increase during downturns and decline during booms.

Here we have focused mostly on the short-run enrolment effects. Perhaps a more pressing concern is whether these short-run enrolment changes lead to long-run differences in educational outcomes. Were this to be the case, it would suggest that higher resource prices could depress the long-run stock of overall human capital in a resource rich economy, providing further evidence of a potential channel by which the so-called "resource curse" operates. We describe briefly some evidence that suggests that higher oil prices that occur when a cohort reaches the age of entering post-secondary education appear to depress this group's educational attainment in the long run (at age 25 and older). This possibility is, however, worth examining in more detail in future work.

It will be of particular interest to revisit this work in the coming years given the magnitude of the drop in oil prices over the past year. The data we have used only go to October 2008, just before the collapse in oil prices and the worsening economic conditions associated with the global financial crisis. The results suggest that if oil prices remain relatively low, Alberta should be preparing for an increase in demand for post-secondary places relative to other provinces – which themselves are likely to see increasing demand for post-secondary places due to the recent economic collapse and increase in unemployment rates. As of August 2009, there are reports of a large rise in applications and number of students accepted into post-secondary institutions in Alberta, with speculation that this pattern is driven by weaker economic conditions (McGinnis 2009). Post-secondary institutions in other provinces have also seen higher applications (Colleges Ontario 2009; *MacLean's* 2009). It would be helpful for future policy-making to see whether these early reports hold and whether the predictions in this paper are borne out by experience in the next few years.

Notes

1. This paper began life as Michal Burdzy's major research paper for his MA in Business Economics at Wilfrid Laurier University. We thank participants at workshops at Wilfrid Laurier University for their helpful comments on earlier versions of this work, and Robert Staples for excellent research assistance.
2. Loken is mostly concerned with how parental income affects educational attainment and does not consider how oil price shocks affect enrolments of youth directly via their own labour market opportunities.
3. Given that the LFS does appear to have some limitations here, it may be worthwhile to revisit this analysis using administrative data on enrolments. For the moment, however, the data are not available for a sufficiently long period of time to enable us to generate reliable estimates from them.
4. We use the sex-specific unemployment rate of 25-34 year old high school graduates as a proxy for the unemployment rate that would be faced by a typical 17-24 year old, because the unemployment rate of 17-24 year olds would be affected by changes in the enrolment rate of that age group.
5. The results are not very different for most models, except those that include cubic province-specific year trends. Regression results incorporating tuition fees are available on request.
6. Real oil prices in 2002 Canadian dollars peaked in July 2008 at $118, above the peak in April 1980 at $109, but the annual averages show oil prices a little lower in their 2008 peak than at their 1980 peak, because of the precipitous decline in oil prices in the second half of 2008. The lowest oil price between

1976 and 2008 came in December 1998, when the price was just $19 per barrel in 2002 Canadian dollar terms.

7. We also ran specifications including the square of the unemployment rate, to ensure that the estimates of the effects of oil prices were not picking up the effect of non-linearities in the effects of unemployment rates. The square of the unemployment rate was never statistically different from zero, and its inclusion had little effect on the estimated coefficient on the oil price interaction term. We also included provincial average undergraduate tuition fees in models estimating the probability of enrolling in university. As noted elsewhere, however, including tuition fees in itself had little effect on the estimated effects of oil prices but did reduce the number of years of data available, which reduced the magnitude of the estimated effect on oil prices slightly and increased the standard error substantially. Results including tuition fees and the square of unemployment are available on request.

8. It is comforting that the results here are consistent with other studies, but these results should not be taken as indicating a causal effect of minimum wages on enrolments; the focus here is on the broader economic effects.

9. This assumption is likely not valid. Our purpose is simply to illustrate the potential magnitude of the Albertan enrolment effect.

10. The school leaving age was increased from 15 to 16 in Newfoundland in 1987, in Quebec in 1988, and in BC in 1990. New Brunswick and Ontario have both recently raised the school leaving age to 18 (in 2000 and 2007 respectively). See Oreopoulos (2006) for details.

11. Mostly because of data availability problems, there is no consistent provincial-level series for average wages, family incomes, or overall government spending on post-secondary education extending back as far as 1976 and up to 2008.

12. LFS data from CANSIM Table 282-0069.

13. Full results are available on request. Note that these estimates depend on the reliability of the data on inward migration. If there are a large number of migrants into Alberta who are not identified as such in Statistics Canada's population statistics, which may be a concern, then this will likely underestimate net migration flows into Alberta in response to oil price increases.

14. Full results are available on request.

References

Bound, J., and S. Turner. 2008. "Cohort Crowding: How Resources Affect Collegiate Attainment." *Journal of Public Economics* 91(5-6): 877-99

Card, D., and T. Lemieux. 2001. "Dropout and Enrollment Trends in the Post-War Period: What Went Wrong in the 1970s?" In *Risky Behaviour among Youths*, ed. J. Gruber, 439-82. Chicago: University of Chicago Press.

Chan, P.C.,W, R. Morissette, and M. Frenette. 2009. "Do Minimum Wages Affect the Enrolment Decisions of Canadian Youth?" Paper presented at Statistics Canada's SocioEconomic Conference, May 2009.

Coelli, M. 2005. "Parental Income Shocks and the Education Attendance of Youth." Mimeo, University of Melbourne.

Colleges Ontario. 2009. "Colleges Experience Major Jump in Applications." News release, 8 January 2009.

Coulombe, S. 2006. Internal Migration, Asymmetric Shocks, and Interprovincial Economic Adjustments in Canada." *International Regional Science Review* 29 (2): 199-223.

Emery, H., and R. Kneebone. 2009. "Will It Be Déjà Vu All Over Again?" *SPP Briefing Papers* 2 (1). Calgary: University of Calgary.

Fortin, N. 2006. "Higher Education Policies and the College Premium: Cross-State Evidence from the 1990s." *American Economic Review* 96 (4): 959-87.

Handa, M., and M. Skolnik. 1975. "Unemployment, Expected Returns, and the Demand for University Education in Ontario: Some Empirical Results." *Higher Education* 4 (1): 27-43.

Kane, T. 1994."College Entry by Blacks since 1970: The Role of College Costs, Family Background, and the Returns to Education." *Journal of Political Economy* 102 (5): 878-911.

Kruger, D. 2007. "Coffee Production Effects on Child Labor and Schooling in Rural Brazil." *Journal of Development Economics* 82: 448-43.

Landon, S. 1997. "High School Enrollment, Minimum Wages and Education Spending," *Canadian Public Policy* 23 (2): 141-63.

Loken, K. 2009 (forthcoming). "Family Income and Children's Education: Using the Norwegian Oil Boom as a Natural Experiment." *Labour Economics*.

MacLean's Magazine. 2009. "Grad School Applications Up." *MacLean's on Campus.* 13 January 2009.

Martinello, F. 2008. Transitions and Adjustments in Students' Post-Secondary Education." In *Who Goes? Who Stays? What Matters? Accessing and Persisting in Post-Secondary Education in Canada*, ed. R. Finnie, R.E. Mueller, A. Sweetman, and A. Usher, 209-38. Montreal and Kingston: Queen's Policy Studies Series, McGill-Queen's University Press.

McGinnis, S. 2009. "Calgary's Jobless Flocking Back to School." *Calgary Herald,* 7 August 2009.

Neumark, D., and W. Wascher. 1995a. "The Effects of Minimum Wages on Teenage Employment and Enrollment: Evidence from Matched CPS Surveys." *Research in Labor Economics* 15: 25-63.

– 1995b. "Minimum Wage Effects on Employment and School Enrollment." *Journal of Business and Economics Statistics* 13 (2): 199-206.

– 1995c. "Minimum-Wage Effects on School and Work Transitions of Teenagers." *American Economic Review Papers and Proceedings* 85 (2): 244-9.

– 2003. "Minimum Wages and Skill Acquisition: Another Look at Schooling Effects." *Economics of Education Review* 22: 1-10.

Oreopoulos, P. 2006. "The Compelling Effects of Compulsory Schooling: Evidence from Canada." *Canadian Journal of Economics* 39 (1): 22-52.

Rees, D., and H.N. Mocan. 1997. "Labor Market Conditions and the High School Dropout Rate: Evidence from New York State." *Economics of Education Review* 16 (2): 103-9.

Wente, M. 2007. "The Horror of Too Many Kids in University." *Globe and Mail,* 12 May 2007.

DATA APPENDIX

Enrolment Data	*Labour Force Survey, Public Use Microdata Files*
Unemployment rate	Annual average unemployment rate of 25-34 year old high school graduates, calculated from LFS.
Minimum wage	The minimum wage applying in July, from the Human Resources Development Canada website, deflated using provincial CPI: http://www110.hrdc-drhc.gc.ca/psait_spila/lmnec_eslc/eslc/salaire_minwage/index.cfm/doc/English.
Oil prices	Annual average spot price of WTI, from Federal Reserve of St Louis. http://research.stlouisfed.org/fred2/series/OILPRICE/downloaddata. This is converted to 2002 Canadian dollars using annual average exchange rates and the Canadian CPI from CANSIM.
Oil intensity of production	Percentage of current dollar gross provincial product accounted for by oil and gas extraction average between 1984 and 1994. Provincial economic accounts, CANSIM Table 3790025.
Educational attainment data	2001 Census.

APPENDIX TABLES

TABLE A1
Estimated Marginal Effects on 17-24 Year Old Male Enrolments (Probit Models)

	Enrolled in Some Educational Program					Enrolled in College Full Time					Enrolled in University Full Time				
	a	b	c	d	e	a	b	c	d	e	a	b	c	d	e
Oil price * oil intensity	-0.054	-0.058	-0.058	-0.051	-0.039	-0.001	-0.001	-0.001	0.004	-0.016	-0.035	-0.032	-0.032	-0.032	-0.035
	(5.07)**	(6.18)**	(6.18)**	(4.68)**	(1.88)	(0.13)	(0.10)	(0.10)	(0.50)	(1.20)	(3.32)**	(4.20)**	(4.19)**	(3.95)**	(2.37)**
Oil price * oil intensity lagged															
One year					-0.016					0.005					0.020
					(0.50)					(0.24)					(0.97)
Two years					-0.012					0.023					-0.011
					(0.46)					(1.48)					(0.60)
Three years					0.006					-0.020					-0.001
					(0.22)					(1.47)					(0.05)
Four years					0.012					0.024					-0.012
					(0.67)					(2.58)*					(0.79)
Unemployment rate (%)	0.390	0.384	0.385	0.396	0.368	0.125	0.120	0.120	0.096	0.072	0.112	0.098	0.098	0.073	0.094
	(6.09)**	(6.28)**	(6.29)**	(6.18)**	(6.70)**	(3.26)**	(3.02)**	(3.02)**	(2.41)*	(1.79)	(2.28)*	(2.08)*	(2.08)*	(1.49)	(1.82)
Minimum wage ($)	0.007	0.011	0.011	0.012	0.009	-0.004	-0.005	-0.005	-0.005	-0.006	0.001	-0.003	-0.003	0.003	0.003
	(1.35)	(2.21)*	(2.21)*	(2.30)*	(1.84)	(2.05)*	(2.09)*	(2.09)*	(2.36)*	(2.85)**	(0.32)	(1.01)	(1.02)	(0.75)	(0.81)
Linear trends		y	y	y	y		y	y	y	y		y	y	y	y
Quadratic trends			y	y	y			y	y	y			y	y	y
Cubic trends				y	y				y	y				y	y

Notes: N = 273433. All specifications include a full set of province and year fixed effects. Point estimates on the oil price * oil intensity interaction variable can be interpreted as the effects of a C$50 per barrel increase in oil prices in a province with oil intensity of production of 20 percent. Robust z-statistics, based on standard errors clustered at the province-year level, are in parentheses. * significant at 5 percent; ** significant at 1 percent.

TABLE A2
Estimated Marginal Effects on 17–24 Year Old Female Enrolments (Probit Models)

	Enrolled in Some Educational Program					Enrolled in College Full Time					Enrolled in University Full Time				
	a	b	c	d	e	a	b	c	d	e	a	b	c	d	e
Oil price * oil intensity	-0.023	-0.028	-0.028	-0.043	-0.034	0.013	0.010	0.010	0.003	-0.015	-0.028	-0.022	-0.022	-0.024	0.008
	(2.15)*	(3.07)**	(3.05)**	(4.87)**	(2.74)**	(2.68)**	(2.07)*	(2.07)*	(0.66)	(1.27)	(2.70)**	(2.80)**	(2.78)**	(3.72)**	(0.64)
Oil price * oil intensity lagged															
One year					-0.016					0.017					-0.031
					(0.89)					(1.36)					(2.29)*
Two years					0.002					0.003					0.011
					(0.11)					(0.21)					(0.95)
Three years					0.002					0.007					-0.021
					(0.10)					(0.54)					(1.88)
Four years					0.006					-0.002					0.000
					(0.48)					(0.19)					(0.03)
Unemployment rate (%)	0.132	0.031	0.032	0.030	0.021	0.021	0.013	0.013	0.001	-0.008	0.113	0.072	0.072	0.030	0.048
	(2.00)*	(0.57)	(0.57)	(0.56)	(0.38)	(0.67)	(0.41)	(0.41)	(0.04)	(0.23)	(2.36)*	(1.53)	(1.53)	(0.66)	(1.03)
Minimum wage ($)	0.005	0.003	0.003	0.004	0.004	-0.011	-0.007	-0.007	-0.006	-0.006	0.002	-0.006	-0.006	0.001	0.001
	(1.07)	(0.82)	(0.82)	(0.81)	(0.81)	(3.74)**	(1.61)	(1.62)	(1.54)	(1.66)	(0.68)	(1.93)	(1.94)	(0.27)	(0.46)
Linear trends		y	y	y	y		y	y	y	y		y	y	y	y
Quadratic trends			y	y	y			y	y	y			y	y	y
Cubic trends				y	y				y	y				y	y

Notes: N = 273300. All specifications include a full set of province and year fixed effects. Point estimates on the oil price * oil intensity interaction variable can be interpreted as the effects of a C$50 per barrel increase in oil prices in a province with oil intensity of production of 20 percent. Robust z-statistics, based on standard errors clustered at the province-year level, are in parentheses. * significant at 5 percent; ** significant at 1 percent.

TABLE A3

Estimated Marginal Effects of Oil Price Changes, by Age and Sex

	N	Enrolled in Some Educational Program				Enrolled in College Full Time				Enrolled in University Full Time			
		a	b	c	d	a	b	c	d	a	b	c	d
Male													
15-16 year olds	76867	0.007 (0.81)	0.000 (0.03)	0.000 (0.03)	-0.006 (0.80)	0.000 (0.09)	0.003 (0.81)	0.003 (0.82)	-0.001 (0.30)	-0.001 (0.80)	-0.001 (0.51)	-0.001 (0.51)	-0.001 (1.37)
17-19 year olds	108647	-0.026 (2.38)*	-0.036 (3.24)**	-0.037 (3.24)**	-0.043 (3.90)**	0.011 (0.86)	0.010 (0.75)	0.010 (0.76)	-0.002 (0.09)	-0.035 (2.36)*	-0.029 (2.49)*	-0.029 (2.48)*	-0.029 (2.64)*
20-21 year olds	67573	-0.029 (2.07)*	-0.032 (2.31)*	-0.032 (2.30)*	-0.017 (0.89)	0.004 (0.38)	0.002 (0.18)	0.002 (0.18)	0.006 (0.62)	-0.029 (2.46)*	-0.025 (2.37)*	-0.025 (2.36)*	-0.016 (1.38)
22-24 year olds	97213	-0.062 (3.30)**	-0.063 (4.46)**	-0.063 (4.45)**	-0.047 (3.05)**	-0.004 (0.76)	-0.004 (0.79)	-0.004 (0.79)	0.011 (2.54)*	-0.038 (3.00)**	-0.038 (3.61)**	-0.038 (3.60)**	-0.043 (2.99)*
Female													
15-16 year olds	73763	0.005 (0.68)	-0.0023 (0.30)	-0.002 (0.30)	-0.018 (2.69)**	0.002 (0.50)	0.005 (1.10)	0.005 (1.11)	0.006 (1.00)	-0.002 (1.88)	-0.001 (1.53)	-0.001 (1.52)	-0.001 (0.89)
17-19 year olds	104836	-0.018 (1.53)	-0.026 (2.11)*	-0.026 (2.09)*	-0.053 (4.71)**	0.037 (3.13)**	0.030 (3.01)**	0.030 (3.02)**	0.022 (2.06)*	-0.048 (3.70)**	-0.038 (4.00)**	-0.038 (3.98)**	-0.039 (4.87)**
20-21 year olds	67944	-0.018 (0.95)	-0.020 (1.14)	-0.020 (1.13)	-0.032 (2.17)*	0.018 (1.45)	0.008 (0.84)	0.008 (0.83)	0.000 (0.03)	-0.029 (1.48)	-0.020 (1.68)	-0.020 (1.66)	-0.025 (1.69)
22-24 year olds	100520	0.000 (0.02)	-0.007 (0.67)	-0.007 (0.66)	-0.003 (0.23)	0.003 (0.60)	0.001 (0.18)	0.001 (0.18)	-0.006 (1.11)	-0.003 (0.30)	-0.005 (0.49)	-0.005 (0.48)	-0.002 (0.26)
Linear trends			y	y	y		y	y	y		y	y	y
Quadratic trends				y	y			y	y			y	y
Cubic trends					y				y				y

Note that all specifications include a full set of province and year fixed effects. Point estimates on the oil price * oil intensity interaction variable can be interpreted as the effects of a $50 per barrel increase in oil prices in a province with oil intensity of production of 20 percent. Robust z-statistics, based on standard errors clustered at the province-year level, are in parentheses. * significant at 5 percent; ** significant at 1 percent.

TABLE A4
Estimated Marginal Effects of Oil Prices in Oil Intensive Provinces on Educational Attainment, by Sex (Census Data)

	Male (N=148,190)				Female (N=143,074)			
	a	b	c	d	a	b	c	d
Dependent variable:								
Years of schooling	-0.413	-0.129	-0.188	-0.187	-0.604	-0.131	-0.175	-0.179
	(3.92)**	(1.92)	(2.86)**	(2.85)**	(4.71)**	(1.91)	(2.93)**	(3.07)**
High school or more	-0.032	-0.013	-0.032	-0.035	-0.028	0.001	-0.016	-0.016
	(3.54)**	(1.27)	(3.37)**	(3.78)**	(2.42)*	(0.06)	(1.06)	(1.09)
College diploma	-0.031	-0.001	-0.013	-0.015	-0.031	0.008	-0.003	-0.003
	(3.88)**	(0.08)	(1.45)	(1.66)	(3.01)**	(0.60)	(0.27)	(0.26)
University degree	-0.009	-0.007	-0.012	-0.014	-0.019	-0.011	-0.016	-0.015
	(1.54)	(1.17)	(1.72)	(2.05)*	(2.32)*	(1.15)	(1.81)	(1.70)
Linear trends	y	y	y		y	y	y	
Quadratic trends		y	y			y	y	
Cubic trends			y				y	

Notes: Each cell shows the estimated marginal effects of the oil price * oil intensity interaction variable (which can be interpreted as the effects of a $50 per barrel increase in oil prices in a province with oil intensity of production of 20 percent) from a separate regression. All specifications include a full set of province and year fixed effects. Robust z-statistics, based on standard errors clustered at the province-year level, are in parentheses. * significant at 5 percent; ** significant at 1 percent.

7

Are Economic Returns to Schooling Different for Aboriginal and Non-Aboriginal People?

Marc Frenette

Le niveau de scolarisation des Autochtones est en général inférieur à celui des autres Cana-diens, et ce phénomène est bien documenté. Par contre, on connaît assez mal les raisons qui expliquent cet écart. Cette étude est la première d'une série de deux où j'analyse cette situation en détail. Dans celle-ci, je me concentre sur un facteur qui pourrait expliquer l'écart : j'émets l'hypothèse selon laquelle les Autochtones retireraient moins d'avantages économiques d'un degré supérieur de scolarisation que les autres Canadiens. Pour vérifier cette hypothèse, j'ai utilisé les données du recensement de 2006. Je n'ai trouvé aucune preuve qui montre de façon systématique que les Autochtones qui ont un degré supérieur de scolarisation profitent moins que les autres Canadiens des avantages économiques que cela apporte sur le marché du travail (en termes de revenus et de risques de se retrouver au chômage). En réalité, à certains égards, les Autochtones profitent même plus que les autres Canadiens d'un degré supérieur de scolarisation. J'en conclus donc que les avantages liés à la scolarisation ne sont pas un facteur qui pourrait expliquer la plus faible scolarisation que l'on observe chez les Autochtones. Ces résultats sont valables pour tous les Autochtones, qu'ils vivent dans des réserves, hors d'une réserve, ou dans des communautés nordiques.

While it is well documented that Aboriginal people generally have lower levels of educational attainment than other groups in Canada, little is known about the reasons behind this gap. This study is the first of two investigating the issue in detail. In this initial paper I focus on one potential reason for differences in educational attainment between Aboriginal and non-Aboriginal individuals: the possibility that Aboriginal individuals reap fewer economic benefits from additional schooling than their non-Aboriginal counterparts. Using the 2006 Canada Census, I find no systematic evidence that Aboriginal people benefit less from additional schooling than non-Aboriginal people in terms of labour market outcomes

Pursuing Higher Education in Canada: Economic, Social, and Policy Dimensions, ed. R. Finnie, M. Frenette, R.E. Mueller, and A. Sweetman. Montreal and Kingston: Queen's Policy Studies Series, McGill-Queen's University Press.

(i.e., earnings and the probability of being unemployed). In fact, Aboriginal people benefit more economically from schooling in some respects. These findings suggest that returns to schooling are not likely to be a factor behind the lower levels of educational attainment among Aboriginal people. Finally, the results hold whether Aboriginal people live off-reserve, on-reserve, or in northern communities.

Introduction

According to the 2006 Canada Census, more than one in five (21.8 percent) off-reserve Aboriginal individuals lived in economic families with after-tax income below the Low-Income Cut-Off (LICO), as depicted in Figure 1. That is about two times the figure for non-Aboriginal individuals (11.1 percent). Among off-reserve Aboriginal people, North American Indians have the highest low-income rate by far (27.6 percent), although a greater proportion of Métis and Inuit people are below the LICO compared to non-Aboriginal people.

Since education is a key component of labour market outcomes, a thorough understanding of the economic returns to schooling experienced by Aboriginal people is required to more fully understand their economic situation. It is also important to understand Aboriginal educational attainment, since this group may represent a potentially large, untapped skilled labour force. Despite the importance of the topic, all we know is that Aboriginal individuals lag behind non-Aboriginal individuals in

FIGURE 1
Proportion in Economic Familes below the Low-Income Cut-Off (LICO)

Proportion

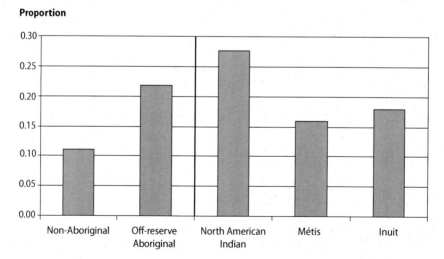

Source: Census, 2006.

terms of educational attainment (O'Donnell and Ballardin 2006; Costa and Siggner 2005; Tait 1999) and literacy (Bougie 2008). We know little about the reasons behind the gap.

One possible explanation for the "education divide" is the possibility that Aboriginal people simply do not reap the same economic benefits from additional schooling as do non-Aboriginal people. This is precisely the issue that is addressed in this study. Why might returns to schooling matter? Although we have limited evidence, we know that returns to schooling tend to vary by other dimensions. For example, we know that boys face lower returns to higher education than girls, and that this plays some role in understanding the gender gap in university enrolment (Frenette and Zeman 2008; Christofides, Hoy, and Yang 2006).

Using the 2006 Census, I find no systematic evidence that Aboriginal people benefit less from additional schooling than non-Aboriginal people in terms of labour market outcomes. In fact, Aboriginal people benefit more from schooling in some respects. Higher levels of schooling are generally associated with larger declines in the probability of unemployment for Aboriginal people. In terms of wages and salaries, both Aboriginal and non-Aboriginal groups have more or less similar returns to schooling. Moreover, among bachelor's degree graduates working full-year and full-time, both groups earn about the same when they have studied in similar disciplines. However, unemployment rates are higher among Aboriginal than non-Aboriginal people, even for the same disciplines. Furthermore, the two groups do not generally study in the same disciplines. Aboriginal people are more likely to choose disciplines such as education, arts, social sciences, and humanities, while non-Aboriginal people are more likely to choose disciplines such as engineering, mathematics, computer science, and physical sciences. These trends are true for men and women, but they are especially true for men. It is generally the case that engineering, mathematics, computer science, and physical sciences lead to higher-paying jobs and are less strongly associated with jobs requiring less education. These findings suggest that returns to schooling are not likely to be a factor behind the lower levels of educational attainment among Aboriginal people.

In the next section I describe the data and methods used in the study. I follow this with a section outlining, in somewhat more detail than has been previously done, the extent to which Aboriginal and non-Aboriginal people differ in their educational outcomes. I then present the main results of the study, which focus on returns to schooling. In the next two sections, I ask (and attempt to answer) two questions that add perspective on the estimates of returns to schooling: "Can self-selection of Aboriginal and non-Aboriginal people in different levels of education explain the results?" and "Are the perceptions of the returns to schooling different for Aboriginal and non-Aboriginal youth?" The study is summarized in the final section.

Methodology

This study primarily uses the Canada 2006 Census of Population micro-data file. I focus on three groups of Aboriginal people: North American Indians, Métis, and Inuit. However, sample size limitations at higher levels of education often require that I combine all three groups to create aggregate estimates. It is important to note that this may miss important differences among the three groups. For a substantial portion of the study, I do not examine Aboriginal people living on-reserve or in northern communities, given that the labour market might be very different in those areas. However, I do include them in a separate analysis later on.

The term "Aboriginal" refers here to identity as opposed to ancestry. Specifically, I look at how respondents answer the question: "Is this person an Aboriginal person, that is, North American Indian, Métis, or Inuit (Eskimo)?"[1]

Respondents could answer:[2]

- No
- Yes, North American Indian[3]
- Yes, Métis
- Yes, Inuit

All results are generated separately by sex. I also include non-Aboriginal people in the analysis, as a benchmark; however, I take a 2 percent random sample of them to save on computing time. (All sample sizes used in the analysis are available upon request.)

Since the focus is on returns to schooling, I select individuals of prime working age (i.e., 25 to 54 years old). Three outcomes are examined in particular, each requiring a different analytical sample. The educational choices of Aboriginal people are examined for the full sample (i.e., all individuals 25 to 54 years old). Although this is not the main focus of the analysis, it is important to highlight these choices in order to set the backdrop for the returns-to-schooling results to follow. The two labour market outcomes included are the unemployment rate, and wages and salaries. The unemployment rate is calculated among individuals who are working during the Census reference week (i.e., 7 May to 13 May 2006), have a job lined up, or are actively seeking employment. Wages and salaries refer to the year prior to the Census (i.e., 2005). To minimize the impact of differences in weeks worked or hours worked per week, I focus on individuals who worked full-year (i.e., 49 weeks or more) and full-time (i.e., 30 hours or more per week, on average). For this part of the analysis, only paid employees are examined (i.e., individuals with positive wages and salaries and zero net self-employment from farm and non-farm sources).

The main outcome examined in the study is a measure of returns to schooling. This refers to the estimated benefit of pursuing additional qualifications, which is calculated from predicted values generated from ordinary least squares regression in the case of the unemployment rate models,[4] and median regression in the case of the wages and salaries models. Note that since we do not have longitudinal data, and since we know nothing about differences in discount rates for Aboriginal and non-Aboriginal people, returns can not be estimated over the life course.

Separate regressions are estimated for Aboriginal and non-Aboriginal people. For each group, predicted outcomes are generated for each level of completed schooling, holding other variables in the model constant. The absolute or relative differences in predicted outcomes across levels of education are interpreted as a measure of returns to schooling, which can then be compared across groups (Aboriginal versus non-Aboriginal).

The categories of completed schooling include:

- Less than a high school diploma
- High school diploma (omitted in the regressions)
- Trade/vocational certificate or apprenticeship
- College certificate
- University certificate below a bachelor's degree
- Bachelor's degree
- Graduate or professional degree

The other variables included in the model are age, age squared, activity limitation (no limitations [the omitted category in the regressions], sometimes has a limitation, often has a limitation), and economic region, which is used to identify the local labour market (59 in total).[5]

At times the analysis also delves deeper into educational choices and their associated labour market outcomes by looking at the major field of study. To reduce the dimensionality of this analysis, I only look at these choices among bachelor's degree graduates. The fields of study are grouped into nine categories:

- Educational, recreational, and counselling services
- Fine and applied arts
- Humanities and related
- Social sciences and related
- Commerce, management, and business administration
- Agricultural, biological, nutritional, and food sciences
- Engineering and applied sciences
- Health
- Mathematics, computer, and physical sciences

Finally, data drawn from the Youth in Transition Survey (YITS), Cohort A, are used to examine two other possible explanations for the results: selection into different levels of education and perceptions of returns to schooling. I describe these data in the relevant sections.

The Educational Attainment of Aboriginal People

Although it is well documented that Aboriginal people generally have lower levels of completed education than non-Aboriginal people (O'Donnell and Ballardin 2006; Costa and Siggner 2005; Tait 1999), previous evidence dates back to 2001 and generally does not consider differences in field of study choices.[6] This section of the study is meant to update our knowledge of the educational attainment of the Aboriginal population in somewhat more detail than earlier works.

In Table 1 I show the distribution of Aboriginal and non-Aboriginal men and women aged 25 to 54 years old by their highest level of education. Aboriginal people are far more likely than non-Aboriginal people to have less than a high school diploma. This is especially the case among Inuit men and women. Specifically, 13.9 percent and 11.4 percent of non-Aboriginal men and women, respectively, have less than a high school diploma. In contrast, 49.9 percent and 48.7 percent (one-half) of Inuit men and women, respectively, have less than a high school diploma. Off-reserve North American Indians and Métis people are as likely to report a high school diploma as their highest level as are non-Aboriginal people; however, this is due to the fact that off-reserve North American Indians and Métis are less likely to pursue further studies once they have

TABLE 1
Distribution of Highest Level of Education

	Men				Women			
		Off-reserve Aboriginal				Off-reserve Aboriginal		
	Non-Aboriginal	N. Amer. Indian	Métis	Inuit	Non-Aboriginal	N. Amer. Indian	Métis	Inuit
Less than a high school diploma	0.139	0.318	0.269	0.499	0.114	0.264	0.209	0.487
High school diploma	0.239	0.243	0.246	0.130	0.248	0.244	0.263	0.144
Trade/voc. cert. or apprenticeship	0.153	0.181	0.202	0.183	0.092	0.100	0.120	0.092
College cert.	0.192	0.160	0.182	0.153	0.234	0.237	0.260	0.199
Univ. cert. below a bachelor's degree	0.042	0.029	0.025	0.014	0.054	0.046	0.043	0.030
Bachelor's degree	0.148	0.048	0.053	0.017	0.170	0.083	0.079	0.039
Graduate or professional degree	0.089	0.022	0.023	0.005	0.088	0.027	0.027	0.011
Total	1.000	1.000	1.000	1.000	1.000	1.000	1.000	1.000

Notes: Aborig. = Aboriginal; N. Amer. Ind. = North American Indian; voc. = vocational; cert. = certificate; univ. = university. The sample includes 25 to 54 year olds. A 2 percent random sample of non-Aboriginal people was taken.

Source: Census, 2006.

completed high school. However, this is not true for trade/vocational certificates or apprenticeships and college certificates: Aboriginal people are as likely as non-Aboriginal people to report these as their highest level. The story is quite different for university qualifications. Non-Aboriginal people are far more likely to report having a university certificate below a bachelor's degree, a bachelor's degree, or a graduate or professional degree. Professional degrees include those in medicine, dentistry, veterinary medicine, and optometry.

The disciplines chosen by Aboriginal people in university are very different from those selected by non-Aboriginal people. In Table 2, I show the distribution of major field of study among bachelor's degree graduates. Aboriginal men are far more likely than non-Aboriginal men to choose disciplines such as educational, recreational, and counselling services, fine and applied arts, humanities and related fields, and social sciences and related fields. On the other hand, Aboriginal men are far less likely than non-Aboriginal men to choose disciplines such as engineering and applied sciences, mathematics, computing, and physical sciences. While the Aboriginal/non-Aboriginal differences are usually in the same direction for women as for men, the magnitudes of the gaps are generally smaller for women.

Taken together, the results in Tables 1 and 2 suggest that, compared to non-Aboriginal people, Aboriginal people are far less likely to obtain a high school diploma, just as likely to obtain a non-university postsecondary certificate, and far less likely to obtain university credentials. Moreover, once in university, Aboriginal men (and to a lesser extent

TABLE 2
Distribution of Major Field of Study among Bachelor's Degree Graduates

	Men		Women	
	Non-Aboriginal	*Off-reserve Aboriginal*	*Non-Aboriginal*	*Off-reserve Aboriginal*
Educational, recreational, and counselling services	0.085	0.165	0.186	0.272
Fine and applied arts	0.032	0.041	0.040	0.031
Humanities and related	0.089	0.124	0.141	0.111
Social sciences and related	0.181	0.283	0.184	0.245
Commerce, management, and business administration	0.229	0.185	0.185	0.180
Agricultural, biological, nutritional, and food sciences	0.049	0.036	0.060	0.035
Engineering and applied sciences	0.215	0.103	0.044	0.016
Health	0.022	0.016	0.118	0.096
Mathematics, computer science, and physical sciences	0.098	0.048	0.043	0.015
Total	1.000	1.000	1.000	1.000

Notes: The sample includes 25 to 54 year olds with a bachelor's degree. A 2 percent random sample of non-Aboriginal people was taken.

Source: Census, 2006.

Aboriginal women) are generally more likely to pick disciplines that are less well-paying compared to other disciplines (Finnie and Frenette 2003) and more likely to lead to under-employment (Frenette 2004).

The Returns to Schooling of Aboriginal People

This section considers the returns to schooling of Aboriginal people. To the best of my knowledge, this topic has not been explored in Canada. However, several studies examine Aboriginal earnings through a different lens. Using the 1986 Census, George and Kuhn (1994) document the size of the wage gap between Aboriginal and non-Aboriginal workers and attempt to explain it with observable characteristics. They note that the size of the gap is small compared to other groups, and that about half of it can be accounted for by differences in factors such as education, language, and region. Kuhn and Sweetman (2002) use the 1991 Census to study Aboriginal earnings in a framework similar to the standard one used in the immigrant earnings assimilation literature. They find support for the hypothesis that earnings of Aboriginal workers benefit from skill/trait acquisition similar to non-Aboriginal workers (i.e., the assimilation theory). Walters, White, and Maxim (2004) use the 1995 National Graduates Survey to examine labour market outcomes of Aboriginal post-secondary graduates in comparison with their non-Aboriginal counterparts. They find that once educational attainment and socio-economic characteristics are accounted for, Aboriginal post-secondary graduates earn more than non-Aboriginal post-secondary graduates. However, Aboriginal post-secondary graduates generally experience poorer employment prospects, as measured by their part-time/full-time status or their probability of being unemployed.

In Figures 2 and 3, I show predicted unemployment rates by level of education for men and women, respectively. Table A1 in the Appendix shows the exact numbers as well as absolute and relative rates of return. First, higher levels of schooling are associated with lower unemployment rates. This is true for non-Aboriginal and Aboriginal men and women. In general, the returns are actually higher for Aboriginal people than for non-Aboriginal people. At the bottom of Table A1, I show absolute and relative rates of returns for three types of decisions: (1) completing a high school diploma (compared to having less than a high school diploma), (2) completing a first post-secondary qualification, such as a trade/vocational certificate or apprenticeship, a college certificate, a university certificate below a bachelor's degree, or a bachelor's degree (compared to a high school diploma), and (3) completing a graduate or professional degree (compared to a bachelor's degree).

The findings suggest that the returns to completing a high school diploma or a university degree are generally higher for Aboriginal people, both in absolute and relative terms. In contrast, the absolute and relative rates of return for completing a trade/vocational certificate or apprenticeship, a college certificate, or a university certificate below a bachelor's degree are generally lower for Aboriginal people. These results are interesting in light of the numbers in Table 1 showing that Aboriginal people are far less likely to complete a high school diploma or obtain a university degree but just as likely to obtain a trade/vocational certificate or apprenticeship or a college certificate as non-Aboriginal people.

FIGURE 2
Predicted Unemployment Rates by Highest Level of Education – Men

Proportion

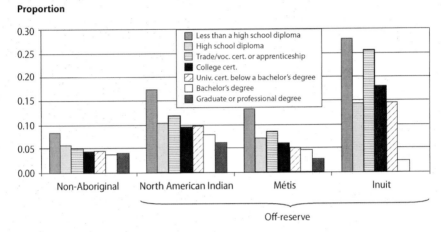

Source: Census, 2006.

FIGURE 3
Predicted Unemployment Rates by Highest Level of Education – Women

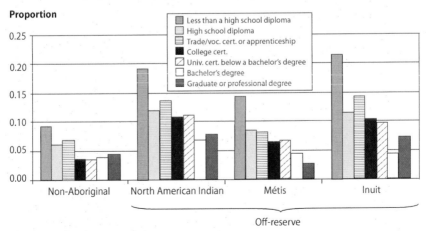

Source: Census, 2006.

In Figures 4 and 5 the focus is on predicted median wages and salaries for men and women, respectively. Table A2 in the Appendix shows the exact numbers, as well as well as absolute and relative rates of return. The three Aboriginal groups had to be combined in this instance due to low sample sizes at higher levels of education. This is because of the focus on full-year, full-time workers. First, the returns to further schooling are large and positive for all groups. Absolute and relative rates of return are shown at the bottom of Table A2 for the median results. They indicate that the returns for Aboriginal people are generally as high or almost as high as the returns for non-Aboriginal people for most thresholds and groups. Although there are some exceptions, there is no systematic evidence suggesting that non-Aboriginal people gain more from higher schooling than Aboriginal people in terms of wages and salaries.

In Table 3, I show unemployment rates by major field of study among bachelor's degree graduates. Note that these are actual numbers, not predicted. In general the disciplines that Aboriginal people are relatively more likely to take are precisely the ones where their unemployment rate is highest. For example, 8.6 percent of Aboriginal people who studied social sciences and related disciplines (a relatively common choice among this group) are unemployed, compared to only 3.9 percent of their non-Aboriginal counterparts. In contrast, only 1.2 percent of Aboriginal people who studied engineering and applied sciences (a much less common choice among Aboriginal people) are unemployed, compared to only 4.5 percent of their non-Aboriginal counterparts.

FIGURE 4
Predicted Median Wages and Salaries by Highest Level of Education – Men

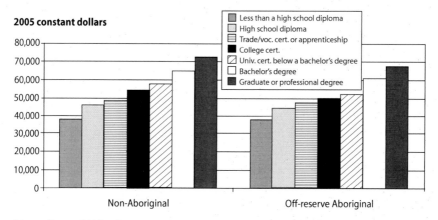

Source: Census, 2006.

FIGURE 5
Predicted Median Wages and Salaries by Highest Level of Education – Women

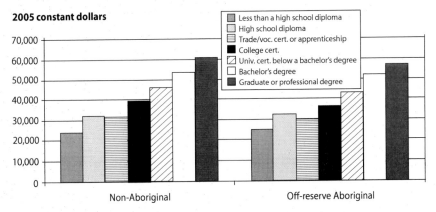

Source: Census, 2006.

TABLE 3
Unemployment Rates by Major Field of Study among Bachelor's Degree Graduates

	Men		Women	
	Non-Aboriginal	*Off-reserve Aboriginal*	*Non-Aboriginal*	*Off-reserve Aboriginal*
Educational, recreational, and counselling services	0.022	0.018	0.025	0.046
Fine and applied arts	0.064	0.123	0.025	0.056
Humanities and related	0.046	0.082	0.053	0.084
Social sciences and related	0.039	0.086	0.046	0.074
Commerce, management, and business administration	0.025	0.068	0.046	0.063
Agricultural, biological, nutritional, and food sciences	0.038	0.000	0.053	0.078
Engineering and applied sciences	0.045	0.012	0.073	0.101
Health	0.009	0.000	0.020	0.030
Mathematics, computer science, and physical sciences	0.061	0.043	0.092	0.025
All fields of study	0.030	0.059	0.048	0.060

Notes: The sample includes 25 to 54 year olds who were in the labour force during the Census reference week. A 2 percent random sample of non-Aboriginal people was taken.

Source: Census, 2006.

Table 4 considers median wages and salaries by major field of study among bachelor's degree graduates. Once again, note that these are actual numbers, not predicted. Here the evidence suggests that non-Aboriginal and Aboriginal people generally earn the same when they study in the same discipline, as long as they both work full-year, full-time. Of course, we know from Table 3 that unemployment is more frequent among Aboriginal people, even within similar disciplines.

TABLE 4
Median Wages and Salaries by Major Field of Study among Bachelor's Degree Graduates

	Men		Women	
	Non-Aboriginal	Off-reserve Aboriginal	Non-Aboriginal	Off-reserve Aboriginal
Educational, recreational, and counselling services	58,470	59,860	53,343	50,771
Fine and applied arts	43,864	50,741	39,012	31,970
Humanities and related	51,691	52,789	42,747	45,862
Social sciences and related	61,843	55,000	49,235	45,947
Commerce, management, and business administration	69,288	51,881	51,109	49,174
Agricultural, biological, nutritional, and food sciences	53,322	52,000	46,442	48,908
Engineering and applied sciences	70,016	68,039	47,319	54,898
Health	67,434	62,749	59,912	59,000
Mathematics, computer science, and physical sciences	64,819	68,103	59,653	63,700
All fields of study	62,609	58,300	50,958	49,630

Notes: Wages and salaries are reported in 2005 dollars. The sample includes 25 to 54 year olds who were employed full-year, full-time with positive wages and salaries and no net self-employment income from farm and non-farm sources in 2005. A 2 percent random sample of non-Aboriginal people was taken.

Source: Census, 2006.

Can Selection Explain the Results?

Since Aboriginal people who choose higher levels of schooling are relatively fewer than their non-Aboriginal counterparts, it is possible that higher-educated Aboriginal people are a relatively more selective group. An important element of this unobserved heterogeneity would be a measure of abilities. Unfortunately, this measure is not available in the Census. As a result, the findings presented so far may simply reflect self-selection.

However, the Youth in Transition Survey (YITS), Cohort A, contains overall reading scores from a standardized assessment administered to students at the age of 15, as part of the Programme for International Student Assessment (PISA). The survey then tracks these same students until age 21 (so far) and asks them about their educational participation since age 15. Although this birth cohort (those born in 1984) is too young to examine on the labour market, looking at their test scores prior to their chosen level of schooling can provide some insight.[7]

In Figures 6 and 7, I plot median overall reading scores at age 15 by the highest level of educational attainment by age 21. Since many students have not yet had time to complete college or university, I show results for students who have simply attended such institutions by age 21.

The results show that, for both males and females, the median test scores of Aboriginal and non-Aboriginal people rise at the same rate in absolute and relative terms. This suggests that for both males and females, more highly educated Aboriginal people are no more selective as a group than non-Aboriginal people with higher levels of schooling.

FIGURE 6
Median Overall Reading Score at Age 15 – Males

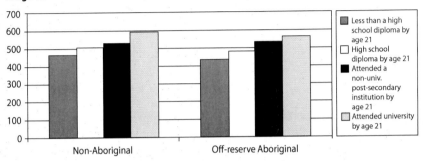

Source: Youth in Transition Survey (YITS), Cohort A.

FIGURE 7
Median Overall Reading Score at Age 15 – Females

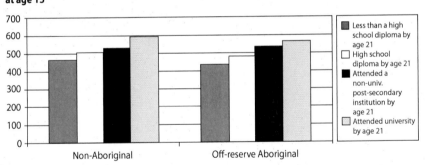

Source: Youth in Transition Survey (YITS), Cohort A.

Perceptions of Returns to Schooling among Aboriginal and Non-Aboriginal People

Although it is clear from the results presented so far that returns to schooling are no lower for Aboriginal people than for non-Aboriginal people, it is still possible that there are differences in the *perceptions* of returns to schooling. Once again, the YITS data are useful here. Students are asked to what extent they agree with the following statement: "Getting a good job later in life depends on my success in school now." This is the closest question relating to perceptions of returns to schooling in the survey.

Although it does not make reference to specific dollar amounts, it does ask the student to relate success in the labour market with success in school.

The results are shown below for males (Figure 8) and females (Figure 9). For males, the distribution of responses is almost identical for Aboriginal and non-Aboriginal youth. Aboriginal females are slightly less in agreement with the statement than non-Aboriginal females. Thus, there is only limited information that the perceptions of returns to schooling are lower for Aboriginal youth.

FIGURE 8
Agreement at Age 15 with the Statement "Getting a good job later depends on my success in school now" – Males

Proportion

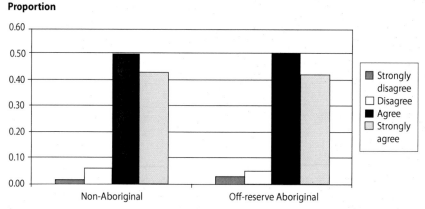

Source: Youth in Transition Survey (YITS), Cohort A.

FIGURE 9
Agreement at Age 15 with the Statement "Getting a good job later depends on my success in school now" – Females

Proportion

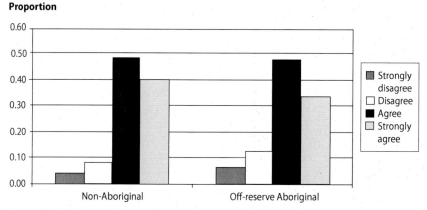

Source: Youth in Transition Survey (YITS), Cohort A.

Aboriginal People On-Reserve and in Northern Communities

To this point, this study has focused exclusively on Aboriginal people living off-reserve and outside of northern communities. The reason is that labour markets are very different in these areas. In this section, I show predicted unemployment rates and median wages and salaries, as well as their associated rates of return for non-Aboriginal and Aboriginal people (split into those living off-reserve, on-reserve, and in northern communities) by highest level of education. Note that low sample sizes among Aboriginal people living on-reserve and in northern communities required that all individuals holding a university degree be combined.

Predicted unemployment rates are shown below in Table 5. Generally speaking, predicted unemployment rates are higher among Aboriginal people living on-reserve or in northern communities than non-Aboriginal people and Aboriginal people living off-reserve. However, our previ-

TABLE 5
Predicted Unemployment Rates by Highest Level of Education – Including Aboriginal People Living On-Reserve and in Northern Communities

| | Men | | | | Women | | | |
| | | Aboriginal | | | | Aboriginal | | |
	Non-Aboriginal	Off-reserve	On-reserve	Northern communities	Non-Aboriginal	Off-reserve	On-reserve	Northern communities
Less than a high school diploma	0.075	0.160	0.326	0.352	0.089	0.174	0.265	0.244
High school diploma	0.049	0.089	0.228	0.265	0.061	0.101	0.174	0.142
Trade/voc. cert. or apprenticeship	0.048	0.106	0.268	0.283	0.065	0.109	0.192	0.241
PS cert. below a bachelor's degree	0.034	0.081	0.184	0.182	0.045	0.087	0.132	0.093
University degree	0.040	0.057	0.115	0.037	0.042	0.057	0.090	0.039
Absolute returns								
High school versus no high school	-0.026	-0.071	-0.098	-0.086	-0.028	-0.073	-0.091	-0.102
Trade/voc./appr. versus high school	-0.001	0.017	0.040	0.018	0.005	0.007	0.018	0.099
PS cert. below a bachelor's degree versus high school	-0.015	-0.009	-0.044	-0.083	-0.016	-0.014	-0.042	-0.049
University degree versus high school	-0.009	-0.032	-0.113	-0.229	-0.019	-0.045	-0.084	-0.103
Relative returns								
High school versus no high school	-0.348	-0.441	-0.301	-0.245	-0.313	-0.420	-0.343	-0.419
Trade/voc./appr. versus high school	-0.024	0.188	0.174	0.067	0.076	0.073	0.106	0.697
PS cert. below a bachelor's degree versus high school	-0.305	-0.098	-0.191	-0.314	-0.257	-0.142	-0.239	-0.343
University degree versus high school	-0.189	-0.357	-0.496	-0.862	-0.311	-0.440	-0.481	-0.723

Notes: Predicted values are derived from regression results that are available upon request. voc. = vocational; cert. = certificate; appr. = apprenticeship. The sample includes 25 to 54 year olds who were employed full-year, full-time with positive wages and salaries and no net self-employment income from farm and non-farm sources in 2005. A 2 percent random sample of non-Aboriginal people was taken.

Source: Census, 2006.

ous findings still hold: the rate of return (in terms of a reduction in the predicted unemployment rate) is generally as large on-reserve and in northern communities as in other areas.

Predicted median wages and salaries appear in Table 6. In terms of differences by level of education, the findings are interesting. For men, predicted wages and salaries are always lowest among on-reserve Aboriginal people and highest among Aboriginal people living in northern communities. Non-Aboriginal people and Aboriginal people living off-reserve stand in the middle. For women, the story is different. Predicted wages and salaries are more or less similar regardless of Aboriginal status.

Regarding relative rates of returns, the patterns are generally the same across Aboriginal status and sex. In other words, the relative returns are generally about as high for Aboriginal people living on-reserve or in northern communities compared to Aboriginal people living on-reserve or non-Aboriginal people. A notable exception concerns the relative returns

TABLE 6

Predicted Median Wages and Salaries by Highest Level of Education – Including Aboriginal People Living On-Reserve and in Northern Communities

	Men				Women			
		Aboriginal				Aboriginal		
	Non-Aboriginal	Off-reserve	On-reserve	Northern Communities	Non-Aboriginal	Off-reserve	On-reserve	Northern Communities
Less than a high school diploma	40,846	37,696	26,645	43,177	24,994	25,113	24,004	25,070
High school diploma	45,390	44,062	30,567	56,177	33,087	32,641	32,397	32,695
Trade/voc. cert. or apprenticeship	49,742	47,125	30,842	57,024	31,119	30,061	31,921	30,151
PS cert. below a bachelor's degree	53,856	50,288	33,565	57,877	40,157	37,075	39,257	36,305
University degree	66,963	62,010	36,585	--	55,084	52,618	45,599	--
Absolute returns								
High school versus no high school	4,544	6,367	3,922	13,000	8,092	7,527	8,394	7,625
Trade/voc./appr. versus high school	4,352	3,063	275	847	-1,968	-2,580	-476	-2,544
PS cert. below a bachelor's degree versus high school	8,466	6,226	2,998	1,700	7,071	4,434	6,860	3,610
University degree versus high school	21,573	17,947	6,019	--	21,997	19,977	13,202	--
Relative returns								
High school versus no high school	0.111	0.169	0.147	0.301	0.324	0.300	0.350	0.304
Trade/voc./appr. versus high school	0.096	0.070	0.009	0.015	-0.059	-0.079	-0.015	-0.078
PS cert. below a bachelor's degree versus high school	0.187	0.141	0.098	0.030	0.214	0.136	0.212	0.110
University degree versus high school	0.475	0.407	0.197	--	0.665	0.612	0.407	--

Notes: Predicted values are derived from regression results that are available upon request. -- = suppressed since cell size is below 30; voc. = vocational; cert. = certificate; appr. = apprenticeship. The sample includes 25 to 54 year olds who were employed full-year, full-time with positive wages and salaries and no net self-employment income from farm and non-farm sources in 2005. A 2 percent random sample of non-Aboriginal people was taken.

Source: Census, 2006.

to completing a university degree versus a high school diploma, which is lower among on-reserve Aboriginal people.

Summary

This study examines a straightforward question: "Are returns to schooling higher for Aboriginal or non-Aboriginal people?" The issue is important, since we know that Aboriginal people are far more likely to drop out of high school and less likely to pursue university credentials than non-Aboriginal people. However, little is known about the reasons behind the education gap. One possible reason is that Aboriginal people may face lower economic returns to higher schooling than non-Aboriginal people.

Using the 2006 Census, I find no systematic evidence that Aboriginal people benefit less from additional schooling than non-Aboriginal people in terms of labour market outcomes. In fact, Aboriginal people benefit more economically from schooling in some respects. The results hold whether Aboriginal people live off-reserve, on-reserve, or in northern communities.

Higher levels of schooling are generally associated with larger declines in the probability of unemployment for Aboriginal people. In terms of wages and salaries, both groups have more or less similar returns to schooling. Moreover, among bachelor's degree graduates working full-year, full-time, Aboriginal and non-Aboriginal people who have chosen similar disciplines earn about the same. However, unemployment rates are higher among Aboriginal than non-Aboriginal people, even when their degrees are in the same disciplines. Furthermore, the two groups do not generally choose the same disciplines. Aboriginal people are more likely to choose disciplines such as education, arts, social sciences, and humanities, while non-Aboriginal people are more likely to choose disciplines such as engineering, mathematics, computer science, and physical sciences. These trends are true for men and women, but they are especially true for men. It is generally the case that engineering, mathematics, computer science, and physical sciences lead to higher-paying jobs and are less strongly associated with jobs requiring less education.

Using data on standardized test score results while in high school, I find no evidence that Aboriginal people who eventually choose to pursue further education following high school are a more selective group than their non-Aboriginal counterparts. This suggests that the results in this study are not likely to be explained by self-selection. Furthermore, there is little evidence that perceptions of the returns to schooling are any different for Aboriginal youth than for non-Aboriginal youth.

Since the findings suggest that the labour market returns to schooling are no less for Aboriginal people than for non-Aboriginal people, it is likely that other factors contribute towards the gap in educational attainment that exists between the two groups. A companion paper in this volume (Frenette 2010) investigates this issue in more detail.

Notes

The author gratefully acknowledges helpful comments by Jane Badets, Torben Drewes, Ross Finnie, Rochelle Garner, René Morissette, Richard Mueller, Daniel Parent, Garnett Picot, Arthur Sweetman, and Nancy Zukewich, as well as participants in one of the Measurement of the Effectiveness of Student Aid (MESA) sessions at the Canadian Economics Association meetings in Vancouver (June 2008) and in Montreal (October 2008), and in the Business and Labour Market Analysis Division Seminar Series. All remaining errors are the responsibility of the author.

1. An alternative would have been to use responses to the ethnic origin question. However, responses to this question are not conveniently grouped into the three major Aboriginal peoples.
2. Respondents could give two answers. To simplify the analysis, I dropped these cases throughout the study, which accounted for less than 1 percent of the sample.
3. This term is synonymous with First Nations.
4. The unemployment equations are also estimated with logit and probit models but are not shown in the study since the results are very similar to ordinary least squares.
5. Note that job characteristics such as industry, occupation, and job tenure are excluded from the wages and salaries models. As such, these returns to schooling should be interpreted as unconditional returns (i.e., not conditional on job characteristics).
6. Wannell and Caron (1994) are an exception. They examine a sample of university and college graduates from the class of 1990 two years later (in 1992), and report "representation rates" of Aboriginal people in various fields of study, as well as unemployment rates and earnings of Aboriginal people in those fields. However, the labour market outcomes are not available for many fields due to small sample sizes.
7. Unfortunately, there is no way to impose the same labour force attachment criteria as with the Census. One option would be to consider the International Adult Literacy Survey (IALSS), but for the most part the assessment in this case is administered *after* respondents have completed their schooling. Since schooling can impact performance on standardized tests (e.g., Frenette 2008), it is preferable to examine scores prior to reaching the age of compulsory schooling, which is largely the case in YITS. (Most youth are 15 years old when they are assessed by PISA.)

References

Bougie, E. 2008. "Literacy Profile of Off-Reserve First Nations and Métis People Living in Urban Manitoba and Saskatchewan: Results from the International Adult Literacy and Skills Survey 2003." Catalogue no. 81-004-XIE. Ottawa: Statistics Canada.

Christofides, L.N., M. Hoy, and L. Yang. 2006. The Gender Imbalance in Participation in Canadian Universities (1977-2003). University of Guelph, Department of Economics Working Paper 2006-10. Guelph, ON: University of Guelph.

Costa, R., and A. Siggner. 2005. "Aboriginal Conditions in Census Metropolitan Areas, 1981-2001: Trends and Conditions in Census Metropolitan Areas." Catalogue no. 89-613-MWE2005008. Ottawa: Statistics Canada.

Finnie, R., and M. Frenette. 2003. "Earnings Differences by Major Field of Study: Evidence from Three Cohorts of Recent Canadian Graduates." *Economics of Education Review* 22 (2): 179-92.

Frenette, M. 2004. "The Overqualified Canadian Graduate: The Role of the Academic Program in the Incidence, Persistence, and Economic Returns to Overqualification." *Economics of Education Review* 23 (1): 29-45.

Frenette, M. 2008. "The Returns to Schooling on Academic Performance: Evidence from Large Samples around School Entry Cut-Off Dates." Catalogue no. 11F0019MIE2008317. Ottawa: Statistics Canada.

Frenette, M. 2010. "What Explains the Educational Attainment Gap between Aboriginal and Non-Aboriginal Youth?" In *Pursuing Higher Education in Canada: Economic, Social, and Policy Dimensions*, ed. R. Finnie, M. Frenette, R.E. Mueller, and A. Sweetman, 175-190. Montreal and Kingston: Queen's Policy Studies Series, McGill-Queen's University Press.

Frenette, M., and K. Zeman. 2008. "Understanding the Gender Gap in University Attendance: Evidence Based on Academic Performance, Study Habits, and Parental Influences." In *Who Goes? Who Stays? What Matters? Accessing and Persisting in Post-Secondary Education in Canada*, ed. R. Finnie, R.E. Mueller, A. Sweetman, and A. Usher, 135-52. Montreal and Kingston: Queen's Policy Studies Series, McGill-Queen's University Press.

George, P., and P. Kuhn. 1994. "The Size and Structure of Native-White Wage Differentials in Canada." *Canadian Journal of Economics* 27 (1): 20-42.

Kuhn, P., and A. Sweetman. 2002. "Aboriginals as Unwilling Immigrants: Contact, Assimilation and Labour Market Outcomes." *Journal of Population Economics* 15 (2): 331-55.

O'Donnell, V., and A. Ballardin. 2006. "Aboriginal Peoples Survey 2001 – Provincial and Territorial Reports: Off-Reserve Aboriginal Population." Catalogue no. 89-618-XIE. Ottawa: Statistics Canada.

Tait, H. 1999. "Educational Achievement of Young Aboriginal Adults." Catalogue no. 11-008-X19980044418. Ottawa: Statistics Canada.

Walters, D., J. White, and P. Maxim. 2004. "Does Postsecondary Education Benefit Aboriginal Canadians? An Examination of Earnings and Employment Outcomes for Recent Aboriginal Graduates." *Canadian Public Policy* 30 (3): 283-301.

Wannell, T., and N. Caron. 1994. "A Look at Employment-Equity Groups among Recent Postsecondary Graduates: Visible Minorities, Aboriginal Peoples and the Activity Limited." Catalogue no. 11F0019MPE68. Ottawa: Statistics Canada.

APPENDIX

TABLE A1
Predicted Unemployment Rates by Highest Level of Education

	Men				Women			
		Off-reserve Aboriginal				Off-reserve Aboriginal		
	Non-Aboriginal	North American Indian	Métis	Inuit	Non-Aboriginal	North American Indian	Métis	Inuit
Less than a high school diploma	0.083	0.173	0.131	0.278	0.093	0.192	0.144	0.215
High school diploma	0.057	0.103	0.072	0.144	0.062	0.119	0.085	0.113
Trade/voc. cert. or apprenticeship	0.051	0.118	0.085	0.254	0.070	0.137	0.081	0.145
College cert.	0.043	0.095	0.061	0.180	0.039	0.109	0.065	0.103
Univ. cert. below a bachelor's degree	0.044	0.097	0.052	0.144	0.037	0.112	0.066	0.096
Bachelor's degree	0.040	0.079	0.048	0.024	0.039	0.069	0.045	0.043
Graduate or professional degree	0.040	0.062	0.028	--	0.046	0.078	0.028	0.073
Absolute returns								
High school versus no high school	-0.026	-0.070	-0.059	-0.134	-0.031	-0.073	-0.059	-0.101
Trade/voc./appr. versus high school	-0.007	0.015	0.013	0.110	0.008	0.018	-0.004	0.031
College versus high school	-0.014	-0.008	-0.011	0.036	-0.023	-0.011	-0.021	-0.010
Univ. cert. below bachelor's versus high school	-0.014	-0.006	-0.020	0.001	-0.025	-0.007	-0.019	-0.017
Bachelor's degree versus high school	-0.017	-0.024	-0.024	-0.120	-0.023	-0.050	-0.040	-0.070
Grad./prof. degree versus bachelor's degree	0.000	-0.017	-0.019	--	0.007	0.009	-0.017	0.030
Relative returns								
High school versus no high school	-0.310	-0.404	-0.450	-0.482	-0.330	-0.378	-0.409	-0.472
Trade/voc./appr. versus high school	-0.114	0.144	0.183	0.767	0.122	0.151	-0.047	0.275
College versus high school	-0.247	-0.077	-0.154	0.249	-0.375	-0.090	-0.241	-0.090
Univ. cert. below bachelor's versus high school	-0.240	-0.056	-0.280	0.004	-0.399	-0.062	-0.225	-0.149
Bachelor's degree versus high school	-0.305	-0.237	-0.335	-0.836	-0.368	-0.423	-0.475	-0.619
Grad./prof. degree versus bachelor's degree	0.004	-0.211	-0.405	--	0.170	0.131	-0.377	0.697

Notes: Predicted values are derived from regression results that are available upon request. -- = suppressed since cell size is below 30; Aborig. = Aboriginal; N. Amer. Ind. = North American Indian; voc. = vocational; cert. = certificate; univ. = university; appr. = apprenticeship; grad. = graduate; prof. = professional. The sample includes 25 to 54 year olds who were in the labour force during the Census reference week. A 2 percent random sample of non-Aboriginal people was taken.

Source: Census, 2006.

TABLE A2
Predicted Median Wages and Salaries by Highest Level of Education

	Men		Women	
	Non-Aboriginal	*Off-reserve Aboriginal*	*Non-Aboriginal*	*Off-reserve Aboriginal*
Less than a high school diploma	38,374	37,700	24,004	25,070
High school diploma	45,543	44,094	32,397	32,695
Trade/voc. cert. or apprenticeship	48,320	47,069	31,921	30,151
College cert.	54,337	49,934	39,257	36,305
Univ. cert. below a bachelor's degree	57,215	51,848	45,599	42,770
Bachelor's degree	64,458	60,630	53,359	51,716
Graduate or professional degree	72,165	66,867	60,542	56,714
Absolute returns				
High school versus no high school	7,169	6,394	8,394	7,625
Trade/voc./appr. versus high school	2,777	2,976	-476	-2,544
College versus high school	8,795	5,841	6,860	3,610
Univ. cert. below bachelor's versus high school	11,672	7,754	13,202	10,075
Bachelor's degree versus high school	18,915	16,537	20,962	19,022
Grad./prof. degree versus bachelor's degree	7,707	6,237	7,182	4,997
Relative returns				
High school versus no high school	0.187	0.170	0.350	0.304
Trade/voc./appr. versus high school	0.061	0.067	-0.015	-0.078
College versus high school	0.193	0.132	0.212	0.110
Univ. cert. below bachelor's versus high school	0.256	0.176	0.407	0.308
Bachelor's degree versus high school	0.415	0.375	0.647	0.582
Grad./prof. degree versus bachelor's degree	0.120	0.103	0.135	0.097

Notes: Predicted values are derived from regression results that are available upon request. -- = suppressed since cell size is below 30; Aborig. = Aboriginal; N. Amer. Ind. = North American Indian; voc. = vocational; cert. = certificate; univ. = university; appr. = apprenticeship; grad. = graduate; prof. = professional. The sample includes 25 to 54 year olds who were employed full-year, full-time with positive wages and salaries and no net self-employment income from farm and non-farm sources in 2005. A 2 percent random sample of non-Aboriginal people was taken.

Source: Census, 2006.

8

What Explains the Educational Attainment Gap between Aboriginal and Non-Aboriginal Youth?

MARC FRENETTE

Dans cet article, j'analyse l'écart entre le degré de scolarisation des jeunes Autochtones et celui des autres jeunes Canadiens. Pour ce faire, j'utilise les données recueillies auprès de la cohorte A de l'Enquête auprès des jeunes en transition (EJET) ; il est noter que ce sondage ne concernait pas les Autochtones vivant dans des réserves ou dans le Nord, et que l'analyse ne tient donc pas compte de ce groupe. Les résultats suggèrent que la plus grande partie (90 %) de l'écart de que l'on observe, chez les diplômés du secondaire, dans le fait de poursuivre ou non des études universitaires dépend de différences liées à certaines caractéristiques données. Le facteur le plus important a trait aux résultats scolaires (et en particulier aux notes obtenues, par opposition aux résultats des tests standardisés). Les différences dans le revenu parental n'expliquent, de façon directe, qu'une très petite partie de l'écart dans la fréquentation de l'université ; mais l'environnement familial (qui peut être influencé par le revenu parental) joue pour sa part un rôle non négligeable dans l'écart observé. Le revenu parental pourrait également influencer les résultats scolaires, mais je n'aborde pas cette question ici. Dans une moindre proportion, l'écart que l'on observe dans le fait de terminer ou non des études secondaires peut aussi s'expliquer par les mêmes différences liées aux caractéristiques mentionnées.

This study examines the gap in educational attainment between Aboriginal and non-Aboriginal youth using the Youth in Transition Survey (YITS), Cohort A. Aboriginal people living on-reserve or in the North are excluded from the survey and thus from the analysis. The results suggest that most (90 percent) of the university attendance gap among high school graduates is associated with differences in characteristics. The biggest factor is academic performance (especially differences in performance on scholastic as opposed to standardized tests). Differences in parental income account for very little of the university attendance gap in a direct way, although the home environment (which may be influenced by the level of parental income) accounts for a non-negligible portion of the

Pursuing Higher Education in Canada: Economic, Social, and Policy Dimensions, ed. R. Finnie, M. Frenette, R.E. Mueller, and A. Sweetman. Montreal and Kingston: Queen's Policy Studies Series, McGill-Queen's University Press.

gap. Parental income may also influence academic performance, although this study does not investigate this possibility. A smaller proportion of the gap in high school completion can be accounted for by differences in characteristics.

Introduction

Education is recognized as a key component of labour market success and thus economic well-being (e.g., Card 1999). It is also well documented that Aboriginal individuals lag behind non-Aboriginals in terms of educational attainment (e.g., O'Donnell and Ballardin 2006). However, less is known about the reasons behind this gap. A companion study in this book (Frenette 2010) demonstrates that the rates of return to schooling are as high (or even higher) for Aboriginal people compared to non-Aboriginal people. Thus, it is unlikely that differential rates of returns explain why the educational attainment of Aboriginal people lags behind that of others.

This study follows earlier work in the Canadian literature focusing on Aboriginal labour market outcomes, including George and Kuhn (1994), Kuhn and Sweetman (2002), and Walters, White, and Maxim (2004). It seeks to explore further the possible reasons behind the education gap by examining the role of socio-economic and academic factors. The study uses the Youth in Transition Survey (YITS), Cohort A, matched with standardized test scores from the Programme for International Student Assessment (PISA). The YITS survey contains detailed background information on youth, high school experience, and most importantly, academic performance measures not usually available in other data sources. Most general population surveys contain very small sample sizes of Aboriginal people, thus impeding meaningful analysis. Fortunately, the YITS is somewhat larger than most surveys and contains several hundred Aboriginal youth. Aboriginal people living on-reserve or in the North are excluded from the survey and thus from the analysis.

The results suggest that most (90 percent) of the university attendance gap between Aboriginal and non-Aboriginal high school graduates can be accounted for by differences in characteristics. Of these, the lower academic performance of Aboriginal youth accounts for almost half of the gap. Interestingly, performance on scholastic tests accounts for a much larger portion of the gap than performance on standardized tests. Differences in parental income account for very little of the university attendance gap in a direct way, although the home environment (which may be influenced by the level of parental income) does account for a non-negligible portion. Furthermore, parental income may also influence academic performance, so that some of its impact on educational attainment may be crystallized in academic performance (e.g., Finnie, Lascelles, and Sweetman 2005). Of course, lower high school completion rates among Aboriginal youth further limit options regarding university attendance. What is behind the lower high school completion rates of Aboriginal youth? The findings suggest that differences in characteristics account for just over one-half (53 percent) of the high school completion gap. Once again, academic performance is a major contributor. Clearly, however, more work is needed to better understand differences in high school completion.

The study proceeds as follows. The next section describes the methodology, including the statistical techniques and data used in the study. The results are presented in the following section, and the study is summarized in the final section.

Methodology

The data are drawn from the Youth in Transition Survey (YITS), Cohort A. This survey was developed in conjunction with the Programme for International Student Assessment (PISA), a project of the Organisation for Economic Co-operation and Development (OECD) that consisted of standardized tests in reading, mathematics, and science. All students wrote the reading test, while half also wrote the mathematics test, and the other half also wrote the science test. The target population consisted of students enrolled in an educational institution on 31 December 1999 who were 15 years old on that day (i.e., born in 1984). The assessment took place in April or May 2000. Furthermore, background questionnaires were administered to students through PISA and the YITS. Parents and schools were also administered questionnaires through the YITS. Students were followed up every two years. To date, we have information up to and including Cycle 4 (youth who were 21 years old as of 31 December 2005). Students who were deemed mentally or physically unable to perform in the PISA assessment and non-English or French speakers with less than one year of instruction in the language of assessment were excluded. Also excluded were students living in the territories or on Indian reserves. Thus, the current study excludes Aboriginal youth who live on-reserve or in the North.[1]

Two educational outcomes are examined in this study: high school completion and university attendance among high school graduates. Both outcomes are measured as of Cycle 4 (when youth were 21 years old). In most general population surveys, the sample of Aboriginal people is too small for meaningful analysis. Although the sample of Aboriginal youth in YITS is not large by any means, it is large enough to produce reliable estimates at the national level for all Aboriginal groups combined (i.e., I can not separate North American Indian, Métis, and Inuit groups in the analysis since these estimates would be unreliable from a statistical point of view) and for young men and women combined. In the analysis of high school completion, there are 428 Aboriginal youth. Among these, 378 had a high school diploma, and these youth are used in the analysis of post-secondary and university attendance.[2] Aboriginal youth are identified by asking parents, "Is this person Aboriginal, that is, North American Indian, Métis, or Inuit?"

In Figure 1, the raw high school and post-secondary/university participation rates are shown. While 93.7 percent of non-Aboriginal youth have completed high school by age 21, only 82.7 percent of Aboriginal youth have done so. The gap is even larger in terms of post-secondary attendance: 80.5 percent of non-Aboriginal youth have attended some form of post-secondary institution compared to only 63.1 percent of Aboriginal youth. Interestingly, the university attendance gap is almost exactly the same in absolute terms: 46.8 percent versus 29.8 percent. To be more precise, the percentage point gap in post-secondary attendance is 17.4 percent, while for university attendance it is 17.0 percent. This implies that the post-secondary attendance gap is fully accounted for by differences in university attendance. In other words, Aboriginal and non-Aboriginal youth are about as likely to attend non-university forms of schooling. This point is also noted in Frenette (2010). As a result the remainder of this study focuses exclusively on high school completion and university attendance.[3]

Many factors may explain the large educational divide between Aboriginal and non-Aboriginal people. Figure 2 shows the differences in the proportion of youth having select characteristics for non-Aboriginal and Aboriginal youth. The sample here includes all individuals, with or without a high school diploma. The actual numbers of the full list of characteristics used in this study is available in the appendix (Table A1). Many of the differences shown in Figure 2 are substantial. For example, Aboriginal youth are twice as likely to grow up in a lone-parent family; are almost twice as likely to have a mother who does not have a high school diploma; are far more likely to have parental income in the bottom quartile of the distribution; are about twice as likely to grow up in

FIGURE 1
Proportion Having Achieved Various Educational Outcomes by Age 21

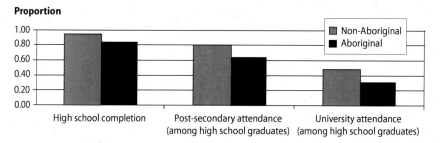

Source: Youth in Transition Survey (YITS), Cohort A.

FIGURE 2
Proportion Having Select Characteristics

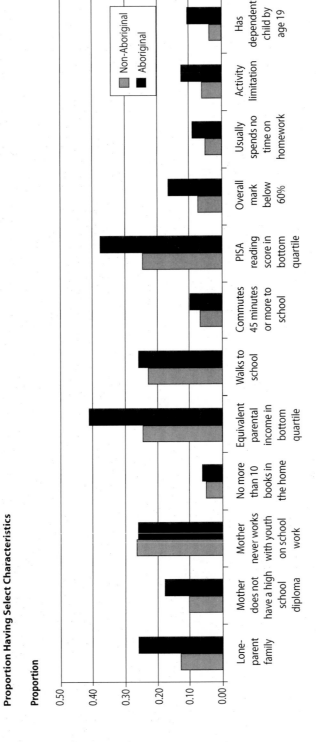

Source: Youth in Transition Survey (YITS), Cohort A.

a home that is more than 80 kilometres from a university; are more than twice as likely to report some form of activity limitation; and are three times as likely to have a dependent child by age 19.

Many of the characteristics described in Figure 2 (and those appearing in Table A1) are strong correlates of educational attainment. To show this, I regress both educational outcomes on the various socio-economic characteristics and present the results in Table A2 in the appendix. Without describing the results in too much detail, it is worth noting that the Aboriginal indicator variable is not statistically significant in the university attendance model. In other words, there is no significant difference in Aboriginal and non-Aboriginal rates of university attendance once differences in characteristics are taken into account. The Aboriginal coefficient is only significant at 10 percent in the high school completion model. Moreover, the point estimate, which is our best estimate, given the data that we have, is still quite a bit lower than zero. In the university attendance model the Aboriginal coefficient is nowhere near being significant, and in any event it is very close to zero.

The main focus of the paper, however, is to try to account for the large differences in educational outcomes. To do so, I turn to a simple decomposition exercise where the gap in the mean educational outcome in question can be expressed as the sum of an "explained" and an "unexplained" component. The explained component is simply the sum of the differences in mean socio-economic characteristics (shown in Table A1), each weighted by "importance" in terms of determining the outcome in question. The weights used are actually the regression coefficients appearing in Table A1. Of course, the results should not necessarily be interpreted in a causal manner. The term "explained" should be interpreted in an accounting sense only. See Frenette (2008) for a more detailed description of this approach.[4]

Results

In this section, I take a significant step toward understanding the gap in educational outcomes between Aboriginal and non-Aboriginal youth. Two outcomes are examined: raw high school completion rates and university attendance rates among high school graduates. The magnitudes of these gaps were shown in Figure 1 in the previous section. In Table 1, I show the decomposition results, including the contribution of specific groupings of factors. The results are more succinctly presented in Figures 3 and 4. In each figure the characteristics are grouped into seven categories, which are somewhat more aggregated than in Table 1: home environment (age of mother of birth, parental presence, maternal education and involvement, and books in the home), parental income, geography (distance to university, commuting mode and time to high school, and residential mobility), academic performance (the PISA reading score and school marks), academic effort (time spent on homework), personal characteristics (activity limitation, sibling order, number of siblings, sex, and the presence of a dependent child at age 19), and an unexplained component. The discussion below focuses on the figures but occasionally refers to some more detailed results from Table 1.

TABLE 1

Decomposition Results of the Educational Attainment Gap between Aboriginal and Non-Aboriginal Youth

Variable groupings	Variable groupings used in Figures 3 and 4	High School Completion (% of total gap)	University Attendance (% of total gap)
Age of mother at birth	Home environment	-0.9	6.2
Parental presence		6.1	3.8
Maternal education		5.1	9.2
Maternal involvement		0.1	0.7
Books		-0.6	0.4
Parental income	Parental income	3.6	3.7
Province	Geography	-4.9	-9.8
Distance to university		--	5.8
Commuting mode to HS		0.6	--
Commuting time to HS		-0.1	--
Residential mobility		4.6	--
Reading score	Academic performance	7.5	12.0
Overall mark		17.9	32.7
Homework time	Academic effort	5.3	13.2
Activity limitation	Person characteristics	0.5	5.5
Sibling order		0.3	-0.7
Number of siblings (including self)		0.0	0.3
Female		-0.2	-0.1
Dependent child at age 19		8.1	6.5
Total explained portion		53.0	89.5
Unexplained portion		47.0	10.5
Total gap		**100.0**	**100.0**

Notes: -- = not applicable. The samples consists of all respondents in Cycles 1 and 4 (high school completion sample) and all respondents in CCycles 1 and 4 who completed high school (university attendance sample). Unless otherwise stated, all variables refer to Cycle 1.

Source: Youth in Transition Survey (YITS) Cohort A.

We now turn to the gap in the high school completion rate (Figure 3). Overall, 53 percent of the high school completion gap can be accounted for by differences in characteristics. The key component here is academic performance, accounting for 25.4 percent of the gap (7.5 percent + 17.9 percent). The other characteristics individually account for smaller portions of the overall gap.

FIGURE 3
Decomposition of Gap in High School Completion Rates between Aboriginal and Non-Aboriginal Youth

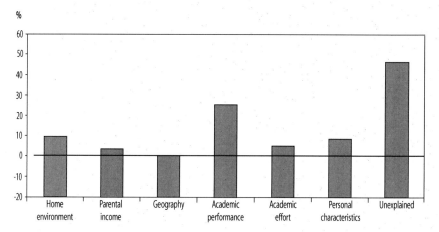

Source: Table 1.

FIGURE 4
Decomposition of Gap in University Attendance Rates between Aboriginal and Non-Aboriginal Youth

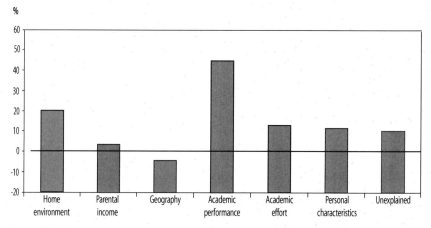

Source: Table 1.

The educational outcome that has attracted the most attention among both researchers and policy analysts is without a doubt university attendance (or completion, when available). One possible reason relates to the high level of economic returns associated with a university degree (Frenette 2010). In Figure 4, I show the decomposition results for the overall gap in university attendance among high school graduates. Overall, 90 percent of this gap can be accounted for by differences in characteristics. Almost half of the gap (44.7 percent) is related to differences in academic performance (12 percent + 32.7 percent). The fact that the overall mark in high school accounts for a much larger portion of the gap than the PISA reading scores is interesting, especially in light of the fact that the opposite was true when I examined the university attendance gap among higher and lower income students (Frenette 2008). There appear to be important implications for the poorer performance of Aboriginal youth on scholastic (as opposed to standardized) tests. To better understand this poorer performance of Aboriginal youth, more detailed information on school level factors is required. For example, detailed information on teacher characteristics (i.e., ethnicity), teaching strategies, and curriculum would be required to understand the relationship between specific school factors and scholastic outcomes of Aboriginal youth. John Richards, who holds the Roger Phillips Chair in Social Policy at the C.D. Howe Institute, notes in the *National Post* of 30 January 2008 that several school level factors may benefit Aboriginal youth in particular; these include incorporating Aboriginal cultural content into the curriculum, engaging Aboriginal parents and local Aboriginal leaders in school affairs, and encouraging teachers to engage Aboriginal students. Richards points to higher results among Aboriginal youth on standardized tests in British Columbia schools that actively pursue such strategies.

Summary

Despite the importance of educational attainment in determining labour market outcomes, we know very little about the reasons behind the gap in educational attainment between Aboriginal and non-Aboriginal youth. Until recently, no data set contained detailed information on a sufficient sample of Aboriginal youth in the process of making decisions regarding their education. The present study fills this gap with data from the Youth in Transition Survey (YITS), Cohort A.

The results suggest that most (90 percent) of the university attendance gap between Aboriginal and non-Aboriginal high school graduates can be accounted for by differences in characteristics. Of these, the lower academic performance of Aboriginal youth accounts for almost one-half of the gap. Interestingly, performance on scholastic tests accounts for a much larger portion of the gap than performance on standardized tests.

Differences in parental income account for very little of the university attendance gap in a direct way, although the home environment (which may be influenced by the level of parental income) does account for a non-negligible portion of the gap. Furthermore, parental income may also influence academic performance, although the current study does not investigate this possibility. Of course, lower high school completion rates among Aboriginal youth further limit options regarding university attendance. What is behind these lower high school completion rates? The findings suggest that differences in characteristics account for just over one-half (53 percent) of the high school completion gap. Once again, academic performance is a major contributor. Future work could look at additional topics related to Aboriginal educational outcomes, namely, high school marks, completing a university degree once begun, and the field of study choice in university.

Notes

The author gratefully acknowledges helpful comments by Jane Badets, Torben Drewes, Ross Finnie, Rochelle Garner, René Morissette, Richard Mueller, Daniel Parent, Garnett Picot, Arthur Sweetman, and Nancy Zukewich, as well as participants in one of the Measurement of the Effectiveness of Student Aid (MESA) sessions at the Canadian Economics Association meetings in Vancouver (June 2008) and in Montreal (October 2008), and in the Business and Labour Market Analysis Division Seminar Series. All remaining errors are the responsibility of the author.

1. The survey design consisted of a two-stage approach. In the first stage a stratified sample of schools was selected to ensure adequate coverage in all 10 Canadian provinces (including adequate coverage of minority school systems in certain provinces). The stratification was based on the enrolment of 15 year olds in the school in the previous academic year. In the second stage a simple random sample of 15 year old students within each school was selected. Given this complex survey design (the clustered sampling within schools as well as the stratified sample of schools in the first stage), variance measures based on the assumption of a simple random sample are incorrect. To address this issue, I estimate variance measures using a Taylor linear approximation. Although much less computationally intensive than the bootstrap approach, the Taylor linear approximation generally yields variances that are slightly higher than the true variances. In other words, significance may be slightly understated in this study. On the other hand, if results are found to be statistically significant, they are almost certainly statistically significant in actual fact.
2. It is tempting to compute a high school completion rate for Aboriginal youth by dividing 378 by 428. However, these are not weighted to match population counts. Because of sample stratification, the relative sizes of the weighted counts in the population are slightly different.
3. Aboriginal people often return to school later in life (Vaillancourt 2005), so that follow-up data would be very useful.

4. Note that the regression coefficients I use are from a pooled model of Aboriginal and non-Aboriginal youth. I also tried regression coefficients from separate models, but these yielded broadly similar conclusions.

References

Card, D. 1999. "The Causal Effect of Education on Earnings." In *Handbook of Labor Economics*, vol. 3, ed. O. Ashenfelter and D. Card. Amsterdam.

Finnie, R., E. Lascelles, and A. Sweetman. 2005. "Who Goes? The Direct and Indirect Effect of Family Background on Access to Post-Secondary Education." In *Higher Education in Canada*, ed. C.M. Beach, R.W. Boadway, and R.M. McInnis. Montreal and Kingston: McGill-Queen's University Press.

Frenette, M. 2008. "Why Are Lower-Income Youth Less Likely to Attend University? Evidence from Academic Abilities, Parental Influences, and Financial Constraints." In *Who Goes? Who Stays? What Matters? Accessing and Persisting in Post-Secondary Education in Canada*, ed. R. Finnie, R.E. Mueller, A. Sweetman, and A. Usher, 279-97. Montreal and Kingston: Queen's Policy Studies Series, McGill-Queen's University Press.

Frenette, M. 2010. "Are Economic Returns to Schooling Different for Aboriginal and Non-Aboriginal People?" In *Pursuing Higher Education in Canada: Economic, Social, and Policy Dimensions*, ed. R. Finnie, M. Frenette, R.E. Mueller, and A. Sweetman, 151-172. Montreal and Kingston: Queen's Policy Studies Series, McGill-Queen's University Press.

George, P., and P. Kuhn. 1994. "The Size and Structure of Native-White Wage Differentials in Canada." *Canadian Journal of Economics* 27 (1): 20-42.

Kuhn, P., and A. Sweetman. 2002. "Aboriginals as Unwilling Immigrants: Contact, Assimilation and Labour Market Outcomes." *Journal of Population Economics* 15 (2): 331-55.

O'Donnell, V., and A. Ballardin. 2006. *Aboriginal Peoples Survey 2001 – Provincial and Territorial Reports: Off-Reserve Aboriginal Population*. Catalogue no. 89-618-XIE. Ottawa: Statistics Canada.

Vaillancourt, C. 2005. *Manitoba Postsecondary Graduates from the Class of 2000: How Did they Fare?* Catalogue no. 81-595-MIE. Ottawa: Statistics Canada.

Walters, D., J. White, and P. Maxim. 2004. "Does Postsecondary Education Benefit Aboriginal Canadians? An Examination of Earnings and Employment Outcomes for Recent Aboriginal Graduates." *Canadian Public Policy* 30 (3): 283-301.

APPENDIX

TABLE A1
Means of Socio-Economic Characteristics

	Sample for High school Completion		Sample for University Attendance	
	Non-Aboriginal	Aboriginal	Non-Aboriginal	Aboriginal
Age of mother at birth	27.450	25.564	27.530	25.804
Lone-parent family	0.130	0.257	0.125	0.229
Two parents, at least one not biological	0.110	0.181	0.102	0.148
Two biological parents	0.760	0.563	0.773	0.623
Mother does not have a high school diploma	0.101	0.177	0.088	0.159
Mother has a high school diploma	0.381	0.416	0.382	0.428
Mother has a non-university post-secondary certificate	0.319	0.287	0.324	0.273
Mother has a university degree	0.198	0.120	0.206	0.140
Mother never works with youth on school work	0.262	0.260	0.259	0.246
Mother works with youth on school work a few times per year	0.236	0.239	0.239	0.235
Mother works with youth on school work about once per month	0.206	0.223	0.209	0.207
Mother works with youth on school work several times per month	0.208	0.183	0.209	0.210
Mother works with youth on school work several times per week	0.087	0.095	0.084	0.103
No books in the home	0.006	0.005	0.004	0.007
1 to 10 books in the home	0.043	0.057	0.041	0.047
11 to 50 books in the home	0.161	0.196	0.156	0.195
51 to 100 books in the home	0.200	0.159	0.200	0.178
101 to 250 books in the home	0.251	0.283	0.253	0.281
251 to 500 books in the home	0.202	0.192	0.207	0.197
More than 500 books in the home	0.136	0.108	0.139	0.096
Equivalent parental income in bottom quartile	0.246	0.408	0.237	0.355
Equivalent parental income in 2nd quartile	0.250	0.268	0.245	0.275
Equivalent parental income in 3rd quartile	0.251	0.201	0.257	0.237
Equivalent parental income in top quartile	0.253	0.123	0.261	0.133
Newfoundland and Labrador	0.021	0.030	0.021	0.032
Prince Edward Island	0.006	0.003	0.006	0.004
Nova Scotia	0.034	0.020	0.034	0.022
New Brunswick	0.026	0.038	0.026	0.044
Quebec	0.235	0.134	0.226	0.106
Ontario	0.377	0.287	0.383	0.300
Manitoba	0.033	0.095	0.033	0.084
Saskatchewan	0.037	0.091	0.038	0.097
Alberta	0.106	0.123	0.105	0.124
British Columbia	0.124	0.180	0.128	0.186
Parental home within 40 km of a university	--	--	0.690	0.534
Parental home between 40 and 80 km from a university	--	--	0.151	0.181
Parental home further than 80 km from a university	--	--	0.159	0.285
Walk to school	0.227	0.257	--	--
Bus to school	0.377	0.419	--	--
Public transit to school	0.122	0.102	--	--
Drive or ride to school	0.249	0.201	--	--

... continued

**TABLE A1
(Continued)**

	Sample for High School Completion		Sample for University Attendance	
	Non-Aboriginal	Aboriginal	Non-Aboriginal	Aboriginal
Bicycle, rollerblade, or skateboard to school	0.022	0.021	--	--
Live in school residence	0.004	0.000	--	--
Commute less than 15 minutes	0.517	0.501	--	--
Commute between 15 and 30 minutes	0.314	0.313	--	--
Commute between 30 and 45 minutes	0.102	0.089	--	--
Commute between 45 and 60 minutes	0.046	0.066	--	--
Commute between 60 and 90 minutes	0.017	0.027	--	--
Commute 90 minutes or more	0.004	0.005	--	--
Number of residential moves	2.009	2.941	--	--
PISA reading score in bottom quartile	0.245	0.373	0.220	0.300
PISA reading score in 2nd quartile	0.252	0.239	0.254	0.259
PISA reading score in 3rd quartile	0.247	0.214	0.257	0.248
PISA reading score in top quartile	0.256	0.174	0.269	0.193
Overall mark below 60%	0.073	0.166	0.058	0.101
Overall mark between 60% and 69%	0.180	0.224	0.165	0.241
Overall mark between 70% and 79%	0.336	0.375	0.343	0.397
Overall mark between 80% and 89%	0.329	0.208	0.347	0.229
Overall mark between 90% and 100%	0.082	0.028	0.088	0.032
Usually spend no time on homework	0.049	0.092	0.043	0.084
Usually spend less than 1 hour per week on homework	0.180	0.280	0.169	0.244
Usually spend 1 to 3 hours per week on homework	0.403	0.405	0.405	0.435
Usually spend 4 to 7 hours per week on homework	0.260	0.187	0.269	0.193
Usually spend 8 to 14 hours per week on homework	0.085	0.027	0.090	0.032
Usually spend 15 or more hours per week on homework	0.023	0.010	0.024	0.012
No activity limitation	0.938	0.876	0.942	0.868
Activity limitation – sometimes	0.050	0.089	0.046	0.089
Activity limitation – often	0.013	0.035	0.012	0.043
Sibling order	1.545	1.499	1.551	1.498
Number of siblings (including self)	2.279	2.253	2.290	2.259
Female	0.507	0.516	0.518	0.520
Dependent child at age 19	0.037	0.106	0.029	0.091
Sample size	13,906	428	13,251	378

Notes: -- = not applicable. The samples consists of all respondents in Cycles 1 and 4 (high school completion sample) and all respondents in Cycles 1 and 4 who completed high school (university attendance sample). Unless otherwise stated, all variables refer to Cycle 1.

Source: Youth in Transition Survey (YITS) Cohort A.

TABLE A2
Regression Results

	High School Completion		University Attendance	
	Coefficient	Standard Error	Coefficient	Standard Error
Aboriginal	-0.052 *	0.028	-0.018	0.034
Age of mother at birth	-0.001	0.001	0.006 ***	0.001
Two parents, at least one not biological	-0.018	0.017	-0.035	0.022
Two biological parents	0.028 **	0.011	0.033 **	0.016
Mother has a high school diploma	0.075 ***	0.014	0.064 ***	0.017
Mother has a non-university post-secondary certificate	0.077 ***	0.015	0.094 ***	0.018
Mother has a university degree	0.075 ***	0.015	0.208 ***	0.020
Mother works with youth on school work a few times per year	0.006	0.008	0.008	0.014
Mother works with youth on school work about once per month	0.002	0.009	-0.016	0.014
Mother works with youth on school work several times per month	0.000	0.009	-0.025 *	0.014
Mother works with youth on school work several times per week	-0.015	0.013	-0.065 ***	0.021
1 to 10 books in the home	0.162 *	0.084	-0.073	0.058
11 to 50 books in the home	0.150 *	0.083	-0.050	0.056
51 to 100 books in the home	0.145 *	0.083	-0.054	0.055
101 to 250 books in the home	0.136	0.083	-0.049	0.056
251 to 500 books in the home	0.134	0.082	-0.030	0.056
More than 500 books in the home	0.135	0.083	-0.035	0.056
Equivalent parental income in 2nd quartile	0.004	0.010	-0.018	0.015
Equivalent parental income in 3rd quartile	0.024 ***	0.009	0.031 **	0.016
Equivalent parental income in top quartile	0.022 **	0.009	0.040 **	0.017
Prince Edward Island	0.000	0.009	0.045 *	0.025
Nova Scotia	-0.029 ***	0.010	0.045 **	0.021
New Brunswick	-0.004	0.009	0.038 *	0.020
Quebec	-0.080 ***	0.010	-0.191 ***	0.019
Ontario	-0.036 ***	0.011	-0.077 ***	0.019
Manitoba	-0.047 ***	0.013	-0.022	0.023
Saskatchewan	-0.028 ***	0.010	-0.040 *	0.022
Alberta	-0.040 ***	0.010	-0.102 ***	0.019
British Columbia	-0.022 **	0.010	-0.121 ***	0.021
Parental home between 40 and 80 km from a university	--	--	-0.081 ***	0.015
Parental home further than 80 km from a university	--	--	-0.059 ***	0.013
Bus to school	-0.011	0.010	--	--
Public transit to school	0.000	0.011	--	--
Drive or ride to school	0.002	0.009	--	--
Bicycle, rollerblade, or skateboard to school	0.015	0.022	--	--
Live in school residence	0.027	0.038	--	--
Commute between 15 and 30 minutes	0.008	0.008	--	--
Commute between 30 and 45 minutes	0.029 ***	0.011	--	--
Commute between 45 and 60 minutes	0.020	0.015	--	--
Commute between 60 and 90 minutes	0.015	0.019	--	--
Commute 90 minutes or more	-0.069	0.062	--	--
Number of residential moves	-0.005 ***	0.002	--	--
PISA reading score in 2nd quartile	0.059 ***	0.011	0.112 ***	0.015
PISA reading score in 3rd quartile	0.068 ***	0.010	0.174 ***	0.016

... continued

TABLE A2
(Continued)

	High School Completion		University Attendance	
	Coefficient	Standard Error	Coefficient	Standard Error
PISA reading score in 4th quartile	0.063 ***	0.010	0.253 ***	0.017
Overall mark between 60% and 69%	0.108 ***	0.022	0.058 ***	0.017
Overall mark between 70% and 79%	0.177 ***	0.021	0.167 ***	0.018
Overall mark between 80% and 89%	0.180 ***	0.021	0.362 ***	0.019
Overall mark between 90% and 100%	0.175 ***	0.021	0.478 ***	0.022
Usually spend less than 1 hour per week on homework	0.017	0.022	0.018	0.023
Usually spend 1 to 3 hours per week on homework	0.043 **	0.021	0.069 ***	0.023
Usually spend 4 to 7 hours per week on homework	0.052 **	0.022	0.132 ***	0.024
Usually spend 8 to 14 hours per week on homework	0.058 ***	0.021	0.235 ***	0.029
Usually spend 15 or more hours per week on homework	0.024	0.027	0.197 ***	0.041
Activity limitation – sometimes	-0.027	0.019	-0.088 ***	0.020
Activity limitation – often	0.024	0.030	-0.184 ***	0.032
Sibling order	0.008 *	0.005	-0.021 **	0.009
Number of siblings (including self)	0.001	0.004	0.017 **	0.007
Female	0.022 ***	0.006	0.073 ***	0.010
Dependent child at age 19	-0.129 ***	0.030	-0.178 ***	0.022
Intercept	0.503 ***	0.091	-0.155 **	0.070
Adjusted R^2	0.164		0.356	
Sample size	14,334		13,629	

Notes: *** = significant at 1%; ** = significant at 5%; * = significant at 1%; -- = not applicable. Ordinary least squares is used throughout. The samples consists of all respondents in Cycles 1 and 4 (high school completion sample) and all respondents in Cycles 1 and 4 who completed high school (post-secondary/university attendance sample). Unless otherwise stated, all explanatory variables refer to Cycle 1.

Source: Youth in Transition Survey (YITS) Cohort A.

9

They Came, They Saw, They Enrolled: Access to Post-Secondary Education by the Children of Canadian Immigrants

Ross Finnie and Richard E. Mueller

Dans cet article, nous examinons le taux de fréquentation d'institutions d'enseignement postsecondaire chez les jeunes Canadiens d'origine immigrante – qu'il soient arrivés au pays avant l'âge de 15 ans ou nés au Canada de parents immigrants. Ces jeunes ont, dans l'ensemble, plus tendance à entreprendre des études postsecondaires – et tout particulièrement de fréquenter l'université – que les jeunes Canadiens de souche. Surtout chez les jeunes d'origine asiatique, mais aussi chez les jeunes d'origine africaine, le taux de fréquentation d'institutions d'enseignement postsecondaire est particulièrement élevé. Parmi les jeunes qui proviennent de pays autres que ceux d'Asie et d'Afrique, le taux, moins élevé, se situe quand même au-dessus de la moyenne de celui de l'ensemble des jeunes immigrants (et est supérieur au taux observé chez les jeunes Canadiens de souche). Il y a toutefois une exception : chez les jeunes qui proviennent d'Amérique latine, le taux est inférieur à celui que l'on observe dans tous les autres groupes. Divers facteurs peuvent expliquer certaines de ces disparités, dont le niveau de scolarité des parents, le revenu parental et les aspirations à un meilleur degré de scolarité que nourrissent les parents immigrants pour leurs enfants. Toutefois, même quand l'on tient compte de ces facteurs, on observe des écarts importants.

In this paper we investigate access to post-secondary education (PSE) among the children of Canadian immigrants, including both children who came to this country by the age of 15 and those who were born in Canada. Both groups are, overall, considerably more likely to attend PSE – especially university – than non-immigrant youth. Asian and African groups (especially Chinese) have particularly high participation rates, while those from other regions have lower but still above average (and above non-immigrant) rates, except for those from the Americas (excluding the United States), who have lower rates than others. Various factors such as parental education, family income, and parental aspirations for their children's PSE attainment explain some of these differences, but important gaps remain even after these factors are taken into account.

Pursuing Higher Education in Canada: Economic, Social, and Policy Dimensions, ed. R. Finnie, M. Frenette, R.E. Mueller, and A. Sweetman. Montreal and Kingston: Queen's Policy Studies Series, McGill-Queen's University Press.

Introduction and Background

Numerous researchers have investigated why new Canadian immigrants have in recent years been faring so poorly in the Canadian labour market compared to both the Canadian-born and past cohorts of immigrants (e.g., Abbott and Beach 1993; Aydemir, Chen, and Corak 2008; Aydemir and Skuterud 2005; Baker and Benjamin 1994; Bloom, Grenier, and Gunderson 1995; Frenette and Morissette 2005; Grant 1999; Li 2001; McDonald and Worswick 1987, 1998; Meng 1987; and Picot 2008). This relatively poor performance has been puzzling to researchers, since these immigrants were admitted to Canada at least in part on the basis of their human capital characteristics (including education credentials) and might thus have been expected to do well. One of the reasons behind their poor outcomes may be due to credential recognition (e.g., Aydemir and Skuterud 2005), and being educated in Canada may help address this issue.

Another line of research has begun to address the outcomes of the children of immigrants, often with a focus on educational attainment, motivated by the expectation that education is likely to be an important determinant of their future economic well-being and social integration (Hansen and Kucera 2004; Bonikowska 2007; Hum and Simpson 2007; Aydemir and Sweetman 2008; and Aydemir, Chen, and Corak 2008). One general finding of this literature is that the children of immigrants have been outperforming non-immigrant Canadians, as well as their immigrant parents, in terms of both education levels and earnings. These Canadian findings stand in contrast to work in Europe, which has found that the children of at least some immigrant groups do not appear to be integrating so successfully into the broader society – either socially or economically (Österberg 2000; Nielsen, Rosholm, Smith, and Husted 2001; and Van Ours and Veenman 2002, 2003).

For these and other reasons, studying the experiences of the children of immigrants is of significance interest. Such research also has the merit of placing immigrant issues generally – and immigrant policy in particular – in a longer-run context, both in terms of concern for the well-being of the immigrants and for their contribution to and integration into the broader society. For example, we might not be quite so concerned about the declining outcomes for recently arrived immigrants if their children are doing well, while the benefits of immigration for Canadians and the Canadian economy might look different in the longer run when their children's outcomes are taken into account.

The educational attainment of the children of immigrants is thus an important area of research. This is as true in Canada as in other countries – perhaps even more so, given that first and second generation Canadians form a sizeable proportion of the Canadian population, about 35 percent of those aged 16-65 years (Aydemir, Chen, and Corak 2009), and given that the country continues to admit the equivalent of approximately 1 percent of its total population in immigration each year.

The contribution of this paper is to address one aspect of this set of issues: access to post-secondary education (PSE) on the part of first generation and second generation Canadian children of immigrants. The former group, for our purposes, includes those who were born outside of Canada and came to the country as immigrants themselves, along with their immigrant parents, arriving by age 15. This group thus completed their secondary school experiences and faced their PSE opportunities in Canada, and comprises what has been called the "1.5 generation" of immigrants (e.g., Aydemir and Sweetman 2008). This separates them from other first generation immigrants who arrived in this country when older, after their schooling was complete (i.e., the "1.0 generation"). Educational attainment and labour market outcomes diverge significantly for these groups, and the Canadian nature of the educational opportunities of the 1.5 generation is clearly key to these differences. The second group (i.e., second generation immigrants) includes those born in Canada to immigrant parents.

We seek to address the following questions: Does access to PSE differ overall for first and second generation children of immigrants as compared to "non-immigrant" (i.e., third generation or higher) Canadians? Do differences exist by region of origin? What are the underlying factors that drive these differences?

We make use of the extraordinarily rich YITS-A dataset, which is comprised of a sample of Canadian students aged 15 in December 1999 followed longitudinally over time. With its expansive set of family and educational background factors, detailed information on post-secondary experiences, and sufficient sample sizes of immigrants (as well as non-immigrants), the YITS-A provides an excellent resource for investigating these questions and allows us to offer a detailed analysis of the comparative PSE experiences of immigrant youth and some of the factors that drive their experiences.

Methodology and Data

The Model and Differentiation of Immigrant Groups

Our analysis is based on a standard empirical model used for analysing access to PSE, in which going to college (including trade school), going to university, or not attending PSE are taken to be functions of different sets of influences. In the specific approach we adopt here, we first include only the immigrant indicators, and then add in family and demographic variables that have commonly been found to affect access (e.g., family income and parental education levels). We then further supplement the models with other variables available in the YITS-A dataset that have been shown in related work to also be important correlates of access to PSE. These include high school grades, PISA (Programme of International Student Assessment) reading scores, high school engagement, parental aspirations regarding their children's education, and other such influences.[1]

This approach allows us first to place in a modelling format the raw differences in PSE access by immigrant group – differences that correspond to what we observe in the simple descriptive data (which we also show). By adding the other background variables, we are able to ascertain to what degree the observed differences by immigrant group are related to the factors included in the models or – conversely – if important unexplained differences remain even after these general determinants of access to PSE (i.e., parental education and so on) are taken into account.

The YITS-A data allow us to sort the individuals in our samples among immigrant groups along two dimensions. First, we can distinguish whether they belong to the (overall) first generation, second generation, or non-immigrant (i.e., third generation or above) groups – each individual fitting into one of these categories. And secondly, among the immigrant groups we can identify the region of origin. Different models are estimated for the two different sets of immigrant identifiers: one set that treats immigrants according to the broader "generational" categories, and another set that differentiates the groups according to region of origin.[2]

The specific countries of origin available in the raw data are combined into nine areas: the "Anglosphere" (all Western English-speaking countries including the UK, the US, Australia and New Zealand), the Americas (excluding the US but including the rest of North, Central, and South America), Africa, China, East and South-East Asia (including India and Pakistan), Other Asia (including Japan and South Korea), Western and Northern Europe, Southern and Eastern Europe, and Others.[3] These groupings were determined by a combination of criteria including geographical proximity, linguistic characteristics, a preliminary analysis of PSE outcomes whereby similar countries were grouped together, and the sample sizes available.

The Data and Samples

The data used in the analysis are taken from the Youth in Transition Survey – Reading or Cohort A (generally known as the YITS-A).[4] The YITS-A is well suited to this application since it follows a representative sample of young people living in Canada at age 15 in 1999 through their high school years and beyond, and includes detailed information on family background, early schooling experiences, participation in PSE, and immigrant status.

When this project was undertaken, four cycles of YITS data were available, corresponding to the initial and follow-up interviews undertaken at two year intervals from 2000 through 2006, at which time respondents were 21, an age at which the great majority of young people have made their PSE decisions.[5] The first cycle in 2000 includes data derived from interviews with not only the respondents but also their parents and high school principals, and also contains the youths' PISA reading scores. Follow-up surveys were carried out with respondents only. The substantial sample size of the YITS-A, approximately 25,000 in the first cycle, provides sufficient numbers of observations to estimate differences in PSE access rates not only by immigrant generation but also by region of origin within these groups.[6]

The PSE Outcomes, the Models, and the Presentation of the Findings

The dependent variables used in our study represent the highest level of PSE in which the individual participated up to the Cycle 4 interview: college (including the relatively small number of individuals in trade school) or university, with university arbitrarily classified as being the higher of the two. Access to these is compared to the baseline outcome of no PSE. Our analysis uses the standard definition of access employed in the literature: whether respondents have at some point been enrolled in (or have "touched") university or college, regardless of whether they completed their studies.

In the analysis that underlies the results presented here, we model college and university attendance jointly. To do so, we employ the multinomial logit approach previously used in Finnie and Mueller (2007, 2008a, 2008b), which treats the particular level of PSE as a jointly determined process along with the decision to go to PSE.[7] We restrict the results presented, however, to the university outcome, primarily because this is where the greatest differences in access rates obtain.[8]

To show the results, we use a series of graphs representing the marginal effects of the indicated immigrant variables (i.e., the indicator variables representing the different immigrant groups) on the probability of attending university, while controlling for the different sets of background and related variables mentioned above. In essence, these graphs show in a simple format the differences in university access rates between the immigrant groups and non-immigrant Canadians – first the raw rates without taking any of the various explanatory variables considered in the analysis into account, and then after the different sets of explanatory variables are added to the model in a stepwise fashion.[9]

Empirical Findings

Descriptive Statistics

The means for the immigrant variables included in the analysis (which represent the distribution of the sample across the different categories) and the PSE access rates for each group are shown in the top part of Table 1.[10] The other variables included in the analysis are shown in the lower part of the table. The distributions and patterns are consistent with what is generally found in the literature, including other work using the YITS-A, but it is the immigrant variables that represent the focus of this analysis.

Both first and second generation immigrants have higher overall PSE participation rates than non-immigrants, their substantially higher university rates driving this difference: 57.0 and 54.3 percent for first and second generation immigrants, respectively, as compared to 37.7 percent for non-immigrant Canadians.

By region of origin, a number of interesting patterns emerge. The overall PSE participation rates of first generation immigrants born in Africa, China, and Other Asia exceed 90 percent, the highest rates in these data. Again, these differences are mostly driven by their higher university attendance rates. China is the most notable of all, with a full 88.3 percent having attended university by age 21, followed by Other Asia at 68.7 percent and Africa at 64.6 percent. The Americas (excluding the US) have the lowest university participation rate (22.8 percent), well below that of the immigrants of any other region. This is also the only group with a participation rate below that of the Canadian-born.

Among second generation immigrants, the results are very similar, although slightly lower university attendance rates are the norm compared to the first generation. The second generation also includes a number of extra sets of results, reflecting mother's origin (regardless of the father's status), father's origin (same), where both parents are from the same region and where both parents are immigrants from different regions. The results are generally quite similar across the different ways of looking at immigration status, as are the results by region – those with one or both parents from China, Africa, or Other Asia have the highest overall participation rates, those from the Americas have the lowest, and the others lie between these upper and lower bounds. The "mother Canadian, father immigrant" group has somewhat higher rates than the converse, while the "both parents immigrant from the same origin" group – taken all together – have rates between these two.

Table 1 also gives the breakdown by region of origin of the immigrant groups: the respondent's own region in the case of first generation immigrants, and the region of origin of the parents in the case of second generation immigrants. The figures here will come as no surprise to students of Canadian immigration. The first generation of immigrants is likely to have been born in Africa, China, or other parts of Asia, whereas the second generation is more likely to have one or both parents from Europe or the Anglosphere. These numbers reflect the general changes in Canadian immigration flows over time.

TABLE 1
Descriptive Statistics

Variable	Mean	No PSE %	Trade or College %	University %
		Participation Rate		
Total		25.0	32.9	42.1
Aggregate Immigrant Indicators				
Non-immigrant	0.716	28.1	34.2	37.7
1st generation	0.081	13.8	29.3	57.0
2nd generation	0.180	16.2	29.5	54.3
Generation unknown	0.024	37.2	33.3	29.5
Detailed immigrant indicators				
1st generation (origin of the student)				
Americas (except USA)	0.010	37.9	39.3	22.8
Africa	0.005	6.7	28.7	64.6
China	0.014	1.4	10.3	88.3
Other East and South-East Asia	0.011	12.6	46.1	41.3
Other Asia	0.018	6.6	24.7	68.7
Western or Northern Europe	0.003	22.9	30.5	46.6
Southern or Eastern Europe	0.012	12.1	35.0	53.0
Anglosphere	0.007	28.5	23.9	47.6
Others/unknown	0.001	13.2	45.1	41.8
2nd Generation				
Origin of the mother				
Mother is Canadian by birth	0.045	14.9	28.5	56.6
Americas (except USA)	0.021	19.4	39.2	41.5
Africa	0.005	2.4	15.8	81.8
China	0.010	5.2	13.6	81.3
Other East and South-East Asia	0.011	11.8	28.7	59.5
Other Asia	0.014	5.5	28.5	66.0
Western or Northern Europe	0.012	16.5	29.3	54.3
Southern or Eastern Europe	0.028	21.9	31.2	46.9
Anglosphere	0.030	22.5	31.2	46.3
Other/unknown/no mom	0.004	19.5	27.0	53.5
Origin of the father				
Father is Canadian by birth	0.031	19.9	29.0	51.2
Americas (except USA)	0.013	18.4	39.4	42.2
Africa 0.006	6.0	15.5	78.5	
China 0.010	5.8	15.0	79.1	
Other East and South-East Asia	0.009	13.9	27.0	59.1
Other Asia	0.014	4.0	28.7	67.3
Western or Northern Europe	0.014	13.4	27.5	59.2
Southern or Eastern Europe	0.032	19.8	30.1	50.1
Anglosphere	0.027	21.8	30.4	47.9
Other/unknown/no dad	0.022	16.1	35.6	48.3
Mixture of the parent(s)' origin				
Mother Canadian, father immigrant	0.045	14.9	28.3	56.9
Father Canadian, mother immigrant	0.031	19.8	29.2	51.0
Both parents imm. but different origin	0.012	23.8	16.8	59.5
Both parents imm. from same origin	0.067	14.1	31.0	54.9
Other/unknown/single parent	0.025	16.2	33.7	50.1
Both parents imm. from same origin				
Americas (except USA)	0.009	19.6	44.7	35.7
Africa	0.003	1.8	15.8	82.4
China	0.008	5.3	13.2	81.5
Other East and South-East Asia	0.008	12.1	30.5	57.4
Other Asia	0.011	4.0	28.3	67.6
Western or Northern Europe	0.002	6.8	36.3	56.9
Southern or Eastern Europe	0.018	23.8	33.0	43.2
Anglosphere	0.007	17.9	40.4	41.7

... *continued*

TABLE 1
(Continued)

Variable	Mean	Participation Rate		
		No PSE %	Trade or College %	University %
Female	0.498	18.8	31.3	49.9
Male	0.502	31.2	34.5	34.3
HS location				
Rural	0.231	32.4	35.4	32.2
Urban	0.769	22.8	32.2	45.0
HS province				
Newfoundland and Labrador	0.020	25.1	30.2	44.7
Prince Edward Island	0.005	22.0	21.3	56.7
Nova Scotia	0.033	22.7	22.6	54.8
New Brunswick	0.027	26.4	24.1	49.6
Quebec	0.226	29.3	40.0	30.7
Ontario	0.375	17.8	36.3	45.9
Manitoba	0.037	32.2	19.9	48.0
Saskatchewan	0.039	32.0	23.6	44.4
Alberta	0.106	33.0	28.0	39.0
British Columbia	0.132	28.2	26.8	45.0
Linguistic minority				
French outside QC	0.028	21.9	34.8	43.3
English in QC	0.020	17.2	40.4	42.4
Family type				
Two parents	0.828	23.7	32.4	43.9
Mother only	0.131	30.8	34.5	34.7
Father only	0.026	30.4	39.9	29.6
Other	0.014	38.4	33.4	28.2
Parent's education				
Less than HS	0.085	51.7	33.0	15.3
Some PSE	0.214	33.9	38.1	28.0
HS completed	0.067	27.5	38.7	33.8
Trade/college	0.311	26.4	37.6	36.0
University - below BA degree	0.047	15.2	31.6	53.2
University - BA	0.183	11.2	26.4	62.5
University - grad	0.093	5.9	14.5	79.6
Other/unknown	0.001	35.4	38.2	26.5
Family income level	1.000			
Extremely low ($0 - 5 000)	0.013	24.8	34.6	40.6
$5 000 to $25 000	0.073	38.0	32.0	30.1
$25 000 to $50 000	0.253	32.6	35.4	32.1
$50 000 to $75 000	0.283	25.7	34.9	39.5
$75 000 to $100 000	0.227	20.0	31.3	48.6
$100 000 and up	0.151	12.4	27.8	59.8
Sample size	16,825	4,211 (25.0)	5,537 (32.9)	7,077 (42.1)

Multivariate Results

Aggregate Immigrant Groups. Figure 1 presents the results obtained with the multinomial logit model using the aggregate immigrant indicators – first generation immigrant or second generation immigrant as compared to the non-immigrant comparison group. The bars essentially represent the differences in access rates for the indicated groups as compared to the non-immigrant group after taking into account the other variables included in the model. The different sets of bars represent the results obtained with the different blocks of regressors included. The first block includes only the immigrant indicators. The second block adds the controls for sex, urban (versus rural) high school location, province of high school attendance, being a member of a provincial linguistic minority (French or English only), and family type.[11] The third block adds parental income, which is captured by a set of categorical variables indicating different income ranges to allow for non-linear effects. The final block adds parental education, again represented by a set of categorical variables (eight in total).

In each case we show the average marginal effects associated with the relevant immigrant indicators, as generated by the appropriate transformations of the regression coefficients obtained with the multinominal logit model employed. We use the word "effects" advisedly, understanding that it represents the relevant correlations or associations found in the data given the models estimated, rather than a necessarily causal relationship as the word might strictly imply.

FIGURE 1
The Baseline Models, First and Second Generation Immigrants (Aggregated)

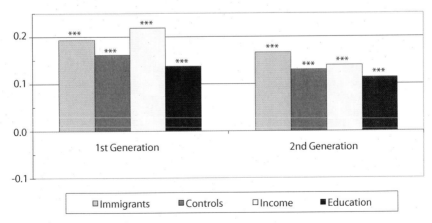

Notes: ***, **, and * denote statistical significance at the 1 percent, 5 percent, and 10 percent levels, respectively. The baseline (comparator) group is non-immigrants and those for whom immigration status is unknown.
Source: Finnie and Mueller, 2009.

The first bar for each group (indicated as "Immigrants" in the figure legend) reflects the overall raw differences previously seen in the descriptive statistics presented above, now seen in a modelling framework. The results thus indicate that first generation Canadians are on average 19.3 percentage points more likely to attend university than non-immigrant Canadians, while those from the second generation show a 16.6 percentage point advantage. Given the mean university participation rate in the sample of 42.1 percent, these are large differences.

The second column adds to the model the set of basic controls representing urban versus rural high school location, province, linguistic minority, and family type. The effects of these variables (not shown here) all appear reasonable, but more interesting to the focus of this paper is that adding them only moderately reduces the marginal effects of the immigrant indicators. After controlling for these factors, first and second generation immigrants remain about 16 and 13 percentage points (respectively) more likely to attend university than non-immigrant Canadians. Stated differently, only about 17 percent of the overall (raw) gap on the part of first generation immigrants and 22 percent of the raw gap for second generation immigrants are explained by these basic control variables (i.e., these are the estimated proportional declines in the immigrant effects between the first and second models). The immigrants' higher rates of living in cities, coming from two parent families, and living in Ontario (all of which are generally associated with higher university access rates for immigrants and non-immigrants alike) account for most of this decline between the two models.

Column 3 adds parental income to the equation. Taking income into account actually raises the first generation immigrant effect by several percentage points. This is an interesting but not surprising result. It is well known that recently arrived immigrants (and hence the parents of the first generation immigrants included in our samples) tend to have lower incomes than the Canadian-born. Since income generally has a positive effect on PSE attendance, taking immigrant families' low incomes into account boosts the "pure" immigrant effect – i.e., they are *especially* more likely to attend, given their low incomes. This effect is weaker for second generation immigrants, because their families have been in the country longer and therefore have relatively higher incomes.

The final column adds the level of education of the highest educated parent to the model. The estimated parental education effects are strong and in fact reduce the income effects substantially (not shown), thus once again reflecting how parental education is the greater of the two influences and that income effects are substantially biased upward if parental education is not included (Finnie and Mueller 2007, 2008a, b). More important here is that including the education variables also reduces the first generation immigrant effect to 13.7 percentage points, and the second generation immigrant effect to 11.4 percentage points. Higher immigrant university participation rates can thus be at least partially ascribed to their parents' relatively high education levels. Still, substantial gaps remain even after taking parental education (as well as the other variables included in the models) into account.

Detailed Immigrant Groups. Next we replace the aggregate first and second generation immigrant indicators with the detailed region of origin indicators for the immigrant children in the case of first generation immigrants (Figure 2), or the region of origin of the parents in the case of second generation immigrants (Figure 3). The different columns of these figures represent the same model progression just seen using the aggregate indicators. In other words, the first column again includes only the immigrant origin variables – capturing the raw, unadjusted differences in PSE participation rates of each of the immigrant groups as compared to the non-immigrant population – and the model is then augmented in a stepwise fashion with the basic demographic controls, the parental income controls, and the parental education controls in columns (bars) 2 through 4, respectively.

Again reflecting the descriptive data seen earlier, the results in the first columns point to large differences in access rates to university by country of origin: immigrants of Chinese and Other Asian origin are considerably more likely to go to university, and in some cases substantially so, regardless of which generation (first or second). So too are second but not first generation Africans and East and South-East Asians. In contrast, the only group with significantly lower university access rates than the

FIGURE 2
Baseline Models, First Generation Immigrants by Region of Origin

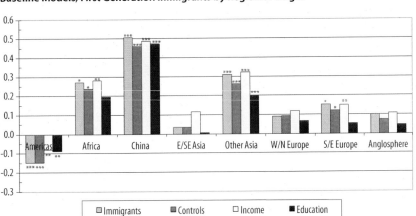

Notes: See notes to Figure 1.

Source: Finnie and Mueller, 2009.

FIGURE 3

Baseline Models, Second Generation Immigrants by Region of Origin

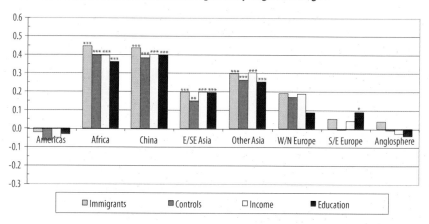

Notes: See notes to Figure 1.

Source: Finnie and Mueller, 2009.

non-immigrant group is the first generation group from the Americas (excluding the US). The other effects are positive but not statistically different from zero.[12]

Working across the models for the first generation groups (Figure 2), the immigrant effects are generally reduced as the other regressors are added, but to different degrees. For China, only a small portion of their significantly higher first generation university participation rate is explained by the different sets of regressors, as the estimated effect falls from 51 percentage points in column 1 to 47 points in column 4. The Other Asia effect, however, falls more, especially in proportional terms, from 31 to 20 percentage points, mainly due to the basic demographic controls and parental education variables (while the income effect again works in the opposite direction). The Southern-Eastern Europe effect goes from a marginally significant 15 percentage points to a non-significant 5 percentage points across the models, the same variables (demographic characteristics, parental education) being responsible. Similarly, the Africa effect goes from a marginally significant 27 to a non-significant 20 percentage point difference.

Among the second generation groups (Figure 3), roughly similar patterns are evident, but with subtle differences. The strongly positive China effect is again reduced by only a small amount as the other regressors are added (from a 44 percentage point difference in university participation rates to 40 percentage points. For the African group the effect is reduced from 45 to 36 percentage points, and for the Other Asia group from 30 to 25 percentage points.

Thus far we can conclude that there are rather large differences in university participation rates between first and second generation immigrant and non-immigrant Canadian youth and that these differences vary a great deal by source region. Further, in some cases a significant amount of the gap is explained by the basic demographic controls included in the models and by parental education levels, while the influence of family income tends to work against first generation immigrants (owing to their generally lower income levels) but not against second generation immigrants (since parent income levels are higher). Finally, despite adding a range of control variables, substantial differences remain, especially for certain groups.

Adding the Grade and Scale Variables: The Role of High School Experiences. We now investigate what happens when the model is augmented to include a variety of other background variables available in the data that could assist in explaining these differences in university attendance rates. These variables are taken (or derived from) the questionnaires administered to the students, their parents, and their high school administrators during the initial cycle of the YITS-A in 2000 and thus correspond to the time when the students were 15 years of age.

The grade variables are self-explanatory. The PISA reading score is that obtained on the standardized international reading test administered to all those included in the YITS. The scale variables relate to different aspects of high school and related life experiences derived from sets of questions designed for constructing these scale variables. A detailed outline of these variables and indices is contained in Finnie and Mueller (2007, 2008a, b, 2009).

Three of these scale measures come under the heading of "high school engagement." "Academic identification" refers to getting along with teachers, having an interest in the subject matter, and to related behaviours and attitudes. "Academic participation" is an aggregate of working diligently both inside and outside of school, such as hours spent on homework, meeting assignment deadlines, and not skipping classes. "Social engagement" is a gauge of social involvement at school including having friends, feeling a sense of belonging to the social aspects of school, and so on.

The second set of scale variables represents "self-perception" and also contains three specific measures. "Self-esteem" is self-explanatory; "self-efficacy" reflects students' responses to questions related to their competence and confidence in performing school work and the results of effort made. "Self-mastery" reflects students' sense of broader control over their life.

The third category of scale measure consists of a single variable, "social support," which measures the availability of assistance from friends and family.

The final set of scale measures, "parental behaviour," consists of three separate measures. "Monitoring behaviour" reflects parents' awareness of what their child is doing and who their child's friends are. "Nurturance behaviour" means what it says. Thirdly, "inconsistent discipline" reflects how parents address their child's inappropriate behaviour.

We recognize that some of these scale and grade variables may be endogenous to PSE decisions (e.g., someone who wants to go to university will presumably attempt to get the grades required to be admitted), but with other variables this is less likely to be the case (e.g., parental behaviour). The basic idea here is to again see how much further the observed gaps can be narrowed by including these variables, thus indicating that the observed differences are related to or work through the variables in question. For example, is it higher grades and academic participation (i.e., hard work) during high school that *allow* the Chinese to go to university at such high rates, or are the immigrant effects still strong even after controlling for this expanded set of control variables? And if the latter is the case, what might be driving these remaining differences?

Figures 4 through 6 show the results for the models that include the grade and scale variables. As with the previous figures, we start with a basic model and then add additional regressors in blocks. The basic model is the final model in Figures 1 through 3. Thus, it includes the immigrant indicators (either aggregated or detailed) as well as the basic demographic and family controls, parental education, and parental income. There are some small difference in these results from those seen previously, since some observations have been dropped due to missing variable values as the additional regressors are added to the models. Note the different scale in the new figures resulting from the smaller gaps being investigated – those that remain after taking the earlier sets of explanatory variables into account.

Figure 4 shows the results for the models that include the aggregate immigrant indicators. First generation immigrants show differences in attending university that are 13.7 percentage points higher than non-immigrants in the first model, and 11 percentage points higher in the last model, while second generation immigrants have university attendance rates in the 9-11 percentage point range above the non-immigrant group across the four models shown. The immigrant effects are thus still substantial after controlling for the grade and scale variables.

That said, we do observe smalls dip in the differences for both immigrant groups when grades are added, suggesting that some of the immigrant differences in participation are in fact related to these variables – i.e., the children of immigrants tend to do well in high school, and those who do well in high school generally tend to go on to university. The scale variables (including the PISA reading score), in contrast, go the other way for first generation immigrants: i.e., the differences get a bit larger,

FIGURE 4
Adding the Grade and Scale Variables, First and Second Generation Immigrants (Aggregated)

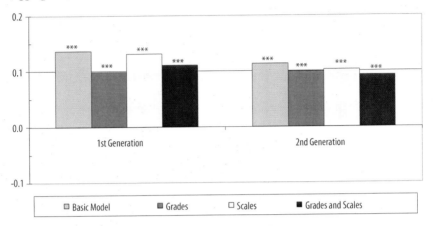

Notes: See notes to Figure 1.
Source: Finnie and Mueller, 2009.

suggesting that these factors tend to work *against* immigrant participation in university. Part of this effect is due to lower PISA reading scores, which makes sense for these recent arrivals, while no such effect is seen for second generation immigrants.

Figures 5 and 6 repeat this exercise using the more detailed immigrant indicators. Among first generation immigrants (Figure 5), the three groups that show significantly different university participation rates in the first column show smaller effects when the grade variables are added. In particular, smaller (i.e., less negative) negative effects for the Americas result, as do smaller positive effects for China. This indicates that some of the differences between groups are related to their high school performances – better than average in the Chinese case, and not as good for those from the Americas – thus leaving a smaller "residual" effect to be picked up by the immigrant variables themselves. The Other Asia difference is, in contrast, much less affected, while the other effects (i.e., for the other regions) – and their changes as the variables are added – are small and/or not very precisely estimated, preventing us from attaching any great importance to these results.

The second generation differences tend to be more consistently cut into with the addition of the grade and scale variables (grades in particular). Still there remain large and statistically significant effects for Africa, China, and East and South-East Asia, even when these additional controls are added.

FIGURE 5

Adding the Grade and Scale Variables, First Generation Immigrants by Region of Origin

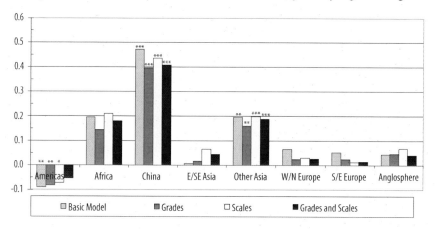

Notes: See notes to Figure 1.

Source: Finnie and Mueller, 2009.

FIGURE 6

Adding the Grade and Scale Variables, Second Generation Immigrants by Region of Origin

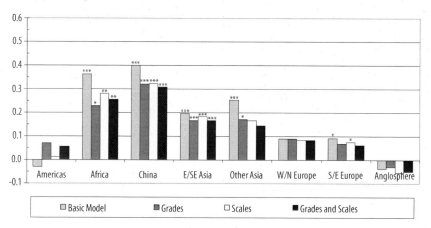

Notes: See notes to Figure 1.

Source: Finnie and Mueller, 2009.

The Role of Parental Aspirations. To try to further explain the gap between first and second generation children of immigrants and non-immigrants, we introduce a series of variables that capture parental aspirations regarding their children's educational attainment. In the YITS, all parents were asked the following questions. First, "How important is it to you that (your child) graduates from high school?" Second, "How important is it to you that (your child) gets more education after high school?" The responses to these questions could be (i) not important at all, (ii) slightly important, (iii) fairly important, or (iv) highly important. Third, "What's the highest level of education you hope (your child) will get?" Here the possible responses were (i) less than high school, (ii) high school completion, (iii) trade or college, (iv) one university degree, (v) multiple university degrees, or (vi) any level of PSE.

The results of adding these variables sequentially to the two models (i.e., the aggregated immigrant indicators and the detailed regions of origin for each generation) are presented in Figures 7 through 9. In all cases we again begin with the basic model, which includes the immigrant variables, demographic controls, and parental income and education, and then add parental aspirations. The first two aspiration variables are combined as there is very little variation in parental aspirations regarding high school completion and the importance of PSE. (Almost all parents want both for their children.)

Given the lack of explanatory power of the educational aspirations for high school and PSE in general just mentioned, it is not surprising that adding these variables does little to change the immigrant effects on access to university, regardless of immigrant generation (Figure 7) or specific immigrant region of origin (Figures 8 and 9). The inclusion of the specific level of PSE hoped for does, however, have an impact – corresponding to the general significance of these variables in the models (and, related, to the greater distribution of responses in the data). The first generation effect in Figure 7 is reduced from 13.7 percentage points with the basic model specification to 5.5 percentage points with all the aspiration variables added, while the second generation effect declines to 6.8 percentage points from 11.3 percentage points.

FIGURE 7
Adding Parental Aspirations, First and Second Generation Immigrants (Aggregated)

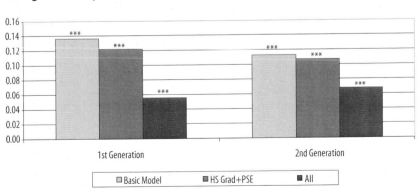

Notes: See notes to Figure 1.

Source: Finnie and Mueller, 2009.

By region of origin, first generation immigrants from the Americas are about 13.9 percentage points less likely to attend university compared to non-immigrants after all the aspiration variables are added (Figure 8), and the effect is now stronger (and also more significant) as compared to when aspirations are not included. The parental aspirations of this group are therefore not likely to blame for their lower than average university access rates – an important result. The only other remaining significant difference among first generation immigrants is for the Chinese, although the effect falls from 47.2 percentage points to 37.4 percentage points with the addition of the parental aspirations, which thus appear to be responsible for a significant share of the large Chinese attendance gap.

Among second generation immigrants (Figure 9), the pattern is similar: most of the effects are diminished with the addition of the parental aspiration variables. Still, even after controlling for aspirations, second generation youth with parents from China, East and South-East Asia, and Other Asia still have large and significant immigrant effects that exceed 10 percentage points, pushing to over 30 points in the case of China. The effect for Africa remains over 20 percentage points, the highest after China, but is statistically significant only at the 10 percent confidence level (i.e., the point estimate is larger but less precisely estimated, possibly due to Africans' smaller sample size.)

FIGURE 8
Adding Parental Aspirations, First Generation Immigrants by Region of Origin

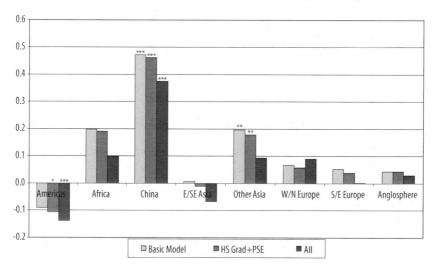

Notes: See notes to Figure 1.

Source: Finnie and Mueller, 2009.

FIGURE 9
Adding Parental Aspirations, Second Generation Immigrants by Region of Origin

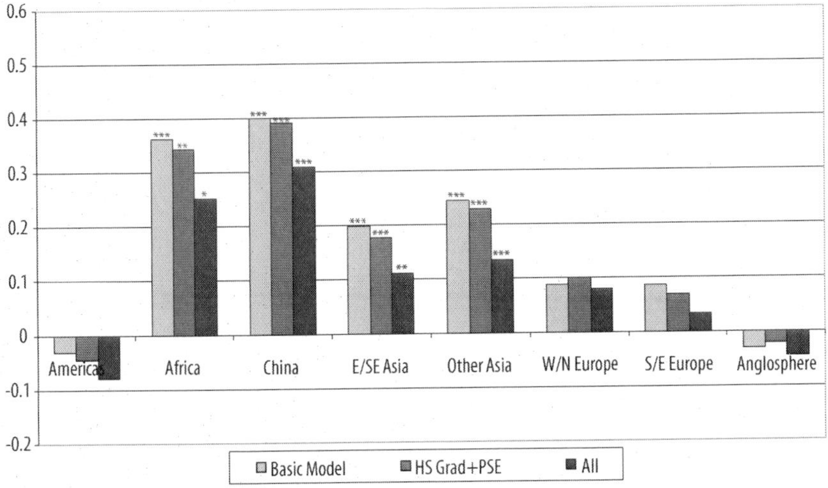

Notes: See notes to Figure 1.
Source: Finnie and Mueller, 2009.

To summarize, parental aspirations are generally an important correlate of a child's access to university, but it is the desired level of PSE completion that is by far the most important influence, and immigrant parents' higher aspirations for their children help explain some of the access gaps we observe. Still, large immigrant effects persist for certain first and second generation immigrant groups, especially those with Asian origins.

Conclusions

In this paper we have used the comprehensive YITS-A dataset to investigate university attendance rates among the children of Canadian immigrants, including both first generation immigrants (i.e., those who came to Canada with their immigrant parents – in this case before age fifteen), and second generation immigrants (those born in Canada to immigrant parents). Overall, immigrant children have significantly higher participation rates than non-immigrant youth, but these differences vary substantially by source region. The Chinese have by far the highest rates of university attendance, followed by those from other regions in Asia and Africa. By contrast, those from the Americas (excluding the US) have university participation rates that are not only lower than those of other immigrant groups but are unique in also having lower rates than non-immigrants. Those from more "traditional" source countries (including Europe and English-speaking countries) have participation rates that are only moderately above the non-immigrant rates.

The many control variables available in the YITS have also allowed us to see how these access gaps are related to a range of factors, including basic demographic characteristics, family incomes, parental education, high school experiences and outcomes, and parental aspirations for their children's education. While these variables help explain the gaps, at least in some cases substantial differences remain between the Canadian-born and their immigrant counterparts, especially those from the regions indicated above, after taking these factors into account. We may also be witnessing non-random immigration flows from various regions. For example, if it is more difficult to get into university in China than in Canada, then the Chinese may migrate to Canada to enhance their children's chances of attending university.

However, there is a very real possibility that the differences by source region reflect cultural factors, including a strong pro-university ethos among most immigrant groups. In a phrase, "they just go." Using a more specific conceptual framework, perhaps immigrants have a sense of identity that propels them toward university education (Akerlov and Kranton 2000, 2005). The literature on cultural capital is also relevant here. Our paper is, however, an empirical one, and we leave it to others to place our findings in the context of such theoretical models.

We do suggest that these results have a number of implications for our understanding of the immigrant experience in Canada and related policy issues. First, our findings suggest that it is probably important to consider the *children* of immigrants, and not simply immigrants themselves, in any full analysis of the social or economic integration of immigrants. Here we agree with Hum and Simpson (2007: 1985), who note that the educational attainment of the children of immigrants in Canada represents "an important legacy of immigration that should not be ignored."

More specifically, our findings suggest that the children of immigrants are likely to enjoy economic success, since university completion is a consistently important predictor of subsequent economic outcomes. We think that this is especially important in a context where there has been a deterioration in the economic outcomes of immigrants in recent years. That said, it remains to be seen if the conjectured successful labour force outcomes of the PSE-educated children of immigrants will indeed be forthcoming (as discussed by Corak in various papers).

Another interesting implication stems from how the Canadian record appears to differ from the European one, where at least by some measures the children of immigrants are facing substantial difficulties. We cannot, however, say why this is so. Does the explanation lie in the manner in which immigrants are received in Canada, which of course has a long history of immigration, even as the face of Canadian immigration has shifted away from the traditional European and "Anglosphere" sources toward Asia, Africa, and the Middle East? Or is the answer more in the qualities of the immigrants we attract and permit to enter, the latter perhaps related to our points system, which favours those with more education and other pertinent labour market skills. Or are other factors at work? Again our research does not answer these questions, but further research would be worthwhile.

An additional implication of our findings is that with the relatively large populations of immigrants permitted to enter Canada – close to 1 percent of the population each year – the high university participation rates of their children may put increasing strains on the Canadian university system, especially those campuses located in Montreal, Toronto, and Vancouver, where most of these new immigrants reside. The concentration of these immigrant children destined for university implies that capacity may have to be expanded or we risk seeing a "crowding out" of non-immigrant youth by the children of immigrants.

According to Citizenship and Immigration Canada (2007), of the 138,257 permanent residents admitted as economic immigrants in 2006, almost 101,000 of these originated in Africa, the Middle East, and the Asia-Pacific region – precisely those regions where we have found university participation rates (and PSE rates more generally) to be highest.[13] With education generally – university education in particular – being an important driving force of the nation's economy, as well as the key to individual success, this is an important dynamic to consider when thinking about the fortunes of immigrants and their long-run impact on the country.

Notes

The authors are grateful for support from Statistics Canada, where both are Visiting Fellows, for the financial support for this project provided by the Canada Millennium Scholarship Foundation through the MESA project, and for the excellent research assistance provided by Yan Zhang and Stephen Childs of MESA. Jane Friesen, Marc Frenette, Harold Henson, Feng Hou, and participants at the special MESA sessions at the Canadian Economics Association Annual Meeting in Vancouver in June 2008 and at the October 2008 MESA workshop in Montreal provided comments that significantly improved this paper. This paper is a modified and abbreviated version of Finnie and Mueller (2009).

1. A more comprehensive treatment of the empirical approach is found in Finnie and Mueller (2009).
2. For the "non-immigrant" groups, the YITS data do not provide information on the origin of the parents, thus providing further rationale for classifying these individuals as such (i.e., the individual and both their parents were born in Canada).
3. A full listing of the countries included in these categories is contained in Appendix 1.

4.   See Finnie and Mueller (2009) for a detailed comparison of the YITS-A and other datasets for the analysis of immigrants' experiences. See also Motte et al. (2008) for a more general discussion of the YITS data.

5.   Other data (including the older YITS-B cohort) show that access rates change only slowly after this age, and the characteristics associated with different access rates generally remain stable after this point.

6.   Non-Canadian citizens, those with unknown immigration status, those who were still continuing in high school at Cycle 4, and those with missing values of the variables used in the models were deleted from the samples. The sample used in the first parts of our analysis contains 16,825 observations, or 96.8 percent of the initial total of those individuals included in Cycle 4, including 8,216 males and 8,609 females. As we add variables to the model, sample size is reduced somewhat due to missing values on these variables. A full accounting of the observations dropped from the sample at various stages of the estimation process is contained in Finnie and Mueller (2009).

7.   We also tested our model against an ordered logit, and found the multinomial logit is indeed appropriate.

8.   It should be noted that when no effect is found on college attendance, this does not mean that there is not an underlying dynamic at work. For example, an increase in (say) parental education is often found to increase the (overall) probability of attending university but not college, with an overall increase in access to PSE. This should be interpreted as a movement from not attending PSE to attending college or university, and an additional movement from college to university. Thus, while the net effect on college attendance may be nil, or even negative, there is still a movement of individuals between these three states, including both shifts (a) toward college (from no PSE) and (b) away from college (toward university). (This interpretation applies to raw participation rates as well, not just model results.) Our model captures the net effects of these flows. Other models focus on other aspects of the access dynamic, or model it in different ways.

9.   It should be noted that our analysis has a very specific cohort interpretation – those 15 year olds included in the YITS-A dataset. Our results will therefore not be directly comparable to other studies that use census (mostly) and other data to look at broader groups of immigrants and non-immigrants.

10. Here we combine male and female observations, owing to the limited number of observations from some source regions. Results by sex (where possible) can be found in Finnie and Mueller (2009), but the results are generally similar for the two groups.

11. "Other" language indicators (i.e., other than English or French) were included in some variants of the models, but these absorbed some of the immigrant effects and thus confounded that focus of the analysis.

12. These results for second generation immigrants are for those individuals having parents from the same origin. For those with parents from different origins (including having one Canadian-born parent) see Finnie and Mueller (2009).

13. The number of economic immigrants admitted includes the principal applicants as well as their spouses and dependents.

References

Abbott, M., and C.M. Beach. 1993. "Immigrant Earnings Differentials and Birth-Year Effects for Men in Canada: Post-1972." *Canadian Journal of Economics* 25: 505-24.

Akerlov, G., and R. Kranton. 2000. "Economics and Identity." *Quarterly Journal of Economics* (August).

– 2005. "Identity and the Economics of Organizations." *Journal of Economic Perspectives*.

Aydemir, A., W.H. Chen, and M. Corak. 2008. "Intergeneration Educational Mobility among the Children of Canadian Immigrants." Analytical Studies Branch Research Paper Series, no. 316, Catalogue no. F0019M. Ottawa: Statistics Canada.

– 2009. "Intergeneration Earnings Mobility among the Children of Canadian Immigrants." *Review of Economics and Statistics* 91: 377-97.

Aydemir, A., and M. Skuterud. 2005. "Explaining the Deteriorating Entry Earnings of Canada's Immigrant Cohorts." *Canadian Journal of Economics* 38: 641-71.

Aydemir, A., and A. Sweetman. 2008. "First and Second Generation Immigration Educational Attainment and Labor Market Outcomes: A Comparison of the United States and Canada." *Research in Labor Economics* 27: 215-70.

Baker, M., and D. Benjamin. 1994. "The Performance of Immigrants in the Canadian Labor Market." *Journal of Labor Economics* 12: 369-405.

Bloom, D.E., G. Grenier, and M. Gunderson. 1995. "The Changing Labor Market Position of Canadian Immigrants." *Canadian Journal of Economics* 28: 987-1005.

Bonikowska, A. 2007. "Explaining the Education Gap between the Children of Immigrants and the Native Born: Allocation of Human Capital Investments in Immigrant Families." Mimeo.

Citizenship and Immigration Canada. 2007. *Facts and Figures: Immigration Overview, Permanent and Temporary Residents, 2006*. Ottawa: Minister of Public Works and Government Services Canada.

Finnie, R., and R.E. Mueller. 2007. "High School Student Characteristics and Access to Post-Secondary Education in Canada: Evidence from the YITS." Mimeo (August).

– 2008a. "The Effects of Family Income, Parental Education and Other Background Factors on Access to Post-Secondary Education in Canada: Evidence from the YITS." MESA Project Research Paper. Toronto, ON: Educational Policy Institute.

– 2008b. "The Backgrounds of Canadian Youth and Access to Post-Secondary Education: New Evidence from the Youth in Transition Survey." In *Who Goes, Who Stays, What Matters: Accessing and Persisting in Post-Secondary Education in Canada*, ed. R. Finnie, R.E. Mueller, A. Sweetman, and A. Usher, 79-107. Montreal and Kingston: Queen's Policy Studies Series, McGill-Queen's University Press.

– 2009. "Access to Post-Secondary Education in Canada among the Children of Canadian Immigrants." MESA Project Research Paper. Toronto, ON: Educational Policy Institute.

Frenette, M., and R. Morissette. 2005. "Will They Ever Converge? Earnings of Immigrant and Canadian-Born Workings over the Last Two Decades." *International Migration Review* 39: 228-58.

Grant, M.L. 1999. "Evidence of New Immigrant Assimilation in Canada." *Canadian Journal of Economics* 32: 930-55.

Hansen, J., and M. Kucera. 2004. "The Educational Attainment of Second Generation Immigrants in Canada: Evidence from SLID." Mimeo.

Hum, D., and W. Simpson. 2007. "The Legacy of Immigration: Labour Market Performance and Education in the Second Generation." *Applied Economics* 39: 1985-2009.

Li, P.S. 2001. "The Market Worth of Immigrants' Educational Credentials." *Canadian Public Policy* 27: 23-38.

McDonald, J.T., and C. Worswick. 1997. "Unemployment Incidence of Immigrant Men in Canada." *Canadian Public Policy* 23: 353-73.

– 1998. "The Earnings of Immigrant Men and in Canada: Job Tenure, Cohort, and Macroeconomic Conditions." *Industrial and Labour Relations Review* 51: 465-82.

Meng, R. 1987. "The Earnings of Canadian Immigrant and Native-Born Males." *Applied Economics* 19: 1107-19.

Motte, A., H.T. Qiu, Y. Zhang, and P. Bussière. 2008. "The Youth in Transition Survey: Following Canadian Youth through Time." In *Who Goes, Who Stays, What Matters: Accessing and Persisting in Post-Secondary Education in Canada*, ed. R. Finnie, R.E. Mueller, A. Sweetman, and A. Usher, 63-75. Montreal and Kingston: Queen's Policy Studies Series, McGill-Queen's University Press.

Nielsen, H.S., M. Rosholm, N. Smith, and L. Husted. 2001. "Intergenerational Transmissions and the School-to-Work Transition of 2nd Generation Immigrants." IZA Discussion Paper Series no. 296.

Österberg, T. 2000. "Economic Perspectives on Immigrants and Intergenerational Transmissions." *Ekonomiska Studier* 102. Göteborg University, Sweden.

Picot, G. 2008. "Immigrant Economic and Social Outcomes in Canada: Research and Data Development at Statistics Canada." Analytical Studies Branch Research Paper Series, no. 319, Catalogue no. F0019M. Ottawa: Statistics Canada.

Van Ours, J., and J. Veenman. 2002. "From Parent to Child; Early Labor Market Experiences of Second-Generation Immigrants in the Netherlands. IZA Discussion Paper Series no. 649.

– 2003. "The Educational Attainment of Second-Generation Immigrants in the Netherlands." *Journal of Population Economics* 16: 739 -53.

APPENDIX 1
Immigration Regions

Region in Model	Region	Countries within Region		
Americas (Except USA)	**North America**	Bermuda	St.Pierre and Miquelon	
	South America	Argentina	Colombia	Peru
		Bolivia	Ecuador	Uruguay
		Brazil	Guyana	Venezuela
		Chile	Paraguay	South America unspecified
	Latin America and the Caribbean	Aruba	Grenada	St.Vincent/Grenadines
		Bahamas	Haiti	Trinidad-Tobago
		Barbados	Jamaica	West Indies
		Cuba	St.Lucia	
	Central America	Belize	Guatemala	
		Costa Rica	Honduras	Nicaragua
		El Salvador	Mexico	Central America unspecified
Africa	**Eastern Africa**	Burundi	Mauritius	Uganda
		Eritrea	Mozambique	Zambia
		Ethiopia	Somalia	Zimbabwe
		Kenya	Tanzania	East Africa unspecified
	Middle Africa	Angola	Congo	
	Northern Africa	Algeria	Libya	Sudan
		Egypt	Morocco	Tunisia
	Southern Africa	Botswana	Lesotho	Republic of South Africa
	Western Africa	Cape Verde Islands	Mali	Sierra Leone
		Ghana	Nigeria	Togo
		Africa unspecified		
China	**East Asia**	Hong Kong	P.R. China	Macao
		Taiwan		
East and South-East Asia	**East Asia**	South Korea	Japan	
		Korea unspecified	Mongolia	
	South-East Asia	Brunei	Malaysia	Thailand
		Indonesia	Philippines	Union of Myanmar
		Kampuchea	Singapore	Viet Nam
		Laos		
Other Asia	**Southern Asia**	Afghanistan	India	Pakistan
		Bangladesh	Iran	Sri Lanka
	Western Asia	Bahrain	Jordan	Saudi Arabia
		Cyprus	Kuwait	Syria
		Iraq	Lebanon	Turkey
		Israel	Qatar	United Arab Emirates
		Asia unspecified		

... continued

APPENDIX 1
(Continued)

Region in Model	Region	Countries within Region		
Western and Northern Europe	Western Europe	Austria Belgium France	Germany Luxembourg Netherlands	Switzerland
	Northern Europe	Denmark Estonia Finland	Latvia Lithuania Codes Norway	Sweden Iceland
Southern and Eastern Europe	Southern Europe	Bosnia-Herzegovina Croatia Greece Italy	Malta Portugal Serbia	Slovenia Spain Yugoslavia
	Eastern Europe	Bulgaria Czech Republic Czechoslovakia Europe unspecified	Hungary Moldavia Poland Romania	Russia Slovakia Ukraine USSR
Anglosphere	Australia and New Zealand	Australia	New Zealand	
	Northern Europe	United Kingdom Republic of Ireland (EIRE)	Ireland unspecified	
	North America	USA		
Others/unknown	Melanesia	Fiji Other		

Part IV

Early Influences
in the Pathways to
Higher Education

10

The Impact of Family Background and Cognitive and Non-Cognitive Ability in Childhood on Post-Secondary Education

PIERRE LEFEBVRE AND PHILIP MERRIGAN

À l'aide des données de l'Enquête longitudinale nationale sur les enfants et les jeunes (ELNEJ), nous tentons d'expliquer, dans cet article, les décisions prises par de jeunes Canadiens (âgés de 18 à 21 ans en 2005) face au choix d'entreprendre ou non des études postsecondaires (EPS). Nous observons que plusieurs facteurs liés à l'appartenance à une famille à faible revenu jouent un rôle majeur dans la décision de ne pas poursuivre des études. Selon nos estimations, la probabilité d'entreprendre des EPS est très faible chez les jeunes qui sont élevés dans une famille monoparentale où la mère est peu scolarisée, qui perçoivent leur état de santé comme étant inférieur à excellent ou très bon, dont le degré d'hyperactivité (chez les garçons) ou d'agressivité (chez les filles) est élevé, et dont les habiletés en mathématiques et en lecture sont faibles.

This paper exploits the Canadian National Longitudinal Survey of Children and Youth (NLSCY) to explain the post-secondary education (PSE) choices of Canadian youth aged 18 to 21 in 2005. We find that several characteristics of low-income families play a key role for schooling attainment. Our estimates reveal that a youth from a single-parent home, with a poorly educated mother, with less than perceived excellent or very good health, with high levels of hyperactivity for males or high levels of aggressiveness for females, and with low math and reading skills has a very low probability of attaining PSE.

Introduction

There is considerable evidence that, on average, youth from lower income families participate less in post-secondary education (PSE) and have lower educational attainment than their better-off peers. Recent studies in child development, using non-experimental panel data, insist on the

Pursuing Higher Education in Canada: Economic, Social, and Policy Dimensions, ed. R. Finnie, M. Frenette, R.E. Mueller, and A. Sweetman. Montreal and Kingston: Queen's Policy Studies Series, McGill-Queen's University Press.

dynamic nature of cumulative learning processes at different stages of the life cycle that determine the level of academic achievement (Todd and Wolpin 2007; Cunha 2007; Cunha and Heckman 2007; Cunha et al. 2006; Heckman and Masterov 2007; Ermisch and Francesconi 2001; Finnie et al. 2008, introduction and all chapters on background, access, persistence, and financial issues on PSE in Canada).

These studies suggest that the shaping of skills and the educational attainment of children are intimately related to the child's family environment at all ages and in particular at early ages (investments, resources, transmitted skills, values, motivation, etc.). Therefore, an especially rich set of data is necessary to address the topic of PSE. The purpose of this research is to estimate the relationship between family background, family income, cognitive and non-cognitive test scores, behavioural scales, parental qualities, quality of schooling at the primary and secondary level, and educational attainment for youth in Canada.

The more specific objectives are, first, to exploit the panel feature of the Canadian National Longitudinal Survey of Children and Youth (NLSCY) and the large diversity of measures collected on the same children and their families over 11 years (six cycles of data from 1994-95 to 2004-05) to better understand schooling transitions and choices of Canadian youth aged 18 to 21 who were last observed in Cycle 6. Second, the research estimates how, in particular, family background, family income, cognitive abilities and non-cognitive abilities as defined in Cunha and Heckman (2006), and behavioural scores are related to PSE choices and can be used as markers for identifying children at risk of not pursuing PSE. We focus on the impact of some variables that are rarely found as a whole in Canadian data sets on education. The NLSCY contains a host of scores on several dimensions such as the cognitive achievement of children (reading and math test scores); behavioural scores that measure the levels of hyperactivity and aggression; scores that measure non-cognitive abilities (self-esteem, the emotional quotient); variables that are helpful in constructing an index of school quality for schools attended by children at the primary and secondary levels; and the dynamics of family structure. The math and reading scores are particularly interesting, because they are computed from repeated objective tests. Also, several of these measures are taken over many cycles, well before respondents must choose their PSE status.

Our goal is to measure the impact of these background family/parental/youth characteristics on the probability of choosing a particular type of PSE (college or university) or of not pursuing PSE after high school graduation, and to derive from the results some policy implications for PSE at both the federal and provincial levels of government. A longer version of this paper (Lefebvre and Merrigan 2008) examines other outcomes such as the probability of high school graduation and of being a high school continuer.

We assess the impact of these different factors using regression analysis. We first estimate, with a multinomial logit model, the probability of not participating in PSE, attending college, or attending university, conditional on graduating from high school. We then proceed with the estimation of a sequential logit model. This latter procedure simultaneously estimates the probability of graduation from high school (HS) and the probability of stopping after HS or participating in PSE. We then compute the effect of key variables on the overall probability of PSE attendance, which is the probability of graduating from HS times the probability of PSE attendance.

The next section of this paper reviews the recent empirical evidence on PSE attendance in Canada. Section 3 presents our research methodology. Section 4 describes the information collected in the NLSCY, the data set available for Cycle 6 respondents, and the variables constructed and used specifically for estimation. The estimation results are presented and discussed in Section 5, and the paper concludes with a discussion of policy implications.

Review of Recent Research

In Canada, studies from diverse data sets (e.g., Survey on Consumer Finances/SCF, Survey of Labour and Income Dynamics/SLID, Youth in Transition Survey/YITS) have analyzed the link between participation in post-secondary education and parental income (Knighton and Mirza 2002; Corak, Lipps, and Zhao 2003; Christofides, Cirello, and Hoy 2001; Frenette 2008; Drolet 2005; Rahman, Situ, and Jimmo 2005). They show that participation rates are higher among youth from high-income families with more educated parents. They also provide evidence that the effects of family income have not varied in the late 1990s and the early twenty-first century.

On the other hand, transitory family income shocks are a crucial factor for PSE, according to the results of Coelli (2005). Tuition fees (given the provincial and time variation of fees observed in Canada) or financial constraints do not seem to be important determinants of participation (Christofides, Cirello, and Hoy 2001; Frenette 2008; Rivard and Raymond 2004). Family background characteristics (e.g., parents' education and family structure) play a larger role for post-secondary participation, as does grade point average in high school (preceding cited studies; Finnie, Sweetman, and Lascelles 2004).

Several studies have been conducted with Statistics Canada's longitudinal Youth in Transition Survey (YITS), which collects unique information on the educational and labour market pathways of a sample of young Canadians first surveyed in 2000 at the ages of 18 to 20 (Cohort B) and at age 15 (Cohort A).[1] Three additional waves (Cycles 2 to 4: 2002, 2004, and 2006) have since been added. The study by Finnie and Mueller (2008) based on the YITS Cohort A is similar to this paper in terms of the diversity of measures used, the objectives, and the methodology. They find that parental income and education are more strongly related to university attendance than college. Adding cognitive, non-cognitive, and behavioural influences (high school grades, academic engagement, self-perception, and the standardized PISA reading test score) in their regression analysis does not affect the influence of family income, while these variables play an active role in PSE access.

Descriptive statistics presented by Shaienks, Eisl-Culkin, and Bussière (2006) and Shaienks and Gluszynski (2007), based on Cohort B of the YITS for Cycles 3 or 4, highlight important facts about high school graduation and participation in post-secondary education. With regards to high school graduation and participation rates, although the usual age of graduation from high school is 18 in most provinces (17 in Quebec), approximately 76 percent of youth received their high school degree in December 1999 at the ages of 18, 19, or 20; 13 percent were high school continuers and managed to graduate four years later (including high school dropouts who returned and completed their degree). Two years later, 2 percent more had graduated, reducing the percentage of dropouts from 10 to 8 percent. A large gender gap in graduation rates at ages 18 to 20 decreases with age but manifests itself again at the PSE level; it is approximately 9 percentage points at ages 24 to 26. Other PSE statistics reveal that the proportion of youth who participate in PSE increases substantially over young adulthood and appears to level off at 24-26 years of age. Concurrently, dropping out of PSE increases with age (15 percent by December 2005 at ages 24-26). University participation and the proportion of PSE graduates who continue are still increasing as of the last survey. A significant gap between young females and males is observed for all types of graduation related to PSE. These statistics show that final schooling decisions are sometimes taken after 21 years old, the age of the eldest individuals in the sample used for this study. Also, it is difficult to measure the success rate in PSE graduation in our sample because PSE participants in the NLSCY are too young and in general are starting PSE studies.

Research Methodology

The youth aged 18 to 21 in Cycle 6 of the NLSCY (2004-05) (the latest wave of data available at the time of this research) were aged 8 to 11 in Cycle 1 (1994-95), and they and their families have (in principle) been surveyed every two years. Unfortunately for our purposes, the attrition rate of youth between Cycles 5 and 6 is very high in contrast to the preceding cycles. For Cycle 5 in 2002-03, 4,424 youth aged 16 to 19 years were surveyed; two years later, in 2004-05, only 2,982 youth aged 18 to 21 are retained in the NLSCY. In addition to attrition, differences in educational systems across provinces also present methodological problems.[2] Although Ontario abolished grade 13 in 2002-03, making its educational system similar to those in the other provinces, there remains the exception of Quebec.[3] We find the sample sizes too small to obtain credible estimates for Quebec youth and therefore exclude those respondents from the analysis.

The simplest modelling approach for the investigation of youths' educational choices is a utility maximization framework with discrete alternatives. For example, in high school teens can choose to drop out or graduate. At a later stage, if they complete high school, they can end their schooling, move to a community college, or attend university. Therefore, assuming independence between schooling decisions at different stages, a logit for the first-stage decision and a multinomial logit for the second can be used to determine the probabilities of graduating HS and then entering PSE.

At each stage, from the estimated models we can measure how the inclusion of current and past values of variables (e.g., test scores, family background, behaviour in the teen years) affects the estimate of the income effect on schooling choices. The main advantage of the NLSCY compared to other data sets is that we can model educational choices in a longitudinal setting as is also possible with the YITS-A or the SLID; that is, we can control for factors occurring ten (or eight, six, etc.) years before schooling decisions are made

We start our analysis by estimating the multinomial logit model with the full sample of 18 to 21 year olds. Conditional on HS graduation, three states are possible: not pursuing a PSE, choosing college, or choosing university. This provides a comprehensive picture of the choices available to this age group.

Estimating post-secondary conditional choices (i.e., given graduation from high school) with a logit or multinomial logit model may lead to biased estimates because of self-selection. Indeed, it is reasonable to believe that unobserved factors that determine graduation from high school will also affect PSE choices, a standard case of selection bias. On average, if selection is based on unobserved ability and if that ability is correlated with family income, the PSE sample conditional on HS graduation would be representative of the population of high income children. However, the sample of low income children having graduated from HS would be biased in favour of high ability children. A comparison of the two groups, in terms of PSE attendance, would bias the income effects downwards. We apply the method of Cameron and Heckman (2001) to correct for this bias and conclude that there is no selection bias[4;] therefore we finish the econometric section of the paper by presenting estimates for a sequential logit that estimates the probability of graduating HS, and then, given graduation from HS, the probability of participating in PSE, assuming no selection bias. This is equivalent to estimating two separate logit models. The interest in doing this is to compute the impact of key variables on the overall probability of PSE attendance, which includes the probability of high school graduation.

Survey, Dataset, and Variables

The data used are taken from Statistics Canada's National Longitudinal Survey of Children and Youth (NLSCY), which is designed to provide information about children and youth in Canada. The survey covers a comprehensive range of topics including childcare; information on children's physical development, learning, and behaviour; and data on their social environment (family, friends, schools, and communities). The NLSCY began in 1994-95 and collects data biennially, and the unit of analysis is the individual child or youth. The person most knowledgeable (PMK) about the child provides the information for each selected child when he or she is between 0 and 17 years of age in the household. The PMK also provides the family information and specific information about himself or herself as well as the spouse.

In addition, respondents between 10 and 17 years of age complete a questionnaire on various aspects of their lives. Youths 18 or older respond for themselves, and the PMK provides no information on the family. Therefore, most current values for the family variables are not observed when the respondent turns 18.

For our purposes, the NLSCY has two main strengths compared to other surveys such as the YITS or the SLID. First, it covers a comprehensive range of topics collected over many waves; some variables relate to non-cognitive skills (e.g., self-esteem and emotional quotient), parenting practices, and behaviours when the youth was a child or a mid-teen, as well as information about schools attended. Second, the survey administered tests measuring "skills": a math test in all cycles for children in grade 2 or above, ranging in age from 7 to 15; a reading test in Cycles 2 and 3 for grade school children; and other cognitive tests or assessments, according to age for those aged 16 to 21. The YITS also includes non-cognitive skills as well as ability measures; the advantage of the NLSCY is that there are more non-cognitive skills data, and data on an earlier time in life.

The NLSCY has weaknesses, however. Although not particular to this survey, some observations are missing for several variables, in particular those regarding schools.[5] For tests such as reading and mathematics, a significant number of respondents have missing scores before Cycle 4 when tests were administered at the children's schools.[6] However, in our case we are using the mean value of the test score over all cycles, minimizing the number of missing values. Because math tests are taken more often than reading tests, the math achievement measurement may be a better reflection of skills than the reading achievement variable. Also, as the math test given the first year was too easy, we then take the mean over several cycles as an explanatory variable.

Sample Used

In Cycle 6 (2004-05) there are 4,695 "longitudinal youth" respondents (as classified by Statistics Canada), which constitute the 16 to 21 year old cohort. After excluding 128 respondents from the cohort because of death or relocation to another country and youth who are 16 or 17 (too young to be in a position to graduate), we are left with 2,982 respondents aged 18 to 21. Table 1 presents their age distribution (approximately 25

TABLE 1
Sample Size, Educational Status and Post-Secondary Education[a] Participation in Percentage by Region, Youth Aged 18-21 Years in Cycle 6 of the NLSCY, 2004-05

	Canada	Quebec	Other Provinces	Women	Men
Observations	2,982	531	1,721	1,591	1,391
Weighted observations[b]	1,509,944	349,943	593,662	736,215	773,729
Age					
18	815	137	460	407	408
	24.8	25.3	24.6	24.7	24.9
19	758	140	440	406	352
	25.5	25.0	25.4	25.6	25.4
20	746	137	426	412	334
	25.1	24.6	25.0	25.1	25.1
21	663	117	395	366	297
	24.6	25.0	25.0	24.6	24.6
Educational status					
High school continuers	310	51	259	132	178
	10.2	9.4	10.4	8.5	11.8
High school dropouts	308	76	232	132	176
	11.4	16.9	9.8	9.7	13.1
High school graduates	2,326	395	1,931	1,315	1,011
	77.2	72.7	78.6	80.9	73.7
High school graduates not attending PSE	505	26	479	220	285
	18.7	9.7	21.3	13.9	23.7
High school graduates attending PSE	1,821	369	1,452	1,095	726
	81.3	90.3	78.7	86.1	76.3
High school dropouts attending PSE	47	14	33	15	32
	1.9	3.0	1.6	5.9	7.5
PSE participation by level					
All	1,868	383	1,485	1,110	758
	64.3	72.3	63.3	70.8	58.2
University	885	93	792	575	310
	30.5	18.5	34.1	35.8	25.4
College	983	290	693	535	448
	33.9	49.4	29.2	35.0	32.8
Proportion attending PSE by level					
University	47.3	27.2	53.9	50.5	43.6
College	52.7	72.8	46.1	49.5	56.4

Notes: [a]PSE is defined as any type of schooling higher than high school. [b]Weighted observations are used (Cycle 6 longitudinal weights) to calculate the percentages presented in this table. Other provinces = all provinces less Quebec.

Sources: Authors' calculation from the NLSCY's Cycles 4 to 6.

percent in each age group), the gender distribution (49 percent female and 51 percent male), and some of the main educational statistics that we focus on in this paper. The relevant proportions are the following: 10.3 percent of the respondents are in HS; 11.4 percent are out of school with no HS diploma; 77.3 percent are HS graduates. For the HS graduates, 18.7 percent had never attended PSE at the time of the survey (autumn 2004/spring 2005), and 81.3 percent can be defined as PSE participants. Approximately 2 percent are PSE participants without a high school diploma. For all provinces except Quebec, university is the choice of 53.9 percent of respondents participating in some kind of PSE, compared to 46.1 percent who choose college. By excluding Quebec, we are left with 2,451 respondents, and keeping only the high school graduates, the sample is reduced to 1,531 (1,473) respondents, which constitute the number used for the multinomial logit estimation (after excluding respondents with missing information).

Variables Used and Descriptive Statistics

Table 2 presents our preferred independent variables used in all the esti-mations presented below, and their definitions. We built our specifications on the basis of experimentation and the previous literature on schooling attainment. The specification includes as explanatory variables family background information: the age of the child, the province of residence in Cycle 1,[7] the PMK's education level, family type in Cycle 1, whether the child experienced a family type change ("separation") between Cycles 1 and 5, the number of siblings, PMK immigrant status, the size of the community, and "permanent" family income (mean income measured over the first four cycles). Other controls are related to behaviours and provided by the PMK: hyperactivity-inattention at ages 8-11, and aggres-sion (conduct disorders and physical aggression) at ages 8-11 for males and 10-15 for females. Other variables are measures of achievement in reading and mathematics, and youth measures of their perceived health,[8] self-esteem, and parental nurturance. Finally, a variable that measures the average of quality of the school the child attended between Cycles 1 and 4 is included. For this variable we construct an index of quality that is described in detail in Lefebvre, Merrigan, and Verstraete (2008).[9] When measures for a particular scale are available for more than one cycle, the regressor variable is the mean value over all available cycles.

In most Canadian studies, only current parental income is available in the surveys. However, mean income over a long period, as used here, is a better proxy for educational resources available to the child at home while growing up.[10]

Table 3 presents descriptive statistics (percentages or mean values) of the variables used in the regressions by gender and educational status observed in Cycle 6. The table shows little regional movement between

TABLE 2
Definition of Control Variables (Reference Category in Parentheses)

Explanatory Variables	Acronym or Definition and Cycle
Age	In C6
(18)	
19	
20	
21	
Provinces	In C1
(Atlantic)	NL, PEI, NS, NB
Ontario	ON
Prairies	MB, SK
Alberta	AB
British Columbia	BC
PMK education	Education of the Person Most Knowledgeable about this child in C1
Primary	<HS
Some secondary	Some HS
(High school diploma)	HS
Some PSE	Some PSE
College diploma	Coll.
University	Univ.
Family type/change	In C1
(One-parent/guardian)	Sgl. parent
Two bio-parents	2 par. bio.
Two parents	2 par.
Separation	Sep. C1-4
Immigrant PMK	Immig. in C1
Sibling	Number of sibling in C1
(0)	Sib. 0
1	Sib. 1
=>2	Sib. 2
Community size	In C1
Rural	Com. Rural
(Small <99,999)	Com. Small
Large =>100,000	Com. Large
Mean School Quality Index	Sch. QI in C1 to C4
(Q1 Fam. income)	Quartile 1 of mean family incomes from C1 to C4, 2002 dollars
Q2 Fam. income	Q2 Fam. Income
Q3 Fam. income	Q3 Fam. Income
Q4 Fam. income	Q4 Fam. Income
(Q1 Math)	Quartile 1 of mean math scores from C1 to C4
Q2 Math	Q2 Math
Q3 Math	Q3 Math
Q4 Math	Q4 Math
(Q1 Reading)	Quartile 1 of mean reading scores in C2 and C3
Q2 Reading	Q2 Reading
Q3 Reading	Q3 Reading
Q4 Reading	Q4 Reading
Health excellent-very good	Mean health status declared by youth excellent or very good/others status in C5 and C6
Self-esteem	Mean general self score according to youth (age 10 to 19 years)
Hyperactivity-inattention	Mean hyperactivity/inattention score according to PMK (age 8 to 11 years)
Aggression 8-11/10-15	Mean conduct disorder-physical aggression score: (age 8-11 boys; 10-15 girls)
Nurturance	Mean parental nurturance score according to youth 10-15 years in C3 and C4

TABLE 3

Descriptive Statistics in Percentage by Gender and Schooling Status by Cycle 6, Youth 18 to 21 Years, NLSCY, Canada Except Quebec, 2004-05

Variables	HS no PSE		College Participant		University Participant	
	Women	Men	Women	Men	Women	Men
18	32	29	12	13	20	20
19	34	28	22	26	26	27
20	20	23	35	27	28	27
21	14	20	31	34	26	26
NL, PEI, NS, NB	12/11	12/10	9/7	10/9	10/11	14/12
ON	38/37	35/36	48/49	43/43	60/62	49/50
MB, SK	13/12	12/12	8/7	7/7	9/8	10/10
AB	20/23	22/26	20/23	19/20	10/8	9/8
BC	17/17	19/19	15/14	21/21	11/11	18/20
<HS	4	5	3	1	1	1
Some HS	15	19	17	11	6	8
HS	24	17	21	20	20	16
Some PSE	31	30	34	30	21	31
Coll.	18	22	18	26	20	19
Univ.	8	7	7	12	33	25
2 par. bio	74	77	79	85	85	86
2 par	5	12	.9	9	7	8
Sgl. parent	21	11	12	6	8	6
Separation	17	24	15	17	6	9
Immig.	20	13	14	21	25	24
Sib. 0	9	11	7	15	9	9
Sib. 1	51	38	46	42	50	44
Sib 2	40	51	47	43	41	47
Com. rural	26	30	25	24	10	17
Com. small	27	26	25	20	18	20
Com. large	47	44	50	56	72	63
Sch. QI	3.7	3.7	3.5	4.0	3.7	4.0
Mean family inc (2002 $)	$58,150	$64,754	$74,274	$71,538	$93,960	$88,878
Q1 Fam. income	34	24	20	21	11	13
Q2 Fam. income	26	28	27	26	30	21
Q3 Fam. income	25	30	28	26	26	26
Q4 Fam. income	15	18	25	27	33	40
Q1 Math	30	15	29	19	7	11
Q2 Math	39	36	37	36	21	25
Q3 Math	29	27	24	24	37	31
Q4 Math	2	22	10	21	35	33
Q1 Reading	34	31	27	32	14	9
Q2 Reading	22	22	28	27	17	20
Q3 Reading	25	24	26	17	29	30
Q4 Reading	19	23	19	24	38	41
Health excellent-very good	55	61	50	67	78	77
Self-esteem	12.4	12.6	12.6	13.1	13.2	13.2
Hyperactivity-inattention	4.6	5.6	4.1	4.7	3.5	3.2
Aggression-11/15	1.0/1.0	1.5/1.4	1.1/0.9	1.3/1.2	0.9/0.3	0.5/0.4
Nurturance	19.8	19.2	20.0	20.6	19.7	21.4
Weighted observations	74,455	119,665	158,413	166,173	221,925	172,374

Notes: Authors' calculation from Cycles 1 to 6 using weighted data and rounding of percentages. See Table 2 for definition of variables. HS Grad =high school graduate; PSE = post-secondary education. In the case of the provincial variables, the first number refers to the proportion living in the province in Cycle 1, the second in Cycle 6.

Cycles 1 and 6. Youth who did not pursue PSE have a lower education PMK, in particular males; the proportion is much lower for youth who are college participants and very low for youth having accessed university. Living in a biological two-parent family (in Cycle 1) is positively correlated with educational attainment. University and college participants are over-represented in the higher quartile of family income. Youth with very good scores in math and reading are more likely to be PSE participants, in particular at the university level. There are slight differences between the means of non-cognitive measures (such as self-esteem) and of the behavioural scales by educational level for both females and males.

Of the scales measuring parental practices, only the parental nurturance score (from youth perception at ages 10 to 15 years) was significant in certain specifications. All scales are significantly correlated, creating collinearity problems for the regression analysis. We retained parental nurturance because the standard deviation was not high relative to the other parental coefficients when all parental variables are included in the regressions. In future work on this topic, clearly some kind of factor analysis should be performed to create a more synthetic scale for parental behaviour.

Socio-emotional behaviours (except hyperactivity-attention and aggression) reported by the PMK when a child was aged between 8 and 11 years were generally insignificant predictors of later academic performance, even among children with relatively high levels of problem behaviour. In the psychology literature, hyperactivity and aggression are variables that are given an important role in child development, particularly in the works of Richard E. Tremblay and his co-authors (Tremblay et al. in press; Fontaine et al. 2008; Leblanc et al. 2008). We therefore included the measure for each of these behaviours in the analysis.

Econometric Results

All estimations use the weights provided by Statistics Canada for parameter estimates and their standard deviations.[11] Therefore the results are applicable to the longitudinal 1994 cohort. All estimations are conducted separately by gender to capture the main elements at the origin of diverging schooling achievements.

Our opening econometric strategy is simple. We estimate for young men and women PSE participation conditional on being a high school graduate with a multinomial logit procedure (again, the three choices are no PSE, college, or university).[12] Our analysis highlights explanatory variables that are in the NLSCY and not in other data sets: in particular, math and reading scores; hyperactivity and aggression; quality of schools; parental nurturance; and quartiles of family income over the first four cycles of the survey. These are particularly interesting because they can inform about the probability of attending PSE when youth are much younger than the age when they must make PSE choices.

Multinomial Estimation Results of Three PSE Outcomes for Youth

Table 4 presents estimated marginal effects on the three estimated probabilities (computed at the mean value of the explanatory variables). We provide two examples to help with the interpretation of the marginal effects. First, the estimated effect for a binary variable is the effect relative to a reference category. In the case of math scores, we estimate effects for quartiles 2, 3, and 4, the reference category being quartile 1. For males, the marginal effect of being in quartile 2 of the math test score on the probability of attaining the university level is 0.367. This means that for males with the same characteristics except the math quartile, the predicted probability of university attendance for those observed in the second quartile of maths scores is 0.367 higher than for those in the lowest quartile of math scores.

Second, for continuous variables such as aggression or hyperactivity, the interpretation is different. Take hyperactivity for males, where the marginal effect on the probability of attaining university level is -0.024. This means that for individuals with the same characteristics except hyperactivity, an increase of the hyperactivity score by 1 will decrease the predicted probability of university attendance by 0.024.

We start our analysis with young men (right panel of Table 3). First, the level of PMK education plays a crucial role for PSE attendance. Very low levels severely reduce the probability of attaining PSE. The estimates show no impact of family type on PSE choices for young men except for the variable separation (indicating that the child experienced a parental breakup or change in family structure during the first four cycles of the NLSCY), which seriously diminishes the probability of attending university (U) by 0.181, while increasing the probability of stopping at the HS level (SHS) by 0.073 and the probability of attending college (C) by 0.108. These latter two results are statistically insignificant at the 5 percent level. This result is similar to that in Coelli (2005), where a period of unemployment by a parent reduces the probability of PSE attendance. The separation may be interpreted as a transition period of low income a few years before PSE choices must be made. Family income quartiles are found to have no effect; this is surprising, because we are using mean income over the first four cycles of the NLSCY, a better proxy of parental financial resources than current income. The presence of several explanatory variables that may be linked to family resources present at earlier ages of the child could explain this result (e.g., achievement in reading and mathematics).

For young women, although there are no statistically significant income effects, the quartile 4 effect is relatively large, around .07, but not precisely estimated. In our opinion, income effects must not be totally ruled out,

of U attendance by a substantial 0.206. This increase is almost totally at the expense of the probability of attending C.

Finally, for girls, for health, behavioural, non-cognitive skills, and family related variables, three stand out. First, very good or excellent health increases the probability of attending U by 0.240 while decreasing the probability of no PSE by 0.061. Second, the measure of aggression for 10 to 15 year olds has a very large negative effect of -0.081 on the probability of attending U. Hyperactivity increases the probability of SHS but the effect is small at 0.006 and not highly significant. It can be large if one compares a pathologically hyperactive girl and an average girl in the sample.

To summarize, for both young females and males, PMK education, experiencing a separation, the size of the residential community, math proficiency, and hyperactivity all matter in various ways. In contrast, family structure, immigration status, reading scores, health, and aggressive behaviour also matter for females. Thus, females are affected by a much larger number of factors than males. Almost all characteristics negatively related to the probability of attending both C and U are particular to low income households, and the negative effects are especially strong for the probability of attending U. This accentuates income inequalities, as earnings for U graduates are higher than for C graduates. Our results also demonstrate that while characteristics linked to low-income households play a crucial role for PSE, the income effects per se are small. This suggests that programs other than income enhancement are necessary for increasing the PSE participation rates for disadvantaged youths.

A Simple Sequential Logit Model

This section presents the estimated effects of the key variables obtained from the estimation of both the HS graduation logit and the PSE multinomial logit. The decision tree estimated is the following: the first branch is graduating HS versus not graduating, while the second is conditional on graduation: stopping education following HS or moving to university or college. Because these logit procedures are estimated with the same youths for both decisions, we chose not to include the 18 year olds since too many are in high school and therefore the high school graduation outcome is not observed. Of course, for several of the 19, 20, and 21 year olds, the final decision concerning their level of education is not taken, implying that we should concentrate on the 21 year olds, the closest to the final decision. In this case, the sample would have been very small, so we decided to include all youth older than 18.

We present estimates of the effects of the key variables on the probabilities of not graduating (NG), of stopping after HS graduation (SHS), of attending college (C), or of attending university (U). To estimate the marginal effects, we start with a baseline case such that the probability of graduating from high school is approximately equal to the percentage of young women graduating (depending on the sample), and we simply change the value of one regressor and recompute the probability. The difference between the new probability and the baseline case is the marginal effect. For the marginal effect of continuous regressors, we fix the value at the mean of the variable for the sample and estimate the marginal effect of a variable by increasing it by one standard deviation, recomputing the baseline probability with this new value, and then finally taking the difference between this probability and the baseline probability. These results appear in Table 5. We compute the effects only for variables that were significant or close (p-value between .10 and .15) to being significant in the sequential logit. The baseline case is a person from Ontario, 21 years old, with a PMK holding a high school diploma but no more, with two biological parents and one sibling, living in a large city, in the second income quartile, second math quartile, third reading quartile, in excellent/very good health, with all continuous variables evaluated at their means.

The baseline probabilities in this table are different from those in Table 1 because the sample does not include 18 year olds, and the base case was chosen so that the estimated probability is equal to the proportion of females with a high school degree (we did not try a base case that would fit to the proportion of all categories).

TABLE 5
Sequential Logit Estimated Base Probabilities and Simulated Effects on Baseline Probabilities

Decision Tree	Schooling Transition				Schooling Transition			
	Dropout of HS	HS Grad	College	University	Dropout of HS	HS Grad	College	University
	Women				Men			
Base probabilities	10	6	53	31	17	20	25	38
	Simulations Results							
Health E-VG=0	+2	+2	+14	-18	+25	-4	-6	-16
<HS=1	+61	0	-42	-20	+44	-5	-10	-29
Univ.=1	-5	-3	-33	+41	-17	-11	-12	+40
2 Par. bio=0	+11	+5	+5	-21	+37	-8	-11	-18
Separation=1	-4	+5	+14	-15	-11	+7	+19	-16
Q4 Math=1	-6	-5	-18	+28	-13	-7	-6	+26
Q1 Reading=1	-3	+4	+10	-12	-10	+1	+25	-16
Hyperactivity +1SD	+1	+2	+1	-3	+2	+8	+2	-12
Aggression +1SD	+3	+2	+7	-11	+6	-2	-3	-2
Nurturance +1SD	-1	0	0	+1	-1	0	0	+1

Notes: HS = high school, grad = high school graduate. The baseline case is a person from Ontario who is 21 years old, has a PMK with a high school degree but no more, has two biological parents, one sibling, lives in a large city, is in the second income quartile, the second math quartile and the third reading quartile, and is in excellent/very good health. All continuous variables evaluated at their means. SD = standard deviation.

Not reporting being in excellent or very good health has a very large effect on the probability of being a dropout for young men, increasing this probability by 0.25 and reducing the probability of graduating from HS, attending C, or attending U, by 0.04, 0.06, and 0.16, respectively. This latter effect is much larger than the estimate found if we only consider the PSE probability computed with the multinomial logit (-.099), because bad health seriously diminishes the probability of graduating from high school. Interestingly, for females the main effect of this variable is to decrease the probability of attending U by 0.18 and increase the probability of attending C by 0.14; therefore for females "poor health" affects the type of PSE but not the probability of attending a PSE level institution.

Having a very poorly educated PMK has dramatic consequences for both young men and women when compared to a youth with a PMK with a HS degree as highest level of education, as it increases the probability of being a dropout by 0.61 for females and 0.44 for males. The proportion of children in this situation is very low, but large enough to be alarming. Again, for both sexes, a university educated PMK will have an enormous impact compared to a mother with a HS diploma. For young women, the main impact is to increase the probability of U attendance by 0.41 and decrease the probability of attending C by 0.33. For young men, the impact is to increase the probability of U attendance by 0.40, but the decreases in the other choices are spread out: 0.17 for not graduating, 0.11 for SHS, and 0.12 for C.

In terms of family type, experiencing a separation is particularly deleterious to a university level education for both sexes; however, it has little overall affect on PSE attendance. A single-mother home compared to a two-biological-parent home has dramatic effects on schooling choices. For females, we observe a 0.11 rise in the probability of dropping out and a 0.21 decrease in the probability of attending U. For males, the increase in the probability of dropping out is 0.37, which is very large. Again, these results are different from the case where the effects are computed on the basis of the multinomial logit results; there, family structure has much smaller effects, in particular for males.

Moving from a quartile 2 math ranking to a quartile 4 ranking has dramatic impacts on the probability of U attendance, increasing it by 0.28 for young women and 0.26 for young men. For reading, the effects are less substantial but remain important. Moving from a quartile 3 ranking to a quartile 1 ranking in reading increases the probability of C attendance for young women by 0.10 and decreases the probability of U attendance by 0.12. There is therefore little impact on the overall probability of PSE attendance. For young men the same is somewhat true, but the large decrease in the probability of being a dropout in favour of C attendance is not credible and is probably the result of the co-linearity of this variable with others. It is a rare instance of a counterintuitive result in this paper.

Hyperactivity strongly affects the outcomes for males but not females. An increase of one standard deviation of the hyperactivity score for males decreases the probability of attending U by 0.12 while increasing the probability of SHS by 0.08, which is considerable. A one standard deviation increase in the mean aggression score computed for males less than 12 years old in our sample diminishes the probability of attending university and increases the probability of dropping out. We do not compute the income effects, as they are far from significant. The sequential logit shows that the total effect of certain key variables on the probability of PSE attendance can be much higher once the probability of graduating HS is integrated in the model.

Policy Discussion and Conclusion

In this paper, we have tried to find the major determinants of PSE choices for young Canadian males and females, using the only Canadian data set, the NLSCY, that contains a lengthy history of childhood experiences as well as measures of different aspects of youths' psychological, socio-emotional, and cognitive development. It was, we believed, important to perform the analysis by gender, as the results differ considerably. For example, levels of aggression have no impact for young men, while they do matter for young women. A large number of variables have impacts that are similar in direction for both genders, but the differences in the magnitude of the impacts are substantial. This necessarily leads to thinking about gender gaps: in general, the explanation as to why young men are losing ground proves elusive.

Given high school graduation, more women choose university than men. Math scores are extremely important for university attendance for males but less so for women; reading scores are important for females, but male attendance is insensitive to them. These findings could be related to the type of academic programs that interest young males and females, but the YITS is a better data set to address the issue of academic program preference. The absence of reading effects for young males is an intriguing result. It must be noted, as explained earlier, that our reading measure covers only two cycles, while our math measure covers four cycles and therefore may be more precise. We do not think that we can infer from these results that better reading skills do not improve educational attainment for males. The two skills are highly correlated, so that identification of reading skills effects is difficult. We are, however, willing to say that math skills are better predictors of educational attainment for males than reading skills.

Although income does not seem to have large effects on PSE attendance or high school graduation, the sign of its effect is generally positive. However, given the very high level of co-linearity of income with other explanatory variables, low t-statistics for income effects are to be expected. We must therefore be careful about concluding that there are no income effects in these models. More importantly, several variables that are characteristics of low-income families play a key role for schooling attainment. For example, being from a single-parent home with a poorly educated PMK and with less than (perceived) excellent/very good health or with high levels of hyperactivity for males or high levels of aggression for young teenage females greatly diminishes the chance of attaining the level of PSE. These results are now becoming familiar throughout the literature. In policy terms, despite the fact that being in a low-income family reduces the chances of attaining PSE, marginally increasing the income of these families (by a few thousand dollars) would have only a minor effect on the probability of attaining PSE.

We find that inequalities in cognitive abilities, good health, and controlling hyperactivity and aggression are more important than income inequalities for PSE; this is particularly true when one is comparing the effect of moving from the the bottom end of the distribution of these scales to the top. It is also known that ability (cognitive and non-cognitive) gaps open up early in life, that chronic health problems early in life are conducive to poor health, and that aggressive and hyperactive behaviours are identifiable at a very early stage in child development. Work by Tremblay et al. (in press) has shown that early interventions can considerably dampen any pathological trajectory of aggression. Also, some periods are "critical" (early childhood periods when investments in certain types of human capital are especially important) for development, while other periods are "sensitive" (periods where investments in human capital have larger effects than in others), to use Cunha and Heckman's (2008, 2007) terminology.

Therefore, policy must be designed to address the problems associated with poorly educated parents or single-parent homes. The types of interventions that seem to work best are those aimed at improving the lot of children as early as possible in their lives (Heckman and Masterov 2007). Clearly, the youths benefiting most from these interventions are from low-income families, as they have the most to gain. On average, youths from middle- and high-income families with two parents are doing very well. Early childhood interventions in the life cycle of disadvantaged children offer a higher return than later interventions such as better schools. Chronic health problems developed early in life are very costly over the whole life cycle. High levels of aggression developed early in life can lead to future criminal behaviour. In short, too many children start grade school with a very small chance of attending PSE.

This does not mean that we should not help low-income students with funding for higher education. It simply means that within a portfolio of interventions geared to helping children attend PSE, proportionally more resources should be devoted to early childhood interventions targeted toward children from low-income families.

A surprising result is that better schools do not seem to have an impact on PSE attendance. However, in recent work Lefebvre, Merrigan, and Verstrate (2008) show that higher quality schools have a positive impact on math scores. Therefore, although our regressions show no direct impact of school quality on PSE, it is possible that there is an indirect effect on PSE channelled by higher achievement in mathematics and reading. In related work, Lefebvre and Merrigan (2009) find that attending private high schools in Quebec, which are heavily subsidized by the provincial government, thus creating a competitive environment for the schooling system, has a strong positive effect on math achievement. That study carefully addresses the issue of simultaneity between private school attendance and achievement in mathematics. Creating a more competitive environment within the schooling sector is achievable by public policy.

Given these facts, it is more difficult for the federal government to directly intervene in this area. Its main tools – fiscal policies and transfers – cannot change the picture of PSE in Canada in any important way. However, there are other ways the government can act. Although some experimental studies have shown that early interventions can change the future prospects of young children, the evidence is mostly American. The federal government should be funding more experimental studies that seek to improve the cognitive and behavioural development of young children.[13] There is no quick-fix fiscal policy that can substantially increase the chances of graduating from high school or attending PSE amongst children with the detrimental characteristics that we have identified.

Finally, we also point out the limits of our study. First, some of the children in the cohort we use for the empirical analysis have not completed their education (10.2 percent of the weighted sample of 1,509,944 respondents). Second, the level of attrition in Cycle 6 compared to Cycle 5 is very high. Furthermore, data for the YITS show that schooling status for a cohort aged 22-24 is more representative of the final level of educational attainment. Therefore, work with Cycle 7 should provide more "final answers" to the questions surrounding PSE. Finally, the non-response rate for math and reading scores as well as non-cognitive skills is high, leading to possible selection bias in the results.

Notes

This analysis is based on Statistics Canada's National Longitudinal Survey of Children and Youth (NLSCY) restricted-access Micro Data Files, which contain anonymized data collected in the NLSCY and are available at the Québec Interuniversity Centre for Social Statistics (QICSS), one of the Canadian Research Data Centres network. All computations on these micro-data were prepared by the authors, who assume the responsibility for the use and interpretation of these data. This research was funded by Human Resources and Social Development Canada. A longer version of this paper is available (see Lefebvre and Merrigan 2008). We thank David Groux for his excellent research assistance, and participants in Statistics Canada Socio-Economic Conference 2008, 5-6 May 2008, Ottawa Congress Centre; MESA Session/Canadian Economic Association Meeting, 7-8 June 2008, UBC, Vancouver. We also thank the MESA Research Committee for inviting us to their session at MESA's Montreal Workshop in October 2008 and for their useful comments as well as those of our discussant, Mike Veall. Finally, we thank the editors, Ross Finnie, Marc Frenette, and Arthur Sweetman, for their constructive criticism and helpful suggestions on an earlier draft, and in particular Richard Mueller, for his very detailed comments and thorough editing of the final draft.

1. A series of research projects using these data sets are ongoing and financed by the Canadian Millennium Scholarship Foundation through the MESA project based at the School of Policy Studies at Queen's University. A first round of findings are presented in a book edited by Finnie, Mueller, Sweetman, and Usher (2008) and summarized in the introduction.

2. In Cycle 5, some Ontario youth are observed in grade 13.

3. Quebec's CEGEPs, which have no tuition fees but charge ancillary fees of the order of $200 to $300 per year, form a distinct schooling level compared to the schooling system in the other provinces. High school graduates must choose between two tracks: a two-year general college program giving access to all university programs (three additional years to obtain a first degree), or a three-year professional/technical college program (all 52 public colleges offer the two tracks) that train skilled technicians who can also access university.

4. We assume that a common unobservable factor determines both the probability of graduating from high school and PSE choice. We also assume that this factor can take only two values: high and low. Because of this assumption, the likelihood function depends on both the probability of graduating from high school and the probability of participation in PSE. Therefore a joint estimation of both probabilities must be achieved to obtain consistent estimates of the parameters of the model. A logit specification is used for each of these probabilities. From the maximization of this overall likelihood function, we estimate the logit coefficients, the probability that an individual is a high or low type, and the parameter associated with being a high or a low type. This is identical to Cameron and Heckman (2001) but with only two outcomes: high school graduation and PSE participation.

5. See Lefebvre et al. (2008) who exploit the longitudinal nature of the school collection information and math test scores.

6. For the tests, consent had to be given by the parent(s) and the school boards. For Cycle 1, the NLSCY received results for about 50 percent of eligible children; for Cycle 2, the percentage was 74 percent and for Cycle 3, it was 54 percent. Since Cycle 4, the test is administered at the home of the child and almost all eligible children passed the test.

7. Using the province of residence at the moment of making the choice of attending a PSE had no impact on the results.

8. We performed regressions with the health status of the child as perceived by the PMK in Cycles 1 to 4 as an explanatory variable, but it was found not to be statistically significant in any of the specifications.

9. The index was constructed from questions asked: to the teacher(s) of the child (years of experience, age, gender) on teaching habits (Do you give homework? Do you ask parents to check the child's homework? Did the

child arrive in class without having finished homework? Do you discipline children because of physical violence/vandalism?), and to the teacher and school principal about the working environment (positive for teachers and pupils, supportive, disciplinary).

10. The results of a separate estimation (not presented here) used quartiles of current family income when youths were aged 14-15 and show that only the highest quartile influenced positively and significantly the university participation rate, but for females only.

11. The standard deviations of the sequential logit, with uncorrelated unobservable error terms, were not computed using the bootstrap weights as the STATA procedure could not implement it; however, the regressions are performed with weights. The sequential logit with a random effect was performed without weights. Since this was done for comparison with the sequential logit with no correlation to ascertain bias, the latter was done without weights as well. No policy analysis is done on the basis of these results.

12. This condition excludes 33 respondents not having this diploma but participating in PSE (31 college and two university students) and 259 high school continuers, the majority of them males.

13. Finnie et al. (2008) suggest random assignment experiments on types of student aid and on other interventions to identify the effects on access to and persistence in PSE.

References

Cameron, S., and J. Heckman. 2001. "The Dynamics of Educational Attainment for Black, Hispanic and White Males." *Journal of Political Economy* 109 (2001): 455-99.

Christofides, L., J. Cirello, and M. Hoy. 2001. "Family Income and Post-Secondary Education in Canada." *Canadian Journal of Higher Education* 31 (1): 177-208.

Coelli, M. 2005. "Parental Income Shocks and the Education Attendance of Youth." Mimeo, Department of Economics, University of British Columbia.

Corak, M., G. Lipps, and J. Zhao. 2003. "Revenu familial et participation aux études postsecondaires." Direction des études analytiques: Documents de recherche. Catalogue no. 11F0019MIF2003210. Ottawa: Statistique Canada.

Cunha, F. 2007. "A Time to Plant and a Time to Reap." Mimeo, Department of Economics, University of Chicago.

Cunha, F., and J. Heckman. 2008. "Formulating, Identifying and Estimating the Technology of Cognitive and Non-Cognitive Skill Formation." *Journal of Human Resources* 43 (4): 738-82.

– 2007. "The Technology of Skill Formation." *American Economic Review, Papers and Proceedings* 97 (2): 31-47.

– 2006. "Investing in Our Young People." Mimeo, Department of Economics, University of Chicago.

Cunha, F., J. Heckman, L. Lochner, and D. Masterov. 2006. "Interpreting Evidence of Life Cycle Skill Formation." In *Handbook of the Economics of Education*, vol. 1, ed. Eric A. Hanushek and Finis Welch, 697-812. New York: Elsevier.

Drolet, M. 2005. "Participation aux études postsecondaires au Canada: Le rôle du revenu et du niveau de scolarité des parents a-t-il évolué au cours des années

1990?" Direction des études analytiques: documents de recherche. Catalogue no. 11F0019MIF2005243. Ottawa: Statistique Canada.

Ermisch, J., and M. Francesconi. 2001. "Family Matters: Impacts of Family Background on Educational Attainments." *Economica* 68 (270): 137-56.

Finnie, R., R. Mueller, A. Sweetman, and A. Usher. 2008. "Introduction: A Framework for Thinking about Participation in Post-Secondary Education." In *Who Goes? Who Stays? What Matters? Accessing and Persisting in Post-Secondary Education in Canada*, ed. R. Finnie, R.E. Mueller, A. Sweetman, and A. Usher, 3-32. Montreal and Kingston: Queen's Policy Studies Series, McGill-Queen's University Press.

Finnie, R. and Mueller, R.E. 2008. "The Backgrounds of Canadian Youth and Access to Post-Secondary Education: New Evidence from the Youth in Transition Survey." In *Who Goes? Who Stays? What Matters? Accessing and Persisting in Post-Secondary Education in Canada*, ed. R. Finnie, R.E. Mueller, A. Sweetman, and A. Usher, 79-108. Montreal and Kingston: Queen's Policy Studies Series, McGill-Queen's University Press.

Finnie, R., A. Sweetman, and E. Lascelles. 2004. "Who Goes: The Direct and Indirect Effects of Family Background on Access to Post-Secondary Education." In *Higher Education in Canada*, ed. C. Beach, R. Boadway, and M. McInnis, 295-338. Kingston: John Deutsch Institute, McGill-Queen's University Press.

Fontaine, N., R. Carbonneau, E.D. Barker, F. Vitaro, M. Hébert, S.M. Côté, D.S. Nagin, M. Zoccolillo, and R.E. Tremblay. 2008. "Females' Hyperactivity and Physical Aggression during Childhood Predict Adjustment Problems in Early Adulthood: A 15-year Longitudinal Study." *Archives of General Psychiatry* 65 (3): 320-28.

Frenette, M. 2008. "Why Are Lower-Income Students Less Likely to Attend University? Evidence from Academic Abilities, Parental Influences, and Financial Constraints." In *Who Goes? Who Stays? What Matters? Accessing and Persisting in Post-Secondary Education in Canada*, ed. R. Finnie, R.E. Mueller, A. Sweetman, and A. Usher, 279-98. Montreal and Kingston: Queen's Policy Studies Series, McGill-Queen's University Press.

Heckman, J., and D. Masterov. 2007. "The Productivity Argument for Investing in Young Children." NBER Working Paper No. 13016.

Knighton, T., and S. Mirza. 2002. "Post-Secondary Participation: The Effects of Parents' Education and Household Income." *Education Quarterly Review* 8 (3): 25-32.

Leblanc, N., M. Boivin, G. Dionne, M. Brendgen, F. Vitaro, R.E. Tremblay, and D. Pérusse. 2008. "The Development of Hyperactive/Impulsive Behaviors during the Preschool Years: The Predictive Validity of Parental Assessments." *Journal of Abnormal Child Psychology* 36 (7): 977-87.

Lefebvre, P., and P. Merrigan. 2009. "Private Schools Do Make a Difference on Math Scores: Canadian Longitudinal Evidence Using the Primary to Secondary School Transitions as an Identification Strategy." Working paper, UQAM, April 2009. (http://132.203.59.36/cirpee/cahierscirpee/2009/2009.htm)

– 2008. "Family Background, Family Income, Cognitive Test Scores, Behavioural Scales and Their Relationship with Participation in Post-Secondary Education: Evidence from the NLSCY." Working paper 2008-30, Cirpée. (http://132.203.59.36/cirpee/cahierscirpee/2008/2008.htm)

Lefebvre, P., P. Merrigan, and M. Verstraete. 2008. "The Effects of Schools and Family Functioning on Math Scores: A Canadian Longitudinal Analysis."

Working paper 2008-22, Cirpée. (http://132.203.59.36/cirpee/cahierscir-pee/2008/2008.htm)

Rahman, A., J. Situ, and V. Jimmo. 2005. "Participation in Post-Secondary Education: Evidence from the Survey of Labour Income Dynamics." Catalogue no. 81-595-MIE2005036. Ottawa: Statistics Canada.

Rivard, M., and M. Raymond. 2004. "The Effect of Tuition Fees on Post-Secondary Education in Canada in the Late 1990s." Working Paper 2004-09, Department of Finance, Ottawa.

Shaienks, D., and T. Gluszynski. 2007. "Participation in Post-Secondary Education: Graduates, Continuers and Drop Outs, Results from YITS Cycle 4." Catalogue no. 81-595-MIE – No. 059. Ottawa: Statistics Canada.

Shaienks, D., J. Eisl-Culkin, and P. Bussière. 2006. "Follow-Up on Education and Labour Market Pathways of Young Canadians Aged 18 to 20 – Results from YITS Cycle 3." Catalogue no. 81-595-MIE – No. 045. Ottawa: Statistics Canada.

Todd, P., and K. Wolpin. 2007. "The Production of Cognitive Achievement in Children: Home, School and Racial Test Score Gaps." *Journal of Human Capital* 1 (1): 91-136.

Tremblay, R E., D. Larocque, M. Boivin, D. Pérusse, M. Zoccolillo, and R.O. Pihl. In press. "Physical Aggression during Infancy and Onset of Male Conduct Disorder." In *A Developmental Approach of Antisocial Behavior*, ed. W. Koops, N. W. Slot and R. Loeber. Abingdon, United Kingdom: Psychology Press.

11

Family Environment, Family Habits, and Children's Cultural Experiences: Is There a Link to Participation in Post-Secondary Education?

STEPHEN CHILDS, ROSS FINNIE, AND RICHARD E. MUELLER

Dans cet article, nous établissons un lien entre la poursuite d'études postsecondaires et divers indicateurs très précis des habitudes des enfants dans leur milieu familial. Parmi ces indicateurs, citons : les types de communication entre les parents et les enfants, le soutien familial à l'apprentissage des enfants, la présence ou non d'un certain nombre de biens matériels à la maison, les habitudes de la famille en matière d'activités culturelles, et les habitudes de lecture des enfants. Les résultats montrent qu'il y a une corrélation importante entre ces facteurs, d'une part, et les résultats scolaires des jeunes au niveau postsecondaire et, en particulier, le fait de fréquenter ou non l'université, d'autre part, même quand on tient compte d'autres caractéristiques importantes des familles, comme le revenu et le degré de scolarité des parents. Cette recherche fournit donc de nouvelles données qui s'ajoutent à la littérature de plus en plus abondante qui traite de l'accès aux études postsecondaires.

This paper extends the growing literature on access to post-secondary education by relating access to a variety of detailed indicators of children's experiences in the family setting. These measures include patterns of communication between parents and children, family support for children's learning, material endowment of the household, and family cultural activities and reading habits. These factors all turn out to be important correlates of post-secondary educational outcomes – university attendance, in particular – even after controlling for other important family characteristics such as income and parental education levels.

Pursuing Higher Education in Canada: Economic, Social, and Policy Dimensions, ed. R. Finnie, M. Frenette, R.E. Mueller, and A. Sweetman. Montreal and Kingston: Queen's Policy Studies Series, McGill-Queen's University Press.

Introduction

Identifying the determinants of participation in post-secondary education (PSE) has long been of interest to academics, policy-makers, educators, parents, and even students themselves. This interest is grounded in the understanding that going to college or university can be a life-changing experience for individuals, and is key to the nation's future economic prosperity. While this paper does not go so far as to identify causal determinants, it does explore correlations (or correlations conditional on observable characteristics) that are useful and insightful, and contributes to literature looking at the determinants of entry into PSE.

Important advances have been made in this area in recent years, especially as research has gone from focusing almost exclusively on the importance of financial factors such as tuition levels, student assistance programs, and family income to investigating early influences, particularly ones related to the family. These influences cause some individuals to begin to think about and prepare for PSE from an early age, while others never make it even to the PSE starting line. This line of research, including important contributions by Nobel laureate James Heckman and various colleagues (e.g., Cameron and Heckman 2001; Carneiro and Heckman 2002), has largely been made possible by the availability of longitudinal datasets. In Canada, this includes the Youth in Transition Survey, which has allowed researchers to link PSE choices to child and family characteristics, behaviours, and experiences.

This research has resulted in an increasing realization that although family income can indeed generate advantages or disadvantages, differences in family background not directly related to income are also important determinants of PSE attainment – and indeed may be the dominant influences. And so when we ask "How do we get more – or the most deserving – students through the doors of our PSE institutions and ensure they are able to complete their programs?" our discussions now commonly include reference to early family-based influences in addition to what might be done in terms of financial incentives, student aid programs, and other financial levers.

Thanks to an emerging body of research using Canadian data, we now know that factors such as parental education, student abilities, attitudes toward school, work ethic, schooling aspirations, and other such influences are strongly related to participation in college and (especially) university. (See the introduction and collection of papers in Finnie, Mueller, Sweetman, and Usher (2009)).

What remains unknown, however, is the precise mechanisms through which these factors work. Is it, for example, parental education per se that determines access to PSE,[1] either through its influence on the formation of preferences or the parental support provided for pursuing higher education? Or does parental education work via its effects on the young person's schooling opportunities at primary and secondary levels, extra-curricular activities, home environment, or some other set of influences? Or is there yet another set of causal relationships involved, for which parental education is merely a marker?

These questions are extremely important not only to our ultimate understanding of the determinants of PSE participation but also to related policy considerations. It is, for example, rather unhelpful to suggest that in order to increase PSE participation rates, we should raise the education level of parents, since this is clearly not possible, at least for a given young person or a given generation of families. But if we understand the environmental factors, family habits, and early experiences that determine who goes to PSE, interventions could conceivably be developed to affect outcomes in line with current policy goals. As noted social thinker Gøsta Esping-Anderson has put it, "We cannot pass laws that force parents to read to their children, but we can compensate" (2002).

The purpose of this paper is to present new evidence on how such background factors are related to access to PSE based on the Reading (or "A") Cohort of the Youth in Transition Survey. The YITS is superbly well suited to this line of investigation, unequalled in this respect perhaps even at the international level.

The measures available include patterns of communication between parents and children (do they talk, how frequently, about what), family support for the child's learning and home resources related to educational activities (e.g., do family members help the child, is there a quiet place to work, a computer, etc.), family wealth (as captured by the presence of certain material goods), "cultural" possessions and activities (having a dictionary in the home, going to museums and concerts, and the like), the child's reading habits (what, how much), and others.

We find that many of these factors are important correlates of educational outcomes. We do not present these results as necessarily representing causal influences, and we recognize the limitations of our analysis. For example, although we include family income as a control variable in our models, it could well be that the relationships between PSE outcomes and the other background variables we investigate are picking up income effects not captured by the particular income measures employed. Or they may be similarly capturing the effects of other parent, family, or background effects not otherwise captured in our analysis.

For example, while how much a child reads or goes to museums might be related to later university attendance, these activities could in turn be correlated with family income or unobserved parental characteristics (e.g., "orientation to learning") that are the actual determinants of access to PSE – not the child's reading or museum attendance habits per se. Alternatively, parents who identify a child who appears to be PSE bound might give that child more exposure to such cultural experiences because they think the child will benefit from those experiences once at

PSE, meaning that causality could run from an early decision to go to PSE to the cultural activities rather than vice versa. Other such spurious relationships might also be driving our results.

That said, we think this paper is useful for how it paints a picture of the kind of family backgrounds and early experiences that are related to attending PSE. While this line of inquiry is preliminary and we cannot infer causality from our results without further research, a better understanding of these relationships could point to certain kinds of policy interventions that might enhance the probability of PSE attendance, especially for those disadvantaged youth who face barriers that run much deeper than being able to afford PSE.

The paper is laid out as follows. The next section briefly reviews the relevant literature. We then discuss the methodology employed, introduce the data used in the estimation of the models, and present the main empirical results. The final section summarizes the findings and draws some implications for policy and future research.

Background Literature and Theoretical Frameworks

A number of recent Canadian studies have gone beyond assessing the importance of financial factors (tuition, student financial aid, family income, etc.) in the decision of young Canadians to pursue PSE and probe influences related to family background. One important consensus that has emerged (Butlin 1999; Drolet 2005; Finnie, Laporte, and Sweetman 2010; Finnie and Mueller 2008a, 2008b, 2009; Frenette 2007, 2008; others) is that parental education is a much better predictor of PSE participation than is parental income. In short, "culture" trumps money, where culture is a shorthand term for the many family influences – apart from those related to income and money, but considering all other factors including parental education – that affect a young person's attitude to and preparation for PSE (Finnie, Sweetman, and Usher 2009).[2]

Perhaps more importantly, the Finnie and Mueller papers, as well as the Finnie, Lascelles, and Sweetman (2005), show that high levels of parental education have both direct and indirect effects on access. Finnie and Mueller show, in particular, that parental education appears to be related to high school grades and PISA reading scores (the international test that YITS participants were given; see further below), which are in turn strongly related to access to PSE, thus pointing to one important channel through which parental education affects access. A myriad of other influences can be imagined – other ways in which parental education might affect PSE outcomes, as well as other aspects of the child's family environment and experiences that might also affect access to PSE.

These family background factors may be seen in terms of several different theoretical frameworks. One is the economic concept of *human capital*, or the knowledge, skills, and abilities that individuals gain, sometimes but not necessarily in the form of investment activities per se (schooling and on-the-job work experience are the classic forms), which subsequently yield a return in terms of labour market earnings. In this case, the "investments" (explicit or otherwise) are those related to the home environment and family based activities and experiences of young people, and the "returns" are the effects of these investments on access to PSE. For example, books are purchased, the child is read to, the child learns; and this learning increases the child's likelihood of going to PSE.

Another framework is provided by the concept of *cultural capital*, rooted in the sociological literature and less familiar to economists. Esping-Andersen (2008, 23) suggests four particular mechanisms through which children's opportunities are transferred from parents: family income, family structure, parental dedication, and cultural capital – the last defined as "the learning milieu within which children grow up."

Cultural capital thus refers to a specific set of ways in which parents pass their social status and economic opportunities on to their children (see, for example, Bourdieu 1983; DiMaggio 1982; Esping-Andersen 2002, 2004, 2008). These processes involve the knowledge, experiences, and connections that help individuals succeed in life, and the earlier "production" of educational outcomes, including PSE, that are important determinants of these attributes. Since highly educated parents tend to provide their children with more cultural capital, this propagates inequality in educational attainment and affects later outcomes (i.e., socio-economic status).

According to Esping-Andersen (2004), cultural capital affects educational outcomes through two mechanisms. The first is through early childhood stimulation, which establishes children's cognitive skills, and the second is the effect of children's "cultural capital stock" on their educational choices. Esping-Anderson thus echoes an important idea previously proposed by Mare (1993), which is that it is critical to overcome the class origins involved in transitions from one level of education to the next, because each outcome is critical to later ones, while the *direct* effects of family background on performance and educational attainment wane.

Esping-Andersen (2004) argues that public policy can be used to break this link between class origins and cognitive and educational inequalities, and that changes in children's early cognitive development could be more effective in untying the "Gordian knot" of social inheritance than (say) simply attempting to ensure the equality of access to education in any formal sense.

In this paper we do not attempt to test these specific theories. Instead, we establish a set of empirical relationships regarding family background and access to PSE which different readers may interpret using either of these human and cultural capital frameworks, a combination of the two, or another paradigm altogether.

Methodology

This paper uses a standard empirical model for estimating access to PSE, which is taken to be a function of a variety of different sets of influences. We work from a baseline set of regressors that have been repeatedly shown to be influential in the PSE attendance decision, and then add the more detailed family background measures available in the YITS-A dataset.

To capture the decision of the type of PSE the individual attends, a multinomial logit model of the following form is used:

$$Y = X_1\beta_1 + X_2\beta_2 + \mu,$$

where Y is the access measure of interest; participation in college, participation in university, or no PSE; X_1 represents the standard variables included in such models, and X_2 represents the added background variables; β_1 and β_2 are the coefficients associated with those variables; and μ is the classical stochastic error term.

Included in X_1 are, most notably, family income, parental education, and family type (two parent versus single parent), which have repeatedly been shown to be important predictors of PSE attendance. Also included are province, language, area size of residence (urban-rural), and immigrant status. These simpler models, which represent the starting point of our analysis, capture the total effects of these variables on access, regardless of the path of those influences (i.e., direct or indirect), while of course also picking up the influences of other omitted factors with which they are correlated.

Our next models include the variables represented by X_2, a total of nine indices that capture the extended background influences discussed above, each one representing a particular set of factors. A description of the nine indices, along with their components, can be found in Appendix Table A1 and are discussed below.[3]

Estimating these two sets of models thus allows us to both broaden our perspective of the family background factors that are related to access to PSE, and to better understand the direct and indirect effects of the conventional family background influences (i.e., income, education, etc.). Our multinomial setup allows the variables included in our models to have different effects on college and university participation (as compared to no PSE), while permitting these processes to be related.

Although the model thus yields a set of estimated relationships that relate each explanatory variable to the probability of not going to PSE, going to college, or going to university, we discuss mainly the university effects. The reason is that the results for university participation are generally larger and more statistically significant than those for college participation and are thus (in our opinion) more worthy of attention.[4]

We repeat that we do not believe we are necessarily estimating causal relationships or "effects" in any true sense of the word, which we use simply to refer to the estimated correlations obtained by our models. First of all, the variables included in our models may be correlated with a range of omitted influences on PSE attendance, including those related to unobserved family background influences or to the individuals themselves. Secondly, at least some of our measures are likely to be endogenous to PSE decisions, even though they are generally captured at age 15, well before PSE decisions are formally made at the end of high school. For example, students who plan to attend university may read more, seek out more cultural events, and otherwise engage in certain activities that will help them to actually get into PSE, be accepted at better institutions, or do better when they get there. Our regressors may thus to some degree be a function of attending PSE rather than determinants of that outcome.

As previously noted, the relationships that we estimate should be of interest all the same. First, we are able to paint a fuller picture of the *correlates* of attending PSE and the types of family backgrounds and experiences that are associated with going on to higher education – and these correlates may point in the directions of further research we need to undertake before ultimately considering policy interventions. Secondly, adding the fuller set of regressors helps point to the channels through which more conventionally measured family characteristics such as family income and parental education may operate to affect children's PSE outcomes.

The Data

The Youth in Transition Survey – Cohort A (or YITS-A) initially interviewed a representative sample of Canadian high school students aged 15 as of 31 December 1999 in early 2000 (Cycle 1). The YITS was carried out in conjunction with the Programme for International Student Assessment (PISA), which was conducted in 43 countries. Unlike the PISA surveys in other countries, however, in Canada these students' parents were also interviewed.[5] Furthermore, the students themselves (although not their parents or school administrators) were followed up in subsequent surveys in 2002, 2004, 2006, and 2008 (Cycles 2, 3, 4, and 5). We chose to observe the respondents' PSE status in the 2006 (Cycle 4) survey as the optimal compromise between the ability to consider different PSE pathways and sample size. In this latter wave of the survey, the young people were 21 years of age, a point at which they have made their initial choices about entering PSE, which is the basis of our analysis.

The dependent variable in our study represents whether the individuals enrolled in college or university at any point over the four cycles of the survey, regardless of whether or not they continued in their studies. This is the standard definition of access to PSE used in the literature; continuing on to graduation and other aspects of "persistence" are normally thought of as being a separate process. We differentiate access to college and university, counting the latter if the individual accessed both.

Our analysis includes information taken from several components of the YITS. Key family background measures such as parental income and education, immigration status, and family structure are taken from the parental questionnaire. Some of the standard controls (such as rural-urban status, province of residence before PSE, and language) are based on the high school attended. PSE attendance information is taken from the student.

Finally, the extended background variables central to our analysis come directly from the PISA component, where students were asked a battery of questions that gave rise to the index variables we employ. The responses of all students across the international scope of PISA were used to standardize these indices, each one having a mean value of zero and a standard deviation of one across all respondents. The value of each index for individual students thus reflects their responses to the questions relative to all other students. See Appendix Table A1 for the variables underlying the construction of each index.

In some other PISA countries, researchers have looked at the effects of these background variables on PISA test scores (reading, math, science), but the longitudinal properties of the YITS allow us to look at their effects on subsequent PSE outcomes – in many ways a much more interesting and more important outcome.

Respondents who are not Canadian citizens and those with unknown citizenship status are dropped from our sample. We also drop those individuals who were still continuing in high school in Cycle 4 because we do not observe any potential transition in to PSE for this group. Finally, the few students for whom information on the highest level of PSE is missing are also excluded from the analysis. These selection criteria result in fewer than 3 percent of eligible observations being removed from the sample.[6]

We include in our samples only those who responded to all four surveys and whose parents participated in the first survey, using the appropriate weights provided by Statistics Canada for attrition and non-response. While attrition from the YITS has been significant (54.7 percent of respondents from the initial survey responded to Cycle 4; see Statistics Canada 2007), the tests performed in Diaconu (2010) suggest the weights meant to adjust for attrition do a good job of preserving access rates between Cycles 3 and 4.

Table 1 contains the summary statistics derived from the YITS, separately for females and males. This final (main) sample, which contains

TABLE 1
Descriptive Statistics

| Variable | Mean | Participation Rate | | |
		No PSE %	Trade or College %	University %
Total		25.0	32.9	42.1
Female	0.498	18.8	31.3	49.9
Male	0.502	31.2	34.5	34.3
Family income level				
$5,000 to $25,000	0.073	38.0	32.0	30.1
$25,000 to $50,000	0.253	32.6	35.4	32.1
$50,000 to $75,000	0.283	25.7	34.9	39.5
$75,000 to $100,000	0.227	20.0	31.3	48.6
$100,000 and up	0.151	12.4	27.8	59.8
Parents' education				
Less than HS	0.085	51.7	33.0	15.3
Some PSE	0.214	33.9	38.1	28.0
HS completed	0.067	27.5	38.7	33.8
Trade/college	0.311	26.4	37.6	36.0
University – below BA degree	0.047	15.2	31.6	53.2
University – BA	0.183	11.2	26.4	62.5
University – grad	0.093	5.9	14.5	79.6
Other/unknown	0.001	35.4	38.2	26.5
HS location				
Rural	0.231	32.4	35.4	32.2
Urban	0.769	22.8	32.2	45.0
HS province				
Newfoundland and Labrador	0.020	25.1	30.2	44.7
Prince Edward Island	0.005	22.0	21.3	56.7
Nova Scotia	0.033	22.7	22.6	54.8
New Brunswick	0.027	26.4	24.1	49.6
Quebec	0.226	29.3	40.0	30.7
Ontario	0.375	17.8	36.3	45.9
Manitoba	0.037	32.2	19.9	48.0
Saskatchewan	0.039	32.0	23.6	44.4
Alberta	0.106	33.0	28.0	39.0
British Columbia	0.132	28.2	26.8	45.0
Linguistic minority				
French outside QC	0.028	21.9	34.8	43.3
English in QC	0.020	17.2	40.4	42.4
Family type				
Two parents	0.828	23.7	32.4	43.9
Mother only	0.131	30.8	34.5	34.7
Father only	0.026	30.4	39.9	29.6
Other	0.014	38.4	33.4	28.2
Immigrant status				
Non-immigrant	0.716	28.1	34.2	37.7
1st generation	0.081	13.8	29.3	57.0
2nd generation	0.180	16.2	29.5	54.3
Generation unknown	0.024	37.2	33.3	29.5

Source: Authors' compilation.

8,518 females and 8,120 males, is used to estimate the baseline models. The samples are slightly reduced in the models that include the extra background variables, due to further missing information. The minimum sample size is 8,370 for females and 7,841 for males. The overall university participation rate of our sample is 42.1 percent (Table 1). For males, the rate is 34.3 percent, and for females it is 49.9 percent.

Results

The Baseline Models

The main estimation results shown in Table 2 report the average marginal probability effects derived from the multinomial logit models, along with their associated standard errors (conventional levels of significance are indicated by asterisks). Results are shown for the different models run for females and males. The interpretation of these effects is straightforward: how much does the probability of the indicated outcome – access to college or university – change with the variable in question?[7] We begin with the baseline model (the first two columns with the "College" and "University" outcomes), for which the findings are comparable to what is found elsewhere in the literature, including other work based on the YITS (e.g., Finnie and Mueller 2008a, 2008b, 2009; Frenette 2007, 2008).

Parental education, measured here by the highest numbers of years of schooling of the mother or father (other particular specifications of the education effects generate similar results), is strongly related to university attendance in particular, with each additional year of schooling associated with a 6.4 percent higher probability of attending university in the case of both males and females (i.e., the .064 shown in the "University" columns under the "Baseline Model" headings). Parental education has no net effect on college attendance, for reasons explained earlier. Family income has a weaker effect than parental education, with a $10,000 increase in income associated with about a 2 percent higher probability of attending university for females (the estimated .0020 times 10), and about one-third this magnitude for males. (It too is unrelated to college attendance.) The gender difference in the income relationship is notable and establishes a theme that we return to below.

In addition, those from urban areas are more likely to attend university and less likely to attend college. In comparison to Ontario, those from the Atlantic provinces are more likely to be university participants, while in the West the opposite is generally the case. Respondents from all provinces, with the exception of Quebec, are less likely to attend college than those in Ontario. Both first and second generation Canadians (i.e., the children of immigrants) go to university at much higher rates, and to college at lower rates, than do non-immigrant youth (see Finnie and

TABLE 2
Multinomial Model Estimation Results: Baseline Model and PISA Index Scores

	Females						Males					
	Basic Model		Separately		Jointly		Basic Model		Separately		Jointly	
	College	University	College	University	College	University	College	University	College	University	College	University
Family income (in $1,000s)	0.000045 [0.0003357]	0.002018*** [0.0004880]			-0.000012 [0.0003272]	0.001337*** [0.0005022]	-0.000048 [0.0002192]	0.000674*** [0.0002434]			-0.000062 [0.0001752]	0.000414** [0.0001916]
Parents' highest level of education (in years)	-0.004 [0.003]	0.064*** [0.004]			-0.002 [0.003]	0.050*** [0.004]	-0.008** [0.003]	0.064*** [0.004]			-0.007** [0.004]	0.051*** [0.004]
HS location – urban (rural)	-0.047*** [0.017]	0.053*** [0.018]			-0.046*** [0.017]	0.040** [0.018]	-0.023 [0.017]	0.078*** [0.016]			-0.022 [0.017]	0.066*** [0.017]
HS province (Ontario)												
Newfoundland and Labrador	-0.140*** [0.026]	0.142*** [0.029]			-0.139*** [0.026]	0.144*** [0.029]	-0.087*** [0.028]	0.118*** [0.029]			-0.081*** [0.028]	0.129*** [0.029]
Prince Edward Island	-0.183*** [0.024]	0.191*** [0.026]			-0.191*** [0.023]	0.203*** [0.025]	-0.189*** [0.025]	0.216*** [0.028]			-0.190*** [0.025]	0.230*** [0.028]
Nova Scotia	-0.184*** [0.023]	0.187*** [0.025]			-0.183*** [0.023]	0.185*** [0.025]	-0.155*** [0.024]	0.162*** [0.026]			-0.157*** [0.024]	0.170*** [0.025]
New Brunswick	-0.168*** [0.024]	0.151*** [0.026]			-0.172*** [0.023]	0.160*** [0.025]	-0.169*** [0.023]	0.145*** [0.026]			-0.160*** [0.024]	0.153*** [0.026]
Quebec	0.012 [0.024]	-0.056** [0.027]			0.005 [0.024]	-0.044* [0.027]	0.020 [0.025]	-0.077*** [0.020]			0.014 [0.027]	-0.057*** [0.021]
Manitoba	-0.161*** [0.024]	0.090*** [0.026]			-0.161*** [0.024]	0.095*** [0.026]	-0.216*** [0.022]	0.112*** [0.027]			-0.214*** [0.023]	0.128*** [0.026]
Saskatchewan	-0.141*** [0.024]	0.077*** [0.027]			-0.147*** [0.024]	0.094*** [0.026]	-0.190*** [0.022]	0.108*** [0.025]			-0.200*** [0.022]	0.133*** [0.025]

...continued

TABLE 2
(Continued)

	Females						Males					
	Basic Model		Separately		Jointly		Basic Model		Separately		Jointly	
	College	University	College	University	College	University	College	University	College	University	College	University
Alberta	-0.073*** [0.025]	-0.049* [0.026]			-0.065*** [0.025]	-0.069*** [0.026]	-0.119*** [0.023]	0.003 [0.022]			-0.122*** [0.023]	-0.011 [0.022]
British Columbia	-0.094*** [0.024]	-0.008 [0.026]			-0.088*** [0.024]	-0.020 [0.026]	-0.106*** [0.024]	0.019 [0.024]			-0.105*** [0.024]	0.007 [0.024]
HS language												
French outside Quebec	0.003 [0.034]	0.023 [0.035]			-0.014 [0.032]	0.051 [0.035]	0.043 [0.034]	0.005 [0.035]			0.023 [0.033]	0.040 [0.040]
English in Quebec	0.012 [0.043]	0.060 [0.055]			0.012 [0.041]	0.054 [0.051]	0.047 [0.037]	0.041 [0.041]			0.063 [0.039]	0.006 [0.042]
Family structure (two parents)												
Mother only	0.025 [0.024]	-0.037 [0.028]			0.023 [0.024]	-0.022 [0.028]	-0.018 [0.024]	-0.047* [0.026]			0.003 [0.025]	-0.045* [0.025]
Father only	0.093* [0.052]	-0.102* [0.057]			0.065 [0.048]	-0.054 [0.056]	0.030 [0.051]	-0.090** [0.045]			0.021 [0.049]	-0.061 [0.043]
Other	0.030 [0.079]	-0.060 [0.087]			0.032 [0.078]	-0.054 [0.080]	0.011 [0.085]	0.000 [0.100]			0.020 [0.091]	0.032 [0.103]
Immigrant status (not an immigrant)												
First generation	-0.078** [0.035]	0.186*** [0.038]			-0.080** [0.034]	0.182*** [0.036]	0.013 [0.034]	0.126*** [0.038]			-0.005 [0.034]	0.123*** [0.037]
Second generation	-0.047** [0.022]	0.130*** [0.025]			-0.038* [0.022]	0.113*** [0.026]	-0.010 [0.021]	0.120*** [0.023]			-0.001 [0.021]	0.109*** [0.022]
Unknown/don't know	0.052 [0.061]	-0.056 [0.066]			0.050 [0.059]	-0.028 [0.063]	-0.059 [0.054]	-0.025 [0.062]			-0.078 [0.052]	-0.032 [0.062]

...continued

TABLE 2
(Continued)

	Females						Males					
	Basic Model		Separately		Jointly		Basic Model		Separately		Jointly	
	College	University	College	University	College	University	College	University	College	University	College	University
PISA index score												
Cultural communication with parents			-0.016** [0.008]	0.076*** [0.009]	-0.016* [0.009]	0.034*** [0.010]			-0.011 [0.008]	0.083*** [0.007]	-0.002 [0.009]	0.044*** [0.009]
Social communication with parents			-0.002 [0.008]	0.061*** [0.008]	-0.005 [0.009]	0.040*** [0.009]			-0.015* [0.008]	0.066*** [0.008]	-0.020** [0.009]	0.036*** [0.009]
Family educational support			0.013 [0.009]	-0.021** [0.009]	0.023** [0.009]	-0.063*** [0.010]			0.015* [0.008]	-0.020** [0.008]	0.020** [0.009]	-0.052*** [0.008]
Family wealth			0.001 [0.011]	0.060*** [0.012]	-0.001 [0.011]	0.049*** [0.012]			0.016 [0.010]	0.025** [0.010]	0.009 [0.010]	0.018* [0.010]
Home educational resources			-0.002 [0.008]	0.073*** [0.008]	0.001 [0.008]	0.047*** [0.009]			0.015* [0.008]	0.049*** [0.008]	0.015* [0.008]	0.023*** [0.008]
Activities related to "classical" culture			-0.008 [0.008]	0.101*** [0.009]	-0.003 [0.009]	0.066*** [0.009]			-0.014* [0.008]	0.075*** [0.008]	-0.008 [0.009]	0.034*** [0.009]
"Classical" culture in the family home			-0.012 [0.008]	0.054*** [0.008]	-0.008 [0.009]	-0.010 [0.009]			-0.012 [0.008]	0.057*** [0.007]	-0.012 [0.008]	0.009 [0.008]
Engagement in reading			-0.005 [0.007]	0.087*** [0.007]	0.002 [0.008]	0.062*** [0.008]			-0.023*** [0.007]	0.091*** [0.007]	-0.026*** [0.009]	0.058*** [0.008]
Reading diversity			-0.009 [0.008]	0.067*** [0.009]	-0.008 [0.009]	0.001 [0.010]			0.006 [0.008]	0.063*** [0.007]	0.017* [0.009]	0.011 [0.008]
Observations	8,518				8,370		8,120				7,841	

Notes: The omitted categories for the different sets of categorical variables are shown in parentheses. The models where the indices are estimated separately also include all of the controls included in the baseline model, but in the interest of parsimony are not included here (there would be a different set for the inclusion of each variable). Sample sizes are not shown for those results for similar reasons, although they differ from the other models only slightly. Average marginal effects are shown, standard errors are shown in brackets, and the asterisks indicate standard levels of statistical signicance: *** p<0.01, ** p<0.05, * p<0.10.

Source: Authors' compilation.

Mueller (2009) and the Finnie-Mueller paper in this volume for more on this), while family structure is unimportant for both males and females.

We have not included in these models students' grades or PISA reading scores, typically found to be strongly related to participating in PSE, since we believe that these measures are themselves at least partly determined by family background factors, including both those represented by the sorts of conventional measures presented here (income, education, etc., as shown and discussed in the Finnie-Mueller papers referenced above) and the more extensive sets of measures to be added below. Adding grades and PISA scores would therefore only confound these relationships. Of course, not including these variables could also bias the other coefficients in the model, but in practice including them did not markedly change the coefficient estimates presented below.[8]

Adding the PISA Indices

Table 2 also shows the results obtained by separately and then jointly adding the nine PISA indices to the baseline model. The effects of the extra background variables are also shown in Figures 1 and 2 (males and females). The bars in each figure show the average marginal effects of each of the indices on the probability of attending university (as also reported in the table). Given the construction of these indices, the correlations shown represent the difference in the probability of accessing university associated with a one standard deviation higher level of the index (see above regarding the construction of the indices and the meaning of the one standard deviation difference). From this point forward, we generally only discuss the correlates with university attendance, since almost none of the indices – whether entered into the model separately or jointly – have much net effect on college attendance.

Almost all of the indices have statistically significant effects, at least on university attendance, for both males and females. And with overall university participation rates being 34.3 percent for males and 49.9 percent for females, the effects represent substantial differences in university access rates for those having higher index values (by one standard deviation) as compared to those having the mean values.

Cultural communication with parents includes measures of the student's responses regarding the frequency of discussions with parents on political or social issues, books, television programs, or movies, and how often they listen to classical music together (see Appendix Table A1). When the variable is included on its own, without the other indices ("Separately" in the table and graphs), students who are one standard deviation above the mean in this regard have an increased probability of university attendance of about 8 percentage points for both males and females. Even after including the other indices ("Jointly"), this factor continues to be important, although its effect is cut in about half.

FIGURE 1
Average Marginal Effects of PISA Indices on University Access, Females

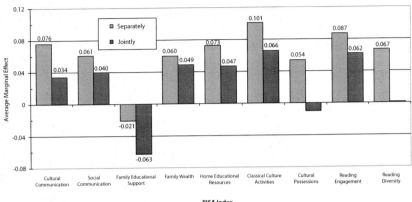

Note: Bars with data labels denote statistical significance at at least the 5 percent level.
Source: Authors' compilation.

FIGURE 2
Average Marginal Effects of PISA Indices on University Access, Males

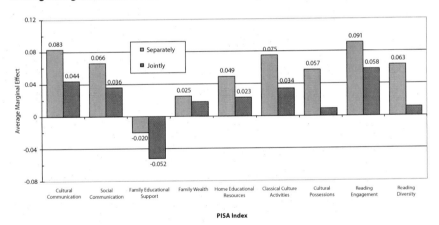

Note: Bars with data labels denote statistical significance at at least the 5 percent level.
Source: Authors' compilation.

Related to cultural communication is *social communication with parents*, which includes measures of the frequency of discussions among students and their parents about school, as well as parent-child conversations in general (i.e., regardless of the topic). Also included is a measure of how often the family eats their main meal around a table together. Again, for both males and females, the association with university attendance is positive: about 6 percentage points, dropping to about 4 when the model is estimated with all the indices included jointly.

Family educational support measures how often members of the family (mothers, fathers, siblings, etc.) help with the student's homework. Those who receive more help are actually somewhat less likely to attend university; interestingly, the effects get larger (and more statistically significant) when the other variables are also included in the model. We interpret these negative effects to be the result of the likely endogeneity of this variable: young people having troubles at school will be in greater need of help from another family member. This conjecture would seem to be consistent with the finding that these effects are substantially reduced when the student's high school grades and PISA scores are included in the models (results not shown here). An alternative explanation could be that parents who are excessively involved in helping their children with homework may not be allowing them to stand on their own two feet. Other reasons for the observed correlation are also possible.

Family wealth includes a diverse set of measures designed to capture the wealth of the student's household by the presence (or absence) of consumer durables (such as cars and dishwashers), household features (such as bathrooms), and technology (cellular phones, computers, and Internet connections). A respondent whose household is above the mean in this measure is more likely to attend university. Recall that these models also include family income as reported by the parents, so these family wealth effects are on top of whatever is captured by that variable. Like the income variable itself, the correlation is considerably more pronounced for females than males (.060 versus .025 in the separate models), and again diminishes once other cultural capital indices are included (.049 and.018), but not as much as the other indices seen thus far.

Likely related to family wealth are *home educational resources*, which measure the presence of a dictionary, a quiet place to study, a desk for studying, textbooks, and hand-held calculators. This index is positively correlated with university attendance, especially for females (7.3 percentage points) as compared to males (4.9 points), which is consistent with the previous findings of stronger income/wealth effects for females than males. Its impact is diminished by about one-third for females when the model is estimated jointly (to 4.7 points), and reduced even more (in relative terms) for males (to 2.3 percentage points).

Classical culture is related to the number of times in the year prior to the survey that the respondents went to a museum or art gallery, opera, ballet, classical symphony concert, or live theatre. Added separately, this index has the strongest correlation with university participation for females: 10.1 percentage points (reduced to 6.6 when other indices are added). For males, the association is weaker (7.5 and 3.4 percentage points, respectively).

A similar measure is the index of *cultural possessions* in the household, which includes classical literature, books of poetry, and works of art. Females and males who score one standard deviation higher on this index have university participation rates of 5.4 and 5.7 percentage points, respectively, higher than those at the mean, but this difference disappears when the other indices are added to the model. These last two sets of results suggest, intriguingly, that actual experiences related to classical culture (i.e., attending concerts, etc.) may be more important than mere ownership of it.

The final two indices capture the respondent's enjoyment of reading and the variety of reading matter. *Reading engagement* is based on questions that ask if the student enjoys reading outside the school context. This variable has a strong correlation with university attendance – approximately 9 percentage points (for both males and females) – and remains strong even when the other indices are included. This result is perhaps not surprising, as reading ability, as captured by the individual's PISA reading score, has previously been shown to have a strong correlation with university access (e.g., Finnie and Mueller 2008a, 2008b).

The second reading index, *reading diversity*, includes the range of the student's reading across six different kinds of material (magazines, comic books, fiction, non-fiction, online materials, and newspapers). There is a positive correlation when this index is specified separately, but it disappears when the other indices are included. This result suggests that it is the activity of reading itself that is important, not the diversity of reading materials.

In reviewing the gender patterns, it is interesting to note that the estimates for wealth, educational resources, and cultural activities are all larger for females – which is consistent with the effect of family income itself – while the rest of the results are more comparable or larger for males. We are currently engaged in pursing the question of why family income effects might be stronger for females than males. Note that this is not the case for the parental education effects, the single most important determinant of access to university, where the results for both genders are almost identical.

Not surprisingly, the associations tend to be weaker when the indices are included individually than when they are included together. This is due to the correlation among the indices and their related effects; they are to some degree capturing similar aspects of the family background and respondents' experiences. The exception to this is family educational support, which actually becomes more negative when the other measures are added.

While we do not attribute causal effects to the estimated relationships, they do paint an interesting portrait of those households whose children have higher university attendance rates. In particular, these families have better (or at least more frequent) communication between parents and their children on a range of issues, the children participate in cultural activities more often, and they enjoy reading. Of lesser importance are family wealth, home educational resources, cultural possessions, and reading diversity. In short, it's not what these families *have* but what they *do* – which is consistent with the more general finding, again reported here, that parental education is more important than family income. Once again, put in crude terms, culture appears to trump money.

The Importance of Parental Income and Parental Education

After adding the cultural capital indices to the model, it is worth assessing how the inclusion of these variables affects the influences of parental income and education. This can give us an idea of the extent to which parental education and family income influence access to PSE through the kind of environment and experiences they provide to children – as captured by the index variables. A similar exercise in Finnie and Mueller (2008a, 2008b) suggested that the effects of parents' education on university attendance appear to operate at least in part (though not wholly) through their children's higher PISA scores, better grades in school, and other related factors, whereas family income had more of an independent, direct influence, which was also smaller overall.

These relationships can be seen by comparing the education and income effects for the baseline model and those obtained for the model with all the indices entered jointly. (No results are reported for the baseline variables when the indices are entered separately, because each one of these estimates is based on a separate regression, which generates a different set of results for these common variables.)

In terms of parental education, an additional year of schooling for the parents increases the probability of attending university by 6.4 percentage points in the baseline model for both males and females. When all the indices are considered, the effect is reduced by approximately 1.3-1.4 percentage points – a decline of 20-22 percent in relative terms.

As mentioned earlier, the effect of parental income differs substantially between males and females. In the baseline model, a female student from a household with $10,000 more in family income is 2 percentage points more likely to attend university, while the comparable difference for a male is less than half that. The proportional effect of adding all the index variables is, however, similar for both males and females: in each case the income effect is reduced by about one-third. (Of course, that represents a larger absolute decrease for females.)

These results thus suggest that parental education and income have substantial influences on university access that operate independently of the other background effects measured here (i.e., the indices), but that those other effects represent one channel – albeit a moderate one – through which wealthy and educated households raise their children's opportunities for access to PSE. Interestingly, the larger proportional decrease in the income effect may suggest that these cultural factors are slightly more strongly related to income and wealth than to parental education, the opposite of what Finnie and Mueller found when looking at high school grades, PISA scores, and various high school experience variables (social and educational engagement, and so on).

It is also worth mentioning that we tried estimating the models with the indices interacted with parental education and parental income (separately), on the grounds that the family background effects might be stronger for individuals from more disadvantaged backgrounds. This was not the case: the effects were not statistically different for the different groups. (Estimating completely separate models for high and low income/education families obtained similar findings.)

Conclusions

For young people, the choice of whether or not to go on to PSE, and if so, which type of institution to attend (college or university), is complex and multi-dimensional, depending on a range of interdependent influences that start early and are to a significant degree rooted in the family (Finnie, Sweetman, and Usher 2009). In this paper we have attempted to extend our understanding of the determinants of access to post-secondary education by looking at the detailed family backgrounds and related experiences associated with subsequent participation in PSE.

Our investigation is consistent with work in the sociological literature on cultural capital, a theoretical model that describes the opportunities that youth gain due to their early family experiences which determine schooling opportunities and, in turn, subsequent life outcomes; this model finds support in the strong intergenerational correlation in education attainment. Our work is, however, in line with economists' concepts of human capital, the development of which may again start early in the family context. The analysis may also be supported by other theoretical frameworks.

Our intention in this paper is not, however, to test competing models of *why* family background matters, but rather to provide new empirical evidence on *how* it matters. More specifically, we estimate the empirical relationship between a range of family background influences and PSE participation by exploiting a detailed set of variables capturing such factors available in the extremely rich YITS-A dataset. We measure the effects of these influences when they are included in our access models – which also control for other, more conventional family influences such as parental education, family income, and family type – individually and then jointly.

The goal is thus to paint a picture of the family backgrounds and early life experiences associated with young people's subsequent access to PSE, and our findings do that. We find statistically significant, and in most cases quantitatively important, associations between participation in PSE (university in particular) and the measures we include, representing communication between children and their parents, family educational support in both time and material resources, family wealth, activities and possessions related to "classical" culture, engagement in reading, and reading diversity.

Effects are estimated separately for males and females, and some interesting patterns are found. In particular, girls' PSE (university) outcomes seem to be more sensitive to the various measures of family wealth, as they are to family income itself, while the influences of the other factors are more similar for girls and boys, as is the effect of parental education, the single most important determinant of who goes to university and who does not.

Although the longitudinal nature of the YITS gives us family background and related information from the student and parent at age 15, well before PSE decisions are formally made in the late teens, we are wary of interpreting the correlations we find as representing causality. The variables we analyze may well proxy for other missing family characteristics that are the true drivers of children's access to PSE – including those related to family income and wealth, to parental values regarding education and the importance of investing in children, or to other specific characteristics or activities not otherwise included in our analysis. In other cases, the variables we include as *determinants of* access to PSE might *stem from* PSE decisions already made (i.e., at a relatively young age), which cause parents or their children to create certain pro-schooling environments or engage in related activities. Other possibilities exist.

Nevertheless, we believe that our results paint a unique and interesting picture of the sort of family environments and habits and related cultural and educational/developmental experiences that tend to lead youth on to PSE, and those that do not. Even though these factors might not be causal, they do point to the *sorts of* factors that might matter, or at least to the environments, experiences, and so on that are *markers for* what truly drives PSE participation. Our work by no means represents the final step in understanding these underlying processes, but it may be a useful step on that important path.

Notes

The authors are grateful for comments received from participants of presentations made at the Organisation for Economic Cooperation and Development (OECD) in Paris, at the Centre Interuniversitaire de Recherche sur la Science et la Technologie (CIRST) at the Université de Quebec à Montréal, at the Graduate School of Public and International Affairs at the University of Ottawa, at the special MESA sessions at the Canadian Economics Association Annual Meetings held in Toronto in May 2009, and at the Society for the Advancement of Behavioural Economics Annual Meetings in Halifax in July 2009. Special thanks go to Keith Banting, Marc Frenette, Barbara Glover, Arthur Sweetman, and Mike Veall for their careful readings of the paper and detailed comments.

1. At this point we use the terms "access" to PSE, "participation," attainment," and other terms interchangeably. The empirical work we present pertains to *access* per se, as it is conventionally defined, as discussed below.

2. We ignore the influence of genetics on PSE attendance throughout the paper.

3. In work in progress, we further disaggregate these indices into their individual components to arrive at an even richer understanding of the specific underlying factors related to PSE attendance.

4. It is not that the various factors do not affect the probability of going to college: they do. But they typically have two effects, the net effect of which is typically small. That is, individuals from higher income families, with more educated parents and so on, are more likely to go to PSE, including both college and university (i.e., a positive effect on college attendance), but they are also more likely to choose university rather than college if they do go to PSE (a negative effect on college attendance), and the overall effect (which is what our models capture) is typically small. Meanwhile, it is not really necessary to present the no-PSE effects, since they are the residual of the university and college effects – any positive effect on the probability of going to PSE (college or university) must be offset by an equal opposing effect on the probability of not going to PSE. Full estimation results (including the college results) are available from the authors upon request.

5. The initial survey and testing component of the YITS and the PISA were conducted at the high school level. The administrators of each participating school were interviewed about the characteristics of the particular school. This rich set of school characteristics is not used in this paper but has been used in the authors' other research.

6. Deceased respondents have also been dropped from the sample. Statistics Canada disclosure restrictions prevent us from providing a specific breakdown of these restrictions. Please direct any specific sample selection issues to the authors.

7. The baseline outcome is no PSE. The change in the probability of this outcome (not shown) is the residual of the college and university effects, the total change being zero due to the nature of the multinomial logit model employed. For any increase (decrease) in the probability of one outcome, there must be an offsetting decrease (increase) in the probabilities of the others.

8. Findings for models that include these variables are available from the authors. In general, the results on the PISA scores, in particular, do not change a great deal. See Finnie and Mueller (2008a, 2008b) for results on the variables included in the baseline models when grades and PISA scores are included.

References

Bourdieu, P. 1983. "The Forms of Capital." In *Handbook of Theory and Research in the Sociology of Education*, ed. J.G. Richardson, 241-58. Westport, CT: Greenwood.

Butlin, G. 1999. "Determinants of Postsecondary Education Participation." *Education Quarterly Review* 5 (3): 9-35.

Cameron, S.V., and J.J. Heckman. 2001. "The Dynamics of Educational Attainment for Black, Hispanic, and White Males." *Journal of Political Economy* 109 (3): 455-99.

Carneiro, P., and J.J. Heckman. 2002. "The Evidence on Credit Constraints in Post-Secondary Schooling." *Economic Journal* 112 (482): 705-34.

Diaconu, V. 2010. "The Effects of Attrition on Access to PSE: Evidence from YITS-A." Mimeo.

DiMaggio, P. 1982. "Cultural Capital and School Success." *American Sociological Review* 47 (2): 189-201.

Drolet, M. 2005. "Participation in Post-Secondary Education in Canada: Has the Role of Parental Income and Education Changed over the 1990s?" Statistics Canada, Analytical Studies Branch Research Paper Series No. 243.

Esping-Andersen, G. 2002. "A Child-Centred Social Investment Strategy." In *Why We Need a New Welfare State*, ed. G. Esping-Andersen, 26-48. Oxford: Oxford University Press.

– 2004. "Untying the Gordian Knot of Social Inheritance." *Research in Social Stratification and Mobility* 21: 115-38.

– 2008. "Childhood Investments and Skill Formation." *International Tax and Public Finance* 15 (1): 19-44.

Finnie, R., C. Laporte, and A. Sweetman. 2010. "Dropping Out and Bouncing Back: New Evidence on High School Dynamics in Canada. In *Pursuing Higher Education in Canada: Economic, Social, and Policy Dimensions*, ed. R. Finnie, M. Frenette, R.E. Mueller, and A. Sweetman, 91-118. Montreal and Kingston: Queen's Policy Studies Series, McGill-Queen's University Press.

Finnie, R., E. Lascelles, and A. Sweetman. 2005. "Who Goes? The Direct and Indirect Effects of Family Background on Access to Postsecondary Education." In *Higher Education in Canada*, ed. C.M. Beach, R.W. Boadway, and R.M. McInnis, 295-338. Montreal and Kingston: McGill-Queen's University Press.

Finnie, R., and R.E. Mueller. 2008a. "The Effects of Family Income, Parental Education and Other Background Factors on Access to Post-Secondary Education in Canada: Evidence from the YITS." MESA Project Research Paper. Toronto, ON: Educational Policy Institute.

– 2008b. "The Backgrounds of Canadian Youth and Access to Post-Secondary Education: New Evidence from the YITS." In *Who Goes? Who Stays? What Matters? Accessing and Persisting in Post-Secondary Education in Canada*, ed. R. Finnie, R.E. Mueller, A. Sweetman, and A. Usher, 79-107. Montreal and Kingston: Queen's Policy Studies Series, McGill-Queen's University Press.

– 2009. "Access to Post-Secondary Education in Canada among the Children of Immigrants." MESA Project Research Paper. Toronto, ON: Educational Policy Institute.

Finnie, R, R.E. Mueller, A. Sweetman, and A. Usher, eds. 2008. *Who Goes? Who Stays? What Matters? Accessing and Persisting in Post-Secondary Education in Canada*. Montreal and Kingston: Queen's Policy Studies Series, McGill-Queen's University Press.

Finnie, R., A. Sweetman, and A. Usher. 2008. "Introduction: A Framework for Thinking about Participation in Post-Secondary Education." In *Who Goes? Who Stays? What Matters? Accessing and Persisting in Post-Secondary Education in Canada*, ed. R. Finnie, R.E. Mueller, A. Sweetman, and A. Usher, 3-32. Montreal and Kingston: Queen's Policy Studies Series, McGill-Queen's University Press.

Frenette, M. 2007. "Why Are Youth from Lower-Income Families Less Likely to Attend University? Evidence from Academic Abilities, Parental Influences, and Financial Constraints." Statistics Canada, Analytical Studies Research Paper Series No. 295.

– 2008. "Understanding the Gender Gap in University Attendance: Evidence Based on Academic Performance, Study Habits, and Parental Influences." In *Who Goes? Who Stays? What Matters? Accessing and Persisting in Post-Secondary Education in Canada*, ed. R. Finnie, R.E. Mueller, A. Sweetman, and A. Usher, 135-52. Montreal and Kingston: McGill-Queen's University Press and Queen's School of Policy Studies.

Mare, R. 1994. "Education Stratification and Observed and Unobserved Components of Family Background." In *Persistent Inequality*, ed. Y. Shavit and H.P. Blossfeld, 351-76. Boulder, CO: Westview Press.

Statistics Canada. 2007. "Youth in Transition Survey (YITS) Cohort A – 21-Year-Olds Cycle 4: User Guide." Accessed at http://bit.ly/cAOXdb, 10 February 2010.

APPENDIX

TABLE A1
Composition of PISA Indices

Index	PISA Code	Components of Index	Valid Responses
Cultural communication with parents	CULTCOM	In general, how often do your parents: • discuss politics or social issues with you? • discuss films, books, or television programs with you? • listen to classical music with you?	Never or hardly ever; a few times a year; about once a month; several times a month; several times a week
Social communication with parents	SOCCOM	In general, how often do your parents: • discuss how well you are doing at school? • eat dinner with you around a table? • spend time just talking to you?	Never or hardly ever; a few times a year; about once a month; several times a month; several times a week
Family educational support	FAMEDSUP	How often do the following people work with you on your schoolwork? • Your mother • Your father • Your brothers and sisters • Your grandparents • Other relations • Friends of your parents	Never or hardly ever; a few times a year; about once a month; several times a month; several times a week
Family wealth	WEALTH	In your home, do you have: • a dishwasher? • a room of your own? • educational software? • a link to the Internet?	Yes/no
		How many of the following do you have at your home? • Cellular phone • Television • Computer • Motor car • Bathroom	None; one; two; three or more
Home educational resources	HEDRES	In your home, do you have: • a dictionary? • a quiet place to study? • a desk for study? • textbooks?	Yes/no
		How many of the following do you have at your home? • Calculators	None; one; two; three or more
Activities related to "classical" culture	CULTACT	During the past year, how often have you participated in these activities? • Visited a museum or art gallery • Attended an opera, ballet, or classical symphony concert • Watched live theatre	Never or hardly ever; once or twice a year; abour three or four times a year; more than four times a year

... continued

**TABLE A1
(Continued)**

Index	*PISA Code*	*Components of Index*	*Valid Responses*
Possessions related to "classical" culture in the family home	CULTPOSS	In your home, do you have: • classical literature (e.g., Shakespeare)? • books of poetry? • works of art (e.g., paintings)?	Yes/no
Engagement in reading	JOYREAD	How much do you disagree or agree with the following statements about reading? • I read only if I have to. • Reading is one of my favourite hobbies. • I like talking about books with other people. • I find it hard to finish books. • I feel happy if I receive a book as a present. • For me, reading is a waste of time. • I enjoy going to a bookstore or a library. • I read only to get the information I need. • I cannot sit still and read for more than a few minutes.	Strongly disagree, disagree, agree, strongly agree
Reading diversity	DIVREAD	How often do you read these materials because you want to? • Magazines • Comic books • Fiction (novels, narratives, stories) • Non-fiction books • Emails and web pages • Newspapers	Never or hardly ever; a few times a year; about once a month; several times a month; several times a week

Source: OECD, Manual for the PISA 2000 Database. Accessed at http://www.oecd.org/dataoecd/47/23/41943106.pdf, 25 February 2010.

12

Can I Get There from Here? Canadian Rural-Urban Participation Rates in Post-Secondary Education

E. Dianne Looker

En matière d'études postsecondaires (EPS), les possibilités offertes aux jeunes Canadiens des centres urbains et à ceux des régions rurales ne sont pas les mêmes. Dans cet article, à partir des données de la cohorte A des quatre cycles de l'Enquête auprès des jeunes en transition (EJET), j'analyse comment ces disparités influencent le choix des uns et des autres d'entreprendre ou non des EPS. J'examine les différences observées entre les jeunes de ces deux catégories dans cinq régions du Canada, d'abord dans le choix d'entreprendre ou non des EPS, et ensuite, parmi ceux qui font des EPS, dans le choix d'entreprendre ou non des études universitaires. Les résultats indiquent que, à part d'importantes distinctions entre le Québec et les autres régions – le système d'EPS n'étant pas le même au Québec que dans le reste du Canada –, plusieurs différences observées entre les jeunes des régions urbaines et ceux des régions rurales dans le choix d'entreprendre ou non des EPS s'expliquent par les caractéristiques des jeunes eux-mêmes et celles de leur famille ; toutefois, la situation est plus complexe quand on se concentre plus précisément sur les études universitaires. De plus, en matière de persévérance pendant des EPS, les données montrent peu ou pas de différences entre les deux catégories de jeunes ; toutefois, cette tendance pourrait changer au fur et à mesure que les jeunes vieillissent (ils n'avaient que 21 ou 22 ans au moment du cycle 4 de l'EJET).

This paper uses data from the four cycles of the Youth in Transitions Survey (YITS), Cohort A, to examine how the different post-secondary education (PSE) options available to youth across Canada affect the rates of participation in PSE of rural as compared to urban youth. The specific issues examined are rural-urban differences in participation in any PSE, and in participation in university in particular, among those who attend PSE within five regions of Canada. Findings show that, apart from some important differences between Quebec (which has a very different PSE system) and other regions, much of the rural-urban difference in participation in overall PSE can be explained by characteristics

Pursuing Higher Education in Canada: Economic, Social, and Policy Dimensions, ed. R. Finnie, M. Frenette, R.E. Mueller, and A. Sweetman. Montreal and Kingston: Queen's Policy Studies Series, McGill-Queen's University Press.

of students and their families in the different regions. For the choice to attend university, the situation is more complex. Moreover, the data show little or no rural-urban difference in persistence, but given that the youth are 21 or 22 in Cycle 4, that pattern may change as they age.

Introduction

This paper looks at rural-urban differences in participation in post-secondary education (PSE) and attendance at university among those who attend PSE in five regions of Canada. Rural versus urban location is one of the many factors known to influence youth's participation in PSE (Andres and Looker 2001; Butlin 1999; Corbett 2000, 2007; Christofides et al. 2001; Looker 1993, 1994, 1997a, 1997b, 2001, 2003, 2007; Rojewski 1999; Tomkowicz and Bushnik 2003; Witko et al. 2006). Much of this difference appears to reflect physical distance insofar as most urban areas have some type of post-secondary institution (often several), while few such institutions are located in rural areas (Andres and Looker 2001; Frenette 2004, 2006). This differential distribution of institutions (which itself varies by type of institution) means that rural youth often have to leave their home community to attend a post-secondary institution, particularly if they want to attend university.

There is also considerable variation in rates of post-secondary education participation across the regions of Canada, and differences in these rates with respect to rural versus urban location within the regions. This variation no doubt reflects in part the differences among the provinces and regions in the availability of PSE options. In much of the literature examining these effects, the focus has been on individual and family level factors that have an impact on rural youth's decisions about pursuing PSE (Cartwright and Allen 2002). Parents in rural areas tend to have lower levels of education (Looker 1994), and rural youth often have lower educational aspirations (Andres and Looker 2001; Looker 1993, 1997b). There has been less focus on the impact of different educational structures in the different regions of Canada (but see Lambert et al. 2004), despite the fact that these structures reflect and can be modified by public policy, while individual and family characteristics are more difficult to change with such policies.

The current analysis has potential policy implications since it considers the relationship of PSE educational structures with the PSE participation and persistence of rural versus urban youth. One of the reasons Alberta and British Columbia have invested so heavily in articulated systems (Dennison and Schuetze 2004; Frenette 2009), which allow university credit courses to be offered in the widely dispersed community college system, is to increase access to university programs for rural youth. University administrators elsewhere across Canada are considering similar options. The CEGEP system in Quebec involves students in PSE in a way that is very different from the systems in other areas of Canada. Discussions about whether similar systems would be advantageous for rural students in other regions need to be based on empirical evidence of the effects of this system on rural as well as urban youth.

The study of rural-urban differences in PSE participation is important for a number of reasons. Not only are rural students under-represented at universities but the dynamic of their decision-making about PSE is very different from that of most urban youth. While some rural youth may share background characteristics with many disadvantaged urban youth (low parental socio-economic status, no history of further education in their family or sub-culture, assumptions that further education is not for "people like me"), their geographical location puts them in a different situation. With the exception of those who live in the few rural communities in Canada that contain a university, most would have to leave their community to pursue a university program. This usually means leaving not only the parental home but also their friendship network of support.

Beyond the impact on individuals, requiring rural youth to leave to pursue PSE has a major impact on rural communities as well. Corbett (2000, 2007) presents a detailed and insightful analysis of how rural youth are "learning to leave" by following dictates that urge them to continue beyond high school. Moreover, as Bollman and Berishi (2000) note, the rate of out-migration from rural and small town areas is higher for each level of educational attainment. In other words, rural youth not only leave to pursue PSE, but once they leave, they are unlikely to return, despite their close ties to their community (Looker 1993). This out-migration of youth is an ongoing issue in Canada: "There has been for some time substantial concern regarding the loss of young people in rural communities" (Dupuy et al. 2000, 1; see also Rothwell et al. 2002).

Thus youth out-migration is an issue not only for those interested in educational policy but for those involved in policies related to rural economic development as well. That is, the "solution" to the problem of rural youth under-representation in certain PSE programs, particularly university, may not be simply to put supports in place to encourage more youth to pursue this level of education and to continue on to graduation. Rather, assuming a will to maintain and revitalize rural areas, initiatives may need to take into account more macro level issues of the health of rural communities and how to keep or attract youth, including highly educated youth, to these areas.

Data and Measures

The data used in this analysis come from the Youth in Transitions Survey (YITS), Cohort A, who were 15 years of age at the time of the first data collection. In 2000, surveys were given to a sample of students, born in 1984, in the ten provinces in Canada. A two-stage sampling procedure was used, with the first stage involving the selection of 1,200 schools. Within each school a sample of the appropriately aged students was selected. Completed surveys were received from 34,275 students in Cycle 1.[1] These respondents were resurveyed every two years, with Cycle 4 data being collected in 2006. Only those who responded in Cycle 3 were contacted in Cycle 4. The Cycle 4 weights have been used in the present analysis, leaving us with a sample of just under 17,000[2] for whom we have data on PSE participation.

Specifically, the analysis examines rural-urban differences in ever participating in any form of PSE, and particularly in ever registering at a university by Cycle 4 of the YITS, when youth would be 21 or 22 years of age. It also considers levels of persistence, keeping in mind that some may re-enter PSE beyond the age of 22.

Measures

The measures used in the analysis are listed here, with the detailed descriptions and source variables from the YITS given in Appendix A.

Dependent Variables. Three dependent variables were used in this analysis:

1. Ever attend PSE (1 = attended, 0 = didn't attend);
2. Ever attend university (1 = attended, 0 = didn't attend) among those who ever attended PSE;
3. Persistence (1 = graduate or continuer, 0 = leaver), among those who ever attended PSE.

Note that the focus of the first two is on PSE and university *attendance*, not the attainment of a degree, diploma, or certificate. The third considers whether, at the time of the Cycle 4 data collection, the young person had left PSE without completing a certificate or degree program. "Persisters" include those who graduated with a certificate or diploma as well as those still registered in PSE. Only leavers who did not graduate are considered "non-persisters." Since Cohort A respondents are just 21 or 22 years of age at Cycle 4, this examination of persistence may be incomplete; that is, many non-persisters may later return to complete their PSE program.

Also note that *type* of PSE and persistence were only asked of those who attended PSE, so the case base on which percentages are calculated varies for the first versus the second and third measures. That is, they are conditional percentages. This fact needs to be kept in mind when considering the results. Attendance at PSE was measured for all respondents, including those who did not, during the time covered by the data collection, complete high school.

Independent Variables. The main independent variable in this analysis is *rural-urban location.* The codes for this in the YITS data were based on the location of high school the respondent attended in Cycle 1 (where 0 = urban, 1 = rural). Note that the measure used was that based on the classification of the *school* in which the young person was registered at the time of the first data collection.[3] Schools in a Census Metropolitan Area (CMA) or Census Agglomeration (CA) are classified as urban; all others are classified as rural (see Appendix A for details). Using this measure, a quarter (25 percent) of the respondents were classified as rural.

Because the YITS classifies schools close to a metropolitan area (those in "Strong Metropolitan Influence Zones") as rural, the results reported here are likely to underestimate rural-urban differences. That is, some of those classified as rural would be seen by themselves and others as urban, and certainly would be within commuting distance of any PSE institution in the nearby urban area. Unfortunately it is not possible to separate out youth in areas more remote from urban areas to see if the patterns for them vary from those reported here.

The other key independent variable is the *region of the country.* In order to maintain a sufficient case base, some grouping of provinces[4] was necessary. Based on the province of last high school attended, five regions were identified: (a) Atlantic (Newfoundland and Labrador, Nova Scotia, New Brunswick, Prince Edward Island); (b) Quebec; (c) Ontario; (d) Prairies (Manitoba and Saskatchewan); and (e) the West (Alberta and British Columbia). The combination of Alberta and British Columbia reflects the fact that both have formal systems of articulation. Quebec has a unique post-secondary system with its CEGEP program, which is coded in the YITS as "college" even if the student is registered in a pre-university program (one option in the CEGEP system).[5] While grouping all four Atlantic provinces together may be problematic, it was done in order to maintain sufficient cases in the various analyses. Of course there are some important differences, with Prince Edward Island and Newfoundland and Labrador having only one university each (albeit with more than one campus, in the latter case) and New Brunswick and Nova Scotia having several, including some with campuses in rural areas.[6]

So, what can the data from the YITS tell us in terms of the systems in the different regions? If one system is better than another at providing access to PSE for rural youth, other things being equal, we should see two patterns. First, rates of PSE participation among rural youth should be higher in that region than for rural youth from other regions, and second, the rural-urban *difference* in participation should be lower in that region. Similarly, if one system is better than others at encouraging rural youth to participate in university and at providing access to universities, then we would expect higher rates of participation in university by rural youth as well as lower rural-urban differences in university participation in that region.

The types of "systems"[7] we have for comparison in the regions identified in this analysis are: (a) a proliferation of PSE institutions in general and of universities in rural areas (as is found in the Atlantic region and Quebec); (b) formal articulation agreements between colleges and universities (as is found in Alberta and British Columbia), which allow for university courses to be taken at colleges; and (c) the system in Quebec whereby the first years of PSE are taken in the CEGEP system, which is part of both pre-university and non-university programs. That is, Quebec essentially has an "articulated" system as well. As noted above, Quebec also has a proliferation of institutions (especially CEGEPs) in rural areas.

If the proliferation of institutions (thereby increasing proximity and ease of access for many rural youth) is key to participation, one would expect participation rates by rural youth to be highest in the Atlantic region and Quebec. If an articulated system attracts more rural youth, we would expect more PSE participation in the West and Quebec. Given that the proliferation in the Atlantic region tends to be of universities, we would expect more university participation of rural youth in the Atlantic region but not necessarily Quebec. Of course, other factors not measured in the YITS (such as tuition, policies on student aid, employment options, and student support, as well as a variety of attitudes held by the students) may also vary across the regions, so this analysis is only a first step in identifying some macro level patterns.

Control Variables. There are also a number of variables that are controlled in the multivariate analyses, given that they are known to be related to rural-urban residence, PSE participation, or both.[8] They are (see Appendix A for details):

- gender/female (0 = male, 1 = female);
- language/English (0 = non-English, 1 = English);
- visible minority (0 = no, 1 = yes);
- immigrant status (0 = non-immigrant/3rd generation or higher, 1 = 1st or 2nd generation immigrant);
- repeated a grade (0 = no, 1 = yes);
- marks in high school (from a high of 6 = 90 per cent-100 per cent or more, to a low of 1 = less than 50).
- parental education (1 = no PSE, 2 = non-university PSE, 3 = university);
- parental income (15 categories in $10,000 increments from 0 = no income to 15 = $150,000 or higher).

Results

Rural-Urban Differences

The first stage is to document the overall rural-urban differences. Table 1 presents the results from three separate analyses: (1) whether the youth ever attended PSE; (2) *among those who attended PSE*, whether they ever attended university; and (3) *among those who attended some PSE*, whether they persisted.

TABLE 1
Urban-Rural Differences in PSE Participation, University Participation, and Persistence

	Attend Any PSE	Attend University	Persist at Any PSE (Grad or Continuer)
Urban	76%***	58%***	87%
Rural	67%	46%	85%
Total	74%	56%	86%
N	16996	12500	12520

Notes: Rural-urban percentage difference: * = sig at .05, ** = sig at .01, *** = sig at .001.
The Ns for university attendance and persistence differ slightly due to differential numbers of missing cases for the two sets of questions.
Source: Author's compilation.

The results indicate differences in both participation measures based on urban-rural location. More urban youth attend some form of PSE.[9] Among those who attend PSE, more urban youth also report attending university at some point (see middle column). The participation rate in both instances is lower (by 9 to 12 percentage points) for rural youth. This pattern is the main point of interest in this paper. Note that the right hand column of Table 1 shows no urban-rural difference in persistence rates. That is, once rural students get to PSE, they are as likely as urban students to persist.

The main focus of this analysis is specifically how these urban-rural differences in participation vary by region of the country. Table 2 gives the relevant results.

Looking first at the measure of whether the young person attended *any* PSE, we can see some consistent urban-rural differences in almost all regions. In all areas, more urban than rural youth report attending a post-secondary institution at some time during or preceding the Cycle 4 data collection in 2006 (although the difference in the Prairies is too small to reach statistical significance). We also see that the participation of rural youth in PSE is highest in the Atlantic region (73 percent) and Ontario (74 percent). It is lower in the remaining three regions (67 percent, 61 percent,

TABLE 2
Urban-Rural Differences in PSE Participation and Persistence by Region

	Attend PSE	Urb-Rural Difference	Attend University	Urb-Rural Difference	Persist	Urb-Rural Difference
Atlantic		4%*		15%***		-1%
Urban	77%		73%		85%	
Rural	73%		58%		86%	
Quebec		11%***		7%**		0%
Urban	72%		44%		82%	
Rural	61%		37%		82%	
Ontario		9%***		22%***		-2%
Urban	83%		59%		89%	
Rural	74%		37%		91%	
Prairies		1%		14%***		3%
Urban	68%		72%		85%	
Rural	67%		58%		82%	
West		11%***		12%***		5%**
Urban	72%		62%		87%	
Rural	61%		50%		83%	
N	16996		12500		12520	

Notes: Rural-urban percentage difference: * = sig at .05, ** = sig at .01, *** = sig at .001.
The Ns for university attendance and persistence differ slightly due to differential numbers of missing cases for the two sets of questions.

Source: Author's compilation.

and 61 percent in the Prairies, Quebec and the West, respectively). The urban-rural difference is largest in Quebec, Ontario, and the West.

These preliminary results suggest that neither Quebec's CEGEP system nor the articulated systems in the West in and of themselves increase access for rural youth as much as the proliferation of PSE institutions in rural areas that characterizes most of the Atlantic region. Note that urban levels of PSE attendance are highest in Ontario and the Atlantic region,[10] suggesting that the situation warrants more detailed analyses beyond these percent differences.

In the middle section of the table we also see an urban-rural difference in university participation among those who attended some PSE. Here the percentages in Quebec are lower than elsewhere, suggesting that starting PSE in a CEGEP does not seem to improve the rates of attending a university. However, this pattern may in part reflect the fact that CEGEP is coded as college in the YITS. That is, taking pre-university courses in Quebec CEGEPs (which can be seen as equivalent to the first year of university in other regions) is not counted as having attended university. Similarly, the somewhat lower levels of university attendance in the West, where under the articulation agreements the first two years of university can be taken at colleges, may reflect the fact that rural youth have not yet attended an institution coded as "university" in the YITS.

Focusing on the urban-rural difference in university participation, it is largest in Ontario (22 percentage point difference), smaller in the Atlantic region and the Prairies (with 15 percentage points and 14 percentage points difference), and smallest in Quebec (7 percentage points difference). This pattern may be surprising given that rural participation in universities is highest in the Atlantic region and the Prairies and lowest in Quebec and Ontario. However, there are also regional variations in the participation of urban youth in universities.

Finally, in the right hand column, there are essentially no urban-rural differences in persistence at PSE in any of the regions except the West. (More detailed analyses document that this difference exists only for British Columbia, with urban British Columbia youth having a persistence rate of 87 percent, compared to 79 percent for rural British Columbia youth.[11]) Given this lack of difference, further analyses of the rural-urban gap in persistence seem unwarranted at this point. The remainder of the paper therefore focuses on differences in participation in PSE and in university.

These preliminary results indicate clear and consistent urban-rural differences in PSE and university participation and some important regional variation in these differences. However, since we know that a range of other factors affect youth participation in PSE, it is important to control for the effects of these variables to see if they account for the regional differences in rural versus urban rates of participation.

Data not shown confirm that the control variables chosen for this analysis, taken individually, are each related to the outcome measures being considered. The only exception is language (measured by language used to complete the first survey), which is not related to whether or not one attends some PSE. The overall patterns are that females are more likely than males to attend some PSE and, among those who attend PSE, to attend university. Those completing the survey in English are somewhat more likely than those who completed it in French to attend university. Youth who self-identify as members of a visible minority group are more likely than others to attend PSE, and to attend university. Immigrants attend more than non-immigrants. Not unexpectedly, those who do less well in high school are less likely to attend PSE and less likely to attend a university; this pattern holds whether one looks at whether they ever repeated a grade or at their marks as of age 15. Finally, those whose parents have higher education or higher income are more likely to pursue some PSE and more likely to attend university.

These findings are not unexpected and reflect the results in the existing literature (e.g., Butlin 1999; Finnie and Mueller 2008; Finnie and Qui 2008; Finnie et al. 2008; Lambert et al. 2004; Looker 1997, 2003, 2007; Tomkowicz and Bushnik 2003). The key question is to what extent these variables account for the rural-urban differences we saw Table 2. To address that question, we turn to logistic regression (since the outcome measures of interest are dichotomies).

Multivariate Analysis

Having examined the bivariate relationships in Tables 1 and 2, we now turn to a multivariate analysis, which shows the simultaneous effect of these measures on the two dependent variables. The first step in the multivariate analysis was to run regressions with all control variables and with rural-urban location as an independent variable for each of the dependent variables, for all respondents across Canada (see Table 3).[12] Then, in order to take into account regional variation in the control variables, two additional regressions were run, including main effects for rural-urban location and region as well as interaction effects for the five regions with this geographic location (presented in Table 4). While it is beyond the scope of any one paper to discuss all the findings in detail, we identify the key points relevant to our discussion of regional differences in rural versus urban location in attendance at PSE and in university.

In the logistic regressions below, the key findings are reported as odds ratios. For example, for the "rural" variable – the odds of a rural youth attending some PSE compared to the odds of an urban youth doing so – if the likelihood of a rural youth attending PSE is equal to the likelihood of an urban youth attending PSE, the odds will be equal, and so the odds ratio will be 1.0. The interesting differences arise when an odds ratio is statistically different than 1.0. Those odds ratios greater than 1.0 (for example, the ratio for females as compared to males, at 1.61) indicate that those in the category of interest (in this case females) are more likely to attend PSE than the other (males), holding the other characteristics controlled for in the regression constant. If an odds ratio is less than 1.0 (as for "ever repeat a grade" at 0.26), it indicates that those in the category of interest (repeated a grade) are much *less* likely to have attended PSE than others (those who did not repeat a grade). The other relevant statistic is Nagelkerke's R^2, which can be interpreted as parallel to the R^2 in an ordinary least squares regression.

As is true in the earlier tables, Table 3 is based on more than one analysis. In this case, there is one regression analysis of those who do or do not attend some form of PSE. A separate logistic regression is then run for university attendance, based only on those who attend some PSE. The two analyses are presented in the one table.

As the top row in Table 3 indicates, the urban-rural difference in attending some PSE is not statistically significant in Canada as a whole once the control variables are taken into account. An overall difference was evident in Table 1; this result in Table 3 suggests that the differences

TABLE 3
Logistic Regression of All Respondents for Attending Any PSE and Attending University

Odds Ratios	Attend Any PSE	Attend University
Rural	0.91	0.73***
Female	1.61***	1.43***
English	1.08	2.13***
Visible minority	2.29***	1.50***
Immigrant	1.31***	1.23***
Repeated grade	0.26***	0.45***
High school marks	2.58***	3.32***
Parental education	1.68***	1.76***
Parental income	1.08***	1.05***
Constant	0.01***	0.00***
Nagelkerke's R^2	0.32	0.35
N	14754	11492

Notes: Odds ratio significance: * = sig at .05, ** = sig at .01, *** = sig at .001.
Source: Author's compilation.

in PSE attendance can be accounted for by rural-urban differences in the student's background characteristics and school performance indicators.

In data not shown, rural youth in the YITS are less likely to be English, a member of a visible minority, or a first or second generation immigrant. They tend to have lower grades; more of them have repeated a grade, and their parents tend to have lower education and income. The only control variable unrelated to rural versus urban location is gender, which is related to PSE participation (with females being more likely to attend). Being English (measured in terms of completing the survey in that language), also an "urban" trait in so far as more urban youth are English, has no effect Canada-wide.[13]

As we see in Table 3, a number of these "urban" characteristics (being a member of a visible minority, being an immigrant, having parents with high levels of education or high income,[14] having high marks) are positively associated with attending PSE. Having repeated a grade (more characteristic of rural youth) decreases the odds of attending PSE, even after other measures are controlled. It is well known that many of these measures affect PSE participation (Finnie et al. 2008; Looker 2003; Tomkowicz and Bushnik 2003); what is important here is that these results suggest a clear link between PSE attendance and attributes that are more typical of urban than rural youth. Further, the lack of a rural-urban difference once these measures are controlled suggests that it may not be rural location per se but other characteristics of rural youth and their families that dominate the patterns of PSE participation.

Next, we look at the patterns for whether or not the student ever attended a university by the time of the fourth data collection. (Keep in mind that in this analysis university attendance was only identified for those who attended some PSE.) In the right hand column of Table 3 we see that the pattern of rural "disadvantage"[15] is present (i.e., an odds ratio of less than 1.0) even after taking into account these control variables. So, while the control measures seem to account for the rural-urban difference in PSE participation, they do not fully account for this location difference in participation rates at university given that these youth have pursued PSE.

The analyses in Table 3 are for Canada as a whole. In order to examine regional differences in the rural-urban patterns of participation in PSE and university, two composite regressions were run, one for each of the two dependent variables, with region and the interactions of region with rural-urban location being explicitly examined. The odds ratios for the interaction terms provide information on the relative rural-urban gap in the different regions. The relevant results are presented in Table 4. Note that the comparisons reported in Table 4 are relative to Quebec (the omitted category).[16]

The first column of results is for "ever attend any PSE." The odds ratios of note are the interaction effects, highlighted in the table. Here we see that the only rural-urban difference (as measured by the regional interaction effect) is the Prairies (relative to the omitted category, Quebec). The odds of a rural young person in the Prairies compared to an urban youth in the Prairies participating in some PSE is higher than the comparable odds in Quebec when other factors, including the overall impact of region, are controlled. Put another way, the rural-urban gap is more pronounced in Quebec than in the Prairies once other variables are controlled. (See Appendix B for details of the patterns by region.)

Other analyses (not shown)[17] document that the *only* other significant rural-urban difference (the only significantly different interaction effect) in terms of participation in some form of PSE, when region and background/performance factors are controlled, is between the Prairies and the West. In this case the rural-urban odds ratio and therefore the rural-urban gap is larger in the West than in the Prairies, with rural youth being less likely to attend in the West. We saw in Table 3 that control variables seem to account for the urban-rural differences in participation Canada-wide, so it is perhaps unsurprising that there are few remaining differences by region.

In university attendance among those who attended PSE, we see a slightly different picture. The pattern in Table 4 suggests that again the odds ratio for the Quebec interaction (the reference category indicating the rural-urban gap) is significantly different not only from the Prairies but also from the interaction terms for all other regions except the West. These odds ratios suggest that, after controls, the rural-urban gap in

TABLE 4
Composite Logistic Regression of "Ever Attend PSE" and "Ever Attend University" with Interaction Effects (Compared to Quebec)

Odds Ratios	Attend Any PSE	Attend University
Rural	0.82	1.05
Atlantic	1.31	5.27***
Ontario	1.24	2.05***
Prairies	0.62**	4.52***
West	0.70**	2.43***
Atlantic* rural	1.12	0.49***
Ontario* rural	1.24	0.46***
Prairies* rural	1.45*	0.49***
West* rural	1.02	0.69*
Female	1.64***	1.43***
English	1.13	1.10
Visible minority	2.40***	1.52***
Immigrant	1.26***	1.38***
Repeated grade	0.27***	0.45***
High school marks	2.58***	3.36***
Parental education	1.71***	1.76***
Parental income	1.08***	1.06***
Constant	0.01***	0.01***
Nagelkerke's R^2	0.33	0.37
N	*14754*	*11492*

Notes: Odds ratio significance: * = sig at .05, ** = sig at .01, *** = sig at .001.
Omitted categories are "Quebec" and "Quebec rural" interaction.

Source: Author's compilation.

Quebec is *smaller* than it is in these other regions. This pattern is consistent with the low rural-urban difference in university attendance in Quebec reported in Table 2.

Quebec rural youth clearly stand out from all others. As is seen from the interaction effects, the rural-urban gap in university attendance in Quebec is smaller than elsewhere in Canada even when one controls for (a) the individual background factors included in the analysis; (b) the overall levels in the region; and (c) the overall rural-urban effect. However, relatively small numbers may be involved in creating this pattern, given the low rates of university participation in Quebec, and it is important to keep in mind the extent to which these patterns are conflated with language.

Discussion and Conclusion

What can we conclude from these results? To answer this we go back to our identification in the introduction of systems that might facilitate access to PSE and to university for rural youth in Canada. We are interested in identifying both which regions have higher participation of rural youth and which have the lowest (or the highest) rural-urban difference.

First we consider access to PSE. There are clearly both regional and rural-urban differences in participation rates. More urban than rural youth pursue some form of PSE. The absolute rates for participation by rural youth appear to be highest in the Atlantic region and in Ontario (see Table 2). However, the results from the multivariate analyses suggest that these initial differences reflect rural-urban differences in individual characteristics, nation-wide and in most regions. (After these multivariate controls, the only rural-urban differences that remain are those between Quebec and the Prairies, and between the Prairies and the West. Given the very different system of PSE in Quebec, the meaning of this difference is very difficult to interpret.)

In other words, these results imply that if the demographic profile and academic performance of rural youth paralleled those of urban youth, then rural youth would attend PSE in numbers comparable to the attendance rates of urban youth in Canada. However, this finding begs the question of what can be done given that the background and school perform-ance of rural youth do *not* match that of their urban counterparts. Rural youth, in fact, come from households with lower levels of education and income. They fare less well in school than their urban counterparts. To what extent, then, is the urban-rural gap in PSE attendance "warranted," and to what extent does it call for policy intervention? That is a question of policy priorities, not data analysis.

In terms of access specifically to university among those who attend some form of PSE, the picture is somewhat different. Here we see a rural-urban gap that persists almost everywhere, even when a range of control variables is taken into account (see Table 3); it is not just a matter of rural youth having different backgrounds or personal characteristics or performance in school. However, the rural-urban gap (as indicated by the region by rurality interaction effects) again highlights the unique system in Quebec.

The relative absence of a rural-urban difference in persistence (docu-mented in Tables 1 and 2) could indicate that once rural youth get into PSE, they are as likely as their urban counterparts to continue. However, the YITS data examined is limited in terms of examining this issue in depth, as the available data reflect the attainments as of age 21 or 22. Ongoing follow-ups of these youth are needed to more effectively analyze rural-urban differences in persistence rates.[18]

Obviously this analysis is just a first step in identifying how educational policy and structures affect the likelihood that rural youth will pursue PSE. The initial suggestion from the patterns in Table 2 is that, if there is an advantage to one type of arrangement over another, the proliferation of options in rural areas seems to be attractive to rural youth. While the articulation systems in Alberta and British Columbia provide such options to some extent, as Andres and Looker (2001) found, this system encouraged rural youth to attend PSE but did not necessarily meet the goal of getting them to continue their university educations beyond the first years at the PSE level. In the current data, based on a more recent national data set, there is little evidence that the articulated system in the West encouraged PSE participation any better than the systems in place in other regions.[19] In the "articulated" CEGEP system in Quebec, the key issue may be that the overall university participation levels are low.

Another matter that needs to be raised here is the tension identified by Corbett (2000, 2007) and by Looker (1993) between the educational aspirations of rural youth (and their parents) and the desire for them to maintain ties to their rural communities. Beyond these desires at the individual level, we know that retaining youth is one of the biggest challenges facing rural communities (Dupuy et al. 2000). As Looker and Naylor (2008) indicate, the "solution" to lower educational aspirations and attainments among rural youth is not simply to put in place policies to get individuals to leave these communities to pursue further education; one has to also take into account the need of rural communities to support and retain their young people, and the desire of many rural youth to live in rural communities once they have completed their formal education. In other words, it is not enough to get the "student to the school," but rather, if rural communities are to be supported, it is important to get the "school to the student" (Frenette 2009, 1).

The proliferation of institutions provides other economic advantages to rural communities: "Rural based colleges are often the only post-secondary institution in the region and play a key role in facilitating a strong rural revitalization strategy through local and regional economic and social development" (Association of Canadian Community Colleges 2007, 1). In other words, the presence of a post-secondary institution may in turn provide employment possibilities in a number of occupations, including those requiring PSE level education, given the range of enterprises in the adjacent area that are required to support such an institution. While this is clearly not the only way of dealing with under-representation of rural youth in PSE and particularly in university, it does appear to be one option. More work needs to be done to identify factors that may affect rural youth participation in PSE in general and universities in particular. This preliminary analysis is a step in that direction.

The next steps for related research could include examining regional and provincial differences, taking into account more details of PSE structure in the different provinces and regions, including tuition costs and student aid provisions, where such information is available. Further down the road, once the respondents are old enough to have completed a university degree, it will be interesting to see the effect of attending a school in a rural versus an urban area on the attainment of a diploma, certificate, or degree program in the longer term. For now, we have established that the patterns of participation of rural as compared to urban students in PSE and in attendance specifically at university do vary in important ways across the different regions of our country.

Notes

This research was financed by the Canada Millennium Scholarship Foundation through the MESA project.

1. See Statistics Canada for details of sampling and data collection for the YITS (http://www.statcan.gc.ca/cgi-bin/imdb/p2SV.pl?Function=getSurvey&SDDS=4435&lang=en&db=imdb&adm=8&dis=2).
2. Note that using Cycle 4 weights means that only those who responded in Cycle 4 are included in this analysis, so the case base will differ from that used in analyses of earlier cycles of YITS.
3. A better measure would be where the student is living. While this information is available from the accompanying parental survey, the case loss (due to parental non-response) argues against using this measure. The two measures are of course highly correlated, and analyses (not shown) document that the key results are consistent whichever measure of rural location is used.
4. As is true in many Statistics Canada surveys, the Northern Territories were not included in the sampling frame.
5. While some CEGEP programs are "pre-university," many universities outside Quebec accept the completion of this two year program as a valid transfer credit equivalent to the first year of university. In this way the system is similar to the articulation system in Alberta and British Columbia.
6. There is also a large francophone population in New Brunswick. Preliminary analyses (see Appendix B) show no French-English differences in rural or urban New Brunswick. Indeed, the only significant English-French differences are in urban not rural Quebec. Given the fact that language is so conflated with province of residence, particularly with residence in Quebec, which has a different structure and pattern of PSE attendance, more detailed analysis of the role of language requires an in-depth examination of PSE in Quebec, a task beyond the scope of this paper.
7. Tuition and tuition supports also vary by region (Coelli 2009). Unfortunately, details of tuition and program length are not easily accessible in the data examined here.
8. There are of course a wide range of other variables that could be included as controls. Aboriginal status is an obvious one. However, the YITS, like many

Statistics Canada data sets, excludes on-reserve First Nations youth as well as any living in the Northern Territories. One could include respondent's educational aspirations, but this would create endogeneity problems. It was felt that the control variables included in the analysis capture the key factors that could help explain any regional rural-urban differences in PSE and university participation, within the constraints of the information provided by the YITS.

9. Note that this measure is of those who by Cycle 4 had ever registered for any form of PSE. These percentages will increase as the youth age and more youth start a program of some ilk. The equivalent percentage who ever attended as of Cycle 3 is 63 percent; by Cycle 4 this had increased to 74 percent.

10. The authors of a Canadian Policy Research Network report (2008) note that based on the 2001 census, more people obtain a PSE diploma, certificate, or degree in Quebec than elsewhere in Canada. It remains to be seen if the educational attainments of the YITS youth will reflect this same pattern.

11. This slight difference in persistence rates (the Alberta urban-rural difference in persistence being 3 percentage points and the British Columbia one being 8 percentage points) is the only statistically significant difference in the dependent variables between the two provinces that comprise "the West." In all other comparisons the rural-urban differences (in PSE and in university attendance) in Alberta and British Columbia are within 4 percentage points.

12. This analysis was rerun separately for each region (see details in Appendix B). Those analyses show that in all five regions, the relationship between rural location and participation in any PSE reduces to non-significance when controls are introduced. For university participation, the rural-urban difference has a statistically significant direct effect even after controls in all regions except Quebec, reflecting the pattern for Canada as a whole reported in Table 3.

13. There is a relationship between language and PSE participation in Quebec (see Table A1 in Appendix B), but only for urban youth.

14. It is important to note that most of the control variables are 0/1 dichotomies. However, parental education has three categories and income has 15. Marks are measured with a six point scale, with 1 being low and 6 being high. The odds ratios indicate the effect of a *one unit* change in the independent variable on the odds of going from 0 to 1 in the dependent variable.

15. Of course, the lower rates of participation of rural youth in university is a "disadvantage" only if one accepts the widely held view that university attendance is "better" (Looker 2003).

16. The decision to use Quebec as the reference category was made on the basis that it showed the most difference from the other regions. The pattern of results would be the same regardless of the region omitted; however, omitting Quebec allows those differences to be more clearly readable from the table.

17. The significance of the other interaction terms (measuring the rural-urban gap) was tested using the Wald test (in Stata).

18. Note that the older cohort of YITS, Cohort B, can be used to examine persistence (Finnie and Qui 2008). However, for this group there is no clean measure of rural-urban location at the initial data collection, since the respondents at 18-20 years of age would not necessarily be living where they attended high school.

19. As noted in the text, the levels of university participation in the West may be underestimated in these data, since students taking university level courses at colleges are not coded in the YITS as having attended university. They would have to go beyond the first two years and actually attend an institution that is coded as a university. Data that allow identification of those taking university level courses at other institutions are clearly needed to complete this picture.

References

Andres, L., and E.D. Looker. 2001. "Rurality and Capital: Educational Expectations and Attainments of Rural, Urban/Rural and Metropolitan Youth." *Canadian Journal of Higher Education* 31: 1-45.

Association of Canadian Community Colleges, 2007. "Rural Poverty." http://www.accc.ca/ftp/briefs-memories/200712_ruralpoverty.pdf (accessed 8 January 2008).

Bollman, R.D., and R. Beshiri. 2000. "Rural and Small Town Canada: A Demographic Overview." Paper presented to the Conference on the New Rural Economy, Alfred, Ontario.

Butlin, G. 1999. "Determinants of Postsecondary Participation." *Education Quarterly Review* 5.

Canadian Policy Research Network. 2008. "From School to the Labour Market in Québec." http://www.cprn.org.

Cartwright, F., and M.K. Allen. 2002. "Understanding the Rural-Urban Reading Gap." Ottawa: Statistics Canada.

Christofides, L.N., J. Cirello, and M. Hoy. 2001. "Family Income and Postsecondary Education in Canada." *Canadian Journal of Higher Education* 31: 177-208.

Coelli, M. 2009. "Tuition Fees and Equality of University Enrolment." *Canadian Journal of Economics* 42 (3): 1072-99.

Corbett, M. 2000. "Learning to Leave: The Irony of Schooling in a Coastal Community: Some Preliminary Findings." Paper presented to the Conference on Rural Communities and Identities in the New Global Millennium, Nanaimo, BC.

– 2007. *Learning to Leave: The Irony of Schooling in a Coastal Community.* Halifax: Fernwood Publishing.

Dennison, J.D., and H.G. Schuetze, 2004. "Extending Access, Choice, and the Reign of the Market: Higher Education Reforms in British Columbia, 1989–2004." *Canadian Journal of Higher Education* 34: 13-38.

Dupuy, R., F. Mayer, and R. Morissette. 2000. "Rural Youth: Stayers, Leavers and Return Migrants." Report by the Canadian Rural Partnership and Atlantic Canada Opportunities Agency, no. 152, Statistics Canada.

Finnie, R., and R.E. Mueller. 2008. "The Effects of Family Income, Parental Education and Other Background Factors on Access to Post-Secondary Education in Canada: Evidence from the YITS." MESA Research Paper. http://www.mesa-project.org/pub/pdf/MESA_Finnie_Mueller.pdf.

Finnie, R., and T. Qiu. 2008. "The Patterns of Persistence in Post-Secondary Education in Canada: Evidence from the YITS-B Dataset." MESA Research Paper. http://www.mesa-project.org/pub/pdf/MESA_Finnie_Qiu_2008Aug12.pdf.

Finnie, R., R.E. Mueller, A. Sweetman, and A. Usher, eds. 2008. *Who Goes, Who Stays, What Matters: Accessing and Persisting in Post-Secondary Education in Canada.* Montreal and Kingston: Queen's Policy Studies Series, McGill-Queen's University Press.

Frenette, M. 2004. "Access to College and University: Does Distance to School Matter?" *Canadian Public Policy* 30: 427-43.

– 2006. "Too Far to Go On? Distance to School and University Participation." *Education Economics* 14: 31-58.

– 2009. "Do Universities Benefit Local Youth? Evidence from the Creation of New Universities." *Economics of Education Review* 28: 318-28.

Lambert, M., K. Zeman, M. Allen, and P. Bussière. 2004. "Who Pursues Post-Secondary Education, Who Leaves and Why." Ottawa: Statistics Canada.

Looker, E.D. 1993. "Interconnected Transitions and Their Costs: Gender and Urban-Rural Differences in the Transitions to Work." In *The Transitions from School to Work*, ed. P. Axelrod and P. Anisef, 43-64. Toronto: Thompson Educational Publishing.

– 1994. "Active Capital: The Impact of Parents on Youths' Educational Performance and Plans." In *Sociology of Education in Canada*, ed. L. Erwin and D. MacLennan, 164-87. Toronto: Copp Clark Longman.

– 1997a. "In Search of Credentials: Factors Affecting Young Adults' Participation in Post-Secondary Education." *Canadian Journal of Higher Education* 27: 2-3.

– 1997b. "Rural-Urban Differences in Youth Transitions to Adulthood." In *Rural Employment: An International Perspective*, ed. R. Bollman and J. Bryden, 85-96. New York: CAB International.

– 2001. *An Overview of Human Capital in Rural and Urban Areas.* Hull: Human Resources Development Canada.

– 2003. "Why Don't They Go On? Factors Affecting the Decisions of Canadian Youth Not to Pursue Post-Secondary Education." Millennium Scholarship Foundation, Ottawa.

– 2007. "Rural-Urban Differences in Post-Secondary Participation and Persistence." Presented to the ARDC Conference on Life Course Transitions of Children and Youth, Halifax.

– Looker, E.D., and T. D. Naylor. 2008. "'At Risk' of Being Rural? The Push and Pull of Rural Ties on Youth." Paper presented to the Canadian Sociology Association meetings, Vancouver, BC.

Rojewski, J. 1999. "Career Related Predictors of Work-Bound and College-Bound Status of Adolescents in Rural and Non-Rural Areas." *Journal of Research in Rural Education* 15 (3): 141-56.

Rothwell, N., R.D. Bollman, J. Tremblay, and J. Marshall. 2002. "Recent Migration Patterns in Rural and Small Town Canada." Ottawa: Statistics Canada.

Tomkowicz, J., and T. Bushnik. 2003. "Who Goes to Post-Secondary Education and When: Pathways Chosen by 20 Year Olds." Ottawa: Statistics Canada.

Witko, K., K. Bernes, K. Magnusson, and A. Bardick. 2006. "Senior High Students' Career Plans for the Future." *International Journal for Educational and Vocational Guidance* 6: 77-94.

APPENDIX A
Measurement of Variables

Dependent Variables

- *Ever attend PSE?* Coded 0 = no, 1 = yes. Uses information from *hedld2*, *hedld3*, *hedld4*. No respondents were in PSE in Cycle 1, given the sampling frame. Since Cycle 4 weights are used, it is the responses to hedld4 that drive the results.

- *Ever attend university*, coded 0 = non-university, 1 = university; only asked of those who attended some PSE. As was done for the measure "ever attend PSE," the measure of "ever attend university" involved working backwards from Cycle 4 responses. Thus the highest level listed in Cycle 4 was used, unless there was no answer (or no PSE), in which case Cycle 3 responses were used. If both Cycle 3 and 4 data were missing (or involved no PSE), highest PSE was based on Cycle 2 responses. Uses *hlpsd2*, *hlpsd3*, *hdpsd4*. The measure of "ever attend university" was created separately from "ever attend PSE" so that the information on university attendance over the four cycles could be captured. Some of those who attended university also attended other forms of PSE.

- *Persistence*, coded 0 = leaver, 1 = graduate or continuer. Since the students would not have started PSE until Cycle 2, the first time they could persist or leave would be Cycle 3. So, this measure is taken from Cycles 3 and 4, using *lpsat3* and *lpsat4*. Note that the non-response for persistence information was slightly lower than for information about whether or not the youth attended university, so the Ns are correspondingly different.

Independent Variables

The main independent variable in this analysis is *rural-urban location*, coded 0 = urban, 1 = rural. The codes were pre-assigned in the YITS data set, based on the location of high school the respondent attended in Cycle 1 (*urbrurmz*). Note that since schools, especially in rural areas, can have large catchment areas, the characteristics of the locale where the students themselves live would be slightly different.

In light of the fact that this is the key independent variable, some additional detail on how it is measured in YITS is warranted. The coding was based on the sampling information about the location of the high school, not respondents' categorization of the location of their school. It was based on the census classification of the school locale.

YITS uses census definitions (for details, see http://www12.statcan.ca/english/census01/products/reference/dict/geo010.htm) for "census subdivisions" – a term "assigned to a municipality not included in either a census metropolitan area (CMA) or a census agglomeration (CA). (A CMA or CA is an area consisting of one or more adjacent municipalities situated around a major urban core. To form a CMA, the urban core must have a population of at least 100,000. To form a CA, the urban core must have a population of at least 10,000.) A municipality is assigned to one of four categories depending on the percentage of its residents who commute to work in the urban core of any census metropolitan area or census agglomeration."

In YITS, CMAs and CAs are coded as urban. The four categories for census sub-divisions (those not classified as a CMA or CA), from strong "Metropolitan influence zone" (MIZ) to no MIZ, are all coded as rural in YITS. Including the strong MIZ zones as rural is likely to minimize the urban-rural differences reported in this paper. However, the more detailed codes are not available in the YITS data.

The other key independent variable is the *region of the country*. Based on the province of last high school attended, using codes from the variable *province*, five regions were identified: (1) Atlantic (Newfoundland and Labrador, Nova Scotia, New Brunswick, Prince Edward Island); (2) Quebec; (3) Ontario; (4) Prairies (Manitoba and Saskatchewan); (5) the West (Alberta and British Columbia).

Control Variables

- Gender (0 = male, 1 = female). Taken from Cycle 1 responses (*st03q01*).

- Language (0 = non-English, 1 = English). Taken from Cycle 1, based on the language used to respond to the survey (*yslangue*).

- Visible minority (0 = no, 1 = yes). Based on the parental responses in Cycle 1 (*visminp1*).

- Immigration status (0 = non-immigrant, i.e., third generation or more, 1 = first or second generation immigrant). Based on information from the youth and the parent (*st16q01, st16q02, st16q03; pd2p1, pd2p2, pd2p3*).

- Ever repeat a grade, coded (0 = no, 1 = yes). Measured in Cycles 2, 3, and 4. If respondents said "yes" in any cycle, they were coded as having repeated a grade (*b2q59, b3q59, b4q59*).

- Marks in high school, from a high of 6 = 90 percent or more to a low of 1=less than 50 percent. Measured at Cycle 1, when youth were 15 years of age (*ysdv_l2*, with the original codes reversed so that a high code indicates a high mark).

- Parental education (1 = no PSE, 2 = non-university PSE, 3 = university or more); uses information from the parental reports *pe1c* and *pe2c*.
- Parental income, 15 categories in $10,000 increments from 0 = no income to 15 = $150,000 or higher, from a recode of the variable *ctid*.

APPENDIX
Supplementary Tables

TABLE A1
Participation in PSE and University in Quebec and New Brunswick by Language and Rural-Urban Location

		English	French	Significance
PSE				
Quebec	Urban	86%	70%	***
N = 3808	Rural	67%	60%	ns
New Brunswick	Urban	74%	75%	ns
N = 453	Rural	71%	73%	ns
University				
Quebec	Urban	51%	43%	*
N = 2615	Rural	48%	36%	ns
New Brunswick	Urban	70%	74%	ns
N = 329	Rural	63%	55%	ns

Notes: Rural-urban percentage difference: ns = non-significant, * = sig at .05, ** = sig at .01, *** = sig at .001.

Source: Author's compilation.

TABLE A2
Separate Logistic Regressions of PSE Participation by Region, with Controls

	Atlantic	Quebec	Ontario	Prairies	West
Rural	0.94 ns	0.85 ns	0.97 ns	1.11 ns	0.87 ns
Female	1.52*	2.17***	1.76***	1.61**	1.37***
English	0.72 ns	2.17***	0.84 ns	0.72 ns	0.92 ns
Visible minority	1.06 ns	2.05**	2.04***	1.43 ns	3.38***
Immigrant	1.04 ns	1.45 ns	1.16 ns	1.36 ns	1.27*
Repeated	0.36***	0.21***	0.32***	0.38***	0.33***
Marks	2.66***	3.69***	2.27***	2.67***	2.42***
Parental education	1.93***	1.87***	1.79***	1.56***	1.53***
Parental income	1.13***	1.10***	1.09***	1.07*	1.05**
Constant	0.01***	0.01***	0.03***	0.01***	0.02***
R^2	0.34	0.45	0.26	0.31	0.30
N	4973	2157	2171	2778	2675

Notes: Odds ratio significance: ns = non-significant, * = sig at .05, ** = sig at .01, *** = sig at .001. Based on five separately run logistic regressions.

Source: Author's compilation.

TABLE A3

Separate Logistic Regressions of University Participation by Region, with Controls

	Atlantic	Quebec	Ontario	Prairies	West
Rural	0.52***	1.04 ns	0.51***	0.49***	0.70**
Female	1.44*	2.00***	1.31***	0.95 ns	1.31**
English	0.86 ns	1.51*	0.91 ns	0.50 ns	0.62 ns
Visible minority	1.02 ns	1.36 ns	1.53***	0.78 ns	1.82 ***
Immigrant	1.99 ns	1.33 ns	1.56***	1.20 ns	1.09 ns
Repeated	0.25**	0.42***	0.15***	0.85 ns	0.85 ns
Marks	3.73***	3.45***	3.70***	2.69***	3.11***
Parental education	1.69***	1.68***	2.05***	1.58***	1.45***
Parental income	1.11**	1.08***	1.05***	1.06 ns	1.04**
Constant	0.01***	0.01***	0.01***	0.02***	0.01***
R^2	0.42	0.32	0.41	0.27	0.31
N	3961	1664	1853	2017	1997

Notes: Odds ratio significance: ns = non-significant, * = sig at .05, ** = sig at .01, *** = sig at .001. Based on five separately run logistic regressions.

Source: Author's compilation.

About the Authors

MICHAL BURDZY is an economist for the Insurance Bureau of Canada. He received a B. Economics (Honours) with an econometric specialization from the University of Waterloo (Canada) and later completed a master's degree in economics at Wilfrid Laurier University.

STEPHEN CHILDS has been a research assistant with the MESA Project since 2008 and divides his time between the University of Ottawa and Statistics Canada. An example of following an alternative post-secondary pathway, he studied computer science, library technology, and history before completing his undergraduate training in economics at Lakehead University. He was awarded the Academic Gold Medal upon the completion of his master's degree in economics at Wilfrid Laurier University.

KATHLEEN DAY is an associate professor in the Department of Economics at the University of Ottawa. She has a PhD in economics from the University of British Columbia. Her research has applied econometric work to a variety of Canadian issues, including interprovincial labour mobility, volunteerism, regional disparities, the relationship between pollution and economic growth and, most recently, post-secondary education in Canada.

TORBEN DREWES joined the Department of Economics at Trent University in 1980 and served as chair of the department from 2002 to 2008. He received a BA in economics from Lakehead University (1975) and a PhD from Queen's University at Kingston (1985). His research has examined interprovincial unemployment disparities, returns to higher education, the gender gap in universities, adult learning, and issues surrounding student financial assistance.

ROSS FINNIE is an associate professor in the Graduate School of Public and International Affairs at the University of Ottawa and a visiting fellow at Statistics Canada, having previously held positions at Queen's University, Carleton University, and Université Laval. His current interests in post-secondary education include access and barriers to PSE, persistence and pathways to completion, student financial aid and its effects on access and persistence, earlier life environments and experiences and participation in PSE, immigrant participation in PSE, the measurement of quality in PSE, students' adjustment to the PSE experience, and other topics. He is one of the principals of the MESA project and is the project's research director.

MARC FRENETTE is a research economist with the Social Analysis Division of Statistics Canada. His primary areas of interest include the economics of education, income inequality, and the consequences of job displacement. He has published research papers in all three areas in government publications as well as in several Canadian and international scientific journals. His work in education has mainly focused on post-secondary access, with particular emphasis on the role of distance to school, family background, academic achievement, and tuition fee deregulation. His current research agenda focuses on understanding the factors linked to learning at all stages of life.

CHRISTINE LAPORTE was educated at Laval University and Queen's University. She is currently a research economist with the Social Analysis Division at Statistics Canada. Her research interests include economics of education and labour supply. She has published research papers in those areas in government publications as well as in Canadian and international scientific journals. Her recent work has focused on access and barriers to a post-secondary education, persistence in apprenticeship programs, and high school dropouts.

PIERRE LEFEBVRE is a professor in the Department of Economics attached to the School of Management at the Université du Québec à Montréal. He has a PhD in economics and specializes in public economics, welfare and poverty, and demographic economics. His work includes the effects of tax reform, cost-benefit analysis of public programs and policies, the effects of welfare programs on marriage and family structure, child poverty, and the use of time among Canadian families with children. His recent studies analyze the impacts of the Quebec's childcare program on mothers' labour supply and child development.

E. DIANNE LOOKER is a professor of sociology and Tier 1 Canada Research Chair at Mount Saint Vincent University. She has studied issues related to the life-course transitions of youth throughout her career, designing surveys and analyzing data from numerous longitudinal surveys on youth in a changing society, often focusing on the particular challenges that rurality presents for youth in terms of educational, occupational, and mobility decisions. She is interested in understanding how the rural experience varies across regions and how shifts, including the move to a more technology-based society, has affected equity for sub-groups of youth.

Felice Martinello was educated in economics at the University of Western Ontario and the University of British Columbia. He is currently a professor of economics at Brock University. He has written on labour unions, wage determination, and union organizing and has recently turned his attention to post-secondary education.

Philip Merrigan has taught since 1991 at UQAM, where he is now a full professor. He received his PhD at Brown University under the supervision of Robert Moffitt in 1993. His areas of expertise are labour economics, applied microeconometrics, public economics, and demography. He has published in the *Journal of Labor Economics* and the *Journal of Human Resources* and has presented work in most of the major international meetings in economics and demography. His most recent research concentrates on the acquisition of human capital for the young and very young across Canada.

Richard E. Mueller is an associate professor of economics at the University of Lethbridge and a visiting fellow in the Social Analysis Division at Statistics Canada. His current research interests include the various determinants of entry into post-secondary education and other related education issues. He holds degrees from the University of Calgary and the University of Texas and has held visiting academic positions throughout the world. His work has appeared in a number of economics and Canadian studies journals and edited volumes.

Christine Neill is an assistant professor in the Department of Economics at Wilfrid Laurier University. She graduated from the University of Queensland (Australia) with a B. Economics (Honours), and went to work as an economist in the Australian Treasury and later the Department of Foreign Affairs and Trade. She completed a PhD at the University of Toronto, specializing in labour and public economics. Her current research focuses on university financing, student loan policies, and individuals' education decisions, with some analysis of Australian policy thrown in for good measure.

Arthur Sweetman is an economist and a professor in the School of Policy Studies at Queen's University. He is cross-appointed in the Department of Economics and the Department of Community Health and Epidemiology. His research interests are broad but primarily involve empirical issues in the areas of immigration, education, labour market, and health policy.

Queen's Policy Studies
Recent Publications

The Queen's Policy Studies Series is dedicated to the exploration of major public policy issues that confront governments and society in Canada and other nations.

Manuscript submission. We are pleased to consider new book proposals and manuscripts. Preliminary enquiries are welcome. A subvention is normally required for the publication of an academic book. Please direct questions or proposals to the Publications Unit by email at spspress@queensu.ca, or visit our website at: www.queensu.ca/sps/books, or contact us by phone at (613) 533 - 2192.

Our books are available from good bookstores everywhere, including the Queen's University bookstore (http://www.campusbookstore.com/). McGill-Queen's University Press is the exclusive world representative and distributor of books in the series. A full catalogue and ordering information may be found on their web site (http://mqup.mcgill.ca/).

School of Policy Studies

Canadian Immigration: Economic Evidence for a Dynamic Policy Environment, Ted McDonald, Elizabeth Ruddick, Arthur Sweetman, and Christopher Worswick (eds.), 2010, Paper 978-1-55339-281-1 Cloth 978-1-55339-282-8

Taking Stock: Research on Teaching and Learning in Higher Education, Julia Christensen Hughes and Joy Mighty (eds.), 2010, Paper 978-1-55339-271-2 Cloth 978-1-55339-272-9

Architects and Innovators: Building the Department of Foreign Affairs and International Trade, 1909–2009/Architectes et innovateurs : le développement du ministère des Affaires étrangères et du Commerce international,de 1909 à 2009, Greg Donaghy and Kim Richard Nossal (eds.), 2009, Paper 978-1-55339-269-9 Cloth 978-1-55339-270-5

Academic Transformation: The Forces Reshaping Higher Education in Ontario, Ian D. Clark, Greg Moran, Michael L. Skolnik, and David Trick, 2009, Paper 978-1-55339-238-5 Cloth 978-1-55339-265-1

The New Federal Policy Agenda and the Voluntary Sector: On the Cutting Edge, Rachel Laforest (ed.), 2009. Paper 978-1-55339-132-6

The Afghanistan Challenge: Hard Realities and Strategic Choices, Hans-Georg Ehrhart and Charles Pentland (eds.), 2009. Paper 978-1-55339-241-5

Measuring What Matters in Peace Operations and Crisis Management, Sarah Jane Meharg, 2009. Paper 978-1-55339-228-6 Cloth ISBN 978-1-55339-229-3

International Migration and the Governance of Religious Diversity, Paul Bramadat and Matthias Koenig (eds.), 2009. Paper 978-1-55339-266-8 Cloth ISBN 978-1-55339-267-5

Who Goes? Who Stays? What Matters? Accessing and Persisting in Post-Secondary Education in Canada, Ross Finnie, Richard E. Mueller, Arthur Sweetman, and Alex Usher (eds.), 2008. Paper 978-1-55339-221-7 Cloth ISBN 978-1-55339-222-4

Economic Transitions with Chinese Characteristics: Thirty Years of Reform and Opening Up, Arthur Sweetman and Jun Zhang (eds.), 2009. Paper 978-1-55339-225-5 Cloth ISBN 978-1-55339-226-2

Economic Transitions with Chinese Characteristics: Social Change During Thirty Years of Reform, Arthur Sweetman and Jun Zhang (eds.), 2009. Paper 978-1-55339-234-7 Cloth ISBN 978-1-55339-235-4

Dear Gladys: Letters from Over There, Gladys Osmond (Gilbert Penney ed.), 2009. Paper ISBN 978-1-55339-223-1

Immigration and Integration in Canada in the Twenty-first Century, John Biles, Meyer Burstein, and James Frideres (eds.), 2008. Paper ISBN 978-1-55339-216-3 Cloth ISBN 978-1-55339-217-0

Robert Stanfield's Canada, Richard Clippingdale, 2008. ISBN 978-1-55339-218-7

Exploring Social Insurance: Can a Dose of Europe Cure Canadian Health Care Finance? Colleen Flood, Mark Stabile, and Carolyn Tuohy (eds.), 2008. Paper ISBN 978-1-55339-136-4 Cloth ISBN 978-1-55339-213-2

Canada in NORAD, 1957–2007: A History, Joseph T. Jockel, 2007. Paper ISBN 978-1-55339-134-0 Cloth ISBN 978-1-55339-135-7

Canadian Public-Sector Financial Management, Andrew Graham, 2007. Paper ISBN 978-1-55339-120-3 Cloth ISBN 978-1-55339-121-0

Emerging Approaches to Chronic Disease Management in Primary Health Care, John Dorland and Mary Ann McColl (eds.), 2007. Paper ISBN 978-1-55339-130-2 Cloth ISBN 978-1-55339-131-9

Fulfilling Potential, Creating Success: Perspectives on Human Capital Development, Garnett Picot, Ron Saunders and Arthur Sweetman (eds.), 2007. Paper ISBN 978-1-55339-127-2 Cloth ISBN 978-1-55339-128-9

Reinventing Canadian Defence Procurement: A View from the Inside, Alan S. Williams, 2006. Paper ISBN 0-9781693-0-1 (Published in association with Breakout Educational Network)

SARS in Context: Memory, History, Policy, Jacalyn Duffin and Arthur Sweetman (eds.), 2006. Paper ISBN 978-0-7735-3194-9 Cloth ISBN 978-0-7735-3193-2 (Published in association with McGill-Queen's University Press)

Dreamland: How Canada's Pretend Foreign Policy has Undermined Sovereignty, Roy Rempel, 2006. Paper ISBN 1-55339-118-7 Cloth ISBN 1-55339-119-5 (Published in association with Breakout Educational Network)

Canadian and Mexican Security in the New North America: Challenges and Prospects, Jordi Díez (ed.), 2006. Paper ISBN 978-1-55339-123-4 Cloth ISBN 978-1-55339-122-7

Global Networks and Local Linkages: The Paradox of Cluster Development in an Open Economy, David A. Wolfe and Matthew Lucas (eds.), 2005. Paper ISBN 1-55339-047-4 Cloth ISBN 1-55339-048-2

Choice of Force: Special Operations for Canada, David Last and Bernd Horn (eds.), 2005. Paper ISBN 1-55339-044-X Cloth ISBN 1-55339-045-8

Force of Choice: Perspectives on Special Operations, Bernd Horn, J. Paul de B. Taillon, and David Last (eds.), 2004. Paper ISBN 1-55339-042-3 Cloth 1-55339-043-1

New Missions, Old Problems, Douglas L. Bland, David Last, Franklin Pinch, and Alan Okros (eds.), 2004. Paper ISBN 1-55339-034-2 Cloth 1-55339-035-0

The North American Democratic Peace: Absence of War and Security Institution-Building in Canada-US Relations, 1867-1958, Stéphane Roussel, 2004. Paper ISBN 0-88911-937-6 Cloth 0-88911-932-2

Implementing Primary Care Reform: Barriers and Facilitators, Ruth Wilson, S.E.D. Shortt, and John Dorland (eds.), 2004. Paper ISBN 1-55339-040-7 Cloth 1-55339-041-5

Social and Cultural Change, David Last, Franklin Pinch, Douglas L. Bland, and Alan Okros (eds.), 2004. Paper ISBN 1-55339-032-6 Cloth 1-55339-033-4

Clusters in a Cold Climate: Innovation Dynamics in a Diverse Economy, David A. Wolfe and Matthew Lucas (eds.), 2004. Paper ISBN 1-55339-038-5 Cloth 1-55339-039-3

Canada Without Armed Forces? Douglas L. Bland (ed.), 2004.
Paper ISBN 1-55339-036-9 Cloth 1-55339-037-7

Campaigns for International Security: Canada's Defence Policy at the Turn of the Century,
Douglas L. Bland and Sean M. Maloney, 2004. Paper ISBN 0-88911-962-7
Cloth 0-88911-964-3

Understanding Innovation in Canadian Industry, Fred Gault (ed.), 2003.
Paper ISBN 1-55339-030-X Cloth 1-55339-031-8

Delicate Dances: Public Policy and the Nonprofit Sector, Kathy L. Brock (ed.), 2003.
Paper ISBN 0-88911-953-8 Cloth 0-88911-955-4

Beyond the National Divide: Regional Dimensions of Industrial Relations, Mark Thompson,
Joseph B. Rose, and Anthony E. Smith (eds.), 2003. Paper ISBN 0-88911-963-5
Cloth 0-88911-965-1

The Nonprofit Sector in Interesting Times: Case Studies in a Changing Sector, Kathy L. Brock
and Keith G. Banting (eds.), 2003. Paper ISBN 0-88911-941-4 Cloth 0-88911-943-0

Clusters Old and New: The Transition to a Knowledge Economy in Canada's Regions,
David A. Wolfe (ed.), 2003. Paper ISBN 0-88911-959-7 Cloth 0-88911-961-9

The e-Connected World: Risks and Opportunities, Stephen Coleman (ed.), 2003.
Paper ISBN 0-88911-945-7 Cloth 0-88911-947-3

Centre for the Study of Democracy

The Authentic Voice of Canada: R.B. Bennett's Speeches in the House of Lords, 1941-1947,
Christopher McCreery and Arthur Milnes (eds.), 2009. Paper 978-1-55339-275-0
Cloth ISBN 978-1-55339-276-7

*Age of the Offered Hand: The Cross-Border Partnership Between President George H.W. Bush
and Prime-Minister Brian Mulroney, A Documentary History*, James McGrath and
Arthur Milnes (eds.), 2009. Paper ISBN 978-1-55339-232-3
Cloth ISBN 978-1-55339-233-0

*In Roosevelt's Bright Shadow: Presidential Addresses About Canada from Taft to Obama in
Honour of FDR's 1938 Speech at Queen's University*, Christopher McCreery and
Arthur Milnes (eds.), 2009. Paper ISBN 978-1-55339-230-9 Cloth ISBN 978-1-55339-231-6

*Politics of Purpose, 40th Anniversary Edition, The Right Honourable John N. Turner 17th
Prime Minister of Canada*, Elizabeth McIninch and Arthur Milnes (eds.), 2009.
Paper ISBN 978-1-55339-227-9 Cloth ISBN 978-1-55339-224-8

*Bridging the Divide: Religious Dialogue and Universal Ethics, Papers for The InterAction
Council*, Thomas S. Axworthy (ed.), 2008. Paper ISBN 978-1-55339-219-4
Cloth ISBN 978-1-55339-220-0

Institute of Intergovernmental Relations

Canada: The State of the Federation 2009, vol. 22, *Carbon Pricing and Environmental
Federalism*, Thomas J. Courchene and John R. Allan (eds.), 2010.
Paper ISBN 978-1-55339-196-8 Cloth ISBN 978-1-55339-197-5

Canada: The State of the Federation 2008, vol. 21, *Open Federalism and the Spending Power*,
Thomas J. Courchene, John R. Allan, and Hoi Kong (eds.), forthcoming.
Paper ISBN 978-1-55339-194-4

The Democratic Dilemma: Reforming the Canadian Senate, Jennifer Smith (ed.), 2009.
Paper 978-1-55339-190-6

Canada: The State of the Federation 2006/07, vol. 20, *Transitions – Fiscal and Political Federalism in an Era of Change*, John R. Allan, Thomas J. Courchene, and Christian Leuprecht (eds.), 2009. Paper ISBN 978-1-55339-189-0 Cloth ISBN 978-1-55339-191-3

Comparing Federal Systems, Third Edition, Ronald L. Watts, 2008.
Paper ISBN 978-1-55339-188-3

Canada: The State of the Federation 2005, vol. 19, *Quebec and Canada in the New Century – New Dynamics, New Opportunities*, Michael Murphy (ed.), 2007.
Paper ISBN 978-1-55339-018-3 Cloth ISBN 978-1-55339-017-6

Spheres of Governance: Comparative Studies of Cities in Multilevel Governance Systems, Harvey Lazar and Christian Leuprecht (eds.), 2007. Paper ISBN 978-1-55339-019-0 Cloth ISBN 978-1-55339-129-6

Canada: The State of the Federation 2004, vol. 18, *Municipal-Federal-Provincial Relations in Canada*, Robert Young and Christian Leuprecht (eds.), 2006.
Paper ISBN 1-55339-015-6 Cloth ISBN 1-55339-016-4

Canadian Fiscal Arrangements: What Works, What Might Work Better, Harvey Lazar (ed.), 2005. Paper ISBN 1-55339-012-1 Cloth ISBN 1-55339-013-X

Canada: The State of the Federation 2003, vol. 17, *Reconfiguring Aboriginal-State Relations*, Michael Murphy (ed.), 2005. Paper ISBN 1-55339-010-5 Cloth ISBN 1-55339-011-3

Canada: The State of the Federation 2002, vol. 16, *Reconsidering the Institutions of Canadian Federalism*, J. Peter Meekison, Hamish Telford, and Harvey Lazar (eds.), 2004.
Paper ISBN 1-55339-009-1 Cloth ISBN 1-55339-008-3

Federalism and Labour Market Policy: Comparing Different Governance and Employment Strategies, Alain Noël (ed.), 2004. Paper ISBN 1-55339-006-7 Cloth ISBN 1-55339-007-5

The Impact of Global and Regional Integration on Federal Systems: A Comparative Analysis, Harvey Lazar, Hamish Telford, and Ronald L. Watts (eds.), 2003.
Paper ISBN 1-55339-002-4 Cloth ISBN 1-55339-003-2

John Deutsch Institute for the Study of Economic Policy

Discount Rates for the Evaluation of Public Private Partnerships, David F. Burgess and Glenn P. Jenkins (eds.), 2010.
Paper ISBN 978-1-55339-163-0 Cloth ISBN 978-1-55339-164-7

Retirement Policy Issues in Canada, Michael G. Abbott, Charles M. Beach, Robin W. Boadway, and James G. MacKinnon (eds.), 2009.
Paper ISBN 978-1-55339-161-6 Cloth ISBN 978-1-55339-162-3

The 2006 Federal Budget: Rethinking Fiscal Priorities, Charles M. Beach, Michael Smart, and Thomas A. Wilson (eds.), 2007. Paper ISBN 978-1-55339-125-8 Cloth ISBN 978-1-55339-126-6

Health Services Restructuring in Canada: New Evidence and New Directions, Charles M. Beach, Richard P. Chaykowksi, Sam Shortt, France St-Hilaire, and Arthur Sweetman (eds.), 2006. Paper ISBN 978-1-55339-076-3 Cloth ISBN 978-1-55339-075-6

A Challenge for Higher Education in Ontario, Charles M. Beach (ed.), 2005.
Paper ISBN 1-55339-074-1 Cloth ISBN 1-55339-073-3

Current Directions in Financial Regulation, Frank Milne and Edwin H. Neave (eds.), Policy Forum Series no. 40, 2005. Paper ISBN 1-55339-072-5 Cloth ISBN 1-55339-071-7

Higher Education in Canada, Charles M. Beach, Robin W. Boadway, and R. Marvin McInnis (eds.), 2005. Paper ISBN 1-55339-070-9 Cloth ISBN 1-55339-069-5

Financial Services and Public Policy, Christopher Waddell (ed.), 2004.
Paper ISBN 1-55339-068-7 Cloth ISBN 1-55339-067-9

The 2003 Federal Budget: Conflicting Tensions, Charles M. Beach and Thomas A. Wilson (eds.), Policy Forum Series no. 39, 2004. Paper ISBN 0-88911-958-9 Cloth ISBN 0-88911-956-2

Canadian Immigration Policy for the 21st Century, Charles M. Beach, Alan G. Green, and Jeffrey G. Reitz (eds.), 2003. Paper ISBN 0-88911-954-6 Cloth ISBN 0-88911-952-X

Framing Financial Structure in an Information Environment, Thomas J. Courchene and Edwin H. Neave (eds.), Policy Forum Series no. 38, 2003. Paper ISBN 0-88911-950-3 Cloth ISBN 0-88911-948-1

Our publications may be purchased at leading bookstores, including the Queen's University Bookstore (http://www.campusbookstore.com/) or can be ordered online from: McGill-Queen's University Press, at **http://mqup.mcgill.ca/ordering.php**

For more information about new and backlist titles from Queen's Policy Studies, visit http://www.queensu.ca/sps/books or visit the McGill-Queen's University Press web site at: **http://mqup.mcgill.ca/**